The Siege of Budapest

THE SIEGE OF
BUDAPEST

One Hundred Days in World War II

Krisztián Ungváry

With a foreword by John Lukacs

Translated from the Hungarian by Ladislaus Löb

YALE UNIVERSITY PRESS

New Haven and London

Copyright © 2002, 2005 by Krisztián Ungváry. Published by arrangement with I. B. Tauris & Co Ltd, London. The original English edition of this book is entitled *Battle for Budapest: 100 Days in World War II* and was published by I. B. Tauris & Co Ltd.

Designed by Sonia Shannon.
Set in Galliard type by Achorn Graphic Services.
Printed in the United States of America

The Library of Congress has cataloged the hardcover edition as follows:

Ungváry, Krisztián.
  [Budapest ostroma. English]
  The siege of Budapest : one hundred days in World War II / Krisztián Ungváry; translated from the Hungarian by Ladislaus Löb ; with a foreword by John Lukacs.
    p. cm.
  Originally published: London : I.B. Tauris, 2002.
  Includes bibliographical references and index.
  ISBN 0-300-10468-5 (cloth : alk. paper)
 1. Budapest (Hungary)—History—Siege, 1945. I. Title.
  D765.562.B8U5413 2005
  940.54′213912—dc22   2004015687

A catalogue record for this book is available from the British Library.

The paper in this book meets the guidelines for permanence and durability of the Committee on Production Guidelines for Book Longevity of the Council on Library Resources.

ISBN-13: 978-0-300-11985-5 (pbk. : alk. paper)
ISBN-10: 0-300-11985-2 (pbk. : alk. paper)

10 9 8 7 6 5 4

Contents

Illustrations

Maps and Map Key

Unit	Infantry	Panzer	Cavalry	Motorised, mechanised or Panzer grenadier	Mountain Army Corps	Assault Artillery	Paratroopers
Army	3	6	Pliev				
Army Corps	7 (Rom)	III	5	2 gd.			
Division	10	13	8 ⚡	Szent László	FHH	I	
Brigade		39	4				
Regiment	38	30	16 ⚡	66		1831 gd.	
Battalion	E		AA8 ⚡			10	II/I
Company							

This table has been constructed on the basis of the units that took part in the siege. Soviet units are marked with a star, Hungarian units with a small coat-of-arms above the flag, and Romanian units are indicated in brackets after the unit number.

BBS	Budapest Security Battalion	**FHH**	Feldherrnhalle
BGB	Budapest Guard Battalion	**gd.**	Guard unit
Gend.	Gendarmerie	**Pol.**	Police
EFS	Europa Flying Squad Battalion	**(Rom)**	Romanian
Univ.	University Assault Battalion	⚡	SS
Res.	Reserve		

Foreword

JOHN LUKACS

The merits of Krisztián Ungváry's work are at least twofold. First: as a military history it is unrivaled. None of the—otherwise quite good—military histories of the battles of Stalingrad or Warsaw or Berlin come close to its minute details and to its vivid reconstruction of where and when and how troops moved and fought. Military historians ought to study *The Siege of Budapest* with jewelers' eyes. So must the people of Budapest, and the diminishing minority among them who experienced its siege sixty years ago (as did I, a historian, who found many details in this superb reconstruction that were new to me).

Krisztián Ungváry's second merit may be even greater. This is not only a military history par excellence but a civil, political, sociographic reconstruction of a dreadful and sordid (and, on occasion, heroic) drama of a siege of a great capital city, inevitably including one million inhabitants whose very existences and minds were involved in a brutal civil war that was at the same time a war within a war. And so not only the extent but the complexity of that dreadful (yes: full of dread—there may not be a better word) drama is without equal, with a meaning that lives even beyond the history of the Second World War.

Such a history, with many of its difficulties, poses a problem for readers thousands of miles and at least two generations away. This is why I have taken upon myself to write a necessary foreword to this magisterial work. To the difficulties of its very complicated subject matter I must now turn.

One is the psychic situation even now. A curious condition—
which, to the best of my knowledge, has not been approached,
let alone analyzed, by psychohistorians—is the distinct reluctance
of many civilian people to talk about their horrible and demeaning
experiences during a war. (A recent description of this phenomenon was made by the excellent German writer W. G. Sebald. He
was astounded by how few German men and women spoke about
their sufferings during the air raids during the war: strange, since
they and we knew of the increasingly indiscriminate bombing of
German cities, and also of the otherwise frequent German ten-
dency to self-pity, especially after their defeat.) Such a psychic condition applies, not exactly but to a great extent, to Budapest and to
much of Hungary in 1944–1945, when the sufferings of war
included, among other horrors, Russian soldiers raping thousands
of women. Shame and fear may perhaps explain this condition of
unspoken or suppressed memories. But in the case of Budapest
there was, and remains, something more than that. For many reasons—political and not only psychic ones—many Hungarians have
not been able or willing to rethink (in plain English, to digest) the
tragic history of their country and of its people in 1944–1945. And
this in a city where a few ruins and many buildings pockmarked by
shellfire from that time are visible even now.

I must therefore briefly sum up Hungary's situation in 1944 and
its then-recent history. Hungary is an ancient nation, considerably (though not entirely) independent during the last decades of
the Austro-Hungarian Dual Monarchy. After the First World War,
for all kinds of reasons, most of these wrong rather than right, the
Western Allies and their newcoming "allies" of Czechoslovakia,
Romania, Yugoslavia, applying the dubious principle of "national
self-determination," decided to amputate the historic Hungarian
state, depriving it of two-thirds of its territory in the treaty of Trianon in 1920, and leaving more than three million Hungarians
under foreign rule. Hungary at Trianon was punished more
severely than was Germany at Versailles. All of this happened soon
after a revolution in Hungary in November 1918 which then
debouched into a short Communist rule in March 1919, after which

a nationalist counterrevolution followed. These traumas—revolutions, defeat, mutilation—marked Hungarian politics during the next twenty years. Hungary was still a "kingdom," but only in name: the head of state was a former admiral, Miklós Horthy, as regent. During the 1920s Hungary recovered—somewhat. During the 1930s the German Reich rose again, led by Hitler; it rapidly became the principal power in Europe, discarding and tearing up one piece of the Versailles treaty after the other. No wonder that the Third Reich had many admirers among Hungarians at that time, especially among the military officerdom. Hitler had no particular sympathies for Hungary; but it was mostly because of the, hardly avoidable, alignment of Hungary with Germany that from 1938 to 1941 some of the lost Hungarian lands were actually reassigned to Hungary.

But now Hungary's fate was already involved with the coming Second World War. When in March 1938 Hitler annexed Austria, the giant Third Reich became Hungary's immediate neighbor. Gradually it was (or at least it should have been) evident that the principal problem for the Hungarian state was no longer the regaining of its lost lands; it was (or at least it should have been) the preservation, in one way or another, of Hungary's independence. This priority was neither acknowledged nor thought about by most of the governing classes, not by many of the Hungarian population, and especially not by the Hungarian military. The latter were largely willing to accommodate themselves and their country to the political strategy of Hitler's Germany (believing, among other matters, that the latter was or would be invincible). Anti-Jewish laws (about which later) were instituted. In November 1940 Hungary joined the so-called Tripartite Pact, the German-Italian-Japanese alliance system. In April 1941 Hungary took part in Hitler's war against Yugoslavia, with which it had signed an "Eternal Friendship Pact" but a few months earlier. (The conservative Prime Minister Count Pál Teleki shot himself.) In December 1941 Great Britain declared war on Hungary, and Hungary declared war on the United States a few days later.

A Hungarian army was sent to Russia to fight alongside the Germans. But in 1942 and 1943 there were subtle changes. A few patriotic (rather than nationalist) conservatives and the regent chose to reduce the Hungarian commitment to Hitler carefully and secretly. There was a new prime minister, Miklós Kállay. There were clandestine attempts to establish contacts with British and American officials. In January and February 1943 Russian forces largely destroyed the 2nd Hungarian Army, which was now compelled to retreat. By tacit consent Hungary and Budapest were not bombed by the British and American air armadas crossing above Hungary. (Budapest experienced one small air raid by Soviet planes in September 1942.) Save for the tragedy of the Hungarian 2nd Army, Hungary and Budapest (including the Jewish population) lived largely, though of course not entirely, unscathed by the war, even as the advancing Russian armies were approaching Hungary from the northeast.

Hitler now had enough. He summoned the regent on 18 March 1944. He ordered Horthy to appoint an unexceptionally pro-German and pro–National Socialist government. The regent thought he had no alternative but to comply. German divisions moved into Budapest and other cities. Soon Budapest was bombed by British and American planes. The humiliation and persecution and suppression of Hungarian Jews was now merciless. On German directives and with the compliance of many Hungarian military and civil authorities, about 400,000 Hungarian Jews were corralled in ghettoes and then deported, most of them to Auschwitz. The great majority of them did not survive the war. The last portion to be collected and deported were the Jews in Budapest, about 160,000 of them. In late June and early July Horthy emerged from his apathy. Spurred, too, by messages from President Roosevelt, the king of Sweden, and Pope Pius XII, he ordered the deportation of Jews from Budapest halted. Seven weeks later Hungary's inimical neighbor Romania turned against Hitler and went over to the Russians. One month later the first Russian troops entered Hungarian territory from the southwest. On 15 October the regent, after woefully inadequate preparations, broadcast Hungary's armistice and surrender to the Allies. Within hours he was surrounded and then arrested by German forces. Within hours the Germans installed a government of the Hungarian National Socialist Arrow Cross movement, whose composition and character included not only fanatics but also criminals. What followed in Budapest were months of terror and then the siege.

The first Russian units approached the southeastern edge of Budapest on 2 November; the full siege began at Christmas; it ended with the German and Hungarian collapse and surrender on 13 February 1945. Meanwhile the hot rake of war had moved over most of Hungary, across burning villages and towns, maiming the lives of millions of people, searing their bodies and their minds. We must say something about that, too, since the Battle for Budapest involved civilians as much (if not more) than soldiers. It was a struggle of armies as well as a struggle of minds.

When the siege of Budapest began, the people of Budapest were badly, indeed tragically, divided. It is not possible to ascertain the accurate proportions of that division. There had been no opinion surveys (also no elections after May 1939). Moreover, divisions and contradictions existed, more than often, within the minds (and hearts) of single persons. Nevertheless I must essay the approximate lineaments of that torn and racked population in my capacity as a historian, as well as in that of a once witness and participant in those memorable months.

I estimate that in the moment the siege began perhaps 15 percent of the (non-Jewish) population of Budapest was willing to continue and to support the war on the Germans' side. These people ranged from fanatics of the Arrow Cross to many other men and women (not necessarily Arrow Cross) who were convinced that the arrival of the Red Army was the very worst prospect that had to be resisted. Another 15 percent had arrived at the very opposite conclusion: that Hungary's alliance with Hitler's Reich was a political and moral disaster that had to be resisted and opposed in one way or another, that the Arrow Cross "government" consisted of criminals, and that therefore the sooner the Russians occupied Budapest the better. (Among this minority Communists and their sympathizers were a minuscule portion.) The rest, perhaps 70 percent of the population (please consider this as a *very* approximate, indeed, arguable rule of one sensitive thumb) were numbed by their circumstances and by events, sometimes willing, sometimes unwilling, to think much ahead, preoccupied as they were with the existing and looming dangers for them and for their families, and without anything like a clear idea for what the end of the siege would bring, confused and divided as their minds were.

Save for these few generalizations there was (and is) no sociographic explanation for these deep, and sometimes fatal, divisions. It may be interesting to note that the remnants of the Hungarian aristocracy were largely anti-Nazi (and therefore, at least temporarily, expecting the Russians), even though their class had the most to lose and fear from a coming Russian and Communist rule—while at the same time pro-German and National Socialist inclinations and even convictions were still widespread among the working classes. (So much for the theories of Marx et al.) The—so-called—Christian (meaning, at that time, non-Jewish and nonsocialist) middle classes were divided, probably reflecting the abovementioned 15–70–15 ratio. So were religious and irreligious people; priests and pastors; teachers and judges and lawyers; civil servants and merchants and policemen, etc., etc. During the siege some of these preferences and opinions would change—because of their very dreadful experiences, to be sure.

And so did their memories—which, as I wrote earlier, so many found it easier to suppress rather than to reconstruct and rethink.

One of these difficulties—persisting to this day, sixty years after these events—involves the state of the Jewish population of Budapest, and their relations with their neighbors. There was this extraordinary condition (for, unlike in science, in history often exceptions rather than rules do matter) that at the end of 1944, when the Battle for Budapest began, the Jewish population there was *the* largest surviving Jewish population in Hitler's Europe, indeed, in *all* of Europe. They had been discriminated against, persecuted, suppressed—many of them had already lost their lives—but most of them were still alive. They were of course fearing for their very lives, and breathlessly waiting for their "liberation," no matter by whom.

The fatal and bitter divisions among and within the people of Budapest were often connected with their physical and mental relationship to their Jewish neighbors. There were many graduations among the Jews themselves. For one thing, it was (and it still is) impossible to ascertain their exact numbers—mostly because of the large number of their intermarriages with Christians, and also because of the considerable number of Jewish Christians—that is, converts. It may be said that before the Second World War the assimilation of Jews, their absorption within the Hungarian people, had been extraordinary. But then modern anti-Semitism was not religious but racial; it was the reaction and resentment against the most assimilated, against the most successfully Hungarian Jews. And Hungarian anti-Semitism, only sporadic before the First World War, got a tremendous boost from the national reaction against the short-lived Communist regime in 1919, in which two-thirds of the commissars had been Jews. The result was the anti-Semitism of the Horthy regime, an official governmental policy, and then the anti-Jewish laws and regulations in 1938–1941, not always responses to German demands, though those did exist. Twenty-five years of anti-Jewish education and propaganda had their influences among many people. And now the fate of the Jews hung by a thread (or, more precisely, by a few frail and silken threads).

Budapest was now ruled by a fanatical anti-Jewish Arrow Cross "government." But this was November 1944. There were— there could be—transports of deportation to Auschwitz no longer. At first the Arrow Cross, on German demands (Eichmann and his cohorts reappeared in Budapest after 15 October), ordered that Jews of all ages and sexes were to be marched on foot, westward toward Austria and Germany. But most of these forced marching orders were then suspended, because they were impractical. By early December, before the actual siege began, the situation of Jews in Budapest was as follows: 1) The government erected an actual ghetto in the, mostly Jewish-inhabited, quarters of the city, whereto most Jews were forced to transfer. No one was allowed to pass through their high wooden palisades, within which about 72,000 Jews were crowded. Most of them survived the battle for

Budapest. On 16–17 January the first Russian troops reached that part of the city. 2) Another 25,000 or 30,000 Jews dwelt in a scatteration of apartment buildings in another portion of Budapest. These "Jewish" houses (marked by a large yellow star on their portals since April) were—a curious practice then—under some kind of "international" protection. The Swedish government (and the brave Raoul Wallenberg, in Budapest through the siege), the Swiss, the Portuguese, the Spanish, and the Vatican legations had declared that, temporarily, Hungarian Jews living in thus designated houses were under their protection. For the sake of maintaining their few existing diplomatic relations with such neutral states the Arrow Cross Foreign Ministry accepted that. The criminal groups did not. On many occasions such gangs invaded these houses in which crowds of Jewish families were cowering; they herded many of them into the wintry streets and marched them to the lower quays of the Danube, murdering them there and throwing their bodies into the icy water. Still, most of the Jews in their "internationally" protected houses survived the siege. (Their brave protector Wallenberg disappeared thereafter.) So survived many other Jews—perhaps as many as 50,000—who, often furnished with false identity papers, were hidden by their non-Jewish neighbors, friends, acquaintances, or were harbored in convents, parish houses, monasteries, and other religious institutions before and during the siege. And so we may essay this observation: within the battle for Budapest, within the clash and crash of German and Russian armies, within a civil war in Budapest rending its people, within those who hoped to end their siege by their "liberation" of a returning German or advancing Russian army, there was this other murderous struggle, often within the very minds of some men and women, between those who were indifferent to the fate of the Jews of Budapest and those who were not. That alone renders the history of the Battle for Budapest so extraordinarily complex, far beyond a chapter in overall histories of the Second World War or of the Jewish Holocaust.

But the fate of the Battle for Budapest was not determined by its population, and not even by the masses of soldiers stumbling and struggling within the city. Much of it was determined by the supreme masters of their armies, by Stalin and by Hitler.

In August 1944 the Russian armies had reached the outskirts of Warsaw. Then Stalin halted their further advance westward. He decided that they should advance into the Balkans, Romania, Bulgaria, Serbia, and then to Hungary. This choice was logical, strategic, and geographic, but also political. The Germans were about to retreat from southeastern Europe (though not from Hungary). No British or American forces would be inserted there to fill a potential military and political vacuum. Churchill knew this. That was one of the two main reasons (the other was the future of Poland) that compelled him to fly to Moscow in October to reach some kind of agreement with Stalin. They did. Stalin agreed to leave Greece to the British, in accord with an agreement (hopefully, but only hopefully, temporary) regulating the British-American and Russian proportions of influence in the Balkans and in Hungary. At first Churchill and Stalin agreed on a 50–50 ratio for Hungary; a few days later Molotov insisted and Eden agreed to revise that to 75–25 in Russia's favor. The Russians had already conquered much of southern and eastern Hungary and were moving toward Budapest. (There was one other factor in Churchill's acceptance of this revision: the collapse of the Hungarian armistice attempt during the very time of Churchill's stay in Moscow.) At the end of October, Stalin ordered and urged Marshal Rodion Yakovlevich Malinovsky, the commander of one of the two main Russian armies in Hungary, to take Budapest as soon as possible. The first Russian advance units reached the outskirts of the capital a few days later; but Malinovsky was, as yet, unable to penetrate and conquer the city, whose real siege began not until Christmas, when the other great Russian army, commanded by Marshal Fedor Ivanovich Tolbukhin, had encircled it from the southwest. Here I must register a slight (very slight) disagreement with my excellent friend Ungváry. Of course Stalin wanted to advance westward as soon and as much as possible. But I do not think that this was his primary concern at that time. Of course he was not pleased with the postponement of his capture of Budapest, with the duration of its siege. But while he was vexed by this circumstance, he was not

particularly grieved by it. The relative slowness of the Russian con-
quest of Budapest is one indirect evidence for that. For once, the
Russians advanced with considerable caution. In any event, Stalin
wanted to make certain that Hungary and Budapest would come
under his control. His minions knew that only too well. One example of their political determination was that they arrested Raoul
Wallenberg and spirited him to Moscow a day or so after the Russian occupation of Pest.

Perhaps more interesting were the purposes of Hitler. His
principal desire was obvious. It was to halt and retard the Russian
advance toward Vienna as much as possible. If that was to involve
the destruction of Budapest, so be it. In this he was, relatively, successful: the siege of Budapest cost the Russians plenty of manpower
and time; it lasted long enough. That is why Hitler forbade the
breaking out of the garrison defending Buda even when two German counteroffensives came near to the city and when such a
break-out was—perhaps—possible. Let Budapest (or at least Buda)
remain a thorn in the Russians' flesh, compromising their progress
to Vienna. Yet it is significant that the greatest German counteroffensive in western Hungary was mounted only *after* Budapest had
fallen. After a few breakthroughs, that last German offensive on the
eastern front—indeed, the last one in the entire war—also failed;
but its significance resides in what it shows of Hitler's mind. His
main (and only) hope—and for years now—was to divide his enemies. To achieve that politically or diplomatically was well nigh
impossible; but perhaps something like this could be achieved by a
sudden great German victory in the field, on one front or the other.
This, and not something like the reconquest of Paris, was Hitler's
purpose for this attack in the Ardennes (the "Battle of the Bulge");
this was his desperate purpose, to inflict a damning blow on the
Russians in western Hungary in March 1945. He did not succeed—
though he delayed the progress of the armies of his enemies somewhat.

Here I must add something seldom or insufficiently re-
counted by historians. This was Hitler's—tacit—consent to the
efforts of some of his cohorts to cause trouble between the British-
Americans and the Russians. There were many instances of this in

1944. So far as Budapest went this may be illustrated by at least two matters. One involves Raoul Wallenberg, who was not even a Swedish diplomat but who arrived in Budapest spurred by his humanitarian convictions and with the help of Jewish and American organizations. The Germans allowed him to travel and to remain in Budapest, and treated him often as if he were a representative of Western Allied interests (which he, in many ways, was). They did this for several reasons, including their wish to cause trouble between Americans and Russians. The Russians knew this (and the Germans made sure they knew), which was the principal reason for their immediate arrest of Wallenberg and for his deportation to Moscow. The other significant matter were the instructions of Heinrich Himmler, who expressly forbade the destruction of the Budapest ghetto and the murder of its inhabitants. (Also: two days before the advancing Russians reached the ghetto there was a plan by some SS units and Arrow Cross to invade the ghetto and massacre its inhabitants. A German major-general stopped this, threatening its eventual perpetrators with arrest.) There are reasons to believe that Himmler's directives were not made against Hitler's wishes.

The siege of Budapest ended on 13 February 1945—the day after the Yalta Conference had ended. Not a word was said at Yalta by Churchill, Roosevelt, Stalin about Budapest or Hungary, which, evidently, were falling entirely under Russian control. Sixty years later, in 2004, the alleged heroism of the last defenders of Buda are still proclaimed and extolled in a few periodicals and by hundreds of demonstrators of Hungarian right-wing organizations. Others in Budapest recall that date (if they recall it at all) as the completion of their "liberation." Yes: there was nothing simple about the Battle for Budapest; and there is nothing simple about its history and the memories of its people.

Preface

The siege of Budapest was one of the longest and bloodiest city battles of the Second World War. From the appearance of the first Soviet tanks on the outskirts of the capital on 3 November 1944 until the capture of Buda Castle Hill on 13 February 1945, 102 days passed (fighting in the city itself began on 24 December, lasting for 51 days). In contrast, Berlin fell within two weeks and Vienna within five days, while Paris and the rest of the European capitals—except for Warsaw—saw no fighting at all. Other German "fortresses"—for example, Königsberg and Breslau—resisted for shorter periods, 77 and 82 days, respectively.

Owing to its geographic bivalence, Budapest (more precisely, the Buda part) has often been besieged. In the course of a thousand years it has experienced more than a dozen sieges of varying intensity. The devastation caused in the Second World War was far worse than any of these. The battle for Budapest was equaled in ferocity only by those for Leningrad, Stalingrad, and Warsaw.

The blockade of Leningrad lasted almost three years, but there was no street fighting. Stalingrad was a battlefield for four months, but the majority of the population had been evacuated. In addition to the soldiers of the German, Hungarian, and Soviet armies, the three-month siege of Budapest engulfed 800,000 noncombatants and was often so vicious that comparisons with Stalingrad began to appear in contemporary soldiers' writings.

The vast majority of the inhabitants of Budapest were not evacuated. At least 38,000 civilians died alongside a similar number

of Hungarian and German soldiers. Thus every other person killed
on the defending side was a civilian. The casualties of the attacking
Red Army were probably of the same magnitude, bringing the
grand total to 160,000.

Archival material on the battle for Budapest, in German,
Hungarian, or Russian, is scarce. Many notes made by soldiers at
the time were lost or destroyed. One of the few documents now
available—the war diary of the Hungarian 10th Infantry Division—
was buried in a Buda courtyard on the orders of chief of staff
Győző Benyovszky and remained hidden for more than four
decades before finding its way to the Hungarian Archive of Military
History in 1986. From the mid-1980s memoirs began arriving at the
archive in increasing numbers, but they were initially banished to
the deepest recesses for political reasons.

For a long time all publications on the battle were designed
for propaganda purposes. The first account with any claim to schol-
arship was Sándor Tóth's *Budapest felszabadítása*, published in
1975. Tóth had been able to inspect Soviet sources only selectively,
however, and had not had any access to German archives. Nor is his
work primarily concerned with what happened in Budapest. Of its
279 pages only 62 refer to the fighting in the city, with the rest
being devoted to political issues and the relief attempts. This is no
coincidence, as Tóth was obliged to keep silent about various
details, and many eyewitnesses could not speak out at the time
when he was writing. Péter Gosztonyi, living in Bern, was free to
undertake research and publish valuable source material and studies from the 1960s, mostly in German and Hungarian. Political
pressure on historians ceased in 1989, but despite a growing interest in military history of the recent past, no comprehensive examination of the battle was carried out in subsequent years. The only
exception was a volume resulting from a conference held at the
Institute of Military History in Budapest in 1994.

My aim in this study was to reconstruct the events of one of
the bloodiest city battles of the Second World War, using all available sources. Owing to the incompleteness of existing official documentation often I had to rely on recollections of participants. In
any event, communiqués written in offices or at battle posts cannot

convey a true impression of the misery of a siege. Personal accounts therefore play a significant part in my study.

I tried to obtain information from both German and Hungarian survivors. But although a heavier burden of fighting was borne by the Germans, accounts by German soldiers proved relatively rare and often inaccurate owing to lack of local knowledge. Recollections of Soviet soldiers were even less readily available. Consequently, I have reconstructed the concrete military engagements mainly from Hungarian narratives.

The history of the battle for Budapest has now aroused considerable interest in both Hungary and Germany. This book has so far appeared in four Hungarian, three German, and one British editions. I am still being approached by survivors with further valuable information. I have also organized successful exhibitions about its subject matter in Budapest and Berlin.

I first wrote this study as a doctoral dissertation at Eötvös Loránd University in Budapest. My research in the Military Archive of the Federal Archives in Freiburg was supported by two scholarships from the German Academic Exchange Service, whose staff, in particular Mr. Brün Meyer, gave me untiring support. I also wish to thank the other institutions and private individuals who supplied me with documents or details of their experiences. Their names appear in the list of sources.

The siege of Budapest is part of Hungarian, German, and Russian history. The tragic and sometimes criminal events still evoke painful memories, which made it particularly difficult, even today, to describe them fairly. With this in mind I would like to thank the following for their technical advice and thought-provoking comments on my manuscript: András Ceglédi, Klaus Ewald, Ervin Galántay, Ferenc X. Kovács, Péter Nádas, György Pongrácz, István Ravasz, Endre Sasvári, Péter Szabó, Sándor Tóth, Rudolf Ungváry, Sándor Vadász, György Válas, Frigyes Wáczek, and Philip Wetzel. My special thanks are due to Professor Ladislaus Löb, the English translator, whose help with the preparation of this volume has far exceeded the requirements of a mere translation and who has also assisted me in correcting various inaccuracies.

The Siege of Budapest

I

Prelude

The General Situation in the Carpathian Basin, Autumn 1944

As a result of the successive defeats suffered by the Germans on the eastern front, Italy, Romania, and Hungary had become increasingly reluctant allies. In all three countries political forces demanding a loosening of the alliance were gaining ground. With the front line approaching the Hungarian border early in 1944, the German Wehrmacht occupied Hungary in order to prevent it from following Italy's example in trying to negotiate a ceasefire with the Allies. Because the occupation of Romania planned by the German leadership failed to materialize, Romania was able to deceive the Germans and join the Soviet side. On 23 August 1944 King Michael dismissed the fascist Prime Minister Ion Antonescu, and Romania severed diplomatic relations with Germany. The German front in eastern Romania promptly collapsed and, after large segments of the German South Ukraine Army Group were destroyed, units of the 2nd Ukrainian Front, encountering practically no resistance to their advance through Romania, arrived at Hungary's Transylvanian border on 25 August. Early in October they also reached the border of the Great Hungarian Plain in the south. On 6 October they began their general offensive with the aim of encircling—together with the 4th Ukrainian Front from the Carpathians—the German and Hungarian troops (roughly 200,000) in Transylvania. The 31 divisions and 293 tanks and assault guns of the German Army Group South in Hungary faced 59 divisions and 825 tanks and assault guns of the 2nd

Ukrainian Front. The respective ration strengths were 400,000 and 698,200.

Along the 160-kilometer front between Makó and Nagyvárad, two armored and two mechanized Soviet corps, with 627 tanks and 22 cavalry and infantry divisions, set out north to meet the Hungarian 3rd Army with its 70 tanks and 8 divisions. The Hungarian front, lacking antitank defenses, was soon torn to shreds, and the Soviet troops were ordered to advance toward Debrecen. In the meantime the Germans had also concentrated forces in the region: Operation *Zigeunerbaron* (Gipsy Baron) was intended to destroy the 2nd Ukrainian Front's units on the Great Hungarian Plain and then, turning south and east, seize the passes in the Carpathians to form an easily defensible battle line. The tank battle of Debrecen took place between 10 and 14 October. Eleven German and Hungarian divisions with 227 tanks and assault guns were outnumbered three times over by 39 Soviet divisions with 773 tanks and assault guns.

Although the Soviet units succeeded in occupying Debrecen on 20 October 1944, they were unable to fulfil their aim of encircling the German 8th Army and the Hungarian 1st and 2nd Armies, stationed in Transylvania and the Carpathians. In addition, the 4th Ukrainian Front under Major-General Ivan Yefremovich Petrov, which should have closed the circle from the north, had made hardly any headway. Thus the German Army Group South succeeded in extricating its troops. After Regent Miklós Horthy's failed attempt of 15 October to break away from Germany and agree to a separate peace with the Soviets, the panzer units that had so far been tied down in the border area added their strength to the German front. By 20 October the Germans had lost only 133 tanks, while the losses of the Soviets amounted to 500—more than 70 percent of their strength. By the end of October the German panzer divisions had encircled General Issa Aleksandrevich Pliev's mechanized cavalry units in the Nyíregyháza region, and the Soviet troops were able to break out only with heavy losses. Even toward the end of the war the Wehrmacht was a formidable force: for each German panzer destroyed, four Soviet tanks were lost. If the Soviet advance had been more deliberate, the Soviet losses would probably have been much smaller.

After the invasion of Hungary, Hitler had appointed Edmund Veesenmayer as his supreme representative in that country. Although Veesenmayer was also obliged to consider the interests of the SS, he essentially determined Hungarian policies. Before the siege of Budapest began, he declared that it did not matter if the city were "destroyed ten times, so long as Vienna could thereby be defended."

Between Baja in the south and Szolnok in the east, only seven exhausted divisions of the Hungarian 3rd Army and 20 tanks of the German 24th Panzer Division were holding their positions against the Soviet 46th Army, as the bulk of the German armored forces had been redeployed to the tank battle of Debrecen. The distance between Budapest and the Soviet lines was only about 100 kilometers. Nevertheless, a Soviet attack was risky, because the German tanks could easily be regrouped to defend the city, while the Soviets no longer had enough armored vehicles to carry out a successful offensive.

While the Soviet occupation of Hungary was continuing in the region beyond the Tisza River and in the southern part of the Great Hungarian Plain, in Budapest and the western parts of the country the Arrow Cross government was establishing its reign of terror.

The Arrow Cross Party had come into being during the second half of the 1930s, through the merger of several far-right groupings. Its emergence was facilitated by widespread disillusionment with the communist republic of 1919, the surviving feudal structures, and the anti-Semitic traditions of Hungarian society. The party was led by Ferenc Szálasi, a suspended general-staff major. In the 1938 elections the party had proved extremely popular in working-class districts, obtaining about 20 percent of the vote. Its program promised land reform, social reforms for workers and peasants, the complete elimination of Jewish influence and the subsequent deportation of all Jews from Hungary, and the creation under Hungarian leadership of a federal state called the Hungarist Carpathian-Danubian Great Fatherland, which was to comprise Hungary, Slovakia, Vojvódina, Burgenland, Croatia, Dalmatia, Ruthenia, Transylvania, and Bosnia. From the National

Socialists it had adopted the Führer and Lebensraum principles: that a nation should unquestionably submit to the absolute rule of its leader and fight to conquer more living space for its expanding population.

Although in reality the fate of Budapest was determined by German military policy, according to the Arrow Cross Party the Hungarian people were now obliged to fight against the violence, looting, and deportation to Siberia that the approaching Soviet army would bring with it. The persecuted Jews saw the advancing Soviet troops as their saviors. The rest of the population, however, had gloomy forebodings. The relative surface calm of Budapest was frequently disturbed as Jews were marched to the ghettos or deported to German camps, columns of refugees left their homes to trek west, and reports of evacuation orders arrived from the Great Hungarian Plain. "We must now be prepared to become a city under siege from one day to the next," the linguist Miklós Kovalovszky noted in his diary, after describing a scene observed in the suburb of Kispest: "The old woman is speaking in tears about the evacuation of Kecskemét. They were able to bring a few pieces of clothing and some food with them, but there wasn't enough time to get the three pigs from the farm. The whole town has become a poorhouse; and what if they have to move on from here as well?"

The Division of Eastern Europe

While the tank battle of Debrecen was raging between the 2nd Ukrainian Front and the German Army Group South, some events that were to prove decisive for Budapest took place in Moscow. From 8 to 18 October 1944 the British Prime Minister Winston Churchill was engaged in negotiations in the Soviet capital. The main issue was the interest of the British and the Soviets in the future of eastern Europe. Churchill explicitly suggested to Soviet premier Josef Stalin that it would be useful to divide the whole area into "spheres of influence." According to eyewitnesses he was slightly inebriated when he scribbled the names of some countries on a piece of paper, together with the respective percentages of influence to be allocated to the Soviets and to "the others," the Western Allies:

Romania 90%–10%
Bulgaria 75%–25%
Hungary 50%–50%
Yugoslavia 50%–50%
Greece 10%–90%

Without any hesitation Stalin placed a checkmark on the historic document. He had a great deal of experience with spheres of interest, having made an agreement about the same issue in 1939, albeit at that time with Nazi Germany. Churchill, worried in one of his clearer moments about the cavalier way in which the matter had been resolved, said to Stalin: "Might it not be thought rather cynical if it seemed we had disposed of these issues so fateful to millions of people, in such an offhand manner? Let us burn the paper." But Stalin replied calmly: "No, you keep it."

But the mistrustful dictator was already thinking of breaking the agreement. The British prime minister had proposed before an advance by British and U.S. troops through the Ljubljana Gap, but each time Stalin rejected this plan for fear that the arrival of the Allies would make the bolshevization of the area impossible. When Churchill again brought up his plan for an invasion of the Balkans, Stalin's reaction was typical. In principle, his "security interests" could not have been harmed by the presence of British and U.S. troops in Hungary and Yugoslavia, where he had promised the Allies a 50 percent share, particularly since the Soviets had already taken Belgrade on 14 October and seemed likely to take the whole territory between the Danube and the Tisza within weeks. If Stalin nevertheless tried to get ahead of his allies—even as far as Austria and Bavaria, which had never been mentioned in connection with the Soviet "sphere of interest"—the reason could only be that he did not mean to keep his word.

The Soviet dictator interpreted his "security interests" rather broadly. It is worth comparing the demands made by the Soviet Union on its neighbors with regard to its alleged security interests in 1939–1940 and in 1944, respectively. Stalin's minimal program of

1944 was almost identical to what he had demanded from Hitler through Molotov: the extension of the Soviet "sphere of interest" to Hungary, Romania, Bulgaria, Greece, and the straits between the Mediterranean and Black seas. By 1944 that list had increased to include Yugoslavia and Albania and with the exception of these two shows a surprising similarity to what Karl Marx had regarded as Russia's "natural frontier" a century earlier. For the sake of this minimal program Stalin was prepared to take considerable military risks. Possession of Budapest was necessary to him not only because of the race against the British and U.S. forces but also for the sake of his "timetable" for the bolshevization of Hungary: "The liberation of the capital from the German fascist yoke would have speeded up . . . the creation of a democratic government . . . and had a favorable effect on some vacillating elements in the bourgeois parties and groupings." The imperialist intentions of the Soviet Union are proven by the significance attributed to the "race" by the Soviets on the one hand and by the British and U.S. leadership on the other. Churchill's Adriatic invasion was the only such operation on the part of the Western Allies, and, unlike Stalin, Churchill sought no revolutionary change of the political situation in the area but only the promised "percentages." For the United States political control over western Europe did not become an issue until much later. The delays to the invasion of Normandy on 6 June 1944 and the total inactivity of the British and U.S. armies between October 1944 and March 1945 also indicate that the British and U.S. general staffs did not consider getting ahead of the Soviets to be a strategic objective.

Plans and Preparations

After the departure of the Allied delegations, Stalin, with his "security interests" in mind, asked his general staff whether there was a realistic prospect of immediately capturing Budapest. A little earlier he had received a report from Colonel-General Lev Zakharovich Mehlis, Stalin's former secretary and the political representative of the 4th Ukrainian Front's commander. Mehlis, whose overoptimistic reports had resulted in military disasters on several occasions, including the ill-fated Crimean operation in 1942, had told Stalin: "The units of the Hungarian 1st Army facing our front are disintegrating and demoralized. Day by day our troops capture 1,000 to 2,000 men, sometimes even more. . . . The enemy soldiers are wandering in small groups in the forests, some armed, others without arms, many in civilian clothes."

As to Stalin's question about the immediate capture of Budapest, Colonel-General Sergei Shtemenko, the first deputy of the Red Army's chief of staff, later recalled: "Without suspecting anything, we replied that it would be most practical to attack from the well-established bridgehead in the Great Hungarian Plain which had been captured by the left wing of the 2nd Ukrainian Front. This would not involve crossing the river, and the enemy had fewer troops here than elsewhere." Stalin ordered an immediate attack, ignoring the reservations of General Aleksei Innokentevich Antonov, chief of the Red Army's general staff, who explained that Mehlis's reports applied only to the Hungarian 1st Army and not to the situation as a whole. On 28 October at 10 P.M. the following telephone conversation took place between Stalin and Rodion Malinovsky, the commander of the 2nd Ukrainian Front:

STALIN: Budapest . . . must be taken as soon as possible, to be more precise, in the next few days. This is absolutely essential. Can you do it?

MALINOVSKY: The job can be done within five days, when the 4th Mechanized Guard Corps arrives to join the 46th Army . . .

S: The supreme command can't give you five days. You must understand that for political reasons we have to take Budapest as quickly as possible.

M: If you give me five days I will take Budapest in another five days. If we start the offensive right now, the 46th Army—lacking sufficient forces—won't be able to bring it to a speedy conclusion and will inevitably be bogged down in lengthy battles on the access roads to the Hungarian capital. In other words, it won't be able to take Budapest.

s: There's no point in being so stubborn. You obvi-
    ously don't understand the political necessity of an
    immediate strike against Budapest.

m: I am fully aware of the political importance of the
    capture of Budapest, and that is why I am asking for
    five days.

s: I expressly order you to begin the offensive against
    Budapest tomorrow!

Stalin then put down the receiver without saying another word.

Experts disagree about whether Stalin made the right decision. When the order to attack was given, the 23rd Rifle Corps,
which had been promised as a reinforcement, was still on its way.
The 2nd Mechanized Guard Corps did not join Malinovsky, who
had no other armored units, until the next day, and the 4th Ukrainian Front, which should have taken part in the encirclement of
Budapest, was unable to reach the Great Hungarian Plain.

The German army command, recognizing the Soviet threat,
had already begun to redeploy its troops on 26 October. By
1 November the 23rd and 24th Armored Divisions had been moved
to the Kecskemét region, and the redeployment of the 13th Panzer
Division, the Feldherrnhalle Panzergrenadier Division, and the
Florian Geyer 8th SS Cavalry Division had also begun. With these
forces, the commander of the German Army Group South,
Colonel-General Hans Friessner, was planning to regain the Great
Hungarian Plain and establish a solid defensive position along the
Tisza.

The offensive, introduced by a brief artillery barrage, started
at the appointed time south of Kecskemét with a northbound
attack by the Soviet 37th Rifle Corps and 2nd Mechanized Corps.
The Soviet tanks soon broke through the Hungarian defenses over
a 25-kilometer stretch. The onslaught continued during the night,
despite an unsuccessful counterattack by the 24th Panzer Division,
but faltered on 30 October when German and Hungarian troops—
particularly antiaircraft artillery—destroyed 20 tanks in the neighborhood of Kecskemét alone. On the same day the Soviet 7th
Guard Army set out to cross the Tisza, gaining ground slowly. On

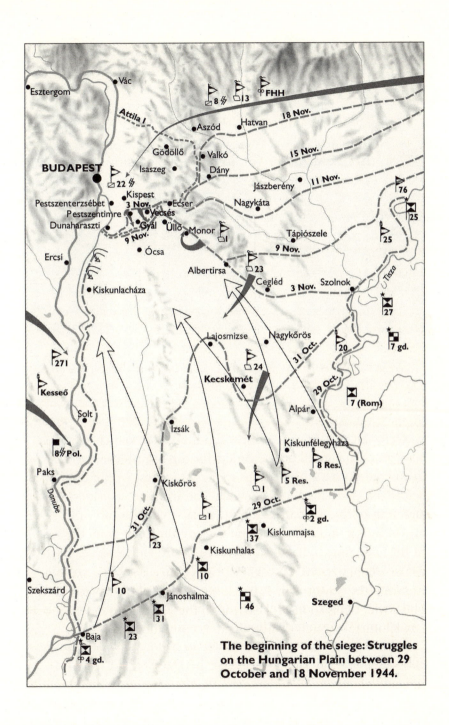

The beginning of the siege: Struggles
on the Hungarian Plain between 29
October and 18 November 1944.

I

Colonel-General Hans Friessner in discussion with other German officers on
Vérmező Meadow

31 October the Soviet troops captured Kecskemét, and on 1
November Malinovsky gave orders for the 4th Mechanized Guard
Corps and the 23rd Rifle Corps to take Budapest within three days,
before the Germans could regroup. The armored vehicles and riflemen transported by trucks and horse carts were to carry out a surprise crossing of the Danube and encircle Budapest from the south.
At the same time the 2nd Mechanized Guard Corps was to overrun
the city from the east. As the majority of Soviet troops were still 40
to 50 kilometers from Pest and there were no bridgeheads on the
Buda side, the plan in practice presupposed that it was possible to
"walk" into the capital without further ado.

The Hungarian and German forces had no chance of successfully defending the region between the Danube and the Tisza. By
31 October, their worn out combat strength amounted only to
some 17,400 men, facing 52,000 soldiers of the Red Army, and they
had only 97 tanks and assault guns, compared with 321 armored

vehicles of Malinovsky's corps (Tables 1 and 2). With the topography practically inviting a large-scale tank attack, the Hungarian defense in that region seemed certain to collapse before long. Nevertheless, the Hungarian (not to mention the German) army still had considerable strength left, as demonstrated by subsequent events in what was to be, for Hungary, the last and most devastating phase of the war. In the initial stages, the Hungarian units on the Danube and their German reinforcements presented a weighty obstacle to the premature Soviet attack, and in any case an early breakthrough by the Soviets would have been almost impossible, because they lacked the necessary resources. A general of Malinovsky's caliber must have known that his objectives were unrealistic. But once Stalin had overruled his objections, he had no choice but to obey.

"They Are Coming!"
The First Soviet Offensive Against Budapest

The Hungarian capital was not entirely unprepared for the Soviet offensive. On orders from the German army supreme command (Oberkommando Heer, or OKH), Colonel-General Friessner had begun to build up a rear defense system in Hungarian territory on 21 September 1944. This consisted of three fortified battle lines: the Margit Line between Budapest and Lake Balaton in the southwest, the Karola Line between the Cserhát, Mátra, and Zemplén Hills in the north, and the Attila Line on the east side of the capital.

The Hungarian general staff had begun to develop the Pest bridgehead on 11 September, and the Attila Line was to provide defense positions for four divisions of six battalions each. It comprised three semicircular belts: the first ran through the villages of Alsógöd, Veresegyház, Maglód, Ecser, and Dunaharaszti; the second through the villages of Dunakeszi, Mogyoród, Isaszeg, Pécel, and Pestszentimre to the suburb of Soroksár; and the third along the edge of Pest itself. The fortifications consisted of earth bunkers, antitank ditches, occasional barbed-wire entanglements, and minefields. After the appearance of the first Soviet troops, work continued: on 1 November, 28,000 men—soldiers of the Slovak Technical Division, specially recruited civilians, and units of the forced labor service—were employed on the earthworks.

The Hungarian supreme command had warned as early as September that Budapest could become a frontline city within days, as the Hungarian 3rd Army was not strong enough to resist the first major attack. On 25 September János Vörös, head of the Honvéd (or Hungarian regular) army's joint chiefs of staff, had cabled to the chief of the German supreme command, Colonel-General Heinz Guderian: "Unless the Hungarian 3rd Army receives significant reinforcements immediately, it is doomed to fall before long. In this event the road toward Budapest, the heart of the country, will be open." On 9 October, Vörös instructed the commanders of the antiaircraft artillery and the available technical units to secure the access roads to Budapest. At the same time he ordered the Hungarian I Army Corps, together with the police, gendarmerie, and antiaircraft units attached to it, to take up positions along the Attila Line, and requested reinforcements from the German Army Group South. Although the Hungarian I Army Corps, located in Budapest, had only administrative functions and no troops of its own, it was temporarily placed in charge of all the Hungarian units in the capital. Today it is difficult to ascertain whether Vörös's real intention was to defend Budapest against the Soviets or to provide support for the ceasefire planned by Horthy. In any case he was aware of Horthy's plans.

On 10 October the Hungarian general staff began to prepare for the siege of the capital. On 12 October the staff of the Hungarian VI Army Corps was ordered to move from the Carpathians to Budapest, as was the Hungarian 10th Infantry Division. The Hungarian I Army Corps was to assume security duties, and the VI Army Corps defense duties. On the same day the 1st Parachute Group, one of the most reliable elite formations in the Hungarian army, was detailed to Budapest, and three antitank gun companies of the 10th Infantry Division were also directed to relocate from their positions in the Carpathians to Budapest with the utmost urgency. Colonel-General Heinz Guderian, commander in chief of the German panzer troops, protested against these measures, probably because the German command was aware of Horthy's ceasefire plans and therefore—despite the approach of the Soviets—primarily interested in forestalling a concentration of Hungarian units in the city. The Germans' decision to concentrate their forces on securing Budapest even at the height of the tank battle of Debrecen suggests that one of their prime concerns was to prevent a Hungarian withdrawal from the war and the loss of their foothold in the Hungarian theater.

Meanwhile, German reinforcements were also on their way to Budapest. These included the 503rd Heavy Panzer (Tiger) Battalion and parts of the 24th Panzer Division. On 13 October the Hungarian general staff gave orders for all mobile Hungarian units to be diverted to the capital. The Maria Theresia 22nd SS Volunteer Cavalry Division, which consisted of forcibly recruited ethnic Swabians living in Hungary, was stationed west of Buda.

According to the diary of the Army Group South, on 25 October the resources available for the defense of Budapest were 26,000 German and some 15,000 Hungarian troops, serving in a variety of units and not all fully trained, and 146 heavy antiaircraft guns, which could also be used against tanks. These were reinforced on 26 October by the 1/I Parachute Battalion from Buda, which took up positions at Dunaharaszti and Soroksár on the Attila Line to cut off the roads to Kecskemét and Solt. Other reinforcements between the end of October and mid-November were the 1st, 10th, 13th, 16th, 24th, and 25th Assault Artillery Battalions, two batteries of the 7th Assault Artillery Battalion with approximately 25 assorted tanks and 2,000 troops, and the 1st SS Police Regiment. The artillery battalions were sent to the less threatened region of Rákoscsaba, Ecser, and Pécel, while the SS police troops were stationed in the suburb of Kispest as reserves. The security forces in Budapest were made up of the 9/II Battalion (Szálasi Bodyguard), the Budapest Guard Battalion, the 201st–203rd Specialized Technical Battalions, the students of the Várpalota Officer-cadet Academy, and three gendarmerie battalions. The 12th Reserve Division, which was being replenished and restructured, also drew back to Budapest. The front line, about 70 kilometers south of Budapest, was being held by the 1st Armored Division, the 23rd Reserve

Division, the 8th Reserve Division, and the exhausted units of the 1st Hussar Division. These forces amounted to some 20,000.

The units stationed in Budapest, with their limited numbers, desultory training, and inadequate equipment, did not represent a serious defense force. Friessner, who realized that the capital would be the next target of the Soviet offensive, wrote to Guderian on 27 October 1944 asking for more units. He was to repeat the request several times during the following weeks, without success.

On 2 November the Soviet mechanized units reached the villages of Dunaharaszti, Alsónémedi, Ócsa, and Üllő, south and southeast of Budapest, and came within 15 kilometers of the city. Kovalovszky described his memories of the first battle sounds heard by the civilian population:

> In the short intervals between air raids I can still hear the constant thunder of guns. Are they firing so intensely at enemy planes that have lost their way? Then I realize that these are not antiaircraft guns. Could the battlefield have gotten so close to us? . . . After the brief lunch break the sirens are silent, but the noise of shooting grows ever more threatening. By now there can be no doubt that it is ground artillery that is firing and not antiaircraft guns, or a big tank battle is going on southeast of us. . . . We are in the battle zone. How long will it last and are we going to survive?

Two paratroopers involved in the action recalled the first appearance of Soviet tanks about 10 kilometers from the city boundary:

> On the afternoon of 2 November heavy gunfire could be heard from the direction of the antitank defense detachment, and soon the road between Soroksár and the defense positions was blocked by the horse-drawn columns of the units retreating from Kecskemét in disarray. . . . We cleared the road, and a little later the first soldiers from the antitank defense position arrived, reporting that the position had been stormed by the Russian tanks.

The five T-34s at the head soon reached the bridge over the antitank ditch. . . . There was deadly silence, and only the droning of the Soviet tanks and the grinding of the caterpillar tracks could be heard. It was already getting dark, but we could see Soviet infantry bent over in the ditches, following the tanks. Our orders were not to open fire on the infantry till the tanks had been shot up. The tanks came in stages, covering each other, but stopped short before the bridge. At that moment the antiaircraft guns hidden in the acacia trees alongside the road began to roar, and the defense units near the bridge discharged their antitank rocket launchers. There was also heavy infantry fire, and the Soviet infantrymen accompanying the tanks threw themselves down on the ground. The unexpected attack immobilized all five tanks.

At nightfall each of the two improvised defense positions of the paratroopers was charged by 20 Soviet tanks:

A chaotic battle raged for several hours. Many tanks were damaged by our antitank mines or guns and towed away. At Soroksár a few tanks managed to break through the defense line, but the Russian infantry got stuck—within assault distance—on the left flank, and the tanks retreated. . . . At Dunaharaszti the attack also collapsed, within assault distance, after a gun battle lasting several hours: the front held and several Soviet tanks were damaged.

On 3 November the Soviet 4th Mechanized Guard Corps broke through the defenses of the 22nd SS Cavalry Division and reached a point six kilometers east of Soroksár, but in the course of the day the paratroopers, led by Major Edömér Tassonyi, regained the lost positions. The Soviet 2nd Mechanized Guard Corps took the villages of Monor, Üllő, Vecsés, Gyál, and Pestszentimre southeast of Budapest, which the combat unit of the Budapest police was trying to defend. Three of the police unit's five obsolete Italian Ansaldo tanks were immediately destroyed, and the first Soviet tank rolled into Üllői Road, one of the main arteries leading into the city. Other formations penetrated as far as Ferihegy Airport, about 16 kilometers from the center. Troops of the 8th SS Cavalry Division and the Hungarian 12th Infantry Division recaptured Vecsés and Monor. Parts of Vecsés fell once more into Soviet hands, but were retaken on 4 November.

The Soviet armored offensive ended on 5 November. Many tanks had been hit, a large proportion of the infantry had fallen behind, the shortage of ammunition and fuel was making itself felt, and the advancing spearheads risked encirclement by the German 1st and 3rd Panzer Divisions. On 8 November the 22nd SS Cavalry Division ejected the Soviet advance guards from their positions along the Attila Line. After the withdrawal of the armored units Soviet infantry companies and battalions continued to attack and penetrate the defenses of the untrained German division, but with the help of the Hungarian paratroopers all such salients were sealed off and destroyed. At the time of the offensive some 13,000 infantry with about 100 tanks and assault guns and 150 guns were regrouped to the Great Hungarian Plain (Table 3).

Further Attacks of the 2nd Ukrainian Front

Colonel-General Shtemenko's memoirs illustrate the general staff reaction to the 46th Army's stalled offensive. As nobody dared to postpone or change Stalin's plan, the only solution was to broaden the attack and try to capture Budapest through an encirclement from two sides rather than a frontal assault. The 6th Guard Tank Army and the 7th Guard Army were to break through in the Hatvan region in the east and reach the Danube north of Budapest at Vác, while the 46th Army was to cross the Soroksár branch of the Danube, take Csepel Island, continue across the Öreg-Duna branch of the river, and attack the capital from nearby Érd in the southwest. The Soviets had stopped their frontal offensive southeast of Budapest on 5 November in order to regroup for an encirclement, which suggests that the strategic command had by now been entirely taken over by military experts who, unlike Stalin, knew what they were doing.

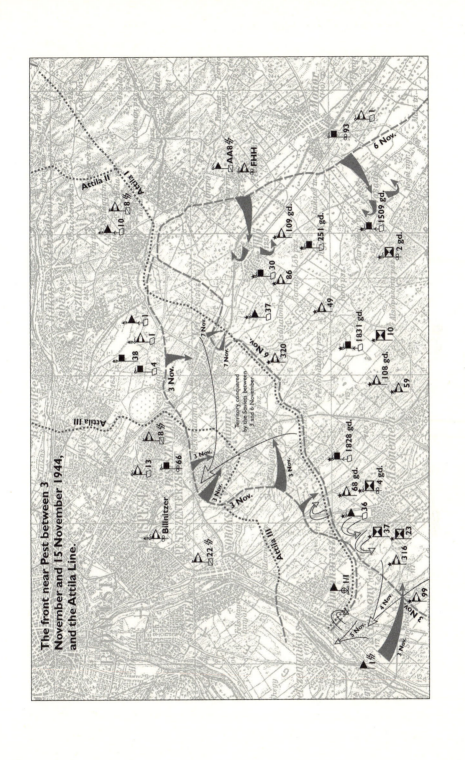

The front near Pest between 3 November and 15 November 1944, and the Attila Line.

Meanwhile, early in November, the German supreme army command had positioned three panzer corps to cut off the access routes to Budapest. The III Panzer Corps, led by Colonel-General Hermann Breith, took on the defense of the capital, while farther east the IV Panzer Corps prepared a counterattack in the Jászberény region and the LVII Panzer Corps in the Cegléd-Szolnok region. The Soviet forces—in particular the 7th Guard Army, which formed the left wing of the 2nd Ukrainian Front; the 53rd, 27th, and 40th Armies; and the mechanized cavalry group commanded by Colonel-General Pliev—were halted by German and Hungarian units as they tried to advance north. Malinovsky's armored units again suffered heavy losses. The German command reported the destruction of 132 Soviet tanks between 31 October and 12 November.

From 8 November Malinovsky's 7th Guard Army and the Pliev Corps renewed their attacks toward Isaszeg and Hatvan. In this region, east to northeast of Budapest, a 50-kilometer front line was defended by only a few Hungarian battalions and the German 13th Panzer Division, 4th and 18th SS Panzergrenadier Divisions, and 46th Infantry Division. Demoralized by the continuous Soviet attacks, many soldiers of the SS panzergrenadier divisions, who had been recruited by force, surrendered or fled. Their condition is illustrated by the following report: "18th SS Panzergrenadier Division . . . consists of ethnic Germans living in Hungary. They cross over to the enemy, their combat value is like a Hungarian division. . . . Strength c. 18,000, 1 rifle per 18 men."

It is not surprising that panic broke out among the untrained and badly equipped SS soldiers, who could only watch their comrades being crushed by the Soviet T-34 tanks as they sought refuge in holes in the ground. Nevertheless, the command of the German Army Group South blamed them for what happened, as Friessner's note to Guderian suggests: "In the 4th SS Police Panzergrenadier Division some commanders have shot themselves because their soldiers had run away. The 18th Panzer Grenadier Division has been a total failure."

The Hungarian 12th Reserve Division, consisting of some 2,000 infantry with 20 guns and still in the process of restructuring, had been deployed early in November to cut off the approach

to Budapest along a line between Pécel, Isaszeg, and, slightly farther to the south, Dány. As this proved insufficient, the Hungarian
1/I Parachute Battalion, commanded by Major Edömér Tassonyi,
was also deployed on 13 November. Until a reinforcement of 600
men arrived on 15 November, the paratroopers, with well-organized
artillery support, held a defense sector between 5 and 6 kilometers
in length by themselves, rebuffing a series of fierce Soviet attacks.
On one occasion the onslaught of the Soviet infantry reached the
Hungarian positions. Tassonyi recalls:

> I turned to the German artillery observer: "Shoot to kill
> at reference point A, at once!"—"But that's your own
> position."—"Never mind, at once!" I looked at my stop-
> watch. Seventeen seconds later our position and the area
> in front of it were under fire from 52 barrels, which grad-
> ually slowed down and after a few minutes decreased in
> range. This barrage scored a direct hit on the Russian
> infantry within assault distance. When I went (more
> accurately, leapt) out after the repulsion of the attack, the
> paratroopers told me they had known that the second
> barrage was their own and there was nothing they could
> do about it. As the firing abated, some had peeped out
> and seen Russian bodies flying through the air and Rus-
> sians in panic trying to dig themselves in. Miraculously,
> our company lost only seven dead and a few wounded in
> the murderous barrage; although a few soldiers had been
> buried by earth they escaped unscathed.

Tassonyi received the First and Second Class Iron Crosses and a
copy of the German Wehrmacht report praising him and his paratroopers. The fighting, however, which continued until 22 November, cost the unit a further 40 percent casualties.

Although the Soviet troops had crossed the Tisza at every
point, they were unable to prevent the Germans from stabilizing the
front and establishing a coherent battle line by constantly regrouping their remaining forces and carrying out successive counterstrikes. The Soviet losses were substantial, but by the end of the
month the German panzer divisions had also been decimated. "The

battalions only numbered 100 to 200 by now. On every 100 meters of front line there were on average only 3.5 of our men. . . . The best panzer units had eight tanks left, the others four or five," Friessner wrote in his memoirs. By the middle of November, the German units stationed northeast of Budapest had retreated to the Karola Line, and in that sector also the front stabilized.

Stalin finally realized that the 2nd Ukrainian Front would not suffice to capture Budapest. On 14 November he therefore placed at Malinovsky's disposal 200 tanks and 40,000 troops from the supreme command's reserves, as well as the 4th Ukrainian Front, at that time stranded in the Carpathians. With the tanks, which vastly outnumbered those of their German counterparts, Malinovsky reinforced the 6th Guard Tank Army in order to encircle Budapest from the north, jointly with the 7th Guard Army, as he had originally planned. But the Soviet forces were unable to break through the defenses from this direction.

The 46th Army's bid to cross the Danube and land on Csepel Island south of the city was more successful. On 6 November a similar attempt by a battalion of the Soviet 23rd Rifle Corps had been foiled by the Hungarian 2/I Hussar Battalion and a rapidly redeployed assault artillery group from Debrecen after the discovery of a Soviet artillery observer hiding in a church tower southeast of the island. Assault artillery lieutenant György Thuróczy recalls:

> The Soviet rifle battalion got stuck in the shallow water near the bank of the Holt-Duna branch, while trying to hide in the thicket of birches, willows, and other water plants. Those who hadn't had time to hide were taken prisoner by us. Most of them were probably over 40, with big mustaches and a meek appearance. Our soldiers offered them rum and patted them on the back in a friendly manner. . . . Our welcoming behavior lured more and more Russkis from their hiding place on the Danube branch. Some were carrying improvised crucifixes made of twigs. . . . There was one Soviet wounded as white as chalk, maybe a sergeant. I still remember his hard, stern gaze and his unyielding face rejecting any

amicable gesture, his mouth clenched with pain. He accepted our prompt medical assistance, but when we offered him some rum, he shook his head without saying a word. The prisoners asked us not to hand them over to the Germans, but the Hungarian army was not allowed to hold prisoners.

The Soviet troops trying to cross the river on 14, 15, 16, and 18 November were repulsed, but by 21 November they were landing on Csepel Island in division strength. Tibor Gencsy, commander of the assault half-company of the Hungarian 4th Hussar Regiment, remembers:

> The renewed enemy breakthrough from the Kis-Duna branch came at dawn the next day. As a reservist I was billeted in one of the schools in Tököl. The regiment commanders were slumbering sweetly behind me. Those in the front lines, Major Mészáros and the other units, offered no resistance. The enemy troops—probably penal companies, saturated with "assault water"—approached the railway line at the end of the village, where I was positioned with my men, in thick clusters. That is why it was possible for one bullet to go through two or three bodies. We reloaded a few times, and they dispersed to try and attack us from behind by going round the village. . . . Then we were pulled out of the village, and the next day there was a counterattack supported by German tanks. The enemy troops were splendidly dug in and this time offered clear-headed and serious resistance. As they sat in their splendidly camouflaged trenches we hit them in the neck and head, but with our weak forces were unable to clean up Tököl completely.

Alarmed by this threat from the south, the German Army Group South detailed the Hungarian 1/II Parachute Battalion, a cadet battalion, and the combat group of the Feldherrnhalle Division to Csepel Island, as well as the 1st and 9th Artillery Battalions and two independent battalions. None of these, however, proved a match for the Soviet 23rd Rifle Corps, which completed the crossing to Csepel Island on 25 November and was joined by troops of the Soviet 37th Rifle Corps. With a number of villages changing hands several times, the front finally came to a standstill between Lakihegy and Királyerdő on the southern edge of the conurbation, when the Soviets had advanced far enough for the substantial Hungarian artillery—supported by speedboats of the river service—to open fire on them with 103 guns from the suburbs of Csepel in the north and Soroksár in the east and from the far bank of the Danube in the west. Nevertheless, the fighting still continued, as Aurél Salamon, a reserve hussar lieutenant, recalls:

> Toward evening the Russian so-called penal battalion (political prisoners) attacked our positions. A horrible bombardment awaited them, with concerted salvos from machine guns, mortars, and dug-in tanks, and even the speedboats on the Danube were showering bullets on them. . . . The attack collapsed after a little while with huge losses. Hundreds of dying and wounded were lying in front of our positions. We could often hear shouts of "bozhe moi" [my God], together with loud, but weakening, calls for help. Our stretcher bearers tried to bring them in, but each time their efforts were rewarded with machine-gun fire. These people simply had to die. We were unable to help them, and by the next day they were silent.

The magnitude of the casualties in general may be illustrated by the fact that the 1,400 men of the Hungarian 1/II Parachute Battalion, who arrived on 28–29 November as reinforcements, roughly equaled in number the entire strength of the hussar division still in action on Csepel Island at the time.

The Second Soviet Offensive Against Budapest: Ercsi and Hatvan

Both Stalin and the Soviet general staff were displeased with the slow progress of Malinovsky's 2nd Ukrainian Front, the strongest of all Soviet fronts. Farther north, the 4th Ukrainian Front was even worse off, having covered only 200 kilometers since August 1944, and having come to a standstill at the Carpathians. The Soviet supreme command sent Marshall Semion Konstantinovich Timoshenko to investigate. Marshall Fedor Ivanovich Tolbukhin, the commander of the 3rd Ukrainian Front operating in Serbia, was also included in the discussions, although he had not so far been involved in the plans concerning Budapest. His role in Hungary was now upgraded because of the 2nd Ukrainian Front's lack of success, and because certain political considerations made a further advance in the Balkans undesirable; in addition, Stalin always liked to incite his subordinates to compete with each other. Timoshenko submitted his report on 24 November:

> The 2nd Ukrainian Front is one of the strongest fronts. It has substantial potential for smashing the resistance of the enemy, but nevertheless has not scored any successes lately. The reasons for this lack of success, in my view, are the following:

> 1. The supreme command—relying on its relatively superior strength—is trying to destroy the enemy formations simultaneously in different areas (Miskolc, Eger, Hatvan).
> 2. This leads to a dispersal of forces, making it impossible for our troops to bring their superior strength to bear. For example, the principal grouping (27th, 53rd Armies, 7th Guard Army), with 24 rifle divisions, 3 mechanized and 1 tank corps, and 2 cavalry corps, is extended as follows:

> > a) in the Miskolc sector the 27th Army on a 50-kilometer front line with 8 rifle divisions,
> > b) in the Eger sector the 53rd Army with 7 rifle divisions on a front line of 45 kilometers,
> > c) in the Hatvan sector the 7th Guard Army with 9 rifle divisions. In the same sector 3 mechanized, 1 tank and 2 cavalry corps are in action.

Thus the rifle units are distributed proportionally among the respective armies and sectors. A somewhat superior strength exists only in the case of the 7th Guard Army, in whose sector Pliev's corps and the 2nd and 4th Mechanized Corps are operating. However, Pliev's corps and the mechanized corps are worn out as a result of protracted fighting and of having to confront superior forces. . . .

3. To some extent the unit commanders and their staffs have been spoiled by events in Romania and Transylvania, and are not therefore handling the cooperation between the different services with due care.

In view of the above I would consider it practical to require the commander of the 2nd Ukrainian Front:

1. to review his earlier decisions and create such formations as will confront the enemy in 2 sectors with absolutely superior strength. The sectors in question are:
a) Hatvan-Balassagyarmat as the principal section and
b) Miskolc as the secondary section.

The Soviets did all they could to ensure the success of the attack. In the Hatvan sector their infantry and tanks outnumbered those of the defense by a factor of nine and their artillery by a factor of eight, compared with a fourfold Soviet superior force in the Carpathian Basin (Tables 4 and 5). The total ration strengths stationed in the Budapest area between 5 November and 24 December amounted to 7 divisions of some 60,000 troops on the German and Hungarian side, and 12 divisions of some 110,000 troops on the Soviet and Romanian side.

The Soviet supreme command had ordered Tolbukhin already in mid-October to halt the advance of the 3rd Ukrainian Front in Yugoslavia after capturing Belgrade, and to make preparations to take part in the operations in Hungary in order to gain access to the Transdanubian aluminium plants and oil fields before pressing ahead toward Vienna or, if necessary, Budapest. It was for this purpose that the 4th Guard Army, stationed in Galicia, had been attached to the 3rd Ukrainian Front on 18 October. On 9 November Tolbukhin's troops had established a bridgehead at Kiskőszeg on the Danube, which they continued to expand. On 12 November Malinovsky had been ordered to hand the 31st Guard Rifle Corps over to Tolbukhin; on 27 November, three days after Timoshenko's report, he had received the same order in respect of the 5th Cavalry Corps. Thus, with the front line gradually shifting west in southern Transdanubia, Soviet forces were in a position to approach Budapest from the southwest.

Soviet headquarters, advised by Tolbukhin, ordered Malinovsky to move the 6th Guard Tank Army, the 7th Guard Army, two mechanized corps, one tank corps, two cavalry corps, and two newly constituted artillery divisions to the Hatvan region northeast of Budapest. Their attack on the eight-kilometer sector of the front chosen for the breakthrough was to be carried out in two waves, the first by six divisions, the second by two divisions, two artillery divisions, and the 6th Guard Tank Army. With a total of 510 tanks and 2,074 guns and mortars, every kilometer of the front line was to be covered by 64 tanks, 260 guns and mortars, and 4,000 infantry. Nearby, over a stretch of seven kilometers, the 53rd Army was to deploy four divisions with 700 guns and mortars. Now Malinovsky had reason to hope that in three or four days his troops would reach Vác and the Ipoly valley, from where they would be able both to overrun Budapest and to advance farther into the Little Hungarian Plain in northwestern Hungary.

By the end of November it was clear that Tolbukhin's troops would capture parts of Transdanubia within weeks or even days, and then advance on Budapest from the southwest. Malinovsky, attacking from the east, was presumably unwilling to share the glory of taking Budapest; that is the only possible explanation for his decision that the 2nd Mechanized Guard Corps and the 46th Army should cross the Danube and encircle the city from the west ahead of Tolbukhin. The senselessness of this strategically unnecessary measure, which cost a great many lives, becomes obvious in view of the fact that by that time the German and Hungarian defense had collapsed south of the point where Malinovsky intended to cross the Danube, and Tolbukhin's troops, advancing at a rate of 10 to 20 kilometers a day, were soon to reach Budapest from the southwest in any case.

Malinovsky ordered the 46th Army to cross the Danube near Ercsi, a village on the west bank close to the southern edge of Budapest, on 4 December 1944. The defenders had been reinforcing their positions for days in anticipation of the attack, which finally began, without any artillery preparation, at 11 P.M. The Soviet assault squads were received by an extraordinary barrage, which destroyed 75 percent of their boats in midriver. The following episode, reported in the Soviet recommendations for the decoration of soldiers, exemplifies the scale of the casualties:

> Toward midnight on 4 December, Sergeant Oleg Niko-laievich Smirnov's pontoon was transporting an assault squad and two guns to the right bank of the Danube. On the way the pontoon was hit. Smirnov received two bullets in the leg, and four of the oarsmen were also wounded. Nevertheless, they managed to land the assault squad and the guns. On the way back the pontoon was hit and Smirnov wounded again. By that time only two of the fighters remained unscathed. Smirnov, gravely wounded, was giving orders to his comrades lying down, but by the time the craft had reached the left bank of the river they could only lift out his dead body.

Several elite companies were lost, and the survivors from others turned back in the middle of the partly frozen river. By the evening of 5 December the Soviet troops had established four bridgeheads, but three were immediately destroyed by swift German counterattacks. On 6 December seven more bridgeheads were established on both sides of Ercsi, although not one member of the first assault company survived the heavy barrage of the defense. Many soldiers were obliged to jump out of their wrecked boats halfway through the journey and continue swimming with their weapons through the icy water. The Soviet losses amazed even their opponents. Hussar Lieutentant-Colonel Emil Tomka wrote in his diary:

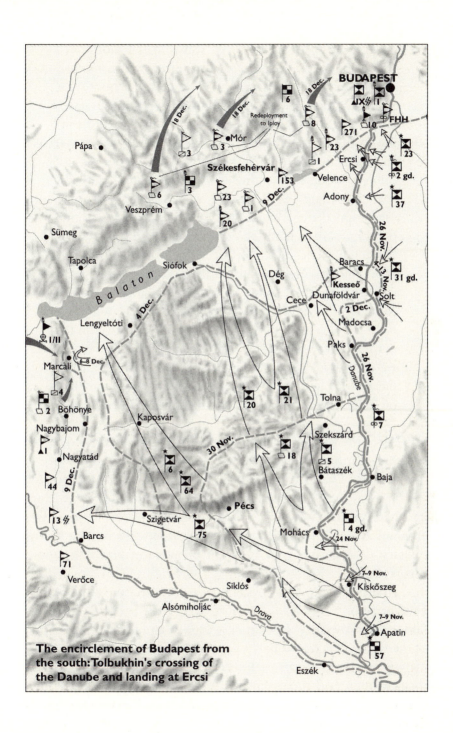

The encirclement of Budapest from
the south: Tolbukhin's crossing of
the Danube and landing at Ercsi

When I went to the northern sector in the morning, I saw a unique sight. Our own artillery was constantly bombarding the Russian crossing point opposite the Szinya farm. German dive bombers were giving assistance, and [Géza] Terstyánszky's three mortars were firing in the same direction. In spite of all this the Soviet crossing continued. The troops were transported not only by assault boats but also by a steam ferry. The packed loading barge was hit by a German bomb and sank immediately, but a little later they pulled another one out from behind the embankment and the crossing continued. The most horrific thing was that the Germans still holding the embankment on this side were firing with machine guns at the disembarking Russian soldiers, of whom only a small percentage could have been left alive, and these were trying to take cover in the densely overgrown river flats, several meters deep in water or mud. As we were watching this, a hussar next to me said: "Lieutenant, Sir, if this is how they treat their own men, what would they do to their enemies?"

After the battle, Malinovsky clearly wanted to gloss over the pointless sacrifice of his soldiers by handing out an abundance of decorations. Thus 115 men, nearly half the soldiers who received the Hero of the Soviet Union medal for actions in specific Hungarian locations, were decorated for participating in the river crossing at Ercsi. The total of those awarded this highest Soviet military decoration up to 1945—in many cases posthumously—was 12,000.

According to Malinovsky's plan the troops crossing the Danube were to reach the Budaörs-Bia area by the end of the second day and the area between Pilisvörösvár and Csákvár by the end of the third. This would have required an advance of 20 to 30 kilometers a day, which can be accomplished by infantry units only if they encounter no enemy forces. In the circumstances this was not possible, because after the crossing Malinovsky's troops would still have had to break through the Margit Line. Presumably he had set such spectacular objectives in order to magnify the supposed importance of the crossing.

The misguided nature of Malinovsky's enterprise is further revealed by the fact that the position of the 46th Army did not stabilize until 8 December, when the units of Tolbukhin's 3rd Ukrainian Front, advancing on the west bank of the Danube, had also arrived below Ercsi. The superior strength of the six rifle divisions and the 2nd Mechanized Guard Corps finally overpowered the drained Hungarian forces—the Hungarian 1st Hussar Division, the German 271st Volksgrenadier Division, and the 8th Panzer Division—but the front came to a standstill at the Margit Line, between 10 and 20 kilometers from the point of the river crossing, where Malinovsky had to hand over his stalled units to the 3rd Ukrainian Front.

An attack of the Hungarian 10th Assault Artillery Battalion, starting between the villages of Baracska and Martonvásár, pushed the Soviet troops back almost as far as the Danube north of Ercsi. A battery of the 1st Assault Artillery Battalion, claiming that it was not adequately employed in its assigned position, joined the attack without orders and destroyed a Soviet group ensconced in Baracska: the battalion's commander, Captain Sándor Hanák, with a self-propelled assault gun, flattened a Soviet antitank gun that was firing at him. The attack was unexpectedly successful: 15 guns were seized or destroyed and some 250 Soviet soldiers killed. As a result, no further Soviet attack took place in this area for a long time, and the daring of the Hungarians was mentioned even in German reports.

Malinovsky's attack north of Budapest was more successful. The German military command had been forced by Tolbukhin's progress to move the 1st and 23rd Panzer Divisions of the German Army Group South from the neighborhood of Hatvan to Transdanubia, and the defense found itself significantly outnumbered.

The attack began at 10:15 A.M. on 5 December, after a heavy barrage lasting 45 minutes. Eight Soviet divisions broke through the German and Hungarian front between Acsa and Galgamácsa, and in two hours established a salient, 12 kilometers wide and between 3 and 6 kilometers deep, pointing toward Vác. At 1:30 P.M.

the Soviet 6th Guard Tank Army was also deployed in the sector of the breakthrough. Friessner requested urgent reinforcements from Guderian: it was imperative to block the Ipoly valley, through which the Soviet tanks could reach the Little Hungarian Plain and threaten Bratislava and Vienna as well as Budapest. The only units that could be detailed to the Ipoly valley immediately, however, were parts of the 24th Panzer Division and an SS brigade of convicts commanded by SS Brigadeführer (equivalent of major-general) Oskar Dirlewanger. Friessner notes:

> When I reached Dirlewanger's staff I was met by a strange sight. The Brigadeführer, a not very appealing adventurer type, was sitting at his desk with a live monkey perched on his shoulder. The monkey was said to have accompanied him everywhere, including Poland. When I discovered that the staff was packing up I ordered them to stay on the spot. . . . The unit was, as suggested before, a wild bunch. One company—communists who were expected to "prove themselves" on the front—had just deserted to the enemy.

Between northeastern Budapest and Vác an enormous gap had opened, which the German Army Group South was unable to fill, as it lacked the necessary reserves. In order to protect at least the northern portion of the Pest bridgehead, the Feldherrnhalle Panzergrenadier Division was transferred from the Csepel front to the Vác region on 6 December, followed over the next eight days by a number of Hungarian units, including the I Special Hussar Battalion, the Army Security Battalion, the IV Pioneer Battalion, and the 1/II Parachute Battalion. By this time, however, the Feldherrnhalle Division was so run down that its entire infantry did not even amount to 30 percent of the combat strength of the Hungarian 1/II Parachute Battalion, whose 1,300 troops were the strongest unit involved in the whole regroupment.

On 9 December the left wing of the Soviet 6th Guard Tank Army reached the Danube at Vác. The assault group of the Feldherrnhalle Division and the 13th Panzer Division tried to counter-attack, but without success. A hastily deployed police training battalion was crushed by troops of the 30th Rifle Corps and the 60 tanks accompanying them: 70 percent of its men were killed or wounded within 24 hours.

In the northern sector of the Attila Line the only defense was provided by two KISKA auxiliary security companies and the 153rd Pioneer Company, which were pulverized by Soviet troops within a few hours. Major-General Günther von Pape, commander of the Feldherrnhalle Division, ordered an immediate counterattack. The task of recapturing the village of Fót was entrusted to the Hungarian II Parachute Battalion, flanked by units of the Feldherrnhalle Division and the Hungarian 10th Infantry Division (with about 15 armored vehicles and 200 German and 600 Hungarian troops). Although the occupiers were supported by 26 batteries and numerous mortars, the paratroopers—together with the remnants of two exhausted German battalions and a panzer company—were able to recapture Fót on 13 December. By the following evening, however, they had been forced to withdraw once more because of the flanks' failure to catch up. From a new position south of Fót, despite almost 40 percent casualties, they carried out a raid and took a number of prisoners, including the Soviet division's operational chief of staff. Pape awarded them 31 First- and Second-Class Iron Crosses and personally delivered a transcript of a Soviet communication monitored by the German division: "I request immediate reinforcement because I cannot fulfil my task in these circumstances. The enemy is as tough as old boots and is offering fierce resistance."

As the focus of fighting shifted toward the northern and eastern parts of the city, the Soviet troops made deep inroads which could no longer be halted. Lieutenant György Thuróczy recalls one of the offensives:

It was already dark when we took over the defense line. The changing of the guard was not betrayed even by the flame of a match. As we groped our way forward in the trenches connecting the separate dugouts, we were suddenly walking on a strange thick material with an uneven surface that felt like textile. When dawn broke we realized that a long stretch of the trench was carpeted with dead German soldiers. . . . The barrage preparing the offensive opened at 8:45 A.M., and for a whole hour, till 9:45, we were bombarded so densely that we couldn't make a move. Then, when the assault of the roaring tanks and the cheering artillery followed, we received no artillery support whatsoever and could only resort to our infantry arms. On our right flank was the defense position of the 1st Battery. To the right of the 1st Battery a platoon of old men of the Territorial Army—horrified by the determined onslaught of the Soviets and lacking a white flag—waved the legs of their underpants at the enemy rushing and clanking toward them. . . . When the attacking Russkis saw the signals of the old soldiers, they immediately formed a wedge of infantry protected by tanks and began to pour behind our defense line through the gap that was offered to them. The 2nd and 3rd batteries, afraid of being encircled, began to retreat. . . .

It was already dark night when we arrived in Pécel, worn out in body and soul. The men went to their quarters and lay down to sleep in their clothes. We officers were summoned to the castle by Colonel-General [Ernő] Billnitzer, the commander of the assault artillery units around Budapest. György Kozma, who had been assigned command of the group, reported on the outcome of the fighting at Tűzberek. The men were worn out and needed to rest. Billnitzer declared: "We mustn't allow the Russians to walk into Budapest." . . .

The men, most of whom were already in a deep sleep, had to be woken, and toward midnight we set out in the damp and cold darkness to form a front line against the Russkis. . . . The enemy's position, firepower, and strength could only be guessed at from the machine guns that started barking a few hundred meters from us and fell silent again after their salvos. . . . Dead beat, we threw ourselves down on the ground and immediately fell into a bottomless sleep. . . .

We were suddenly woken. Soon it would be full daylight and we had to dig ourselves in.

Between 15 and 24 November some Soviet troops near Isaszeg and Valkó had been replaced with Romanians. The attacks continued with equal violence, and the Hungarian defense also became more stubborn. In early December, between Maglód and Vecsés in the less endangered southeastern section, the Hungarian 1st Armored Division and the assault artillery battalion attached to it even launched a counterattack, which proved surprisingly successful and for which Captain Frigyes Wáczek of the general staff was awarded the Officer's Cross of the Hungarian Order of Merit.

A gap between Valkó and Dány east of Isaszeg was to have been closed and the two villages recaptured through a counterattack. Although Hungarian troops recaptured Valkó, however, the action stalled before reaching its objective because the 13th Panzer Division and the Feldherrnhalle Panzergrenadier Division, lacking infantry, could provide only a few tanks in support. The Soviet counteroffensive, which began on 18 November, broke up a Hungarian battalion of reserve units and convicts, pushing its remnants back to the hills east of Isaszeg. An improvised company laid down its arms and surrendered. The 8/I Battalion, which had only recently been replenished with civilian prisoners and had not received any food for two days, was destroyed, and the surviving units of the 9th Infantry Regiment scattered by continuous Soviet attacks.

On 5 December the Soviet and Romanian forces launched a general offensive in the region surrounding Isaszeg and penetrated the lines of the Hungarian 10th Infantry Division and 12th Reserve Division at several points. The 10th Infantry Division alone came under fire for 45 minutes from more than 100 guns. Along the 2.5-kilometer section chosen for that attack, seven Romanian battalions and cavalry battalions charged the positions of two Hungarian battalions. The 8/II Battalion lost 50 percent of its men in one day, and the 36/II Battalion, with the exception of five men, joined the attackers. Although the positions were recaptured in several counterattacks, the lines had to be pulled back, because a number of Soviet armored units that had broken through farther east were approaching the small town of Gödöllő north of Isaszeg.

On 9 December the German command promised to withdraw the 10th Infantry Division for a rest, but this was prevented by a Soviet breakthrough between Vác and Veresegyház, and by 11 December fighting was in progress on the perimeter of Gödöllő itself. As a result of heavy losses, the remnants of the 10th Infantry Division's regiments were converted into battalions of less than 50 percent of normal strength (300 to 500) attached to German battalions. With supplies and administration remaining the only duties of its command, the division in practice ceased to exist.

The 12th Reserve Division, which had arrived in early November in a wretched condition after being almost wiped out in the battle of Debrecen, was in an even worse plight. Because of the incessant Soviet and Romanian attacks, it had to abandon Isaszeg on 12 December and could retain a foothold only in the hills to the north. Although Isaszeg was temporarily recaptured through a German counterattack on 15 December, the front of the 12th Reserve Division, whose battalions numbered only between 100 and 200 by that time, remained the most vulnerable point of the bridgehead.

The Third Stage of the Operations
Soviet and German Strategic Plans and the Breakthrough

Following Timoshenko's report of 24 November—which recommended, among other things, that Malinovsky should not disperse his forces—the Soviet general staff gave orders for the preparation of a renewed assault on Budapest on 12 December. Based on Timoshenko's suggestions, the frontline commanders Tolbukhin and Malinovsky drew up concrete plans for an offensive of four armies on two fronts.

From the south, in Transdanubia, where over a stretch of 100 kilometers the Margit Line was defended by only some 7,800 exhausted men of little combat value (Table 6), two army corps of the 3rd Ukrainian Front were to attack in the direction of Székesfehérvár, the 18th Armored Corps was to advance north toward the Danube, and the 2nd Mechanized Guard Corps was to turn east toward Buda. North of the Danube, the 2nd Ukrainian Front was to move toward Esztergom. The capture of the encircled capital was to be shared by both groupings: the left flank of the 3rd Ukrainian Front was to close the outer encirclement ring by the fifth or sixth day, while the right flank was to take Buda and the 2nd Ukrainian Front was to take Pest, on the eighth or ninth day. To simplify the command structure, Tolbukhin had earlier been placed in charge of all the units operating in Transdanubia, including Malinovsky's.

The German army command realized in good time what the Soviets had in mind. The Department of Foreign Armies East (Abteilung Fremde Heere Ost) signaled the planned Soviet offensive as early as 12 December. Two days later, Colonel-General Maximilian Fretter-Pico, commander of the German 6th Army, warned that the 36-kilometer section of the Margit Line between Lake Velence and Budapest, which was defended by only 2,250 German and Hungarian troops, could be penetrated by any sizable Soviet thrust.

The Germans had already sent substantial reinforcements to Transdanubia, with the intention of regaining the lost territories and creating a solid battle line along the Danube which could be held with a smaller combat strength. Guderian's ultimate reason for so doing was to save troops, for he had always regarded Hungary as a secondary theater of war. The German units concerned were three panzer battalions, the 4th Cavalry Brigade and the 3rd, 6th, and 8th Panzer Divisions, in total numbering some 400 tanks and 40,000 men. Furthermore, the Hungarian Szent László Division was also due to be deployed in this region. In principle they had a fair chance of success, because the advance of the Soviet mechanized units had resulted in a highly vulnerable bulge. Although various options were discussed, the German supreme command, following Hitler's orders, chose the operation codenamed *Spätlese* (Late Harvest), which was to take place between Lake Balaton and Lake Velence; the idea of an attack toward the northeast was dropped because by then the status of the Pest bridgehead was regarded as uncertain. Bad weather and lack of fuel and ammunition, however, forced postponement of the attack, first to 20 December and then to 22 December.

The successes of the 2nd Ukrainian Front at the Ipoly River further weakened the prospects of the German attack. This induced Guderian to send north the 8th Panzer Division, those sections of the Szent László Division already present, and the armored grenadiers attached to them. Surprisingly, these units were split on Guderian's own orders: the armored grenadiers were detailed to try to prevent a breakthrough at the Ipoly, while the tanks remained in the neighborhood of Székesfehérvár to intervene in the battle at the appropriate time. The 4th Cavalry Brigade was left to deal with emergencies near the southwest corner of Lake Balaton. Thus by the middle of the month the attacking formation was entirely devoid of infantry, and the troops arriving in the north were used to support those defending the front, rather than to mount an attack.

Guderian's measures were subsequently criticized by former combatants as well as by military historians. They proved a momentous disadvantage to both the armored units and the infantry, which were separated from their original environment and forced to fight under unfamiliar commands in unfavorable circumstances. The chief asset of an armored division is its combination of mobility and firepower, but this can be maximized only in cooperation with the infantry, which alone is able to defend any captured territories. Moreover, the armored trucks transporting the infantry can come into their own only in a truly offensive strategy. Guderian denied these benefits to his troops; there can be no logical explanation for this unless one assumes that he had been ordered to do so, although the supreme command must have known that his forces were not sufficient to defend Budapest at the Margit Line and at the same time prevent a Soviet breakthrough toward Vienna at the Ipoly. Under the circumstances he could only hope for a miracle that would allow him to gain time and start an offensive of his own later on.

But the Soviet generals did not leave him any time. Taking advantage of the greater mobility of their T-34 tanks in the field, they set their troops in motion on 20 December despite the bad weather. North of the Danube, Malinovsky's 7th Guard Army broke through toward Esztergom on the first day, and the 6th Guard Tank

Army, under Colonel-General Andrei Grigorevich Kravchenko, took Léva and crossed the Garam River on the second day.

The assault of Tolbukhin's 3rd Ukrainian Front on the Margit Line began on 20 December at 9:20 A.M. after a 40-minute artillery barrage. The 3rd Ukrainian Front—with five times as much infantry and artillery, and three and a half times as many tanks and assault guns in the main fighting area—vastly outnumbered the defenders. The Fretter-Pico Army Group had not been surprised by the offensive, but a lack of infantry left it with limited scope for preparation. Major-General László Kesseő, commander of the Hungarian forces between Lake Velence and Baracska, may also

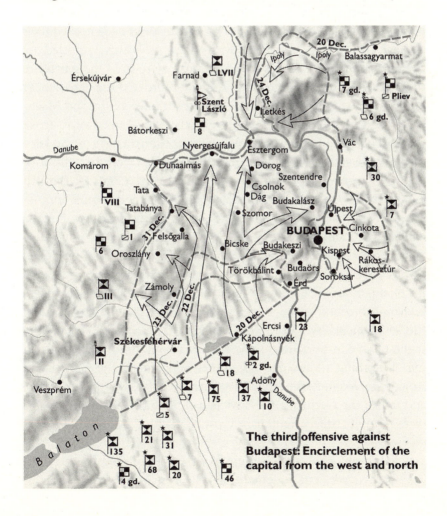

The third offensive against
Budapest: Encirclement of the
capital from the west and north

have assessed the situation correctly, because on 19 December he lay down his command and departed for an unknown destination.

Each kilometer of the front line came under fire from between 99 and 160 guns and mortars. As the diary of the 2/I Hussar Division reports, during the breakthrough at the village of Kápolnásnyék in the main trajectory of the attack, the Soviet generals chased their own infantry into the drumfire, so that "hussars who had taken cover in the ditches were dragged out by the Russians," while "it was no longer possible to step out of the houses to ask what was going on, because one house after the other collapsed, burying those inside."

On 20 December, counter to plans, the breach achieved by Soviet infantry units was only between five and six kilometers wide, because concerted counterattacks by German tanks had checked their advance. The onslaught of the Soviet rifle corps, however, eroded the defenses of the Germans, who lacked infantry to hold the territories they occupied. On 21 December, Tolbukhin ordered the deployment of mechanized units, and on 22 December 82 tanks of the 2nd Mechanized Guard Corps and 228 tanks of the 18th Tank Corps broke through between Érd and Lake Velence, capturing a territory 60 kilometers wide and 30 kilometers deep. Also on 22 December, the 20th and 31st Guard Corps and the 7th Mechanized Corps of the 4th Guard Army—the latter comprising 107 tanks and assault guns—attacked Székesfehérvár, where fierce street fighting ensued. For the defense the Germans deployed several commando units using captured Soviet uniforms and T-34 tanks, which had originally been reserved for a German offensive, but they could stall the Soviets only for brief periods. The devastating casualties the Soviet command was prepared to countenance in its relentless attacks may be explained by the Soviet mentality. Despite the well-known communist slogan "the highest value in Socialism is the human being," human life as such meant nothing to the Stalinist leadership. Unlike the British and Americans, Stalin had no need to consider public opinion at home, and unlike the Germans, the Soviets had no serious shortage of soldiers. Assault artillery lieutenant György Thuróczy recalls:

> In front of the defense line is a well-established double barbed-wire entanglement, and in front of this a pile of

Russian soldiers' bodies in the most unimaginable postures. They are victims of who knows which futile attack
wave. . . . I have hardly got out of the sidecar when I see
two assault artillery men pulling a writhing human wreck
from among the dead. They have probably cut through
the barbed wire and now they are carrying the twitching
body through the gap and laying it down on the outer
edge of the trench. The young soldier, with his shaven
head and Mongolian cheekbones, is lying on his back.

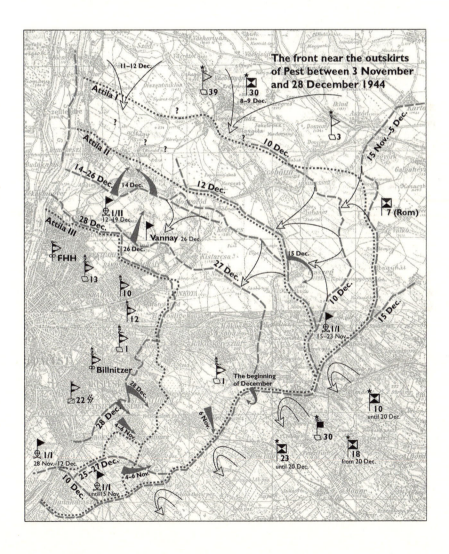

The front near the outskirts of Pest between 3 November and 28 December 1944

Only his mouth is moving. Both legs and lower arms are missing. The stumps are covered in a thick layer of soil, mixed with blood and leaf mould. I bend down close to him. "Budapesst . . . Budapesst . . ." he whispers in the throes of death. . . . In my head one thought revolves: he may be having a vision of "Budapesst . . . Budapesst" as a city of rich spoils and beautiful women. Then, surprising even myself, I pull out my pistol, load it, press it against the dying man's temple, and fire.

Although the breakthrough took longer than the Soviets had planned, the Fretter-Pico Army Group, plagued by a shortage of reserves, in particular infantry, was unable to profit from the delay: only in the Székesfehérvár region did it slow down the Soviet advance. Tolbukhin thought it most profitable to press the offensive on the right flank. He ordered the 2nd Mechanized Guard Corps to avoid local encounters and to move north as fast as possible in order to take the region of Bicske—the most important railway junction in the direction of Budapest—while the infantry was to reach a line 10 to 15 kilometers west of the outskirts of Budapest by the evening of 22 December. Despite desperate counterattacks by the 8th Panzer Division, Bicske fell on 23 December. By 24 December the attacks of Malinovsky's Soviet and Romanian troops on the Pest bridgehead had produced no significant results; on the Buda side Tolbukhin's 23rd Rifle Corps, after taking Érd on the previous day, stalled at the mine barriers near the southwestern edge of the city. Nevertheless, the road to Budapest from the west was now clear.

The Dilemma of the German and Hungarian Leadership

In contrast to the military command, neither the German nor the Hungarian political leadership had been prepared for Budapest becoming a frontline city. Strangely enough, in this respect the views of the regent Miklós Horthy coincided with those of Ferenc Szálasi, the extreme right-wing politician and leader of the fascist Arrow Cross Party, who toppled Horthy through a pro-German coup on 15 October 1944. Szálasi stated soon after his rise to power that he "would regard it as necessary to hold Budapest only if any offensive operations were to be undertaken from there. However, if this is not intended, Budapest must definitely be evacuated and we must make a strategic retreat to the Transdanubian hills." Although Szálasi is generally considered a fantasist, as a trained general-staff officer he was able, on some occasions, to assess the situation realistically. At a press conference early in November, for example, he said: "The Germans want to gain time by defending Budapest."

On 2 November Szálasi convened a crown council meeting in Buda Castle. Having taken his oath as leader of the nation, he delivered a lecture on relations between Hungary and Japan and then left with his retinue without commenting on the military situation. By that time, the thunder of guns could already be heard in the Castle District. On 3 November he summoned Friessner and asked him to forward a statement to the highest German authorities. Friessner signaled:

> In view of the fact that the battle is now raging in the suburbs of Budapest, [Szálasi] stresses that these developments are not his fault but a legacy of the previous regime. . . . He regrets that the German leadership intervened so late in Hungarian affairs. At this point his present government can only engage in damage limitation in an attempt to prevent the collapse of the nation; really constructive work is no longer possible.

Szálasi further claimed that he would be able to call up as many as 300,000 men, but the arms would have to be provided by the Germans.

Szálasi's unwillingness to defend Budapest had less to do with the likely devastation than with his conviction that the population—in his words, the "metropolitan mob"—might try to stab the defenders in the back, and that there would not be enough forces to suppress insurrection. His suspicions were not entirely unjustified, because by that time his Arrow Cross Party had lost much of its popularity among the inhabitants of Budapest. His views were shared by the leaders of the German Army Group South, who on 26 November sought guidance from the German supreme command as to what should be done if unrest erupted among the population. The answer was that the "metropolitan mob" should either be evacuated or kept under control by force. Lacking troops for such a task, Friessner asked for an SS general with experience in keeping law and order to be detailed to Budapest, together with "assault pioneer battalions, as in Warsaw." He also requested the supreme command's permission to retreat to the west bank of the Danube should the inner defense ring be broken—a request which was refused. As Friessner was above all else concerned to avoid street fighting, he stressed the untrustworthiness of the population. He could have made a stronger case on military grounds, but then the responsibility for surrendering Budapest would have rested with his own troops, which he presumably did not dare to risk.

The Hungarian military leadership also rejected the idea of street fighting, believing that Budapest could be defended only through the Attila Line. Early in December, the Hungarian divisions defending the capital were ordered to disarm workers in the public utilities (BESZKÁRT [Budapest Transport] employees, streetcar conductors, firemen, and the like) as Budapest was to be declared an open city.

Hitler alone insisted on defending Budapest. On 30 October this task had been assigned to the III Panzer Corps headed by Colonel-General Hermann Breith, which had been regrouped from the 6th Army and to which the Hungarian divisions retreating to the city were attached. Likewise, on 30 October the Budapest Corps Group had been constituted from the staff of the Hungarian VI Army Corps and the German police and flying squads stationed in Budapest, with Karl Pfeffer-Wildenbruch, who had previously commanded the Waffen SS in the Hungarian hinterland, in charge. His full title was SS Obergruppenführer and General of the Waffen SS and Police; the rank of Obergruppenführer in the SS was equivalent to Lieutenant-General. As Pfeffer-Wildenbruch was an experienced police officer, his appointment indicates the German leadership's fears of subversion.

On 4 November the German 153rd Field Training Division—which would have been useless against Soviet troops but was particularly well suited to put down an insurrection—had been moved to Budapest, and on 10 November the command of the IX SS Mountain Army Corps had been transferred from Zagreb in order to increase the German domination over the Budapest Corps Group. The powers of Colonel Ernő Csipkés, the Hungarian city commander, had been restricted to military security and administration. The Hungarian VI Army Corps had been precluded from taking independent strategic action and left in control only of supplies to its own troops, before being incorporated on 21 November into the Hungarian I Army Corps, which was serving under Colonel-General Iván Hindy as a purely administrative body. These measures had provoked strong protests from the Hungarian general staff because they excluded the Hungarian command from the decision-making process and ran counter to all previous agreements.

On 23 November, Hitler had issued his first directive that no house in Budapest be abandoned without a fight, regardless of any civilian losses or material damage. On 1 December his order number 11 arrived, declaring Budapest a fortress and expressly appointing SS Obergruppenführer Otto Winkelmann—who was already in charge of all the German police and SS units in Hungary—commander of Budapest and thus the superior of Pfeffer-Wildenbruch and the IX SS Mountain Army Corps. The Budapest forces were subordinate to the 6th Army but were entitled to take independent action subject to prior consultation. They were to prepare the city's squares and buildings for the defense, repulse any incursions, keep the German and Hungarian gendarmerie and police on the alert in case of any unrest, and develop the communication system. Hitler's order also promised the dispatch of special units.

The absence of a clear distribution of powers within the German command is sharply illuminated by the allocation of the task of defending Budapest to three different organizations without any precise definition of the remit of each: the Wehrmacht (III Panzer Corps), the Waffen-SS as represented by Pfeffer-Wildenbruch (Budapest Corps Group), and the diplomatic wing of the SS as represented by Winkelmann. This redundancy can be explained only partly by the almost hysterical fear of a popular uprising on the part of some authorities—for example, the Hungarian Arrow Cross Party and the German security service. Above all, it was probably due to the polycratic structures of the Third Reich, which allowed the SS, the SA, the Wehrmacht, and the local *gauleiters* to seize a variety of powers and to engage in fierce power struggles, which Hitler's central will failed to curb in any significant degree.

On 4 December Szálasi accepted Hitler's decision, although Guderian was still saying that he wanted to keep the enemy out of the city. On this occasion it was announced that in any districts about to be abandoned the bridges and public utilities would be destroyed. The notion of declaring Budapest an open city was rejected by German diplomats on the grounds that in Germany, too, every town would be defended to the last brick. Friessner repeatedly asked for the front line to be pulled back, but his request was turned down.

On 5 December, Winkelmann was obliged to resign his post, which he had held for only four days, because his doubts about the chances of defending the city and his recommendation to abandon the Pest bridgehead were not to Hitler's liking. In his place Hitler appointed Pfeffer-Wildenbruch. On 12 December, because of the catastrophic situation in Transdanubia, the command of the III Panzer Corps was withdrawn from Budapest (although its divisions remained behind), and the Budapest Army Corps, led by the IX SS Mountain Army Corps and Pfeffer-Wildenbruch, took over the operations as an integral part of the German Army Group South. Although Pfeffer-Wildenbruch was now in overall charge, Winkel-mann continued to interfere; he did so for the last time on 22 December, when, against Hitler's orders, he tried to convince Friessner of the necessity of abandoning the Pest bridgehead.

The German Army Group South had no illusions about holding Budapest. As early as 1 December, Friessner had ordered the evacuation of all military and civilian agencies, declaring: "The remaining departments must be fully mobile. All German female assistants must leave at once. I . . . shall hold the battle commander personally responsible for ensuring that in the event of a possible battle for the city there shall be no despicable occurrences of German personnel fleeing in a manner likely to damage the reputation of the German Reich and the Wehrmacht."

On 6 December, Colonel-General Fretter-Pico asked for permission to retreat to the inner defense ring of the Attila Line, because he feared a Soviet breakthrough. Hitler refused, arguing that this would deprive the defense of the necessary operational depth. After the breakthrough at Hatvan the situation deteriorated, as the defenders did not have enough troops to man the 20-kilometer battle line that had developed near the northern part of Budapest. On 9 December 1944 Soviet heavy artillery began to bombard the northeastern area of the city. As a first sign that the battle of life and death had begun, the Germans formed flying squads made up of cooks, clerks, and mechanics: thus the Feldherrnhalle Division was able to scrape together seven companies, and the 13th Panzer Division four companies. On 12 December the possibility of a German attack from the Pest bridgehead with the promised reinforcements was also raised but rejected, not least because it was doubtful whether the eastern part of Budapest would then still be in German hands. In other words, the defense of Budapest was by now regarded as unrealistic.

By the beginning of December the Abwehr section of German intelligence, expecting the city to fall shortly, had begun to organize a network of agents with instructions to install 19 stores of explosives at the main traffic junctions and prepare plans for blowing up the most important buildings. The handling of the charges was to be the task of civilians—men and women—recruited for the purpose, who were to communicate only through intermediaries and who did not know each other. However, there is no record of any successful operation of this kind.

From the outset, the defenders had been confronted with a superior force. Between 5 November and 24 December, 7 German and Hungarian divisions, with a ration strength of some 60,000, faced 12 Soviet and Romanian divisions with some 110,000 troops. The smaller German contingent was obliged to bear the larger burden of the fighting and intervene to bail out the badly equipped and demoralized Hungarians.

The Hungarian losses may be illustrated by the following examples. The 12th Reserve Division, which had hardly been reorganized after being shattered at Nagyvárad, had lost 50 percent of its 2,100 infantry by mid-November, while the 10th Infantry Division, which had begun with 4,000 men, had been reduced to one battalion in each regiment in the encounters at Gödöllő in the first half of December. Both divisions had borne the brunt of the Soviet and Romanian onslaught, although the somewhat less exposed German units had not fared much better. Over a three-month period the 10th Infantry Division (the strongest Hungarian unit defending Budapest) lost 99.9 percent of its combat strength: at the end of October it had set out with a ration strength of some 15,000; by the beginning of February its last remaining combat unit numbered 18 men.

The morale of the Hungarian troops also gave cause for concern. According to the war diary of the German Army Group South, 100 members of the 12th Reserve Division had fled or crossed over to the enemy on 19 November and were followed between 22 November and 4 December by 1,200 members of the 10th and 12th Divisions. Most of these were either untrained substitutes or soldiers separated from their units who had been ordered into action once more. Such cases receive particular emphasis in German reports, which give the impression that only Germans were fighting, and not that more than 60 percent of the infantry engaged at the bridgehead were Hungarian. In fact various Hungarian units—the paratroopers, the 6th, 8th, and 38th Infantry Regiments, the 1st Armored Division, and the 10th Reconnaissance Battalion—were sometimes praised even by the Germans for their successful counterattacks.

The desertions drove the divisional commander, Major-General Kornél Oszlányi, to distraction. On 26 November, in a fit of anger, he declared that he "would not ruin his military career by accepting such a shower" and elegantly divested himself of the command by reporting sick. He was succeeded by Major-General József Kisfaludy, and from 15 December by Sándor András, a colonel in the air force general staff. In the Hungarian I Army Corps, Hindy persuaded Captain Ferenc X. Kovács to become the provisional head of the operational section because his predecessors had "moved on west, after looking around for a few days." In the 1st Armored Division nobody was willing to accept the position of chief of staff for more than one day, until Frigyes Wáczek—a captain in charge of the general staff's operational section—alone failed to report sick when he was appointed to that position.

As a result of casualties, the designation of units no longer corresponded to their actual strength in terms of equipment and numbers. Both the German and the Hungarian command sought urgent replacements for the exhausted Hungarian units, but the reinforcements arriving regularly had to be deployed immediately without any possibility of forming reserves, and the lack of arms and training made it difficult to replenish even the 10th Infantry and 12th Reserve Divisions, which were regarded as priorities. Because the badly trained and older reservists as a rule ran away from the battle line on the very first day, the Hungarian command intended to make use of 2,000 Arrow Cross Hungarist volunteers, who had been assembled in the Danube Bend and Szentendre Island north of the capital and were expected to have more staying power. The Vannay Battalion of 500 trained and 250 untrained paramilitaries was ordered to join the 10th Infantry Division, and the deployment of two other paramilitary formations, the Prónay Commando Unit and the Morlin Group, was also contemplated.

However, all this could only delay the catastrophe. By December 1944 the German and Hungarian troops in Budapest had used up almost all their supplies. Even those who still wanted to fight were driven into one of the most terrible city sieges of the Second World War not by the hope of victory but by a courage born of despair.

2

The Encirclement

Hungarian *drôle de guerre:*
Christmas 1944 in the Budapest Cauldron

Soon Edó comes back with a splendid Christmas tree.
He got it for 10 pengős, it wasn't cheaper even in peacetime. "Just take it," the woman had said to him, "it
doesn't matter any more, the Russians are already in
Budakeszi." Naturally we thought this was an exaggera-
tion and didn't take it seriously. . . . Radio Budapest had
been broadcasting Christmas carols with organ music.
—Blanka Péchy

By 24 December 1944 the Soviet troops had reached the eastern edge
of Pest and were closing in on Buda from the west. Although the
siege had already lasted six weeks, the local inhabitants had taken
no notice of the events and blithely continued their Christmas preparations right up to the moment the first soldiers of the Red Army
arrived to put an end to the idyll. The behavior of the German and
Hungarian military leaders was even more absurd. Although they
were informed daily of the approach of the Soviets, as late as Christmas Eve they had still not stationed a defense force worthy of the
name in Buda or made any other realistic efforts to protect the capital against any attack from the west. It was only thanks to the Soviets'
overcautiousness and shortage of infantry to accompany the armored
units that the T-34s did not roll immediately into the Castle District,

from which they were only three kilometers by the afternoon of Christmas Day. They had to pay dearly for missing this opportunity: after Christmas it took them three days to capture the first of those three kilometers and 48 days to capture the next, and in fact they never reached the walls of the Castle itself before the capitulation of Germany.

In contrast to Pest, then, where the German general staff had at least made some theoretical plans for the defense, albeit without taking many practical measures, in Buda there were only a few trenches and bunkers between János-hegy Hill and Hármashatár-hegy Hill, and no defense plans whatsoever.

The Soviet breakthrough near Lake Velence on 20 December prompted the command of the German Army Group South to ask Guderian for permission to move the 8th SS Cavalry Division west. Guderian refused, arguing that this operation would weaken the defense in the east. On 21 December the command of the German Army Group South requested permission to relocate the Feld-herrnhalle Panzergrenadier Division, but the general staff again refused.

Meanwhile, the army corps of the 3rd Ukrainian Front had begun its advance north through a gap that had opened between Lake Velence and Martonvásár. After taking Martonvásár, the front pushed northwest, occupying a number of small villages on the way, and by the evening of 22 December it was threatening Bicske and Bia. When Colonel-General Friessner, renewing his plea for the relocation of the 8th SS Cavalry Division, pointed out that Budapest would be encircled within a few days, Guderian yet again refused and exclaimed angrily: "I can't understand why such a large panzer army, unequaled anywhere on the eastern front, is unable to stop the enemy." He was forgetting that the panzer forces were not accompanied by the necessary infantry.

On 23 December, a performance of *Aida* took place in the Budapest Opera. A member of the audience recalls: "Before the second act an actor dressed as a soldier appeared in front of the curtain. Conveying greetings from the battle front to the half-empty house, he expressed his pleasure at seeing that the spectators were now considerably calmer and more hopeful than a few weeks earlier, and he confidently promised that Budapest would remain Hungarian and our wonderful capital had nothing to fear." Performances in the other theaters and in the cinemas also continued.

On the morning of 23 December the Soviet troops took Székesfehérvár. A few hours later they reached Bicske, Herceghalom, and Bia, severing the principal railway link between Vienna and Budapest and leaving the Esztergom-Budapest line, which could carry considerably less traffic, as the only supply route to the capital. In the afternoon German resistance in Herceghalom and Bia ceased. In the evening the Soviet 18th Tank Corps bypassed Bicske and overran the defenders from behind: the speed of this advance is demonstrated by the fact that the Soviet infantry did not arrive in Bicske until the morning of 25 December. Late on 23 December units of the 2nd Mechanized Guard Corps were also threatening the commune of Páty, north of Bia. The Soviet armored spearheads were advancing at a rate of between 20 and 40 kilometers a day, letting a second wave capture the bases they had missed. By the morning of 24 December this method had brought them from Páty to Budakeszi through the forests of the Buda Hills, while the German and Hungarian troops were still resisting in some pockets around Érd, Törökbálint, and Budaörs, east of Bia.

The German Army Group South and Pfeffer-Wildenbruch managed only hesitant and inadequate countermeasures. They decided to "prevent an enemy advance north and east by fast-moving actions of the armored group of the Feldherrnhalle Panzergrenadier Division in the Bia sector." The combat force removed from the Pest front in this manner comprised at most 12 self-propelled 15cm Hummel (Bumble-bee) guns, 12 self-propelled 10.5cm Wespe (Wasp) guns, 10 to 15 tanks, and 100 armored personnel carriers. Although they temporarily recaptured Törökbánya and broke through the Soviet front somewhat farther north, in the long run they were no match for three Soviet rapid deployment corps pressing ahead toward Budapest from a distance of 20 kilometers. The prospects of the depleted Hungarian Budapest Guard Battalion, ordered from Csömör on the Pest side to Hűvösvölgy Valley north of Budakeszi, were no better. The request of the IX SS Mountain Army Corps's command for the 8th SS Cavalry Division to be relocated from Pest was, as always, refused by Hitler through Guderian. Instead, some small Hungarian units, such as the 4th and 21st Artillery Battalions, were ordered to Bicske, as if these could have repulsed a tank attack.

In a fit of rage, Hitler relieved Fretter-Pico and Friessner of their posts, appointing Panzer General Hermann Balck (Army Group G) and Infantry General Otto Wöhler (8th Army) in their places. This made no difference, however, as Fretter-Pico and Friessner had already done all that was humanly possible: they had even tried to predict the course of events, hoping that Hitler would send further reinforcements. But Hitler was only seeking scapegoats for the continuous defeats, for which he himself was ultimately responsible, and he did not even bother to give reasons for his replacement of the generals.

On 24 December at 1:10 P.M. Lieutenant-General Helmuth von Grolman, Friessner's chief of staff, phoned Guderian, urging him to reconsider: "The capital has never been defended from the west. The commander of the SS police forces, Obergruppenführer Winkelmann, believes that the Reichsführer [Himmler] would certainly approve such a decision. A decision must be made with the utmost urgency to extract at least one division and direct it to the Buda side." After 45 minutes Guderian took it upon himself to approve the relocation of the 8th SS Cavalry Division. At that time he had other great worries. The new German attack in the Ardennes appeared likely to fail, and the Soviet units at the bridgeheads on the Vistula were believed to be preparing an attack on Berlin. Guderian therefore desperately wanted to break off the offensive in the west and transfer the combat forces in question to the east, though not to the Carpathian Basin. He expected a Soviet attack on 12 January 1945 and was soon proved right. Hitler, however, remained convinced that the defense of Budapest was more important. "This is the biggest bluff since Genghis Khan. Who invented this nonsense?" he shouted and, ignoring Guderian's protest, ordered the last reserve on the eastern front, the IV SS Panzer Corps (which incidentally was stationed at the location of the subsequent Soviet attack), to depart for Hungary. With things going wrong in the Ardennes, Hitler's last hope, which had assumed obsessive proportions, was a victory in Hungary. Given that the Hungarian army was still supplying 35 percent of the artillery and 30 percent of the infantry of the joint forces in the Carpathian Basin, Hungary's continuing support was essential for the Germans, and the fall of Budapest would have seriously demoralized the Hungarian soldiers.

At 4:50 P.M., when Soviet tanks had already reached the Szépilona streetcar depot and were only 5 kilometers from Buda Castle, Hitler finally approved the relocation of the 8th SS Cavalry Division but did not give permission to abandon the Pest bridgehead, although both Guderian and Balck considered this the most appropriate step. Instead he ordered two infantry divisions to be dispatched to Hungary and promised to liberate Budapest. For him, as for Stalin, Budapest was a political issue far beyond Central Europe. While Hitler was still dreaming of saving the Third Reich in Hungary, Stalin was trying to push ahead toward western Europe as far and as fast as possible.

The German and Hungarian commands knew how far the Soviet troops had advanced. Nevertheless, they did nothing to avert the impending catastrophe. Hindy's failure to act is understandable, for he had no authority to do so. Orders could be given by Pfeffer-Wildenbruch alone, so only a personal initiative by him could have resolved the situation, but as we shall see, he lacked the necessary qualities.

It has been claimed that the appearance of Soviet troops in Buda struck the German and Hungarian commands like a bolt out of the blue. This is patently wrong. On 23 December Hindy and Pfeffer-Wildenbruch knew that the Soviet troops were between 20 and 40 kilometers from Budapest, and they may also have been informed that the exhausted remnants of the 271st German Volksgrenadier Division southwest of Buda no longer had any serious combat value. Captain Zoltán Mikó, head of the sabotage section of the Hungarian general staff, was aware of the imminent encirclement, and so were the German divisional staffs. Reports were being sent constantly not only by railway employees and gendarmes in the area but also by Pfeffer-Wildenbruch's personnel.

On 22 December, even before Budapest was encircled, Pfeffer-Wildenbruch requested aerial delivery of supplies. On 23 December German antitank guns were stationed in two places at Budagyöngye on the road to Budakeszi. On the same day the supply units of the Hungarian 10th Infantry Division received orders from the Hungarian I Army Corps to send reconnaissance units to the Piliscsaba-Perbál-Zsámbék and Perbál-Budajenő routes north of Páty, and about midday Lieutenant József Bíró, adjutant to the command of the 10th Infantry Division, was ordered by the corps command to commence reconnaissance activities. At 10 P.M. the chief of staff, Captain Győző Benyovszky, personally visited the baggage train in Pilisszentiván to alert all units.

On the morning of 24 December the patrols reported the appearance of Soviet forces from the villages of the Zsámbék Basin between Bicske and Budaörs. Even closer to Budapest, in the suburb of Pasarét, the chief quartermaster of the 1st Panzer Division saw "German antitank guns and assault guns racing toward Hűvösvölgy Valley, and German and Hungarian cars, trucks, and mechanized dispatch runners rushing from Hűvösvölgy toward Széna Square." The reason was that orders to leave the city immediately had been given to the German supply units and the non-combat units of the 13th Panzer Division by Pfeffer-Wildenbruch and to the Hungarian army's supply units by the Hungarian command. The German supreme command, on its own initiative, had detailed a navy commando unit from Lübeck specializing in underwater blasting to Hungary to prepare the destruction of the bridges in Budapest and Esztergom, and on Christmas Day the unit, led by First Lieutenant Tegethoff, was already in Vienna. All this is further proof that the OKH in Berlin was well aware of the impending encirclement.

Typically, no discussions about the possible prevention of the encirclement had taken place between the general staff departments of Pfeffer-Wildenbruch and Hindy. This was mainly due to mutual distrust and, on Hindy's part, to an indifference which had been growing since the end of October. Right at the beginning Hindy's control over the Hungarian troops had been taken away from him and his role restricted to administration.

Pfeffer-Wildenbruch told his Hungarian partner nothing and treated him in a markedly condescending manner. This was probably one of the reasons why the Hungarian general just watched events passively.

On the same morning the Budakeszi gendarmerie advised the staff of the Hungarian army corps billeted in the Notre Dame de Sion convent that the first Soviet tanks had been sighted nearby. Lieutenant-Colonel Ferenc Szögyény, commander of the South Buda antiaircraft unit, was unaware of this and ordered his adjutant, Lieutenant Géza Pintér, to drive to Budakeszi in order to inspect potential positions for antiaircraft guns. Pintér, traveling through the western residential quarters, got as far as the Szépjuhászné-nyereg Saddle:

> There I was unexpectedly stopped by a first lieutenant. I got out, and he asked me where I was going. I said, to Budakeszi to inspect positions. It could have been about half past ten. "You won't be going there," he said, "because, in case you didn't know, you're already at the front line." I said: "How come?" "Look back," he said, "the German SS are behind you." . . . The lieutenant asked me for my two hand grenades, because he said he didn't even have a pistol.

Shortly after 10:30 A.M. the first Soviet soldiers appeared in front of the Szépjuhászné-nyereg Saddle. By midday all resistance had ceased, and by 1 P.M. the first Soviet tanks, slowly rumbling down Budakeszi Road, had reached the junction with Hidegkúti Road. At the filling station beneath the streetcar depot a Hungarian tanker had just begun to siphon off gasoline. A heavy gun battle developed between the German soldiers, who took cover behind the tanker, and the Soviet tanks, which had pushed ahead without infantry support. Meanwhile gasoline was running from the pump and the tanker onto the road.

The Soviet infantry also began to advance from Budakeszi. Some tried to follow the tanks along the Budakeszi road but were left behind, while others set out toward Svábhegy Hill through the Budakeszi Forest. Late in the morning, eight antiaircraft guns positioned in Csillebérc were also attacked by infantry. As the position of the guns did not allow firing at a low angle, the crew destroyed the breech mechanisms and retreated. In the early afternoon, according to eyewitnesses, civilians waiting for their train at the Széchenyi-hegy terminus of the Cogwheel Railway were dumbfounded when they discovered Soviet advance guards with submachine guns in their midst. The military command, although aware of the imminent Soviet onslaught, had been unable to warn the dispersed units—with fatal consequences for many.

Lieutenant Pintér got back to Hidegkúti Road by making a long detour. An 88mm antiaircraft gun in front of the pharmacy in the Szépilona quarter had just set a Soviet tank on fire. Higher up, alongside Budakeszi Road, three or four more Soviet tanks were lurking. A few blocks farther, in Tárogató Road, Soviet shells were suddenly landing near the German first-aid station. A phone call to the command of the Feldherrnhalle Division was answered to the effect that the situation remained unchanged and there was no cause for concern. When an ambulance driver reported that he had come under fire a few kilometers west, nobody believed him. The German chief medical officer again phoned the divisional command, where "the affair was declared to be a pathological fantasy. At the very same moment a shell detonated in front of the building, shattering all the windows and severing the phone link."

At about the same time a BESZKÁRT employee phoned the Hungarian corps command in the Notre Dame de Sion convent from the terminus of the number 81 streetcar line in the Zugliget quarter: "Do you know that the Russians are here? They're here at the streetcar terminus, they've stacked their rifles and are distributing food. What am I to do?" Captain Ferenc X. Kovács, who took his call, merely said: "Nothing. Try to be as inconspicuous as possible, so that nothing happens to you. There's nothing else I can do." Subsequently Kovács also started phoning to find out what was happening. Several times he was answered in Russian: "After my phone calls I went to Sándor Horváth [the army corps's chief of staff] to report. He was also surprised but could do nothing. He may have spoken to Lindenau, but he didn't order me to communicate anything to the Germans." The German corps command heard about the arrival of the Soviets in similar fashion, through a phone call from a policeman posted at the Szépilona streetcar depot, who had had a bad fright when the first T-34 tank had aimed its gun at him.

On the same afternoon the German corps command began to relocate the 8th SS Cavalry Division to Buda, although Hitler's approval arrived only a day later. A reconnaissance detachment drafted from reserves took up firing positions in the Hűvösvölgy Valley and Rózsadomb Hill areas, as did an antiaircraft detachment in Móric Zsigmond Square soon after. The relocation was slowed down, however, by heavy traffic and crowds of civilians hurrying to do their Christmas shopping. At about 6 P.M. the passengers of the Cogwheel Railway on Svábhegy Hill had a strange experience as they were returning home with their Christmas presents. A reconnaissance unit of eight men, led by First Lieutenant Andrey Ilyich Kozlov, had reached the terminus, where Christmas trees and

2

Staff Captain Ferenc X. Kovács, chief of operational section,
Hungarian I Army Corps

3

Staff Captain Győző Benyovszky, chief of staff, Hungarian 10th Infantry Division

roasted chestnuts were still on sale, without being involved in any fighting. The civilians waiting for the train did not notice anything unusual about the Soviet soldiers as they got on in their white winter overalls. The train was already on its way when one passenger realized that the soldiers were not wearing German or Hungarian uniforms inside their overalls. Panic ensued, somebody pulled the communication cord, and the Soviets got off after relieving some passengers of their watches. As the train continued its journey, the guard told new passengers coming aboard that the line was now being run by the Soviets. The news spread through the besieged city like wildfire.

In Széna Square there were tumultuous scenes. Artillery lieutenant Béla Czeczidlowszky remembers:

> The people were very nervous. In Ostrom Street Arrow Cross Party members were getting into their cars and disappearing, and a police officer was carrying a sack of flour on his back. That was when I realized what, in

God's name, was going on here. . . . Tasziló Tarnay, head
of a mortar battery, was in position and bombarding
Hűvösvölgy. The Zöld Hordó Inn was still open, and
I was able to eat a goulash.

Between 3 and 4 P.M. a gun battle erupted near the Szépilona
streetcar depot between the approaching Soviet infantry and the
German units moving into position. At the same time the Arrow
Cross's Hungarist combat group on Svábhegy Hill received an
alarm signal. Led by its commander Antal Ostián—the Arrow
Cross Party's chief of propaganda—the group was probably trying
to escape from the capital when it became involved in a gun battle
with Soviet troops near the Széchenyi-hegy terminus of the Cogwheel Railway, and several of its members, including Ostián himself, were killed. The remnants took up firing positions in the
gardens along Mártonhegyi Road.

At 5 P.M., on the orders of Emil Kovarcz, the Minister for
Total Mobilization, the members of the I University Assault Battalion, who were spending the holiday at home, were alerted
through the "snowball" method: each student receiving the message passed it on to two others, so that within the hour all three
companies were assembled. Although István Zsakó, the Arrow
Cross Party's youth leader, offered the students the opportunity
to leave the capital together with the Arrow Cross units, Lieutenant Gyula Elischer, the battalion commander, decided that they
should stay behind. Transported by truck, the students reached the
Budagyöngye suburb from Hűvösvölgy Valley at 8 P.M. Private
Gyula Kamocsay recalls:

> When we looked farther down, where Budakeszi Road
> and Hidegkúti Road meet, we saw a kind of river begin-
> ning to flow, and that river was—on fire. Something
> down there was burning, actually burning, with blue
> flames. . . . "Never mind, lads, our trucks are big
> enough, the time is 5 past 8, the direction is toward the
> fire"—with this he [Elischer] got into the first truck and
> drove off straight at the fire. . . . We'd just got into the
> thick of the confusion, bang into the middle of the fire,

when a German suddenly jumped up in front of us—
"Stop!"—The drivers put on the brakes, around us
everything was gushing and swirling. One of the Germans said that there were many wounded, and they
immediately started grabbing and throwing the unfortu-
nate half-dead onto the open trailer behind us, where we
had a few barrels of diesel oil.

While we were standing there—the loading took
two or three minutes—I looked toward Budakeszi Road
on the right and noticed three burned-out tanks on the
bend. . . . As soon as these tanks had been hit the oil in
them must have run down the road and been set alight
by a grenade.

The students sealed off Hűvösvölgy Valley and sent patrols to the
Szépilona-Budagyöngye area. One patrol captured two men in
civilian clothes speaking Russian; another blew up a Soviet tank
near Budagyöngye with a hand grenade. A gendarmerie battalion,
which had assembled on Vérmező Meadow the same evening, took
up positions near the Bolyai Academy, János Hospital, and the
Cogwheel Railway and began to mount reconnaissance actions.

According to instructions from the Germans, the 600 men
making up this unit were to hold a front line stretching between
four and five kilometers to the northern edge of Budaörs and to
take part in a counterattack the next day. The student László Zolnay set out at 8 P.M. to visit his relatives in the Pasarét quarter, and
met total chaos on the way:

I tried to walk along Olasz Avenue. Across the entire
width of the street a mass of military formations and
vehicles was rolling along, together with hordes of ethnic Swabian peasants from Budakeszi escaping, mainly
on foot, with their bundles piled high on their backs. It
was almost impossible to find a gap and make headway
against this ubiquitous torrent. The terrified screams of
the fleeing mass were accompanied by the increasing
rattle of guns and occasional explosions from Szépilona.
I tried to make more progress by turning off toward

Városmajor Grange, but here too legions of refugees were rolling toward the city center.

I pushed my way through, along one of the side streets . . . and carried on with my pistol in my hand. . . . When I reached Marcibányi Square I was blinded by a searchlight and had to stop. Then I saw that the square was full of waiting military formations.

Luckily I was questioned by a Hungarian officer. I told him that I was trying to go to Pasarét for Christmas but couldn't find a way. He didn't make me show my identity papers but said he doubted that I would be able to get through . . . because the Russians were already in Pasaréti Square and I would be shot dead in the dark by either the one or the other side.

On the same day, the Soviet command launched heavy attacks against the Pest bridgehead in order to prevent the Germans from regrouping. Simultaneously the systematic bombardment of the whole capital began. The commander on the Buda side, however, decided to stop at Szépilona. He had good reason for so doing, because by that time only about 20 of his tanks, with minimal infantry support, had reached Buda. A street battle fought solely with tanks—which are vulnerable in the narrow passages between the houses—is always risky. On this occasion the Soviets had already lost several T-34s, although they had not advanced very far into the city, and without more infantry it was doubtful that they could control even those parts of Buda that they had captured. Some sources give a different reason: according to these the Soviet troops, suddenly faced with civilians carrying valuables, stopped their advance in order to rob them. In fact they did not stop to pillage but pillaged because they had had to stop to await the main force.

For one group of people more than any other, the Jews, the arrival of the Red Army meant liberation. Unlike the military command, the Arrow Cross militia were surprised by the appearance of Soviet troops in Buda, and many potential victims owed their lives to the ensuing confusion. The first were probably the inmates of a

Jewish children's home in Budakeszi Road, where their parents had left them before they themselves were deported or imprisoned in a ghetto. In the early morning of 24 December, Arrow Cross men burst into the home and lined the children up but departed when they heard the rapidly increasing thunder of guns; the children in their turn saw the first Soviet tanks rattling along the village street in the late morning. On the same morning Arrow Cross men appeared in the Jewish children's homes in Munkácsy Mihály Street in Buda and marched the children together with their caregivers— a group of more than 100—to the courtyard of the Radetzky Barracks, where a machine gun ready to fire was awaiting them. When news of the Soviet approach came in the early afternoon, however, the mass murder was called off and the group herded to the ghetto in the VII District. Sadly, thousands of other Jews did not live to see the Soviet victory. Their fate will be discussed later.

The Encirclement of Buda
The Outer Ring

West of Budapest, the Germans and Hungarians were no match for the Soviets pushing north toward the Danube and Esztergom in the Christmas period. Their joint strength, facing Tolbukhin's 133 tanks and 19,000 infantry, amounted to no more than 91 tanks and assault guns, and some 3,700 infantry of poor quality (Table 7).

On 24 December some units of the Soviet 18th Tank Corps and 31st Rifle Corps were advancing east toward Buda without encountering much opposition, while others were steadily moving north along the fringe of the Buda Hills. In the afternoon the 32nd Mechanized Brigade, approaching from Páty, reached Perbál and Tök; a vanguard battalion of the 110th Tank Brigade arrived in Tinnye; the 181st Tank Brigade crossed the border of Komárom-Esztergom county near Szomor; and the 170th Tank Brigade was pushing ahead toward Bajna. In the early evening advance guards appeared in Jászfalu, and the tanks leading the assault destroyed the locomotive of the last train from Esztergom to Budapest, forcing the passengers to seek shelter in the village. By late evening the road to Vienna was under sporadic fire near Pilisvörösvár, where the chaotic encounter between the columns of vehicles moving outward from the customs point at Üröm and those forced to turn back from Pilisvörösvár was eerily illuminated by Soviet signal rockets.

On 25 December, early in the morning, wedges of Soviet tanks advancing west reached Tatabánya, Tarján, Szomor, Dág, and Csolnok. Others, moving north, crossed the Budapest-Esztergom railway line midway between the two cities. Most of these continued toward Dorog, while the right wing turned east toward the villages in the Pilis district and the Danube Bend. At 7 A.M. the right wing took Piliscsaba with little resistance, then continued its advance across the wooded heights toward Pilisvörösvár. The tanks reached Pilisszentiván in the evening and within hours severed the macadamized road leading from Pomáz via Pilisszentkereszt to Esztergom; some reconnaissance platoons infiltrated Pilisvörösvár itself during the night. On the southeastern edge of Dorog the 170th Tank Brigade, held up until evening by a German antiaircraft gun and a few Hungarian assault guns, lost four T-34s. After the capture of several villages west of Dorog during the day, however, by 7:30 P.M. Dorog too was in Soviet hands, with several hundred goods-laden wagons stranded at the railway station.

At 1 A.M. on 26 December the Soviets reached Esztergom-Tábor, and by morning the siege of Esztergom had begun. The officers of the Hungarian 23rd Reserve Division stationed in the city decided to surrender, but the commander could not make up his mind to give the order: finally, while fighting was already in progress nearby, he decided not to go through with the plan that he himself had approved just minutes before, as this would have been incompatible with his officer's oath and his loyalty to his German brothers-in-arms. The division, with hardly any combat troops left, withdrew across the Danube at the last moment. At 7:30 A.M. the Germans also pulled out, blowing up Mária Valéria Bridge behind them. A few hours later the whole of Esztergom was in Soviet hands. With the capture of Esztergom, the outer encirclement ring round Budapest was closed.

On the morning of 27 December the Soviet 170th Tank Brigade continued its advance west, seizing three wagonloads of

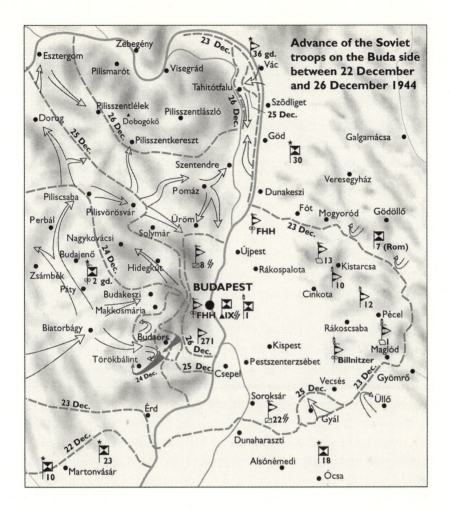

Advance of the Soviet troops on the Buda side between 22 December and 26 December 1944

German tanks and armored vehicles awaiting repairs at Süttő station. The German Pape Division Group, which had arrived in the area between 24 and 26 December—consisting of the remnants of three Panther tank divisions, three battalions that had been moved west from Budapest on 24–25 December, some tanks allocated but not delivered to the 8th SS Cavalry Division and the 13th Panzer Division, and a number of flying squads—had managed with difficulty to close off the passes in the Vértes Hills and secure the Tata-Tatabánya area. Lacking infantry, it could not mount any counterattacks and was finding it increasingly difficult even to hold the territories it was occupying. This situation was to persist until reinforcements arriving in stages from 28 December stopped the Soviets at the eastern approaches to Komárom.

The Soviet command anticipated that the Germans would try to relieve Budapest and decided to concentrate on preparing the defense of the outer encirclement ring, rather than trying to advance any farther. Therefore the battle lines consolidated and Soviet attacks continued only between Mór and Lake Balaton.

The Inner Ring

On 24 December, Soviet mechanized units, mainly from Budakeszi, had reached western Buda. Christmas Eve fell on a Sunday and, with the guns thundering in the distance, the streets were almost deserted. Most of the residents hardly realized that in a matter of minutes their world had been turned upside down. Those who noticed Russians hurrying past the garden fences in padded suits and carrying submachine guns with unfamiliar round cartridge drums, or who were startled by tanks clattering along the main road, rang up their friends and relations to tell them the news, their voices trembling with bewilderment, fear, or—in some cases—joy. In the city center, during the late afternoon and evening, word spread among the civilians that Budapest had probably been encircled. In his apartment in the Castle District of Buda, the liberal politician Imre Csécsy noted: "The guns were roaring without a break till midnight. Sometimes we also heard the rattle of machine guns. This is the most beautiful Christmas music. Are we really about to be liberated? . . . God help us and put an end to the rule of these gangsters. May the drumfire grow stronger by the morning and the city fall." Others were more cautious: "We were so afraid of the Russians that we dismantled the Christmas tree."

At dawn on 25 December, Soviet units, pushing north through the forest from the Szépjuhászné-nyereg Saddle toward Hűvösvölgy Valley, surrounded a platoon of the Hungarist central combat group, commanded by Pál Prónay, which had been stationed for guard duty in a villa at the junction of Hidegkúti Road and

Nagykovácsi Road. The Arrow Cross men, first in the garden and then in the villa itself, fought until the morning of 26 December, by which time all fifty or so of them had been killed.

Farther south, Soviet artillery, catching up from Bia, took Budaörs and continued its strike toward Törökbálint. Other Soviet units, in action between Martonvásár and the Danube and reinforced with troops crossing the river from Csepel Island, pushed north, occupying the suburbs of Budatétény and Budafok and beginning to threaten the suburb of Kelenföld. The Hungarian 206th Antiaircraft Battalion, according to Soviet reports, disobeyed an order to withdraw, and with its 16 guns joined the enemy north of Érd.

The German corps command, overrating its chances against what Pfeffer-Wildenbruch supposed to be inferior forces, tried to hold up the Soviet troops through a counterattack from Törökbálint. But the remnants of the 271st Volksgrenadier Division retreating from the south and the Galántai Police Battalion had no serious combat strength left. Lieutenant Dénes Horváth, in charge of an antiaircraft position in the Kamara-erdő Forest, was about to blow up his guns, which had been fixed in concrete, when he received orders for his battery to support the planned counterattack:

German infantry were due to arrive at the artillery position at about 21:00 hours to provide infantry protection. On my return from the German battle post I restored the six guns of one of our batteries to fire readiness. Platoon commander Sergeant Gerhard . . . reported that a disorganized group of 150 to 200 men was coming toward the artillery position on the highway. I ordered Gerhard not to shoot, because I thought they were German troops coming to give infantry support to the battery during the counterattack in the night. When the tip of the group was about 100 meters from the gun positions, we saw in the light of a signal rocket that they were Soviets. At the same moment we came under extremely heavy infantry and mortar fire, which our surprised men immediately returned with the infantry arms at their disposal. As this was going on, a German infantry platoon arrived from Törökbálint, but in such a battle-weary condition that it could only cover the retreat of some of the gun crews. The Soviet units penetrated the firing position and captured part of the crew.

During the same morning the Soviet 18th Tank Corps continued its drive north, while the 2nd Mechanized Guard Corps, with about 80 armored vehicles, reached the northern and western districts of Buda, capturing the villages of Pesthidegkút and Nagykovácsi. In the early afternoon Soviet soldiers raised the red flag on the lookout tower on János-hegy Hill, and the restaurant at the foot of the tower was ablaze. By evening a large portion of Budafok and the railway station in the next suburb, Albertfalva, were in Soviet hands. Soviet infantry invaded the area of János Hospital and from the chapel opened fire on Olasz Avenue and Városmajor Grange. Only the armored group advancing in Budakeszi Road undertook no further attack that day and the next, being satisfied with securing Budakeszi Road and Hidegkúti Road.

The 8th SS Cavalry Division and three Hungarian battalions, hastily relocated to assist the University Assault Battalion, could offer Buda only scanty defense. With these units, reinforced by seven assault guns and a platoon of the city command, Lieutenant-Colonel László Veresváry launched a counterattack near Soviet-held Zugliget and succeeded in establishing a thin battle line. Units of the Vannay Battalion closed off Városmajor Grange and drove out the Soviet forces ensconced in János Hospital. Some guns of the 1st Assault Artillery Detachment secured the approach to Hűvösvölgy. Soviet advance infantry units had taken the convent on Svábhegy Hill on 24 December. When units of the Székelyudvarhelyi Gendarmerie Battalion reached Svábhegy Hill, they were surprised to find Soviet troops awaiting them. In the ensuing gun battle the gendarmes suffered heavy losses and were forced to withdraw at every point. In the evening the first troops of the German Europa Flying Squad Battalion arrived at Rózsadomb Hill to take over the defense between Bimbó Road and Olasz Avenue from the students. The local civilians suddenly found themselves on the edge of the front, as Endre Sasvári, a local resident, remembers:

> On the morning of 25 December three or four gen-darmes were running down Bürök Street, shouting: "the Russians are coming, save yourselves!" An hour later a tired man of about 40 in a mechanic's suit appeared, asking for food because he had gotten stuck on Márton-hegyi Road. He told us that his buddy was also hiding in the neighborhood. They could have come from the Turán tank stationed up at the terminus of the Cogwheel Railway.
>
> After lunch we heard trotting noises from Bürök Street. . . . I looked out, and a big group of German sol-diers was stopping in front of the house. An officer stepped forward and inquired: "Where are the Rus-sians?" He asked for some water and said: "Budapest is encircled." Then they set out at the double toward Svábhegy Hill. When they got to the house at number 71 shooting suddenly started.

But the civilians in those districts of Buda that had so far been spared apparently refused to acknowledge what was happening: "The residents of one building complained to Gyula Elischer [the students' commander] because a group, ordered into action, fired a few rounds at a mound of sand by the roadside to test their weapons. When the civilians were told that the Soviet forces were only a few hundred meters away, they were quite surprised." Until 25 December the university students' patrols had held a line stretch-ing from János Hospital, along the Lipótmező quarter, to Pusz-taszeri Road almost entirely on their own. It was only by chance that Taszíló Tarnay, commander of the 21st Artillery Battalion's mortar battery, realized that Soviet infantry riflemen had begun an attack, and by letting loose a volley from his mortars prevented them retaking János Hospital.

By 25 December no streetcars were running in the streets. A few lines had tried to start up early in the morning, but had immediately been stopped by the constant shelling. The only public transport still operating was the suburban railway between Budapest and Szentendre and, at least in the morning, the small ships plying on part of the Danube. Electricity, water and gas supplies, and telephone services were maintained, however, despite the increasing bombardment. Along the outer sections of Üllői Road people evicted from the suburb of Pestszentimre in the defensive belt of the Attila Line were escaping toward the inner districts of the city.

Although by this time the German high command, billeted in Buda Castle, was less than three kilometers from the front line, only after these events were reinforcements detailed to Buda. The Soviet forces, consisting mainly of infantry, retreated from the front line, which was patrolled every four or five hours by sizable German platoons. Because each party regarded the other as stronger, neither attempted a serious push ahead.

The Gestapo departments and the divisions' assembly, repair, and supply units had left Budapest for Esztergom on the evening of 24 December. They had been joined by several thousand members of the Arrow Cross Party with their families, and by members of the Arrow Cross youth organizations. On the order of Mobilization Minister Emil Kovarcz, the Hungarist recruits (between 1,500 and 2,000 men) promised to the Hungarian 10th Infantry Division as reinforcement had also been withdrawn, but units of the Hungarian 8th Infantry Regiment stationed in Buda brought them back as instructed by the divisional staff. On the evening of 25 December two German Panther tanks, lent to the Hungarians for a reconnaissance mission, encountered scarcely any obstacles in getting to Pilisszentkereszt, and reached the Hungarian lines at Komárom, on the Danube west of Esztergom, one day later. After dark the last local train, blacked out and full of refugees, left for Szentendre.

On the morning of 26 December Soviet units captured Pilisvörösvár and, meeting practically no defense, occupied the villages of Csobánka, Üröm, Pomáz, and Budakalász. Most of the refugee trains only reached Pomáz. Other groups found the roads to Esztergom either cut off by Soviet troops or blocked by stranded

German and Hungarian vehicles, and only a few, dodging Soviet tanks, got through.

The last group of Arrow Cross men to escape made it to the village of Dobogókő. After taking shelter in the tourist hostel they dispersed: some miraculously reached the German lines at Komárom on 28 December, while others filtered back to the capital and threw away their uniforms. A Hungarian battalion retreating from Szentendre Island tried to break through to Esztergom, but at the request of the Hungarian authorities in Szentendre, decided to surrender. At about 12:30 P.M. the first Cossack reconnaissance unit appeared in front of the Szentendre presbytery. On 27 December Soviet armored units also reached the Danube. The encirclement of Budapest was complete.

The German units and four Hungarian pioneer companies attached to them had begun to evacuate Szentendre Island on 25–26 December. The Soviet 25th Guard Rifle Division, which had crossed the Danube branch at Vác, had carried out an initial reconnaissance operation on the island on 25 December, followed by larger Soviet forces the next day. In a small skirmish, a unit led by Guard Sergeant Kuzhabai Zhazhikov captured the majority of the company defending the Danube bank, for which he received the Hero of the Soviet Union medal. In Tótfalu "the parish priest and the notary received the Russians, who didn't hurt anybody but ordered all the mills to grind flour and sent the [Hungarian] national guards on patrol with white armbands." The bridge near Tahi, which had been mined, was saved by Izabella Boros, a local resident, who cut the fuses. The disarmament of the German and Hungarian troops trapped in the Danube Bend took until 30 December. Between 24 and 30 December, according to Soviet sources, 5,390 were taken prisoner. Finally, Kisoroszi at the tip of the island was occupied on 3 January 1945.

Besiegers and Besieged
The German and Hungarian Troops

The debate about the exact number of troops defending Budapest continues to this day. Contemporary Soviet press notices mention some 70,000 prisoners. Malinovsky reported 188,000 defenders and a total of 138,000 prisoners. The German Army Group South, on 31 December, wrote about 50,000 Hungarian and 45,000 German troops trapped in the encirclement. The command of the Hungarian I Army Corps tried to take stock of its units on several occasions, but in the confusion achieved meager results. Even Sándor Horváth, the army corps's chief of staff, had to confess his bafflement: "During the seven weeks of the siege I was unable to obtain any convincing information about the combat strengths of the units in action within and outside the battle order or about the arms and ammunition situation. The corps's quartermaster, General Staff Captain Dezső Németh, after repeated efforts could only establish that the ration strength was fluctuating around 40,000." Such disparities cannot be attributed merely to the loss of documents. Nor is it sufficient to argue that originally the Hungarian I Army Corps had been an administrative entity without troops of its own, and that the troops trapped in Budapest were there merely as a consequence of the Soviet attacks. It is true, however, that the army corps only "owned" the Budapest Guard Battalion and was so short of soldiers that it had to draft, for intelligence duties, some female students of a Transylvanian university who had fled to the capital.

Many of the Hungarian units trapped in Budapest tried to evade the fighting. In reviews of their manpower and arms they concealed their true strength. When drawing their rations through the Hungarian I Army Corps they inflated their numbers, while in communications to the Germans they understated them. On 14 January 1945 the combined combat strength of the 10th Infantry Division and the 12th Reserve Division was reported to the corps as 300, though the 10th Infantry Division alone had at least 3,500 soldiers within the cauldron. Normally, the combat strength—which includes all the deployable infantry units, but not artillery men, crews of baggage trains, signalers, pioneers, or divisional staffs—is between 50 and 60 percent of the ration strength, which comprises all uniformed soldiers. In this instance, however, nobody in the corps command seems to have noticed that the combat units did not even amount to 10 percent of the ration strength.

Generally, combat units suffer greater losses than others. In the absence of regular reinforcements they must be replenished from the divisions' service units. In the German army, service units were regularly combed for this purpose, but among the Hungarians such a procedure was rare. The 10th Infantry Division managed to scrape together a combat force of only 200 to 300, while the overwhelming majority of its soldiers did not go into battle. This is not surprising, because by that time the Hungarian military command considered it pointless to continue the struggle.

The Hungarian forces defending Budapest on Christmas Day 1944 had a ration strength of 55,100 and a combat strength of 15,050—somewhat less than the statutory ration strength of two divisions (60,000) and the approximate combat strength of one (15,000). While the 15,050 Hungarian combatants represented 30 percent of the combined combat forces defending Budapest, their share of artillery equipment was significantly larger, with 60 percent of the guns belonging to Hungarian units. However, not all took part in the action: the 4/2 artillery battery, for example, did not fire a single shot after 30 December, although it had enough ammunition, four guns, and a number of artillery observers. In addition, the Hungarians lost their men and equipment faster than the Germans.

The combat value of the Hungarian units in the Budapest cauldron was largely determined by the fact that roughly 50 percent of the ration strength were not trained for infantry action and 16 percent were recruited only during the siege. The latter made up 30 percent of the total Hungarian combat strength of 15,000, which in turn was only about 40 percent of the total ration strength of 38,100 (Table 8). A significant number of units that took no part at all in the action included the KISKA auxiliary security force, numerous police officers, and the students of the military institutes, numbering about 17,000. These could have been usefully deployed in action only if they had been equipped with heavy weapons and trained in their use. Even then, however, the majority would probably have stopped fighting at the first opportunity. By the second year of the war the rank and file had no longer understood why they were obliged to fight. After Horthy's failed cease-fire attempt of 15 October 1944 the combat value of Hungarian troops declined ever further. With the exception of certain units, they either surrendered or stood their ground only if they were supported or forced by the Germans.

Among the original noncombatants, KISKA was the successor to the National Guard, which had been formed on 25 September 1944 of men who were not eligible for active service and had either volunteered or been conscripted for security and guard duties. They were given food and pay, wore uniforms or civilian clothes with armbands, carried arms requisitioned from civilians, and received their orders from the heads of the paramilitary groups or factories and businesses in their districts. On 3 December the Szálasi government had dissolved the organization because it had been infiltrated by deserters, persecution victims, resistance fighters, and other dissidents; its replacement, KISKA, became an integral part of the Honvéd army, numbering 7,000 noncombatants. Generally there was one KISKA battalion in each city district, but universities and other institutions had units of their own. When KISKA also proved unreliable, it was dissolved on 6 January 1945.

The police combat groups were similarly made up of men who were originally noncombatants. Although at the time of the encirclement their ration strength was 7,000 and their official combat strength 1,630, their combat value was minimal because of inadequate training and equipment. Their independent operations disintegrated within a few hours with great losses: 50 percent were killed or badly wounded.

One exception to the rule was the assault artillery. Although its equipment consisted mainly of small arms, it had considerable combat value thanks to its high motivation. In January 1945 it was still being joined by volunteers—young paramilitaries, students from military academies and high schools, and soldiers who had lost their own formations—because it offered better food, more humane treatment, and proof of identity in case of police raids. In November 1944 Captain Sándor Hanák recruited an armored grenadier company of soldiers cut off from other units, and in early December First Lieutenant Tibor Rátz, commander of the I/3 Assault Artillery Battery, escaped from Pest with his unit to join in the attack of the 10th Assault Artillery Battalion at Baracska because he felt that his assault guns were underemployed.

The regular divisions, on the other hand, comprised many Hungarian soldiers who did not want to fight. A characteristic example is the 1st Armored Division, which in early December showed a ration strength of 14,000, but reported only 2,038 infantry to the Germans. By late December there had been 80 desertions, but no investigations followed. The staff and almost 600 reserves of the 10th Infantry Division's 6th Infantry Regiment (6/I and 6/II Battalions) did not fight at all from 24 December to the end of the siege, and the 10th Reconnaissance Battalion remained a "hidden unit" of whose existence the Germans were never informed. Most units kept two different sets of troop and weaponry accounts. As early as November three colonels and five lieutenant-colonels of the 12th Reserve Division had been discharged or court-martialed, and by the end of December the battalions numbered only 30 to 40.

Strangely enough, neither the German nor the Hungarian military leaders made any attempt to change this situation and accepted the reports—although they must have known that they were false. Lieutenant József Bíró, a divisional adjutant, writes in his memoirs: "The Germans were satisfied with the token actions of our three battalions and even defended the commander of the 18/I Battalion, which had retreated without permission, when Arrow Cross men informed on him." Many members of the higher military echelons were only carrying out routine administrative duties, being interested mainly in minimizing their losses or, to put it more simply, in surviving the war.

The German military authorities took every opportunity to blame the Hungarians for the defeats. Their reports suggest that the entire responsibility for the defense of Budapest rested on German shoulders, and they repeatedly refer to desertions on the Hungarian side, forgetting that Germans too were deserting, if in smaller numbers. Conversely, several Hungarian officers state in their memoirs that the desertions were due, at least in part, to the arrogance of the Germans, the subordinate position of the Hungarians, and the virtual elimination of the Hungarian command. By the end of December many Hungarian units had been split into companies or even smaller formations and placed under German orders, although in some cases remnants of other units (chiefly the officers) and even civilians had joined German units of their own free will.

Soviet reports about Hungarian desertions also give a false picture, because for political purposes prisoners of war are often presented as if they had voluntarily deserted. Soviet reports about the combat strength of the enemy are equally unreliable. According to documents in Soviet archives, in Pest the defenders lost 35,840 dead, 291 tanks and assault guns, 1,419 guns, and 222 armored trucks. In fact, the defenders had no such quantities of military hardware in the entire cauldron, and if we add to the alleged dead the 25,000 prisoners taken by the Red Army in Pest alone, these claims prove even less tenable.

The Germans and Hungarians in Budapest during the Christmas period were relatively well supplied with guns (nearly 500 between them) and tanks and assault guns (about 220). On the whole, the Germans' training and equipment, as well as their morale, was better than that of the Hungarians. Nevertheless, they too had their share of difficulties. Their greatest problem was lack of infantry. Their ration strength of some 42,000 was made up mainly of cavalry, artillery, and armored units (Table 9). Of the Feldherrnhalle Panzergrenadier Division's four panzer grenadier battalions, one was not in Budapest and the combined combat strength of the other three was barely more than 500; one panzer grenadier battalion of the 13th Panzergrenadier Division had also remained outside the encirclement.

The combat value of the German units was uneven. It was highest among soldiers from the Reich serving in units with a long tradition. One such unit was the 13th Panzer Division, more than 20 members of which were awarded the Knight's Cross and three the Oak Leaf medal. Others were the 8th SS Cavalry Division and the Feldherrnhalle Panzergrenadier Division, which had originally consisted of SA members, although by 1944 it had been all but destroyed three times (first at Stalingrad) and reinforced with new recruits. The combat value of some 10,000 other troops was impaired by lack of training and equipment, and the unit with the lowest combat value was the 22nd SS Cavalry Division, which consisted of ethnic Germans who could not even speak the language and were the most frequent deserters.

The SS units comprised almost all nationalities—in addition to ethnic Germans, press-ganged French Alsatians, Hungarians, Serbs, Slovaks, and Romanians, and Finnish, Flemish, Swedish, and Spanish volunteers. The baggage trains of the SS divisions included Russian, Ukrainian, Tatar, and other auxiliaries. One artillery detachment consisted mainly of Poles, and several of its members were buried in Polish uniforms with German insignia. The 22nd SS Cavalry Division was totally demoralized by early November, and the 1st, 6th, and 8th SS Police Regiments, recruited in Hungary, were extremely unreliable. Behind the 8th SS Police Regiment at the Solt bridgehead, machine-gun positions were set up with orders to fire on any movement that looked like desertion. During the last days of the siege some of these troops even mutinied against their officers. The main reason for the low morale was that the majority of the SS soldiers concerned had been recruited in Hungary and felt no sympathy for Germany. In spring 1944 the Hungarian government had agreed to place all the country's ethnic Germans liable for military service at the disposal of the SS, even though most of them wished to serve in the Hungarian army. The minority that regarded Nazi Germany as their real homeland had already volunteered for the SS in 1941–1942. By 1944 the ethnic German villages had to be searched with a fine-tooth comb for any men available to serve in the SS.

The ideological warfare waged on the eastern front had disastrous consequences for many German soldiers, who resisted to the bitter end not only out of a sense of duty and loyalty but also because they feared the worst from the Soviets. Each side portrayed the soldiers of the other as sadistic criminals, who had to be exterminated. The Nazis tried to moderate this approach somewhat after 1943, but the Soviet propaganda continued to identify the Nazi political system with the German people as a whole. That is why even those German units with low morale chose to fight rather than surrender. A particularly large number of SS soldiers and Russian and Ukrainian auxiliaries chose suicide rather than capture.

Many were seen putting their last submachine-gun cartridge on one side for that purpose.

Supplies for the troops also created serious problems for the German and Hungarian commands. Budapest was a fortress only on paper, and the stockpiling of food to last several months was never even begun. Many of the existing stocks, including both food and military necessities, were kept in the outer districts of Buda and fell into Soviet hands between 24 and 26 December. After Christmas, in an act of deliberate sabotage, Captain Dezső Németh, quartermaster of the I Army Corps, moved the Hungarian stocks to locations where they could soon be found by the Red Army. When the encirclement was completed, the defenders had 450 tons of ammunition, 120 cubic meters of fuel, and 300,000 rations—enough for about five days.

The German and Hungarian commands could not even think of feeding the civilian population. The minimum of food and ammunition required by the encircled troops was calculated as 80 tons per day. Because of limited airfield capacity, 20 tons were to be parachuted in and the rest delivered by Ju-52 air freighters and gliders. Emergency landing zones and parachute dropping points were established at the Racecourse, the North Csepel recreational airfield, the site of today's People's Stadium, and the Kisrákos drill ground in Pest, and in Tabán Park and Vérmező Meadow in Buda. The capital's larger aerodromes had been taken by the Soviets earlier: Budaörs on 25, Ferihegy on 27, and Mátyásföld on 30 December.

The first air delivery arrived on 29 December 1944. It was flown in by the Budapest supply group of the German 4th Air Fleet, which had been set up on the same day under the command of Lieutenant-General Gerhard Conrad. The group had some 200 aircraft of various kinds and flew 61 missions a day on average, of which 49 were successful. Until the capture of the Racecourse in early January there were even some days with up to 93 landings. The greatest losses were suffered by the gliders. Thirty-two of the 73 DFS-230s never reached Budapest, and the remainder either disintegrated on crash-landing or ended up in the wrong place. They were piloted by NSFK (National Socialist Flying Corps) members aged 16 to 18, most of whom had volunteered out of youthful bravado.

Of the required daily supplies only 47 tons on average could be delivered. Although 86 percent of this was ammunition, the German heavy artillery dropped out of the action in the first week of the siege. As no horse fodder was available, the garrison's horses (roughly 25,000) became food for humans. In January the Germans were still carefully guarding a dozen pigs—for the city command and its entourage—at the southern edge of Buda Castle. A company sergeant major of the Hungarian 12th Reserve Division remembers: "The most dangerous and most successful undertaking of my life was when one night, to feed my hungry soldiers better, I stole a pig from the Germans with a few of my lads." By the end of January all central stores were exhausted, and the only food available was carrots—originally kept as animal feed—and horse meat. However, even these were so scarce that by the last weeks of the siege most of the soldiers were starving.

The total supplies flown in weighed 1,975 tons, including 417 tons delivered by Hungarian pilots. The parachutes carrying ammunition canisters were red, those carrying food canisters white. During the last week of the siege several thousand canisters were dropped under cover of darkness, but only a few reached the troops. Some were blown by air currents into Soviet-held areas, and the search for the others could not begin until morning, by which time civilians had pilfered the food, despite the threat of capital punishment. The contents of those that were found intact could not be distributed because of a lack of fuel and constant artillery bombardment. Sometimes the canisters carried surprising objects: Iron Crosses, for example, or yellow flags to mark unexploded shells. A Knight's Cross for Pfeffer-Wildenbruch was dropped three times before it reached him.

The Soviet and Romanian Units

The Soviet and Romanian troops also varied in quality. Some units were first class, but the fighting morale of others was no higher than that of the worst Hungarian units. The Soviet supreme

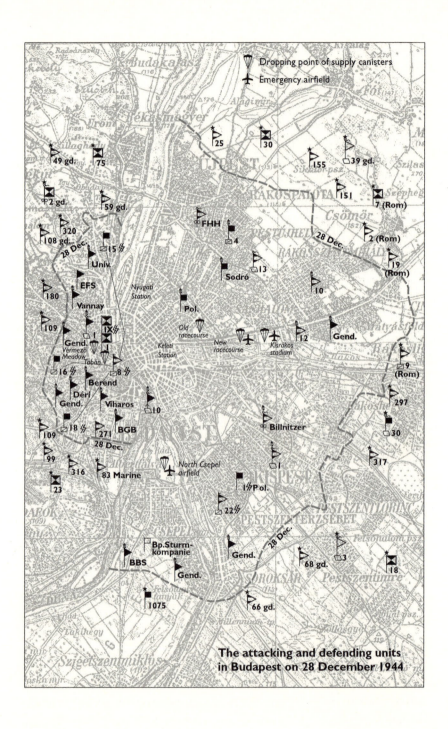

Dropping point of supply canisters

Emergency airfield

49 gd.
75
2 gd.
59 gd.
320
108 gd.
28 Dec.
15
Univ.
EFS
Vannay
180
109
Gend.
I
IX
16
8
Berend
Déri
Gend.
Viharos
10
109
18
271 BGB
99
28 Dec.
316
83 Marine
23

FHH
4
Sodró
13
Pol.
Old racecourse
New racecourse
Nyugati Station
Keleti Station
Vermező Meadow
Tabán
Kisrákos stadium

25
30
155
39 gd.
151
7 (Rom)
28 Dec.
2 (Rom)
19 (Rom)
10
12
Gend.
9 (Rom)
297
30
317

North Csepel airfield
Billnitzer
1
1 P ol.
22

BBS
Bp.Sturm-kompanie
Gend.
Gend.
1075
66 gd.
Gend.
28 Dec.
68 gd.
3
18

**The attacking and defending units
in Budapest on 28 December 1944**

command always reinforced the divisions in the main line of an attack, but other units could rarely count on this. Tank, cavalry, and mechanized guard corps were reinforced with highly trained and motivated recruits, while the reinforcements of the rest included children and old people, drafted indiscriminately. The men in liberated Soviet territories were immediately pressed into service. According to German intelligence 40–70 percent of the troops in 15 reinforced divisions opposing the German Army Group South came from recaptured territories. Soldiers freed from German prisoner-of-war camps in Romania were redeployed with hardly a rest. Thus of 960 prisoners taken by the Hungarian 1st Armored Division in November–December 1944, only 160 were first-timers, while 400 had already been captured once and 400 twice. The Soviet command allocated a large number of Soviet troops and tanks to strengthen the Romanian 7th Army Corps because it mistrusted the equipment and fighting spirit of the Romanians. The majority of Tatar, Estonian, Latvian, Lithuanian, and Caucasian soldiers also felt unenthusiastic about the war, and the morale of the Moldavians and Ukrainians was particularly low. Before an attack, in some units, soldiers were pulled out of the ranks and shot for alleged cowardice. The smallest offenses were punished with ten years' hard labor, converted to three months in a penal company, where the chances of survival were particularly slim. To improve morale before an attack, the Soviet commanders often distributed large quantities of alcohol among the soldiers and set up an armed cordon to prevent any of them trickling back. More than once after a failed attack they ordered their heavy weapons to fire on their own returning infantry.

To escape from such conditions, many Soviet and Romanian soldiers absconded or changed sides, although the Hungarians doing the same in the other direction outnumbered them. The reason Soviet and Romanian defectors often gave to German interrogating officers was that they "wanted to live." Lieutenant József Bíró remembers: "During one of our successful counterattacks 70 Russians crossed over to us. They told us that if they had tried to retreat instead of holding their positions they would have been shot. That is why they were more afraid of going back than forward."

From early November 1944 to late January 1945, the Soviet and Romanian combat forces were constantly being regrouped for the continuing assaults on both Pest and Buda (Table 10). On 1 January 1945 the commanders of the two Ukrainian fronts had some 177,000 Soviet soldiers at their disposal for the siege. While 67,000 men performed infantry duties on the Pest side and 70,000 on the Buda side, 40,000 were engaged on the two fronts as members of the artillery, air force, and navy. Theoretically the Soviet divisions were much smaller than the German and Hungarian. The German divisions originally formed in 1944 numbered 12,500, the Hungarian 20,000, and the Soviet 9,389. These figures are deceptive, however, because most Soviet supply units were directly attached to armies or fronts rather than forming integral parts of divisions; moreover, the total strength of a Hungarian division was so great because the Hungarians tried to compensate for the shortage of heavy weapons by increasing the numbers of infantry armed with rifles. In a Soviet infantry division only 150 men belonged to the supply services and 109 to the medical services, as opposed to 1,113 and 628, respectively, in a German division. The combat strength of a German division was 7,706 and that of a Soviet division 7,509.

By the end of November 1944, Malinovsky's divisions had been dangerously depleted. Although they had received 800 men on average in reinforcements, they still numbered about 4,500, which was their original strength at the start of the attacks. This in practice meant a loss of 20 percent over three weeks. Between 24 December 1944 and 11 February 1945, the total ration strength of the Soviet and Romanian forces declined from 177,000 to 75,000, and their combat strength from 100,000 to 36,000. This compares with a decline from a ration strength of 79,000 to 32,000 and a combat strength from 35,000 to 11,000 for the German and Hungarian forces in the same period (Table 11).

It should be noted that the Soviets, unlike the Germans, were often able to repair their damaged equipment. Their 70 light, 32 heavy, and 10 self-propelled batteries not only outnumbered the 45 light and 15 heavy batteries of the defenders but also remained in battle-ready condition, while the German and Hungarian units lost

30 percent of their guns in the early days of the siege. In addition, the Soviets had enough ammunition and were able to take better care of their wounded. Most of the Red Army's supplies could be obtained from the occupied territories. Apart from flour, sugar, tobacco, and war matériel, everything was requisitioned locally. Sometimes the Soviets paid for requisitioned goods, but this had only symbolic value because the banknotes printed by the military were not covered—which was one of the reasons why in 1946 Hungary was to experience one of the worst periods of inflation in history.

As shown above, the Soviet troops vastly outnumbered the Germans and Hungarians, but their numerical superiority was less decisive than might be expected. In any city battle the defenders have the enormous advantage of being able to form locally superior forces through rapid and concentric regrouping. The presence of roughly double the number of Soviet soldiers therefore proved sufficient solely because the Germans and Hungarians not only were disproportionately short of ammunition and thus unable to make the best use of their heavy weaponry but also evaded action on many occasions. In different circumstances the attackers would have needed three times as many troops as the defenders to succeed. In earlier sieges of Budapest, or those of Berlin, Breslau, or Posen in the Second World War, the attackers outnumbered the defenders by up to a factor of ten.

The German and Hungarian Commands

On 25 December the Soviet artillery began to bombard the convent of Notre Dame de Sion on Sashegy Hill, where the Hungarian Army Corps was billeted. Hindy and his general staff transferred to Sándor Palace in the Castle District in Buda, while most sections of the corps command were stationed at various points in the city. The German corps command established itself in Werbőczy Street not far from Hindy. Early in January both corps commands moved into the air raid shelter in the tunnel under Castle Hill. The two-story shelter had its own ventilation system and electricity generator, which continued to function throughout the siege. The German command occupied the lower level, the Hungarian the upper. Even here Pfeffer-Wildenbruch maintained his bureaucratic habits, with anterooms, secretaries, and fixed office hours.

As suggested earlier, there was little cooperation between the commands. The German command issued orders without taking any notice of the Hungarians' wishes, and the German troops rode roughshod over the needs of the population and the capital, requisitioning property and blowing up buildings for no good reason. Until the forced joint move to the tunnel, briefings were given only by two German captains, and neither Pfeffer-Wildenbruch nor his chief of staff, Lieutenant-Colonel Usdau Lindenau, thought personal contact with the Hungarian command necessary. Nor did the German and Hungarian commands exchange any information about their reports to the outside world, in which they criticized each other.

There were also tensions within the German command. Pfeffer-Wildenbruch, who never left the shelter, distrusted his own officers and kept a constant check on them. He reprimanded Colonel-General Gerhard Schmidhuber for "carelessly reducing the division's combat strength" by airlifting an officer chosen on social grounds out of the encirclement with the 13th Panzer Division's war diary and other documents on 30 December. He repeatedly complained about the discrepancy between the ration strength and the combat strength of the division and refused to accept the result of the ensuing investigation, which contained a detailed account of all its units. After an inquiry which followed the break-out, Major Mitzlaff, chief of staff of the 8th SS Cavalry Division, recorded his impressions as follows:

> Pfeffer-Wildenbruch is . . . not a leader of men. In any
> case it is a novelty for a commanding general not to leave
> the tunnel for six weeks. This also spread to the officers
> of his staff, who visited their troops only as a formality
> after the award of the Knight's Cross. There was partic-
> ularly harsh criticism of the chief of staff, Major [later
> Lieutenant-Colonel] Lindenau. It was said that he lacked

4

Karl Pfeffer-Wildenbruch, commander of the IX SS Mountain Army Corps

the necessary seriousness. They had always been calm and confident in total ignorance of the situation.

The commanders of the various units differed widely in background and character. Pfeffer-Wildenbruch was born in 1888, the son of a doctor. In the First World War he had served as a lieutenant, and he subsequently joined the newly established security police. Between 1928 and 1930 he worked in Chile as a gendarmerie instructor. From 1939 to 1940 he commanded the SS Police Division and then became chief of the colonial police department in the corps of the Reichssicherheitshauptamt headed by the Reichsführer SS, Heinrich Himmler. At that time the Reichssicherheitshauptamt was contemplating the establishment of an African colonial police force. On 27 August 1943 Pfeffer-Wildenbruch was appointed commander of the Latvian VI SS Army Corps, which he commanded until 11 June 1944 at the comparatively quiet front of the German Army Group North. He came to Budapest in September 1944 to help foil Horthy's attempt to make peace with the Allies and to direct the creation of new armed SS units. Horthy's failure and the ensuing political events which favored the Germans would not have been enough to make him an important figure in the defense had not the Soviet troops reached the periphery of the capital two weeks later.

Pfeffer-Wildenbruch was not a member of the National Socialist Party and never used the "Heil Hitler" salute. As an experienced police officer he was appointed commander of the Budapest Corps Group in the hope that he would be able to prevent any unrest and desertions. Like the pedantic official he was, he insisted on strict observation of all the rules. In 1940, for example, he sentenced a soldier to ten days' detention for taking a pound of coffee from an empty apartment. His subordinates had a very low opinion of him. Lieutenant-Colonel Helmut Wolff remembers with bitterness: "To every helpful suggestion we got dirty and arrogant replies. Pfeffer-Wildenbruch always lied in his reports. For example, Keleti Station fell two days later than he reported. All his reports were so exag-

5
Lieutenant-Colonel Usdau Lindenau (in captain's uniform), chief of staff, IX SS Mountain Army Corps

gerated that even his adjutant, shaking his head, declared that he would never dare to report such things." According to Colonel-General Balck, the tune in Budapest was called by a "civilian" or, at best, "political" general and his chief of staff, both of whom were "unable to cope with the situation" but "could not be replaced," as there were no more suitable candidates within the encirclement. Although Balck was biased against all SS generals, his criticism was not without foundation. In 1955 Pfeffer-Wildenbruch was one of the last Soviet prisoners of war to be released, and in 1971 he was killed in a traffic accident in West Germany.

Pfeffer-Wildenbruch's chief of staff, Usdau Lindenau, aged 30, was one of the youngest staff officers in the German army, and had excellent credentials. He arrived in Budapest from Vienna on 19 December 1944. Although he did not belong to the SS, his promotion to the IX SS Mountain Army Corps was not unusual: as the SS had no general-staff academies, its high officers often came from the Wehrmacht.

The commander of the 8th SS Cavalry Division was SS Brigadeführer (equivalent to major-general) Joachim Rumohr. The son of a farmer, he was born in Hamburg in 1910. In 1930 he joined the Nazi Party, and a little later the SS. Since the beginning of the Second World War he had gained considerable experience as commander of various units. During the break-out he was wounded and subsequently committed suicide.

The commander of the 22nd SS Cavalry Division was SS Brigadeführer August Zehender, born in Württemberg in 1903. He joined the army in 1918, aged 15, and served as a sergeant until 1933. After being discharged with distinction he joined the Nazi Party and in 1935 became an SS Hauptsturmführer (equivalent to captain). During the Second World War, he served as a battalion and regiment commander until November 1944: when he saw the failure of the break-out he also committed suicide.

The commander of the 13th Panzer Division, Colonel-General Gerhard Schmidhuber, was born in Prussia in 1894. In 1914 he became a reserve officer. In 1920 he left the army, but he rejoined in 1934. He served as a battalion and regiment commander in France and the Soviet Union and was repeatedly decorated.

6
Colonel-General Gerhard Schmidhuber, commander of the
13th Panzer Division

During the siege, troubled by the memory of having purloined a Persian carpet in Gödöllő, he tried to salve his conscience by giving Captain Benyovszky 100 pengős to help a poor man. He took part in the first wave of the break-out and was killed in Széna Square.

The commander of the 66th Panzergrenadier Regiment of the 13th Panzer Division, Major (later Lieutenant-Colonel) Wilhelm Schöning, was born in Gumbinnen (East Prussia) in 1908. During the siege he was also put in charge of the other regiment of the division, so that he temporarily performed the duties of Schmidhuber, who in his turn assumed command of all combat groups on the Pest side, which included Schöning's unit. Having been wounded several times, Schöning managed to reach the German lines after the break-out from Buda. He was pursued by memories of the siege until he died in 1987 in Bochum.

7

Lieutenant-Colonel Wilhelm Schöning, commander of the 66th Panzergrenadier
Regiment of the 13th Panzer Division

The commander of the Feldherrnhalle Panzergrenadier Division, Major-General Günther von Pape, was born in Düsseldorf in 1907. As a regular officer he commanded several companies, battalions, and regiments in the Second World War. Because of his outstanding record he was awarded the Knight's Cross and the Oak Leaf medal. On 23 December 1944, when he was detailed to organize the Feldherrnhalle Panzer Corps, his command was taken over by Lieutenant-Colonel Helmut Wolff, the commander of the Panzergrenadier Regiment. Wolff escaped during the break-out and died in 1989 in Germany as a retired Bundeswehr general.

Lieutenant-Colonel Herbert Kündiger, acting commander of the 271st People's Grenadier Division, rose from the lowest ranks to staff officer and also received the Oak Leaf and the Knight's Cross. His division was only partly trapped in Budapest and was reconstituted outside the encirclement under its original commander, Major-General Martin Bieber.

8

SS Unterscharführer Adolf John, aged 19

9

Adolf John, 55 years later

10

Banquet of officers and officer cadets in the 1930s. The bald man in lieutenant-
colonel's uniform in the second row is Iván Hindy, subsequently colonel-general
and commander of the Hungarian I Army Corps.

Between the Hungarian and German command structures
there were some noteworthy differences. In particular, the highest
rank a Hungarian officer could reach by the age of 40 was that of
lieutenant-colonel, and Ernő Billnitzer for one was 50 when he
became a general. The German army had lieutenant-colonels aged
30 and generals aged 40. This was one of the reasons why the German officers were much more dynamic and had more stamina than
the Hungarians.

Colonel-General Iván Hindy was born in Budapest in 1890. In
1909 he became a cadet sergeant. In the First World War he
received a commission as a first lieutenant and the class III Iron
Crown—a high honor, considering his rank. After the war he
became a counterintelligence officer, and in 1924 the annual ap-
praisal undergone by every officer described him as

> a determined, mature, open character. He is cheerful,
> with a lively temperament. He has an outstanding intel-

lect, great military talent, and a powerful and quick
mind. He is extremely conscientious and hardworking.
. . . In combat he has proved a brave, calm, and circum-
spect commander, whose personal courage has made him
a model for his subordinates. . . . His behavior as a superior is strict, consistent, and just. He has a very positive
effect on his subordinates, for whom he shows great concern. As a subordinate he is obedient and disciplined.

Despite his excellent record he was unable to obtain a higher
position in the army, possibly because of his modest results in the
staff-officer examination. In 1928 he quit the counterintelligence
service, and for four years he taught German in the Ludovika Military Academy. In 1932 he obtained a law degree and was appointed
adviser on discipline and questions of honor in the supreme command of the Honvéd army before being made head of the same
department. In 1936 he was characterized as an "excellent" staff
officer and in 1940 as "an officer with mature views and under-
standing, a strong sense of responsibility, a high degree of consci-
entiousness and initiative . . . capable of passing objective and fair
judgments." In 1942 he was promoted to major-general and placed
in charge of the Hungarian I Army Corps.

During Horthy's ceasefire bid on 15 October 1944 Hindy
played an important part, when on his own initiative he arrested his
commander, Lieutenant-General Béla Aggteleky, who had given
orders to eject the German units that were about to occupy Sashegy Hill and the Citadel in Buda before instructions had been
issued for the Hungarian breakaway. Hindy was probably talked
into the arrest by Lieutenant-Colonel Sándor Horváth, the chief
of Aggteleky's general staff and an Arrow Cross sympathizer.
When Aggteleky issued his order, Horváth protested, and when
Aggteleky insisted on it being carried out, Horváth left the room.
Half an hour later Hindy and two other officers suddenly opened
Aggteleky's door. As Aggteleky recalls, Hindy was their spokesman:
"'I invite the lieutenant-general and the I Army Corps to join the
Hungarist party.' . . . . 'No, no and no,' I said. Whereupon Hindy:
'Lieutenant-General, hand over the command to me.' At the same

time Captain Czech jumped behind my desk and tore the telephone cable out of the wall. He or another took my pistol holster from the hook."

Shortly after, Hindy addressed a meeting of the 60 officer members of the staff:

A conspiracy against our German comrades is being prepared here. Aggteleky could have opposed the traitors but did not do so. On the contrary, he sided with the traitors. Unfortunately the regent is being influenced by cliques of Jewish agents and defeatists and is not prepared to dissociate himself from these criminal cliques. The radio proclamation is treason. It's possible that the regent doesn't even know about it; otherwise, it would have been read out by him and not by a common newsreader. To prevent this treason I had to take over the command. I expect the officers of the army corps to support me.

The next day Hindy was officially in command of the corps, and 15 days later he was promoted to lieutenant-general.

Hindy's behavior shocked several of his acquaintances. He had been commonly known as modest and quiet, a perfect gentleman, and nobody could understand why he had sided with the Arrow Cross. Asked why he had accepted the command, he answered:

I spent a lot of time at my desk in the Ministry of Defense, dealing with dull and stupid questions of honor. I was always longing to be on the battlefield, but my application was constantly rejected. But my wish always remained the same: to become a commander of troops one day and to reach the highest rank I possibly could. The 15th of October gave me the opportunity. I became a lieutenant-general and commander of the defense of Budapest. I accepted this appointment as a soldier, regardless of politics or the system of government. I fulfilled my dream, and am now going to pay for it with my life.

Hindy was probably unable to admit the real motives for his conduct even to himself. It is unlikely that a soldier who had never been a careerist would have betrayed his regent and his commanders out of ambition. More probably his decision was motivated by his blindness about the Germans and his fundamental rejection of the Soviet system. In this he was by no means alone: many officers who supported neither the Arrow Cross nor the Germans behaved similarly. Gyula Földes, captain of the bodyguard, who was known for his absolute loyalty to the Horthy government, had found himself in a deep inner conflict when he received orders to take action against the Germans, and later committed suicide. The NCOs of the 2nd Árpád fejedelem Hussar Regiment, who all came from peasant families in the Hungarian Plain and were not interested in politics, on hearing the regent's proclamation sent a delegation to their officers, asking for permission to join the Waffen SS if Hungary were to capitulate.

Hindy was not an Arrow Cross fanatic but a typical professional officer of his day. His outlook had been shaped by the Hungarian Commune of 1919 and by 25 years of anticommunist education: "To my mind communism meant nothing but robbery, murder, and above all a total lack of religion and a moral slough," he confessed when he was being questioned by the People's Court, which sentenced him to death on 15 October 1946 and later had him executed. He did not abandon this conviction even when he had lost his illusions about the Germans and realized more and more that all the sacrifices had been pointless. His official reports clearly demonstrate his growing insight into the senselessness of the struggle. By mid-January he described the devastation of Budapest as a fait accompli, and by the beginning of February he dismissed the relief attempts, which Hitler kept promising on the radio, as "fairy tales." In the last phase of the war he even described the Soviet troops in more positive terms than the Germans. His fear of Bolshevism and his sense of impotence, however, made him incapable of taking an independent stance against the ally. From the moment of his arrest he had no illusions about his fate. He said to a friend:

> I told the secret police everything as it really happened. I almost dictated my confession to them. They were surprised. I denied nothing, changed nothing of the truth. They were interested only in a brief period: from 15 October 1944 to the end of February 1945. Four months. My interrogators knew very well that my life before 15 October 1945 was immaculate. I was always against extremes, as you will remember. Even after 15 October I didn't take any part in the atrocities, but tried to prevent them whenever I could. I accepted the command of the defense of Budapest as a soldier. That's all. My case doesn't need any witnesses, either for or against me. What I am going to say is the truth. I shall be sentenced to death and executed.

As Hindy had been invested with "full authority for Hungarian affairs in the territory of the capital and royal residence of Budapest" by the Arrow Cross leadership, the orders for the massacres that followed bear his name. He saved a number of Jews, personally calling on the lawyer László Varga to buy the necessary passes. They were obtained for him free of charge by Sándor Keresztes—50 years later honorary president of the Hungarian Christian Democratic People's Party—who was working in the Interior Ministry at the time. In return he issued certificates of exemption for László Varga and one of his colleagues, although he must have known that both were deserters. But this was not enough.

Hindy embodies the failure of the right-wing Hungarian officer. Although as a private individual he rejected the excesses and bloodbaths, he nevertheless became responsible for them. As commander he lent his name to the crimes of the Arrow Cross militia, instead of resigning when he saw that he could do nothing to stop them.

The chief of staff responsible for upholding the fighting discipline in the capital was Lieutenant-General Imre Kalándy, president

II

Lieutenant-General Imre Kalándy (in major-general's uniform), commander
of the unit responsible for combat discipline

of the Hungarian Boxing Federation, who was already 69 at the
time of the siege. Having served as an assault-company and battalion commander in the First World War, he was one of the most
decorated Hungarian officers. The moment he heard of the encirclement he asked Hindy to assign him to a fighting unit, declaring
that he was still in good health. He was one of the few commanders who regularly visited the front line: "As a soldier he was practically indestructible. His car was hit daily, but if it was hit in front
he was sitting in the back, and if it was hit in the back he was sitting in front next to the driver. His face and hands were full of
wounds. When he had no car he traveled by bicycle, and when he
had no bicycle he walked." On 17 January 1945 he was gravely
wounded. His command passed to Major-General Andor Szőke,
who in his turn was wounded in the fighting near Déli Station.
Kalándy was taken prisoner in the break-out and, debilitated by

12

Lieutenant-General Ernő Billnitzer (in major's uniform), commander of the
assault artillery

dysentery, died on a forced march. Szőke died in April 1945 in
Szolnok.

Lieutenant-General Ernő Billnitzer, commander of the assault
artillery, was born in Fiume in 1889. In the winter of 1942–1943 he
served on the Don as an artillery corps commander. In September
1944 he was commissioned to organize and command the assault
artillery, which was the youngest arm of the service. He was the
only member of the general staff to escape during the break-out,
but he was caught near Perbál. In 1948, one month after being
freed from prison camp, he was arrested and sentenced in a show
trial to three and subsequently eight years' imprisonment. As his
sentence included forfeiture of all his assets, he became a hospital
porter after his release. In the 1960s Major-General András Zákó,
one of the leaders of the military emigration to the West, tried to
persuade Billnitzer to spy for Western intelligence. Billnitzer, 70
years old and worn out both mentally and physically, refused and
informed the authorities. The affair was exploited for propaganda

13

Colonel Sándor András, commander of the Hungarian 10th Infantry Division

purposes, and in exchange he was given an apartment and a modest pension. He died in 1976 in Budapest.

Colonel Sándor András, an infantry lieutenant since 1918, served in the air force after the First World War; it was being organized in secret because of conditions imposed by the treaty of Trianon. He was trained in Italy and took part in the Spanish Civil War as an observer. In November 1942 he became the air force chief of staff, but he was removed from this post under German pressure and instead made head of the War Academy. When the academy was closed in November 1944, he took over the command of the 10th Infantry Division's infantry units, and on 26 November he succeeded Major-General Kornél Oszlányi as commander of the entire division. On 15 January 1945 he crossed over to the Soviets. Later in the same year he was appointed chief of staff of the new Honvéd army, but he resigned when the communist press started a campaign against him following his criticism of the Department of Military Policy's methods of interrogation. On 19 December 1946 he was arrested and in a show trial given a death sentence, which was commuted to life imprisonment. During the 1956 revolution, on 31 October, he was released from Vác prison and after the revolution was suppressed, he escaped to Canada. In 1978 he returned to Eisenstadt in Austria, where he died in 1985 at the age of 87.

Lieutenant-Colonel László Veresváry, commander of the Budapest Security Battalion, was one of the most brutal officers. He had served on the front since March 1944 and was put in charge of the security battalion on 17 October. In his unit, forced laborers or soldiers were regularly executed as a deterrent to misbehavior. He even sentenced one of his ensigns to death for cowardice and after pardoning him bullied him until he committed suicide. He constantly abused his soldiers, both verbally and physically, and refused them even a five-minute rest to smoke a cigarette. On one occasion he was seen walking up and down the Lágymányos railway embankment, riding crop in hand, issuing commands to his soldiers in a hail of bullets. Later on, when his battalion had been pulverized, he became the much hated commander of the unit responsible for the immediate defense of the Castle District. A gendarmerie officer remembers, "Veresváry, the terror of the Castle . . . came twice a day to see us in the cellar, and before he arrived the sentries would shout: 'Look out, Veresváry is coming!' He always boasted of having a list of three battalions in his bag, all of them dead. He had a nasty appearance, thick-set, arrogant, and with a scornful face . . . always ready to find something to pick on. . . . We were so fed up with him that one group decided to do him in next time he came." This did not happen. Having ordered his soldiers to break out, Veresváry himself joined the enterprise and, according to eyewitnesses, was shot dead by Soviet troops southwest of Piliscsaba between 15 and 17 February 1945. Toward the end of January 1944 he had received the Cross of the Hungarian Order of Merit for his "heroism."

The Soviet Generals

Little is known about the Soviet generals engaged in the siege of Budapest, in part because of limited access to Russian archives, but mostly because memoirs published in the Soviet Union lack

14

Marshal Rodion Malinovsky, commander in chief of the 2nd Ukrainian Front,
briefing his officers. Behind him, on the right, Major-General Ivan Afonin, commander of the "Budapest Group."

personal information. We have detailed knowledge only of the marshals of the Ukrainian fronts.

Marshal Rodion Yakovlevich Malinovsky was born in Odessa
in 1898. He served in the First World War from the outset and went
to France in 1916 as a soldier of the Russian Expedition Corps. On
his return in 1919 he immediately joined the Red Army. In 1920, as
a noncommissioned officer, he was sent to commander training
college, and in 1930 he graduated from the Frunze General Staff
Academy. By 1936 he had already become chief of staff of an army
corps, and he was sent to Spain as a military adviser, working there
until 1939. He soon became a major-general, and in March 1941 was
made commander of the 48th Rifle Corps deployed against Romania. The 9th Guard Army, which was attached to his corps, was the

15

Marshal Fedor Tolbukhin, commander in chief of the 3rd Ukrainian Front,
surrounded by his officers

strongest of all Soviet armies. After becoming commander of the
6th Armored Guard Army and holding seven other appointments
within a short period, he commanded the 2nd Guard Army at Stalingrad. In 1942 he was promoted to army general and in May 1944
to marshal and commander of the 2nd Ukrainian Front. The liberation of Odessa and the operations at Iasi-Kishinev, which almost
completely destroyed Friessner's South Ukraine Army Group, are
linked to his name. After the capitulation of Germany, Malinovsky,
as supreme commander on the Transbaikal front, led the main
strike against the Japanese Kwantung Army. Until 1955 he was commander in chief of the Far Eastern Troops, and in the wake of the
XX Communist Party Congress, he became first deputy minister of
defense. As a supporter of Nikita Khrushchev he obtained the post
of defense minister, which he occupied, unaffected by Khrushchev's
fall in 1964, until his death in 1967. He was twice awarded the Hero
of the Soviet Union medal.

Marshal Fedor Ivanovich Tolbukhin was born in Androniki in the Jaroslav region in 1894. In the First World War he served as an ensign and then as a staff captain, and he was known to care deeply about his soldiers. After the 1917 revolution he performed organizational duties. In 1919 he was posted as a staff officer to the northern, eastern, and Karelian fronts. Because of his personal courage he was awarded the order of the Red Flag. He subsequently graduated with distinction from the Frunze General Staff Academy and held various posts in the general staff. In 1941 he became chief of staff of the Transcaucasian Front and the Caucausian Front, and in

16
"I am fighting, you must work for victory," poster of the Fellowship
for the eastern front

1942 of the Crimean Front. After the evacuation of Crimea he was appointed commander of the 57th Rifle Army. He was engaged with his troops in the battle of Stalingrad from the very beginning and played a decisive part in repulsing the German relief attacks. Afterward he commanded several other fronts before taking over the command of the 3rd Ukrainian Front in May 1944.

Because of his levelheadedness, his composure, and his ability to get along with people, Tolbukhin was regarded as an excellent military leader. He proved his mettle in January 1945 when, despite Stalin's permission to withdraw, he chose to keep his troops in southern Transdanubia, although they found themselves in a critical situation as a result of the third German relief attempt. With this decision he put his own life on the line because Stalin showed no mercy for failures. Beginning on 16 March 1945, he and Malinovsky took part in the offensive against Vienna. After the war he became commander of the Soviet Army Group South stationed in Hungary, and from 1947 until his death in 1949 he headed the Transcaucasian Military District.

Special Units of the Defense

When Budapest became a frontline city, several individuals began to organize special volunteer corps outside the battle order. The first of these initiatives came from Lieutenant-Colonel Pál Prónay, who was 70 at the time. Prónay had set up a volunteer corps against the communists in 1919 and another against the Austrians in 1921. After losing his fighting unit in the latter operation, he made many unsuccessful attempts at setting up others. Without the opportunity to assert himself in battle his life became a series of scandals in public places, murky affairs of honor, and court cases lasting decades. He actually came to blows in the street with one of his opponents in litigation.

Following the German occupation of Hungary, Prónay again tried to set up a unit, but in vain. After the Arrow Cross coup of 15 October 1944 he applied for arms to Emil Kovarcz, the new minister for total mobilization, and personally stood up in Apponyi Square to recruit followers. But even this attempt almost failed. First Lieutenant Vilmos Bondor describes his impressions as follows: "The lack of discipline was striking. The comrades gathering round the old man were of advanced age and knew little about modern tactics, although they made up for it by constantly interfering."

Captain Zoltán Mikó, who was responsible to the general staff for organizing commando units, refused to supply arms to Prónay, who was in any case unable to carry out a proper recruiting and training program and was abandoned by most of the men he had managed to recruit. His company commander, László Vannay, fell out with him within a few weeks and proceeded to organize a detachment of his own, and the students who had originally joined him transferred to the University Assault Battalion. When he began to accuse Vannay of poaching his soldiers and to hurl abuse at Gyula Elischer, the students' leader, his officers were obliged to physically restrain him. With a broad-brimmed Boer hat, a studded belt, high boots, an enormous holster, and a riding crop, he made the rounds of various commands, but was refused support by all, including Hindy:

> He told me that he had a permit from the government to set up a special detachment, for which he requested weapons. I told Prónay that I knew nothing about any government permit and thought it strange that he was asking me for equipment if he had a permit from the government, because the government must have known that I had no surplus weapons or clothing. In response to my inquiries Prónay stated that he could muster about 1,500 men. I have always had an aversion to any detachments recruited in this manner, and I refused Prónay tactfully in view of his age. I asked the corps quartermaster if he knew anything about Prónay's detachment, because somebody would have had to feed them. I was told that Prónay's people were drawing rations for 1,500. . . . Soon after, I discovered that they could account for only 100 to 120 men, who were not even armed.

During the siege Prónay became lethargic, and he only rarely visited the corps command. His detachment was officially merged

17
László Vannay, commander of the Vannay Battalion

with the Armed National Service on 7 January 1945. He was last seen in the break-out and, according to some accounts, died in Kútvölgy Valley.

László Vannay did better. He had also had a brush with the law, when on 22 July 1932 he was sentenced by a court-martial to degradation and six months' detention for masterminding a right-wing coup. Previously he had caused a stir when he had insulted the liberal-democratic politician Vilmos Vázsonyi in the street and narrowly missed hitting him in the face. In the 1920s he had been busy organizing paramilitary units to circumvent the Trianon treaty. In 1938 he was involved in the creation of the Ragged Guard in Upper Hungary and then carried out successful guerrilla actions in Sub-Carpathia. In 1943 he began to think of setting up an assault battalion on the instigation of Zoltán Nyisztor, a pioneer lieutenant-colonel who had served as an observer with German pioneer assault troops in the siege of Voronezh. Nyisztor had suggested the creation of similar units in Hungary to the chief of the Hungarian general staff, Colonel-General Ferenc Szombathelyi, on the grounds that in a territory with few natural obstacles most of the battles to come would be defensive actions around housing developments. When Szombathelyi did not reply, Nyisztor put the idea to Vannay.

Vannay was among the first to salute Szálasi in Buda Castle after the Arrow Cross coup. On 20 October 1944 he was granted permission by Emil Kovarcz to set up an independent assault battalion, for which he recruited Arrow Cross members from the public services, the association of veterans of the eastern front, young paramilitaries, students from military academies, and boys aged 15 to 18. The local knowledge of volunteers from the post office, the fire brigade, the water works, and other utilities was indispensable in city fighting—particularly in tunnels and culverts. Vannay introduced the "uncle system," whereby boys younger than 18 were attached to men of 35 to 45, who trained them. Two "uncle-and-kid" pairs made up the smallest tactical unit, three a squad, and nine a detachment. Training began on 1 December at the Újlak brick factory. Vannay had obtained instructors and arms from the 22nd SS Cavalry Division. The methods were so tough that several trainees suffered injuries: some were shot in the buttocks while crawling through barbed-wire entanglements, others fell off the roofs they had to climb in pouring rain.

Vannay solved the problem of food supplies in his own way. First, he seized the Szentkirályi Street store of kosher schnapps, goose liver, and other provisions confiscated from Jews, which brought immediate protests from the district's Arrow Cross authorities. When this proved insufficient, he took the staff of the Tímár Street bakery into "protective custody" and forced them to work day and night for his battalion. The same fate befell the cake shop in Bécsi Road and the 23rd Honvéd catering section, over which he had a fierce argument with Colonel Csipkés, the city commander. The battalion's identity cards and forged accounts were printed by employees of the Kánitz printing works in Vadász Street, whom he had also taken into "protective custody." He was a rabid anti-Semite, but this did not prevent him from letting a certain Uncle Roth and his wife prepare the stamps for the documents and run the kitchens; in exchange, the Jewish couple received the same rations as everybody else and were never hurt. There is posi-

tive proof, however, that 46 people rounded up in Margit Boulevard were executed in the cellar of the Toldy High School and on
the Danube embankment by some of Vannay's men.

Thanks to the kosher supplies, the battalion acquired a reputation for feeding its soldiers better than the regular army. By the
time it was officially named Hungarian Royal Vannay Flying Squad
Battalion on 22 December, it numbered 638 members. For a long
time Vannay followed the example of Hitler and Szálasi by wearing
a tunic without rank insignia. There were several complaints, but
Vannay, in protest against his sentence of 1932, refused to appear in
a normal military uniform until he was rehabilitated. After Christmas, Szálasi formally promoted him to major.

The Vannay Battalion was the only unit with its own security
section, comprising about ten men whose task it was to execute
captured deserters and Soviet soldiers caught in civilian clothes.
The head of this section, Captain Ferenc Gyulay-Molnár, monitored Soviet radio messages, Captain Szekeres conducted coun-
terpropaganda by loud hailer with the help of two Ruthenian
soldiers, and First Lieutenant Endre Kovách took charge of recruitment.

On 24 December the bulk of the battalion was stationed near
János Hospital to close off the access to Buda from Hűvösvölgy
Valley. On 25 December, however, when the stabilization of the
Buda front would have been paramount, three of the four companies were ordered to join in the counterattack of the Hungarian
10th Infantry Division near Csömör east of Pest. On 26 December
the counterattack recovered the original Hungarian positions, but
they were abandoned again when Soviet tanks broke through the
line of the Hungarian 12th Reserve Division. Vannay's units suffered significant losses, and he withdrew the remainder to Buda
without informing anybody. The sources contradict each other
about what followed. We only know for certain that the Honvéd
army officers accused Vannay, who had been slightly wounded, of
running away, while Vannay blamed them for the failure of the
counterattack and the loss of one of his companies.

Subsequently, the Vannay battalion sustained heavy casualties
in the ferocious encounters in Buda, where it was positioned in

18

Ervin Galántay, dispatch runner of the Vannay Battalion, as a cadet
at the Kőszeg Military Academy in July 1943

what was probably the most exposed section of the defense ring. To compensate, Vannay raided the cellars where people had taken refuge and sent whomever he thought fit to the front line with a rifle and no training. To prevent desertions, he announced to the Soviets by radio that the Vannay Battalion would take no prisoners, with the result that the Soviets also showed no mercy to any captured members of the Vannay Battalion, regardless of whether they were fighting of their own free will. Late in December, the students of the Salesian boarding school were drafted into the battalion. Most of the young men, untrained and in civilian clothes, were killed within a few days—a particularly large number died in Széll Kálmán Square in late January. By the time of the break-out those left alive numbered only 100 to 120, with a substantial proportion wounded. Vannay himself was killed in Kútvölgy Valley. Many survivors were later tried by the People's Court for taking part in atrocities.

The student György Deutsch—later the owner of the famous Four Seasons Restaurant in New York—was a special case. Having escaped from the forced labor service, he joined the Hungarist Legion and then the Vannay Battalion. Shortly before the fall of Pest he absconded but was caught and, in a "medical examination," found to be a Jew. Although he claimed to belong to the sect of Transylvanian Sabbathists (who were not regarded as "racial Jews" in spite of being circumcised), he was taken with some others to the Danube to be executed, but managed to escape once more.

The Hungarist combat groups of the Arrow Cross Party were a mixed bunch. They included several flying squads, some equipped with *panzerfausts* (similar to bazookas), but these were deployed only as security patrols behind the main defense line. The majority of party members preferred to engage in violence against defenseless people. Of the 2,500 activists in the six combat groups no more than 700 actually came into contact with the Soviets, and that generally when the Soviets attacked them. There were a few, however, who not only accepted the Arrow Cross ideology but were also prepared to risk their lives for it. Béla Kollarits was one of them, as Ensign István Szalay, his adjutant, remembers:

> In civilian life Kollarits was legal adviser to the German aircraft factory in Csepel. In military terms he was a nobody and had never served in the Hungarian army. He had fought in the Spanish Civil War with a German flying squad. When Szálasi came to power, he reported for duty and was immediately made a first lieutenant. He was assigned to propaganda and traveled the battlefield in a car, egging on the soldiers with a loudspeaker. On his way home from one of his trips, he noticed that the Russians had reached the Lágymányos railway embankment. Determined to defend his house, he went to the Ludovika Military Academy, picked 25 loafing soldiers . . . and with them joined in the defense of the embankment.

The University Assault Battalion came into being in very different circumstances. According to regulations introduced after

15 October 1944, all men were obliged to report for duty in the Armed National Service. Several units, including KISKA, were formed in order to satisfy these regulations—but sometimes also in order to evade them. This gave a new impulse to the creation of the University Assault Battalion. On 5 October, Reserve Lieutenant Gyula Elischer, a former student at the Technical University, obtained a permit from the Ministry of Defense to form a battalion. Toward the end of October the group, which by then numbered 500, was adopted in the battle order as the Royal Hungarian I Honvéd University Assault Battalion and thus became a unit of the regular army rather than of any particular faction. Many of the students who joined had previously belonged to the Levente organization of young paramilitaries or the National Guard. The battalion included 12 men above the rank of private, with an officer corps consisting of two reserve lieutenants and two reserve ensigns. As the promised evacuation to Germany continued to be delayed, other university students offered themselves, and soon the organization of the II University Assault Battalion began. Elischer writes:

> I and a few others wanted to believe in the possibility of an Anglo-Saxon thrust as in a miracle. Facing the reality was simply too awful. . . . I could not identify with the Arrow Cross, but I could accept a Stalinist communist occupation even less. . . . In 1941 I had been one of the first to cross the Russian border. As a reconnaissance officer I witnessed some terrible atrocities committed by the retreating troops, or rather by the political units. Everything I saw of Stalinist communism filled me with horror. Professor Ferenc Orsós, a member of the Katyn international commission, was a colleague of my father's, and I first heard from him what had happened to the Polish officer corps. . . . I hoped that it would be possible to hold our unit together till the end of the war. If it were transferred to Germany for training, I thought, an efficient unit would be able to fight its way through to the Anglo-Saxon lines.

Most of the battalion's organizers were committed anticommunists, but they were not right-wing extremists. Elischer, for one, was revolted by the treatment of Jews he had witnessed on a trip to Germany in 1942, and the battalion gave shelter to some Jewish men and a social-democratic youth leader wanted by the Gestapo.

On 5 December, Lajos Sipeki Balás, a third-year student of mechanical engineering and an engineering-corps captain, took over the command of the original battalion, while Major Lajos Csiky became commander of the second. The first 200 recruits were outfitted within five days. Each received a sheepskin jacket, pioneer boots, and an overcoat with pioneer insignia. Although weapons were in short supply, the students found other ways of acquiring fairly adequate equipment. They even obtained rifles with telescopic sights from the Buda shooting range; being familiar with technology, they did not need much training in their use.

Sipeki, with his frontline experience, insisted that his unit should not be sent into battle before completing its training. This landed him in heated arguments with Kovarcz and other Arrow Cross leaders, who demanded immediate deployment, but he resisted these demands and also prevented individual actions by students, which he knew would only have led to pointless slaughter. Unlike him, the majority of the students had no conception of what war was really like. Most had not been soldiers before and, full of romantic ideas, awaited their baptism of fire.

On 24 December, Kovarcz and the Arrow Cross youth leader István Zsakó alerted the battalion to the Soviet breakthrough and invited the students to leave the capital together with the Arrow Cross youth organizations. The students' commanders faced a difficult choice. According to plans, the battalion should have gone to a training camp in Érsekújvár after Christmas, but there were various arguments in favor of staying, as Elischer, who made the decision to do so, notes:

> Leaving Budapest together with the Arrow Cross youth—
> with party organizations, perhaps the Gestapo, and others like it—would have compromised every member of

the battalion once and for all. I did not want that to happen under any circumstances. . . . I thought that the first battalion must be kept out of the fighting as long and as far as possible. Perhaps there would still be a chance to leave the encirclement and accomplish our original ideas. If it were unavoidable, it would be better to die fighting than to be captured or to allow ourselves to be butchered as a disgraced unit.

I believed that every day we could hold up the communists would help the cause of Hungary and Europe.

Elischer and his companions must have realized that the longer they held out, the longer the sufferings of the population of Budapest—in particular the Jews—would continue, and the closer the city would come to being reduced to a heap of rubble. They believed that in both human and moral terms they were choosing the lesser evil, and were prepared to risk their own lives in the process. Their feelings about communist rule were too strong to let them opt for an alternative that posterity might have regarded as more justifiable.

Finally, the special units also included the Morlin Group, named after Imre Morlin, an artillery captain who later became a priest. This group consisted of some 120 cadets, military academy students, and soldiers who had been separated from their units. Equipped with panzerfausts, two 7.5cm antitank guns, and a considerable number of light weapons, it was attached to the 10th Infantry Division with the task of destroying any Soviet tanks penetrating into the city. Desertions from this group were rare: even boys aged 14 to 18 fought to the last bullet, and many were killed. After the capture of Morlin on 15 January, however, the group disintegrated. Some members ended up in the Budapest Security Battalion, and several died on the Lágymányos railway embankment.

3

The Siege, 26 December 1944–11 February 1945

The Hostilities on the Pest Side Beginning 24 December 1944
The Penetration of the First and Second Defense Belts of the Attila Line

With Budapest completely encircled by Christmas, the scene was set for an all-out siege. On the Buda side, the advance that had begun with Marshal Tolbukhin's attack on the Margit Line on 20 December had soon stalled because of a lack of infantry. On the Pest side, Marshal Malinovsky's 2nd Ukrainian Front was scheduled to start its offensive concurrently with Tolbukhin's, and to have taken the whole of Pest by 23 December. In fact, Malinovsky's troops were unable to score any substantial successes until the German command moved part of its forces from Pest to Buda in January. By 24 December, Malinovsky's three rifle corps had only penetrated the positions of the Hungarian 1st Armored Division between Ecser and Vecsés southeast of the city and begun a significant strike against the Hungarian 10th Division between Csömör and Fót to the northeast. This sector, where developed areas alternated with deep wedges of vacant land, constituted one of the most important lines of attack. With its fields and pastures, which extended as far as the suburb of Pestújhely, it was extremely vulnerable to tank offensives, as the Soviet advances in January were to prove.

The Soviet offensive along the entire length of the Pest bridgehead began on 25 December. South of Mogyoród, a short distance from Csömör, the German troops retreated and the attackers advanced over a breadth of 500 meters. In the evening, Captain Sándor Német, with eight men and two German assault guns, recovered the territory, but two companies of the Hungarian 18/I Battalion were captured.

Despite some local successes of the defenders, the Soviet and Romanian troops ensconced themselves almost everywhere in the first and second belts of the Attila Line, particularly in the central and northeastern sectors of the bridgehead. The third belt, however, along the edge of the suburbs, was still in German and Hungarian hands, as were parts of the first belt between Vecsés and Pécel, and of the second between Soroksár and Maglód.

When the 8th SS Cavalry Division had been relocated to Buda on 24 December, the defense of the first and second belts—both constructed mainly on vacant ground between villages—had become so thinly spread that only one infantryman was available for every 100-meter stretch. The defenders therefore retreated to the second and third belts, which were tighter and easier to hold. The retreat took place under constant attacks, with considerable casualties. Between the retreating groups large gaps opened, and the connecting wings of the 22nd SS Cavalry Division and the 13th Panzer Division between Kerepesi Road and Üllői Road, two major arteries leading into the city from the east and southeast, were repeatedly separated. The Soviet attack also made the withdrawal of reserves impossible, so that maintaining links between the two divisions remained an acute problem.

On 26 December, between Fót and Pécel on the northeastern front, Soviet and Romanian attacks carved out a number of salients 300 to 600 meters in depth along the lines of the Hungarian 4th Hussar Regiment, 10th Infantry Division, and 12th Reserve Division, when T-34 tanks overran the scantily manned trenches and opened fire on the defenders from the rear. In the central sector of the same front, near Csömör, the troops of the 8/III Battalion were surrounded and pulverized, although they had knocked out 3 of the 12 attacking tanks with their light weapons. Between 10 and 15 Soviet tanks also assaulted the lines of the 4th Hussar Regiment north of Csömör. Two were smashed by the hussars' panzerfausts, but the rest broke through. The staff of the 4th Hussar regiment, stationed in a nearby winery, escaped capture only because Lieutenant Ernő Kammerer, who jumped out of a window and was handed a panzerfaust, destroyed a tank that was attacking the building. A fortified hill northeast of Csömör also fell. The Soviets, for their part, suffered heavy losses, which are ignored in their bland reports:

> When several attempts to take the fortified hill had failed, Sergeant [David Sergeievich] Merkviladze asked for permission to try again with a platoon. After receiving permission they approached the enemy positions on the hill under cover of fog to within 20 to 30 meters and requested artillery fire. . . . They held out successfully on the captured hill for about five hours until the arrival of their own subunit, during which time they foiled two enemy assaults.

Merkviladze was awarded the Hero of the Soviet Union medal.

A counterattack by the Vannay Flying Squad Battalion, launched on the same evening, was initially successful, and the positions of the 8/III Battalion at Csömör were recaptured. But Soviet and Romanian troops, piercing the line of the 12th Reserve Division near Sashalom, threatened to encircle Vannay's men, who retreated after one of their companies had been crushed and their commander wounded. The Germans had sent to assist them only three armored artillery trucks, which were no match for the Soviet tanks.

On the southern front, some parts of the Hungarian 1st Armored Division were relocated to guard the sector between the village of Lakihegy and the suburb of Királyerdő, which included the emergency airfield on Csepel Island, the first to be put into service after the closure of the encirclement.

On 27 December Soviet and Romanian forces broke through the line of the 12th Reserve Division in the third defense belt and took the eastern suburbs of Rákoskeresztúr and Újmajor. On the same day, troops of the Soviet 18th Rifle Corps took Vecsés and established a deep salient stretching as far as the southeastern suburbs of Pestszentlőrinc and Rákoscsaba. From the southern suburb of Budafok on the west bank, a Soviet raiding party tried to cross the Danube eastward to Csepel Island but was repulsed in close-quarter fighting by Hungarian antiaircraft artillery.

Leaders of the German Army Group South and the Budapest garrison agreed that it was not possible to maintain the entire Budapest bridgehead. Both believed that a retreat would stabilize the situation, as shorter concentric lines could be held by smaller forces. The most practical solution would have been abandoning the Pest bridgehead altogether in order to develop the defense of Buda and prepare for a break-out. But the chief of staff of the German Army Group South, Lieutenant-General Grolman, advocated a fast retreat, while the head of the Budapest garrison, Colonel-General Balck, favored a slower method.

Although Hitler's order of 24 December had prohibited any reduction in the Pest bridgehead, the IX SS Mountain Army Corps began planning a break-out. As it was impossible to comply with Hitler's demand that both Buda and Pest be held until relief arrived, the corps had no other choice. On 26 December the underground telephone lines between Budapest and the headquarters of the German Army Group South were still working, and about noon Radio Budapest announced that the defenders were going to break out. This was probably done on Pfeffer-Wildenbruch's instructions, although according to his own memoirs it was on 27 December that he decided to disobey Hitler. On 28 December another order arrived from Hitler, categorically forbidding the break-out.

In view of Hitler's repeated orders to the contrary—issued not only on 24 December but also on 23 November, 1 December, and three times on 14 December—one may wonder why the commanders of the IX SS Mountain Army Corps nevertheless began preparing for a break-out. They may have been hoping that Hitler would see the dramatic deterioration in the situation and authorize the break-out at the last moment; on 24 December the 8th SS Cavalry Division received his permission for a withdrawal after it had actually begun to move. The predicament of the commands, which were constantly having to revise earlier orders, can be attributed to Hitler's habit of leaving nothing to the military and reserving the right to direct operations at all levels, down to individual battalions. As his messages from distant Berlin always arrived late, some of the more self-reliant generals acted on the assumption that the order they wanted would arrive after the event. The command of the IX SS Mountain Army Corps, however, believed in the promised relief and lacked the confidence to disobey the Führer at the crucial time.

The Hungarian command had no say in the matter. The reports of the Hungarian I Army Corps show that Hindy and his general staff advocated a break-out as early as 26 December, but Pfeffer-Wildenbruch replied that he was not entertaining such an idea "for the time being." Typically, the German general considered it unnecessary to give his Hungarian colleague any reasons for his decision.

The onslaught of the Soviet and Romanian troops at the eastern edge of Budapest continued on 28 December. The Hungarian 1st and 13th Assault Artillery Battalions between Pécel and Ferihegy, unable to close the gap left by the withdrawal of the 8th SS Cavalry Division, were wiped out. In contrast, parts of the 16th and 24th Assault Artillery Battalions managed to hold out and even eject the occupiers of Rákoskeresztúr and Újmajor.

Meanwhile, at the northeastern edge of Pest, Soviet troops had expanded their front line along the Szilas stream and all but destroyed the two Hungarian battalions facing them. Nearby at Rákosszentmihály, the Germans attempted five counterattacks, all of which foundered on strong Soviet resistance. Second Lieutenant Nikolai Hodenko knocked out three armored vehicles single-handed: it was partly for this that he was awarded the Hero of the Soviet Union medal. The security battalion of the Hungarian I Army Corps was also smashed: 300 to 400 soldiers sent as replacements crossed over to the Soviets, the commander became ill, and by 30 December there were only seven officers and 40 privates left. The Romanian 2nd and 19th Infantry Divisions captured Pécel and Kistarcsa and reached the edge of the eastern suburb of Cinkota, where extremely heavy fighting ensued. After three assaults Cinkota was finally occupied during the night of 29–30 December, but the Romanian 2nd Infantry Division was so worn out that it had to be withdrawn from the front at once. East and southeast of

Pest, Maglód and Gyál fell into Soviet hands on 28 December, and there was fighting in the streets on the periphery of Pestszentimre immediately northwest of Gyál. The nearby railway bridge across the Danube was blown up by the defenders because Soviet troops had reached its Buda end.

After these events the Soviets announced by loudspeaker that parley delegates were to arrive next day. Leaflets were dropped from aircraft, urging the German and Hungarian troops to surrender.

Intermezzo: The Parley Delegates

Malinovsky wanted to capture Budapest as quickly as possible in order to continue his thrust toward Bratislava and Vienna. Both he and Tolbukhin knew, from their experience of Stalingrad, that the siege would be lengthy and fighting in the city costly, but never before had the Red Army besieged a European metropolis with a million inhabitants. In fact, the situation was so complex that it finally took 15 Soviet and 3 Romanian divisions to capture Budapest.

On 29 December the Soviet command, with Stalin's agreement, called upon the garrison to surrender. The terms were generous. The Hungarians would be released forthwith and the Germans repatriated to Germany immediately after the war. All would be allowed to keep their uniforms and medals, and officers even their side arms. Food would be provided for all, and the wounded and sick would receive medical attention without delay. The ultimatum should have been delivered by two Soviet captains, Miklós Steinmetz in Pest and Ilya Afanasevich Ostapenko in Buda, but both parley delegates were killed and their mission failed.

The Soviet command accused the Germans of murdering the delegates, and for half a century communist historians were to cite the incident as a prime example of the "Nazi fascist atrocities." In Hungary until the fall of communism in 1989, students in every school were regularly reminded of the "murder" of the two men, and at the scene of the alleged crime imposing monuments were erected to commemorate them. The communist propaganda was false, but the fact remains that the delegates were killed. Thus their story is equally apt to illustrate the irrationality of war, as well as both the lapses of survivors' memories and the distortions of communist propaganda.

Steinmetz, a Hungarian by origin who had grown up in the Soviet Union, had served in the Spanish Civil War as Malinovsky's interpreter and later as an intelligence officer. His mission failed even before he could reach the German lines. First Lieutenant Gyula Litteráti-Loótz, commander of the antitank detachment of the Hungarian 12th Reserve Division, writes:

> In the morning one of my gun commanders reported that a Russian jeep with a white flag was approaching. . . . One hundred fifty to two hundred meters ahead of us in the direction of the Russians, clearly visible to the naked eye, antitank mines had been laid out on the cobbles of Üllői Road like a chess board. . . . The purpose of the mines was to make the Soviets, if they were attacking with tanks, stop in front of the mine field and offer a firm target, at least for a short while. To our immense surprise the jeep in which I observed two seated men—the driver and another next to him who was waving a white cloth attached to a stick—merely slowed down in front of the mines and then tried to pass between them at walking speed. . . . There was dead silence; not a shot was fired by either side. It all happened in a fraction of a second. There was a huge bang, whitish-gray smoke, the front of the car reared up, and the white flag presented a grotesque sight as it flew through the air in a high arch. When the smoke had cleared the wrecked car was standing in the middle of the mine barrier. The two Russians were sitting in the jeep, slumped motionless against each other. The mine had exploded on the left-hand side of the car; the driver had probably hit it with his left-hand front wheel.

Litteráti-Loótz's memories prove highly problematic if one tries to reconstruct the events on the spot. From his fighting position, as he specifies it, he could not have seen what he describes because his view would have been obstructed by a rise in the road and a five-meter difference in elevation between him and the first Soviet line. In addition, his outlook was restricted by the fact that the road bends north at an angle of about 5 degrees rather than running straight, as on the map published by Gosztonyi. Given these and other inaccuracies, he either mislocates his fighting position or gives an incorrect account of how the delegates died—or both.

Let us assume that Litteráti-Loótz has mislocated his fighting position. If, as he says, the mines on the road were visible to the naked eye and he was able to distinguish the two persons in the jeep, he could indeed not have been more than 150 to 200 meters away, but then a 2.5-meter rise in the street would have hidden the jeep until it was 20 to 30 meters from the mine barrier, leaving a maximum of ten seconds before the explosion—not enough time for him to observe the approach of the jeep, identify its occupants, and watch them slalom around the mines.

Unlike Litteráti-Loótz's position, the place where the delegates died can be determined precisely. The mine barrier was situated at the crossing of Üllői Road and Gömbös Gyula Road. This is the highest point in the neighborhood, from which the road dips east and west. The mines could not have been laid farther east because then the slope would have made it possible for the Soviets to remove them unobserved; moreover, any Soviet tanks slowing down in front of the mines would have been sheltered by the slope from the defenders' antitank weapons. Laying the mines farther west would have been pointless because the nearest road junction in that direction was too far away.

Let us now assume that Litteráti-Loótz's account of the delegates' death is wrong. Given the terrain, the delay between the delegates' appearance and their death must have been extremely short and, with slight snowfall, fog, and a temperature of about 25 degrees Fahrenheit, visibility was very low. A nervous antitank gun commander might therefore immediately have opened fire on the approaching vehicle. At a postmortem, two bullets from a light weapon were found in Steinmetz's body that had certainly not been fired by any member of Litteráti-Loótz's group. Antitank guns are always positioned behind the first battle line, which in this instance ran alongside the mine barrier in Gömbös Gyula Road. It is possible that the soldiers in the first line saw the delegates coming and, mistaking the discharge of an antitank gun for a signal, also began to shoot, hitting Steinmetz, who may already have been dead. It is equally possible, however, that no antitank gun was fired, because the shortage of ammunition would have made a gun attack on a jeep unjustifiable.

Exactly what happened will never be known. The most likely explanation is that Litteráti-Loótz's account is incorrect in both respects, although the jeep may really have hit a mine.

The group led by the other delegate, Captain Ostapenko, was initially more successful. Although they came under fire, none of them was hurt, because the bullets landed in front of their feet. In a second attempt, they reached the German positions without being shot at. A Major Shakhvorostov, the 318th Division's head of intelligence, had been informed by telephone of the death of Steinmetz and his companion, but he did not stop Ostapenko's group.

First Lieutenant Nikolai Yeoktisovich Orlov, who survived the mission, has reported the events in detail. The delegates were blindfolded by the Germans and driven to the 8th SS Cavalry Division's command post on Gellért-hegy Hill. After a polite introduction Ostapenko handed the ultimatum to the most senior officer, who immediately contacted Pfeffer-Wildenbruch. Ostapenko then spent almost an hour in informal conversation with German staff officers. After Pfeffer-Wildenbruch's negative reply the delegates started their return journey: "When Ostapenko had put the envelope back into his map case, the lieutenant-colonel offered each of us a glass of soda water," Orlov recalls. "We accepted with pleasure and poured the welcome drink down our dry throats. The Germans blindfolded us and, taking us by the arm, led us out of the building. They sat us again in a car and we set off." The delegates soon reached the German front, where they were received by SS Scharführer Josef Bader, an NCO of the 8th SS Cavalry Division, who recalls:

My commander ordered me to take the delegates back to no-man's land, where I had first met them. We walked.

The closer we got to our first lines the more intense the Soviet shelling became, although a few hours before, when the delegates arrived, it had died down completely. Now they were battering our first lines again. I suggested to the Soviet captain (who spoke flawless German) that we should halt and wait for the shelling to stop before we continued. I also said that I couldn't understand why his people were firing so heavily on our positions although they must have known that their delegates had not yet returned. But the captain said that he had strict orders to return to his people as soon as possible. I ordered the group to stop, took off their blindfolds, and told them that I had no intention of committing suicide and was not going any farther. I let them cross the no-man's land. I must stress that nobody on our side fired. The pause in the firing was complete, and one could only hear the detonations of the enemy shells. The group started to cross a little square. When they had gone about 50 meters, a shell struck from the side. I threw myself flat on my stomach. When I looked up I could see only two soldiers walking on. The third was lying motionless in the road.

Orlov's recollection is similar:

When they had led us to the first line they took off our blindfolds, and we started walking toward our people. We walked much faster on our way back than on the way there. We may have been about halfway when Captain Ostapenko turned to me and said: "It looks as if we've made it. We've been lucky once more." As soon as he had spoken these words there were three enormous explosions. Splinters and bullets were whistling around us. Captain Ostapenko turned toward the Germans and fell on the road.

In the intense shelling a German artillery observer and several German soldiers were also wounded. To all appearances the source of the shelling was an uninformed Soviet battery, although it could have been the Hungarian antiaircraft guns that were also stationed in the area. According to a Soviet postmortem, two splinters and four bullets were lodged in Ostapenko's back. If this is true it strengthens the possibility of Hungarian involvement, as it is unlikely that the bullets could have been fired from the Soviet side.

In any event neither Ostapenko nor Steinmetz and his driver were deliberately killed by the Germans. In all probability their deaths were caused by chance and carelessness. The Nazis were responsible for the death of millions of people, but they never murdered any parley delegates during the war.

According to eyewitnesses a third delegate, an officer of the Soviet 30th Rifle Corps, arrived on horseback with a white flag and was led to Colonel-General Schmidhuber, the commander of the German 13th Panzer Division. In the name of his corps the officer, who is described as having been slightly drunk, offered a three-day ceasefire to enable the Germans to prepare their capitulation. Schmidhuber telephoned Pfeffer-Wildenbruch, suggesting that he "pretend to accept the offer in order to gain at least three days of truce during which the problems of manning the front line after the regrouping of troops can be solved. The fortress commander brusquely replied that such a proposition was entirely out of the question. The Russian officer was taken prisoner." Nothing more is known about his fate.

On 31 December 1944 Radio Moscow broadcast a detailed report of the deaths of the delegates. As a result the supreme command of the Wehrmacht launched an investigation—which actually produced further fabrications in addition to those already in circulation. Based on Pfeffer-Wildenbruch's comments, the Balck Army Group sent the following telegram to Berlin:

> They did not send two Soviet officers but four German prisoners of war as delegates. These were initially ordered by the Budapest command to be shot, but were then handed over by the army high command to the secret field police in Vienna. According to latest reports these four prisoners of war are to be delivered immediately

through the SS and police high command in Vienna to the Führer's headquarters for interrogation. In accordance with the documents held here, the following can be noted with reference to the alleged murder of Soviet parley delegates which was strongly emphasized by Soviet radio on 31 December 1944:

The dispatch to the city of Soviet delegates, as announced by the Soviets, did not take place.

This is one of those well-known Soviet misrepresentations designed to serve as a propaganda lie, hypocritically legitimizing the Soviet craze for the destruction and devastation of European cultural shrines and the environment.

Thus Pfeffer-Wildenbruch denied the very existence of any official Soviet delegates, although he certainly knew about Ostapenko and probably about the others. He lied to his superiors in order to cover himself because he was aware that the delegates were protected by international law. By suggesting that the Soviets had used German prisoners as delegates—which would have been a contravention of international law on their part—he heightened the total-war psychosis which made it inconceivable for the defenders to capitulate. As a result of his false report, the German supreme command cabled to the commanders on the eastern front that the outcry over the death of the delegates was nothing but Soviet war propaganda, and on 17 January 1945 the supreme command forbade all "fortresses" and army groups to receive Soviet delegates, arguing that the Soviet Union, by its use of German prisoners, had repudiated its international obligations.

The four German prisoners of war are not mentioned anywhere else, and Pfeffer-Wildenbruch did not speak of them either. We may safely rule out a deliberate German propaganda lie, as a U.S. historian has examined the files of the section concerned and found no propaganda reports whatsoever. The Soviet authorities were also silent, either because using these prisoners as delegates would have been illegal or because they did not exist. The Red Army frequently sent prisoners to demoralize the enemy, but in

Budapest these were primarily Hungarians. Strangely enough, on 21 January, Pfeffer-Wildenbruch ordered the Hungarian I Army Corps's chief of staff to deliver all the documents relating to the delegates to his own command. The purpose of this directive is not known. Nor could Hindy, in his evidence before the People's Court, explain it.

It is possible that all the parties were lying, but about different aspects of the matter. Litteráti-Loótz may have been trying to cover up his, or his unit's, responsibility for the death of Steinmetz. The Soviet commanders may have known that at the time of Ostapenko's death their units were shelling, and it was also not in their own interest to press the issue of the four German prisoners. Pfeffer-Wildenbruch may have been trying to supply propaganda material in his own bureaucratic way. In addition, the Soviets' preparation of the mission had been inadequate: they could have invited Pfeffer-Wildenbruch by radio to receive the delegates, but they did not. Nor can the defenders be held responsible for constructing a mine barrier, or for Steinmetz's imprudence in trying to cross it.

It is striking that the war crimes with which the German military command was later charged did not include the murder of the delegates, and no similar case is documented during the entire war. Pfeffer-Wildenbruch, who was tried in Moscow, was not questioned about the matter, and Hindy, who was sentenced to death by the Hungarian People's Court, was not charged with this particular crime. To all intents and purposes Pfeffer-Wildenbruch had unconditional orders to hold Budapest, and therefore had to reject the ultimatum.

The Soviet judiciary nevertheless exploited the affair, as it did other cases in which innocent German officers were executed. In Budapest the scapegoat was Captain Erich Klein, commander of the I Artillery Battalion of the Feldherrnhalle Division. In 1948, as a prisoner of war, he was charged with the death of Ostapenko. Despite physical torture he refused to plead guilty but nevertheless received a death sentence, which was later committed to 25 years' imprisonment. He was released in 1953. His rehabilitation by the Russian military prosecutor in 1993 confirms that the charge against him was pure fiction.

19
Captain Erich Klein, commander of the I Artillery Battalion,
Feldherrnhalle Division

The Siege of Pest, First Phase: 30 December 1944–5 January 1945

The Soviet offensive began promptly the day after the rejection of the ultimatum. On the ground nearly a thousand guns opened fire, and in the sky bombers droned continuously, dropping their deadly loads. The barrage lasted between seven and ten hours daily for three days, and the intervals were filled with constant air raids. Nearly a million people took refuge in overcrowded cellars, many of which received direct hits, killing their occupants. Civilians ventured into the streets only when it was absolutely necessary, hugging the walls as they hurried to fetch water from a standpipe or bread from one of the bakeries that had been ordered by the Arrow Cross regime to remain open.

In the city center the streets were covered in a jumble of broken glass, torn overhead streetcar cables, toppled lampposts, and other objects that had lost their original purpose. The rubble was interspersed with dead bodies in torn, soiled, and bloodstained clothing, frequently with their necks and chests exposed and their pockets turned inside out in the search for their identification disks, personal documents, and valuables. Their eyes were wide open, their hands waxen yellow, their ears and noses bloody. They were lying in pools of blood and strangely contorted postures where the force of the explosions had thrown them, and many had lost an arm or a leg. Houses were aflame. Where shells had exploded, bluish-yellow gunpowder vapor lingered in the air. Mountains of refuse piled up, no longer collected by the municipal services.

The Soviet troops had been reinforced with large quantities of heavy weapons as well as fighter and bomber aircraft. The infantry was supported by a complete air corps, two artillery divisions, and various other units, amounting to a total of 15 artillery or mortar brigades and regiments. Each artillery division consisted of three artillery brigades equipped with 36 pieces of ordnance—76mm guns, 122mm howitzers, and 152mm heavy howitzers, respectively—and complemented by a heavy mortar battalion. The rifle corps were supported by tanks that probably belonged to the 39th Tank Brigade of the Soviet 23rd Tank Corps, and some other tank and assault gun regiments. In the whole territory of Budapest some 200 Soviet tanks were put out of action, which suggests an attacking force of more than one tank brigade.

The German and Hungarian defense, in contrast, could not even muster enough ammunition for its remaining heavy weapons, so the artillery was allowed to fire only a limited number of rounds per day. Heavy-mortar ammunition had run out completely by the end of December.

On the morning of 30 December the Pest front lay east of a semicircular line that bulged out along the edge of the suburbs of Rákospalota, Rákosszentmihály, Mátyásföld, Pestszentlőrinc, Pest-szentimre, and Soroksár. During that day, the Soviet offensive gained a significant amount of ground in the eastern and southern sectors, where the front of the Hungarian 12th Reserve Division was repeatedly overrun, and the Hungarian 10th Infantry Division, with only three fighting battalions left, found itself in a critical situation. The Hungarian 8/III Battalion, surrounded in Csö-mör, was obliged to break out, losing a large part of its combat force in street fighting. Continuing the attack that had begun at Christmas between Fót and Csömör, Soviet infantry supported by tanks stormed across the fields bordering the Szilas stream west of Mátyásföld, toward Pestújhely. The Hungarian 18/I Battalion took up new positions alongside the detached houses in Rákosszentmi- hály but by evening had been practically annihilated near the local church, although the Soviets also suffered significant losses. A group of Soviet soldiers who had advanced as far as the church were encircled as a result of German and Hungarian counterstrikes, and broke out only after asking their own artillery to fire at them, continuously adjusting the direction of the fire as the battle pro- gressed. Captain Nikolai Leonteievich Nikolaichuk was awarded the Hero of the Soviet Union medal for organizing this action. The 13th German Panzer Division also launched counterattacks. The first of these stalled. The second, led by Lieutenant-Colonel Ekesparre, chief of the general staff, captured the western section of Rákosszentmihály but stalled again after the destruction of four or five German tanks and nine armored trucks.

On 31 December a German and Hungarian counterattack resulted in the recapture for one day of the western section of Mátyásföld and its airfield, but nearby Cinkota fell into Soviet hands. Farther south, the 22nd SS Cavalry Division evacuated Pest- szentimre, and in the outer section of Üllői Road the Soviets advanced several hundred meters toward the inner city. Farther north, near Rákoskeresztúr, the Hungarian 24th Assault Artillery Battalion, commanded by Major Barnabás Bakó, repulsed an at- tack, causing the Soviet troops considerable losses. One Russian major committed suicide before he could be taken prisoner.

On 1 January 1945 the line of the Hungarian 10th Infantry and 12 Reserve Divisions between Rákospalota and Pestszentlőrinc became the prime target of the Soviet push toward Pestújhely. The attackers crossed the Circular Railway at several points, and some of their tanks reached the Rákos stream. The first building within the administrative boundaries of Pest was taken by Guard Sergeant Adavkin's assault group north of Sashalom. On the same day, the Soviet 297th Rifle Division, which had so far been kept as a second echelon, launched an attack somewhat farther south through the

New Communal Cemetery. Captain György Péchy, the commander of the Hungarian 38/III Battalion, remembers:

At dawn the battle line skirted the eastern edge of the New Cemetery facing Ferihegy. The battery took up position in the morgue. I had been allocated 30 extra Hungarist novices.

At 8 o'clock such an artillery and mortar barrage began as I had never experienced on Hungarian soil. The earth in the cemetery was shaking. The men leapt back from their positions, seeking cover in the ditch of Kozma Street. We also ran there from the morgue and took cover. The Russian infantry attack began. From the ditch we all opened fire on the enemy racing toward us. I directed the fire of the men by my side as if I had been a platoon commander. Majors [Gusztáv] Kajdy and [Ferenc] Joó did the same. Our vigorous and accurate fire worked, and we stopped the attack. . . .

In the early afternoon a Soviet tank appeared and breached the stone wall of the brickworks yard. From a German Tiger tank hidden on the other side of the brick kiln an NCO crept to the wall. When he had ascertained the position of the Soviet tank he waved to guide the Tiger's gun toward it. The Soviet tank was destroyed with one shot. At dusk we moved into the round kiln, where workers from the houses nearby had also taken refuge.

About midnight the enemy unexpectedly attacked. We took up firing positions in the corridor around the kiln. The Russians were driving Hungarian prisoners ahead of them, who were shouting: "We're Hungarians." We shouted back that they should throw themselves on their stomachs when they heard "Lie down!" Under our continuous submachine gun salvos the Russians retreated. Some of the prisoners escaped. We then succeeded in clearing the area of the brickworks through a hand grenade counterattack. . . . Next day I and my remaining 15 men withdrew.

Between 2 and 3 January the Soviet thrust toward Pestújhely made further progress. The attackers broke through at several points on the Rákos stream, although five of their six tanks in the first wave were destroyed by soldiers of the Hungarian 10th Infantry Division. Soviet and Romanian infantry penetrated the first defense line and opened fire on it from behind, forcing the Hungarian 6/III Battalion to withdraw in a fierce street battle.

By 3 January heavy engagements had reduced the combat strength of the Hungarian 12th Reserve Division to between 10 and 25 men in each battalion, and on that day alone 307 Hungarians were taken prisoner by the Romanians. Despite repeated German and Hungarian attempts to drive them back across the Rákos stream, the Soviets continued to widen their salient. To secure their position, they redeployed the exhausted Romanian 2nd Division, which had been withdrawn two days earlier. Major-General Grigori S. Lazhko, the commander of the Soviet 30th Rifle Corps, threw into battle the Soviet 36th Guard Rifle Division, which had meanwhile been placed in his charge, and crossed the Rákos stream and the Circular Railway. Farther south his units were steadily advancing toward Pestújhely. The 18th Rifle Corps came within 500 meters of the emergency airfield on the Racecourse, leaving the emergency airfield on Csepel Island the only possible landing site. A counteroffensive by the 13th German Panzer Division toward Alsórákos failed: the tanks that had penetrated as far as the railway embankment were destroyed by the Soviets, and a massive mortar barrage prevented the infantry following them.

One of the most daring exploits of the siege took place at that time. A 40-ton motor barge manned by Russian SS volunteers and carrying ammunition began a 140-kilometer journey from Győr, slipping through the mine barrier on the Danube and running aground 17 kilometers from Budapest near the village of Leányfalu. It was only thanks to the gaps in the Soviet occupation of the villages along the Danube Bend that the enterprise did not end in disaster. With the help of a Hungarian assault-boat platoon, the crew transported part of its cargo into the city, probably under cover of the trees in the flood plain. Attempts by the SS to organize further transports failed, and a tug was later sent to salvage the stranded barge.

The Soviet corps commanders had introduced various measures in preparation for street fighting. Their experience, particularly in Stalingrad, had shown that the most practical approach was to split the enemy units into small portions and liquidate these individually. Accordingly, in each Soviet division a special assault group was formed of 15 to 50 riflemen and a number of technicians, equipped with a submachine gun, one or two light machine guns, an antitank gun, a flamethrower, and one or two direct-fire guns.

As rifle divisions in the main trajectory of an attack normally proceeded over a strip measuring 400 to 800 meters in width and bounded by parallel streets, the strength of the attackers had to be at least three times as great as that of the defenders. The command staffs had to be positioned immediately behind their units because in the volatile situation communications were extremely difficult to maintain. Since subunits making sudden advances were frequently separated from one another, each regiment was allocated a fast-moving reserve formation—comprising a submachine gun company, a reconnaissance detachment, and a technical crew—which could urgently intervene to close the gaps in critical situations. The artillery observers had to be posted in the front line because the view was almost completely blocked beyond 100 meters by buildings and enormous clouds of dust rising after the impact of projectiles.

The daily reports of both sides convey a uniformly inaccurate picture of the shifting fronts. In the ocean of houses the constantly changing main combat lines could be located only vaguely. In addition, advance guards and patrols occupied or held positions in front of the main combat lines when the occasion arose. Any maps showing the fronts therefore are no more than rough guides.

For a long time operations were hampered by the lack of coordination between the attacking army corps. While the Soviet 30th Rifle Corps and the Romanian 7th Army Corps received their orders from the Soviet 7th Guard Army, the Soviet 18th Special Rifle Corps was under Malinovsky's direct command. On 11 January, on the recommendation of the Soviet general staff, Malinovsky consolidated the attacking forces into the Budapest Group, with the Soviet 18th Special Rifle Corps's staff in charge. The corps's

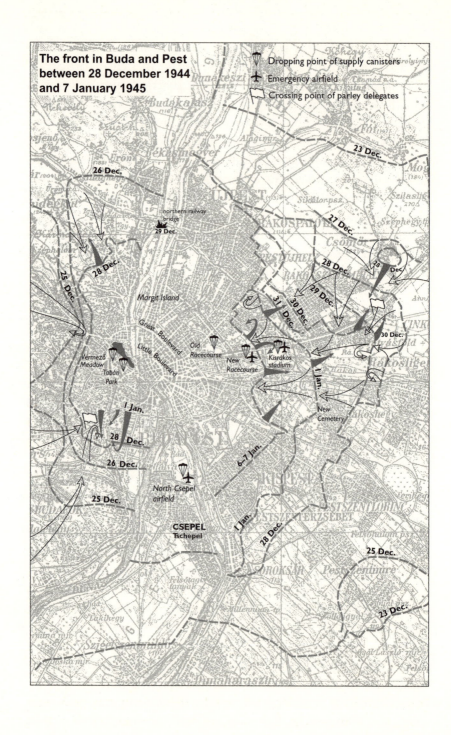

The front in Buda and Pest between 28 December 1944 and 7 January 1945

Dropping point of supply canisters
Emergency airfield
Crossing point of parley delegates

26 Dec.
23 Dec.
27 Dec.
northern railway bridge
29 Dec.
28 Dec.
28 Dec.
25 Dec.
Margit Island
28 Dec.
29 Dec.
30 Dec.
31 Dec.
30 Dec.
Great Boulevard
Little Boulevard
Old Racecourse
Vérmező Meadow
Tabán Park
New Racecourse
Kisrákos stadium
1 Jan.
New Cemetery
1 Jan.
28 Dec.
26 Dec.
6–7 Jan.
25 Dec.
North-Csepel airfield
1 Jan.
28 Dec.
25 Dec.
CSEPEL
Tschepel
23 Dec.

commander, Lieutenant-General Ivan Mikhailovich Afonyin, was appointed to head the group.

The German corps commands had very little scope for influencing events. In early January it was still possible to make phone calls, and Hungarian members of the reconnaissance units frequently obtained valuable information by ringing up residents of Soviet-held areas. By mid-January, however, most telecommunications had been destroyed, and contact with the fighters on the front line could be maintained only through messengers. In the opaque mass of buildings, information about Soviet advances was delayed. The command therefore was increasingly transferred to the combat groups, which, despite their limited resources, were frequently able to recapture the most important buildings and thoroughfares.

To prevent desertions, the Hungarian soldiers were attached in small groupings to the German units. The German command reinforced the defense with technical barriers and cordons. Key junctions, streets, and squares were blocked with electric fences, mine barriers, tank traps, and barricades. Behind the fighting units the activities of Soviet infiltrators were to be foiled by a second defense line of police, gendarmerie, and other units with inferior combat value such as the II University Assault Battalion.

Within the boundaries of Pest six largely parallel and semicircular defense lines were developed, starting from and returning to the Danube. The first skirted the perimeter of the southern suburbs to Rákos Station and then northwest along the Rákos stream; the second took in Könyves Kálmán Boulevard, Hungária Boulevard, and Róbert Károly Boulevard; the third branched off from the second near Józsefváros Station and continued along Dózsa György Street and Dráva Street; the fourth followed Haller Street, Orczy Road, Fiumei Road, Rottenbiller Street, Szinyei Merse Street, the Ferdinánd Bridge across the railway line, and Csanády Street; the fifth ran along the Great Boulevard (comprising Ferenc Boulevard, József Boulevard, Erzsébet Boulevard, Teréz Boulevard, and Szent István Boulevard); and the sixth along the Little Boulevard (comprising Károly Boulevard, Múzeum Boulevard, and Vámház Boulevard). They all contained only makeshift temporary fortifications, however, occasionally complemented by mine barriers or electric fences.

Early in January the command of the IX SS Mountain Army Corps ordered the remnants of Lieutenant-Colonel Kündiger's 271st People's Grenadier Division from Buda to Pest. The commander of the 13th Panzer Division, Colonel-General Schmidhuber, was placed in charge of all the units in Pest. By then the Hungarian infantry regiments were reporting ration strengths of only 150 to 200, equipment averaging five light machine guns, one heavy machine gun, and four or five mortars—and their numbers were declining. On 7 January the combat strength of the 13th Panzer Division was 887 and that of the Hungarian 10th Infantry and 12th Reserve Divisions was 507; on 14 January the Kündiger Group's combat strength was 225 and that of the Feldherrnhalle Division, including the Hungarian units attached to it, was 865. Estimating the combat strength of the 22 SS Cavalry Division at about 800 and that of other frontline units at 400, we obtain a total of 3,684. Thus the combat strength of the whole Pest garrison roughly equaled that of one complete Soviet division.

Pfeffer-Wildenbruch did not trust Schmidhuber, and therefore attached SS Oberführer (equivalent of colonel) Helmut Dörner to the divisional staff as "political officer." Since Dörner also had military duties, he was made commander of a combat group formed from remnants of the 13th Panzer Division. This did not, however, reflect the true power relationships: although Dörner was technically Schmidhuber's subordinate, he was able to order Schmidhuber, who had moved his command post away from the battle, to relocate to Pest on about 10 January.

The Siege of Pest, Second Phase: 5–18 January 1945: Fighting in the City Center

The noose around the Pest bridgehead tightened and lost its semicircular shape as the attack in the northeastern sector continued. By 5 January, Soviet tanks had carved a deep salient through Pestújhely as far as the Zugló quarter in the inner city. North of the salient, the Germans and Hungarians were still holding Újpest and the western corner of Pestújhely and Rákospalota, and south of the salient the Racecourse, the area near Örs vezér Square, Kőbánya and a large part of Kispest and Pestszenterzsébet. Farther south, on the Danube, Soroksár was about to be encircled at any moment. West of Soroksár, the main defense line ran through Királyerdő Forest and Lakihegy on Csepel Island. A report of the IX SS Mountain Army Corps reads:

> The focus of the battle of Budapest has shifted to the eastern bridgehead. Fighting continues with undiminished ferocity, with heavy enemy artillery and mortar fire. Significant losses on both sides. Apart from a small loss of territory it has been possible, despite the extremely tight ammunition situation, to maintain our position against strong enemy attacks on the entire eastern and northeastern front. . . . Supplies very tight, artillery ammunition available only for one more day. Some types of ammunition used up.

In Zugló, where street fighting went on all day, First Lieutenant István Mányoki's assault artillery group lost 70 percent of its 120 soldiers in several unsuccessful counterattacks.

On 6 January, early in the morning, the 22nd SS Cavalry Division abandoned Soroksár. In the densely built-up areas of Pestszenterzsébet and Kispest, house-to-house fighting slowed down the Soviet advance, but at the outer edge of Kőbánya the defense line almost disintegrated because the five-kilometer stretch leading to the Hungarian 10th Infantry Division's sector in Zugló was held by only a few hundred men. Eastern Kőbánya fell to the Soviets before the 22nd SS Cavalry Division could intervene. During the day Soviet troops also captured northern Kőbánya and Rákosfalva, which enabled them to keep the emergency airfield on the Racecourse out of action by bombarding it from both north and south.

On the same day the defenders were obliged to abandon central Kőbánya and eastern Zugló. From Zugló and Pestújhely, Soviet assault units started to advance toward Rákosrendező Station, and it was evening before the German 93rd Grenadier Regiment could halt them. At the northern edge of Zugló the Hungarian 6/III

Battalion, with heavy losses, held its position, which was illuminated by the enormous flames of a burning timber yard nearby. In Pestszenterzsébet, Soviet troops, breaching the line of the Hungarian 12th Reserve Division, took the Hofherr-Schranz factory—the last plant still producing spare parts for tanks and functioning as a tank repair workshop.

The emergency airfield in the northern part of Csepel Island had been within range of Soviet artillery since 6 January, and from 7 January could no longer be used. The Germans therefore started fierce counterattacks to regain the Racecourse with its airfield. The commander of the 66th Panzergrenadier Regiment, Major Schöning, considered the attack pointless because he saw no possibility of taking the buildings left and right of the Racecourse. A fierce argument broke out between him and Schmidhuber, who insisted on the execution of the order. The infantry needed for this action could be provided only by withdrawing the II/66 Grenadier Battalion from the defense and hoping that the Soviets would not notice its absence. Ten assault guns of Assault Artillery Captain Sándor Hanák's company and a German and Hungarian combat group of some 200 were positioned behind the wooden fence of a stadium. Hanák observed the events through a gap in the fence:

> As soon as we had taken position we were told that the Russkis were approaching singing. And really, they were coming across the open track, singing and arm in arm. They were going to attack, presumably in an alcoholic state! I ordered the guns to open fire. Kicking the fence down, we fired fragmentation grenades and machine-gun volleys into the mass. They ran to the stands, where there was a terrible bloodbath when the assault guns fired at one row of seats after another. The Germans reported about 800 of them dead.

German and Hungarian casualties were also great, as Schöning remembers: "The attack collapsed after less than an hour in a hurricane of Russian artillery fire. Reconnaissance Unit 13 made hardly any headway, II/66 together with the very bravely attacking Hungarian assault guns gained the far side of the Racecourse but could not hold it. In the evening we had an incomplete defense line across the Racecourse, stands and stables." Lack of infantry made further advance impossible, and the Racecourse could not be re-captured.

On 7 January, Soviet and Romanian troops advanced farther in Zugló, while in Kőbánya, the 22nd SS Cavalry Division and Lieutenant-General Billnitzer's Hungarian assault artillery troops started nine unsuccessful counterattacks before finally abandon-ing the district in the evening. Fighting continued near Kőbánya-alsó Station and the MÁV (Hungarian State Railways) housing estate, as well as along Vaspálya Street and the railway embank-ment parallel to it. Most of the 22nd SS Cavalry Division was wiped out. In Kispest and Pestszenterzsébet, Soviet rifle guard divisions were pressing ahead, and the SS Mountain Army Corps signaled:

> Desperate street fighting is raging in Kispest. South of Déli Station two incursions have been dealt with through counterstrikes. Despite rigorous combing of staffs and rear services, the bases that make up the front line are daily becoming thinner owing to heavy losses. The supply situation is extremely critical, in particular for lack of adequate ammunition supplies by air. . . . Total casualties from 24 December to 6 January 5,621.

On 8 January the Soviet troops achieved only small successes, mainly at the line of the 22nd SS Cavalry Division, where they finally captured Kispest. Near Józsefváros Station, German infantry, supported by three assault guns of the Hungarian 1st Assault Artillery Detachment, recaptured the MÁV housing estate. Here a lance-corporal of the 66th Grenadier Regiment had held an impor-tant building single-handed by running up and down while firing, in order to suggest that a German soldier was hiding behind every window: he later received the Knight's Cross. Soviet troops, break-ing through at the railway embankment, entered Népliget Park south of the housing estate. At Rákosrendező Station, west of Pestújhely, more significant breakthroughs followed. Units of the 7th Romanian Army Corps attacked the post office's vehicle depot in Egressy Road and by the evening, in hand-to-hand fighting, had taken the post office building.

From the attacks on Zugló it became obvious that Malinovsky intended to split the Pest bridgehead in two. While the territory held by the defense from north to south still measured 15 kilometers, the Soviet spearheads advancing from the east were already within 4 kilometers of the Danube. A number of counterattacks against the Zugló salients indicate that the German command was fully aware of the danger, but none of the counterattacks achieved lasting success.

On 9 January the Soviet 30th Army Corps, with overwhelming strength, began a general attack through the side streets of Csömöry Road to capture Rákosrendező Station. They stalled in the morning but, according to a Hungarian report, the pressure grew heavier and heavier during the afternoon, and it became clear that the "enemy was trying to cut off the troops in Rákospalota and Újpest in order to split the Pest bridgehead. They therefore constantly increased the pressure toward Rákosrendező Station by deploying more troops, tanks, flamethrowing tanks, and flamethrowers, and reached the station. Some enemy patrols also infiltrated Városliget Park during the afternoon." In order to prevent an encirclement, Major-General Schmidhuber gave orders for the immediate evacuation of Újpest. He intended to pull the front back to the northern line of the railway ring, and he succeeded in temporarily recapturing Magdolnaváros Station in the process. By evening, however, Soviet tanks were again ensconced among the goods cars in the railyard.

Meanwhile in Zugló the Soviets occupied every house, and the front moved to the railway embankment in Mexikói Road. Nearby, the Romanian 7th Army Corps, having captured the Racecourse, crossed Hungária Boulevard at the Kerepesi Road junction. German infantry, assisted by Hungarian assault guns, retook the northwestern part of Népliget Park. In southern Pest the front stabilized along Határ Road. At the same time the evacuation of Csepel Island began; the island had become untenable as a result of the Soviet advances in both Pest and Buda. The remnants of the decimated German 93rd Grenadier Regiment were incorporated in the 66th Regiment.

The IX SS Mountain Army Corps bombarded the staff of the German Army Group South with desperate messages: "Unless supplies arrive by air, the ammunition for machine guns, mortars, and field guns will only last until 9 January, other ammunition until 12 January, horse fodder and fuel until 10 January, food until 11 January. In Budapest there are 3,880 wounded, 1,400 of them stretcher cases. The situation demands an early solution."

During the night of 10 January the Feldherrnhalle Division withdrew from Újpest, but was unable to hold its defense positions on the northern railway embankment. Soviet troops moving south in pursuit breached the defenses around Angyalföld Station and reached the Rákos stream near Lehel Street. They also took Rákosrendező Station. Soviet and Romanian troops crossed Hungária Boulevard at the intersection with Mexikói Road and entered Városliget Park. The 2nd Company of the Budapest Police Assault Battalion and some 300 gendarmes ejected them and took up positions on the northeastern edge of the park. Joining the counterattack of the 13th Panzer Division, they advanced to Amerikai Road and Korong Street, where one of their small Ansaldo tanks—already obsolete in the Abyssinian war of 1935–1936—was destroyed and half of the men killed. A Soviet counterthrust in division strength pushed the exhausted group back across the park to Aréna Road, where it was relieved by Tibor Kubinyi's Budapest Assault Company, which promptly launched a counterattack and, backed by two German tanks, recaptured about half the park. There was also heavy fighting for Népliget Park. In southern Pest, Soviet guard rifle divisions advanced along Soroksári Road toward Ferencváros Station. Meanwhile the evacuation of Csepel Island was completed.

On 11 January fighting began in the culverts of the inner districts of Pest. Soviet reconnaissance patrols squeezed through the narrow passages, surfacing under cover of night among the ruins behind the front line. In Angyalföld the Soviet 25th Guard Rifle Division broke through the defenses on the Rákos stream. In the deserted streets to the southwest the Germans retreated from one factory after another toward Róbert Károly Boulevard. The Soviet troops followed relatively slowly, so that the two sides were separated by a wide stretch of no-man's land.

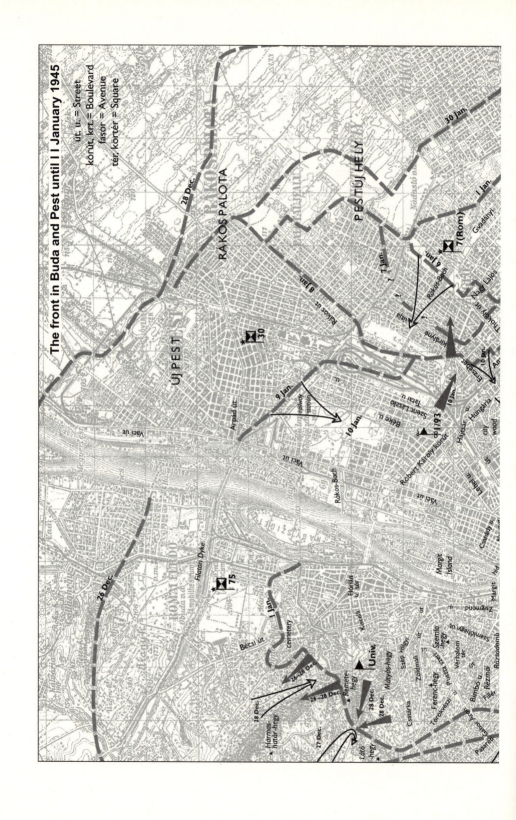

The front in Buda and Pest until I I January 1945

út, u. = Street
kórút, krt = Boulevard
fasor = Avenue
tér, körtér = Square

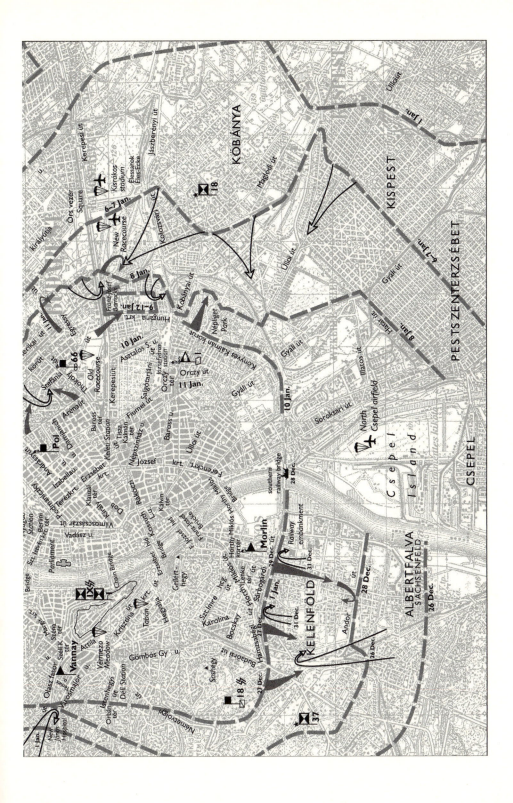

An encounter that was to last several days began in Városliget Park and Angolpark, and in Vidámpark amusement park the Hungarian 7th Assault Artillery Detachment lost all its assault guns. Józsefváros Station fell into Soviet hands. Kerepesi Cemetery was taken by the Soviets in close-quarter fighting after pioneers had blasted a gap in the surrounding wall, while the 13th Panzer Division withdrew to Fiumei Road. Police units attached to the Hungarian Zrínyi assault guns to compensate for the lack of infantry recaptured the western part of Orczy Square. The Hungarian 10th Infantry Division carried out a successful counterstrike in the Törökőr area and regained the positions lost on the previous day. The tug sent to recover the motor barge stranded in the Danube at Leányfalu was hit on its way, and the crew rejoined the relief armies after swimming to the bank near Visegrád and slipping through the Soviet lines in the Pilis Hills.

On 12 January, on the Angyalföld front, the Feldherrnhalle Division retreated to a line formed by Dagály Street, Frangepán Street, Jász Street, Szabolcs Street, and Aréna Road. A large portion of Városliget Park was now in the hands of the Soviets, who had also taken Rottenbiller Street. The Hungarian 10th Infantry Division held its position at the intersection of Hungária Boulevard and Stefánia Road but was left out on a limb, with Soviet troops in its rear at Városliget Park and the Fiumei Street edge of Kerepesi Cemetery. The 13th Panzer Division and members of the Morlin Group launched a counterattack but stalled after retaking half of the cemetery. A more successful counterattack of the Kündiger Group and the Hungarian 1st Tank Division from Üllői Road reached Orczy Square and the southwest corner of Népliget Park and recaptured most of the Tisztviselőtelep estate.

Around midday, German armored vehicles with flamethrowers set the stalls in Teleki Square alight, and Hungarian soldiers manned the two barricades erected there. Soviet troops opened fire on the square, where a building next to the barricades went up in flames and the positions had to be abandoned. A counterattack failed, leaving a large gap in the southeastern section. Although the front line had moved toward the west three days earlier, it was only now that the Romanian 7th Army Corps managed to capture the

Ferenc József Barracks between Kerepesi Road and Hungária Boulevard, with each room being fought for so fiercely that in one of the attacking companies all officers and NCOs were killed.

Three times the defenders sent motorboats to unload the barge stranded at Leányfalu. Although these returned filled with ammunition, it was not possible to recover everything. Daring civilians with wheelbarrows had constructed makeshift pontoons and helped themselves to part of the cargo, which included, among other things, grated cheese labeled "Wiener Molkerei" (Vienna Dairy).

On 13 January the IX SS Mountain Army Corps signaled to the army group: "The battle of Budapest has reached its climax. The eastern bridgehead is unceasingly battered by waves of attacks with maximum artillery, fighter aircraft and tank support. . . . By day traffic is paralyzed by continuous air raids concentrating on the Danube bridges. Some of the bridges are badly damaged. The loss of the eastern bridgehead must be expected soon after 15 January."

20

Teleki Pál Street, 5 January 1945. Carts and horses of the Hungarian artillery

In the XIII District the Feldherrnhalle Division halted the Soviet advance along Dagály Street, Lehel Street, and Szabolcs Street. In the VI and VII Districts the Soviet commander, Lieutenant-General Afonyin, directed his main forces against Nyugati Station and Erzsébet Boulevard. By evening the front line was running along Bajza Street, Rottenbiller Street, and Damjanich Street, and all but the southern rim of Városliget Park was in Soviet hands.

In the southern section of the bridgehead, Soviet units pushed the Germans and Hungarians back as far as Orczy Square and retook the Ludovika Academy. Farther north, they made a deep dent in the defense toward the city center and captured Horváth Mihály Square. The Morlin Group failed to mount a counterattack because the firing pins of its antitank guns had been removed by saboteurs. From Hungária Boulevard the Hungarian 10th Infantry Division withdrew to Keleti Station to avoid encirclement. Repeated counterattacks by Sándor Hanák's assault artillery unit delayed the Soviet and Romanian advance, but Ferencváros Station fell. Civilians were forced out of cellars and made to walk ahead of the attackers urging the defenders to defect. Some buildings between Podmaniczky Street and Rákóczy Road changed hands as many as five times.

On 14 January, at 4:30 A.M., a building at the corner of Klotild Street used as a military hospital received a direct hit. The ammunition store on the mezzanine exploded, burying some 300 patients and staff. Fighting continued unabated, as reported by the Hungarian and German army corps commands: "The whole day was marked by enemy terror bombing. Squadrons of enemy aircraft dropped bombs, and fighter planes strafed the streets. This resulted in devastating losses and conflagrations." "All the artillery ammunition is used up, infantry ammunition is running out and can be preserved only through prohibition on firing; the fuel is finished, provisions are extremely critical, the situation of the wounded is disastrous."

In Angyalföld the Feldherrnhalle Division, threatened with encirclement, hurriedly retreated from Róbert Károly Boulevard toward Csanády Street and Ferdinánd Bridge. In the VI and VIII districts, Soviet and Romanian troops reached Vörösmarty Street,

21
Soviet heavy artillery attacking Budapest city center

Rózsa Street, Izabella Street, Rottenbiller Street, and Bethlen
Gábor Street, and captured Keleti Station. The remnants of the
Hungarian 10th Infantry Division began to relocate to Buda. In the
southern section the bulk of the Hungarian 1st Mechanized Rifle
Regiment was encircled behind the ruins of Ferencváros Station. As
the Soviet troops now posed an immediate threat to the city center, Lieutenant-General Billnitzer was ordered to close off the
Great Boulevard with the remnants of the assault artillery detachments, two pioneer battalions, and some assault-boat squads. The
boulevard had previously been mined and the streets leading out
from it barricaded.

On 15 January the Soviets captured Nyugati Station. In the
south they reached the eastern rim of Kálvin Square. Some units
entered the National Museum through the drains, but withdrew
when seven or eight guns of the Hungarian 10th Assault Company
opened fire on them. Remnants of the 22nd SS Cavalry Division
resisted along Lónyay Street and Mátyás Street. In Rákóczy Road

and elsewhere civilians were forced to walk ahead of the Soviets calling on the defenders to surrender.

In Tavaszmező Street the Soviets stormed the command post of the Morlin Group. The Hungarians first mistook them for Germans and were able to stop them in hand-to-hand fighting only at the barricade at the corner of Rigó Street and József Street. As Soviet troops were already in the Great Boulevard, the residue of the Morlin Group was encircled but managed to break out thanks to two crates of hand grenades and a Zrínyi assault gun. According to reports of the IX SS Mountain Army Corps, the battle continued "with undiminished ferocity in the shelled, bombed, burning center of Pest. In constant attacks the enemy penetrated as far as the buildings east of Kálvin Square."

In the evening, Colonel Sándor András, the commander of the Hungarian 10th Infantry Division, and Major Béla Botond, the chief of staff, called an officers' meeting in the cellar of the General Credit Bank, at which they announced that the Germans had lost

22
Soviet pioneers and minesweeping dogs in Budapest city center

the war. They contacted the Soviets and adjourned to András's apartment. József Bíró, the adjutant of the operational staff, remembers András's last conversation: "'Is there anything left in the box?' 'A little alcohol, food, cigarettes, and cigars.' 'Divide it up between the men. Don't see me home. God be with you. Don't say anything to anyone.' He shook hands and left the Credit Bank cellar. I was surprised at being trusted with his secret."

General-staff captain Győző Benyovszky, who could not bring himself to defect, reported the "disappearance" of the commander and the chief of staff to the army corps command, but no action was taken. One reason why the two officers had not attempted to carry any of their units with them may have been that the close links between the Hungarian and German troops would have made a collective defection impossible. In any case, the gap between them and their soldiers by then was so wide that they were hardly able to give them orders. András himself remembers:

> When I had left the cellar of the bank and arrived on the square in front of the Vigadó Concert Hall, I was faced with a Neronian sight. The hotels along the Danube embankment were on fire. . . . The dark Buda side provided an eerie background to the flames. . . . My first interrogation was held in a shelter. . . . I was questioned by a Soviet colonel. My hands were tied behind my back, and during the interrogation somebody tried to take my watch from my wrist. Through the interpreter I asked the colonel if I could give the watch to the person in question as a "souvenir." The colonel shouted at my guard, and the watch remained in my possession. While I was still awaiting my fate, a guard thrust his hand in my coat pocket. I grabbed his hand and noticed that he was putting biscuits in my pocket.

During the night, the Germans and Hungarians withdrew from Rákóczy Road to the Great Boulevard in order to avoid encirclement. Horthy Miklós Bridge was blown up by the Germans. The II University Assault Battalion was shattered and its remains incorporated in the Hungarian 12th Reserve Division. At József

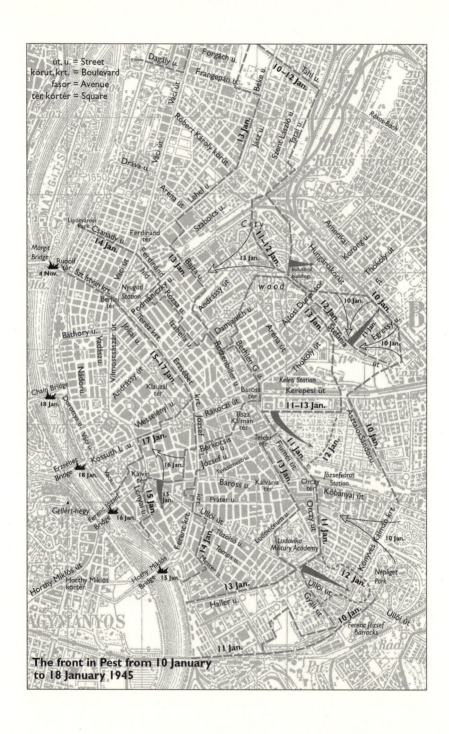

**The front in Pest from 10 January
to 18 January 1945**

Boulevard survivors from the Morlin group, joined by assault-artillery troops, held up a Soviet assault.

On 16 January encounters continued along the Great Boulevard, Rákóczy Road, Kálvin Square, the National Museum, and Vámház Boulevard. The 13th Panzer Division's report reads: "Forays in Erzsébet Boulevard have been contained in heavy fighting. Fighting is intensive around breaches east of Berlin Square and on the Danube (northern section)." A combat group of the 13th Panzer Division was surrounded near Kálvin Square, and various attempts to rescue it failed.

During the night Ferenc József Bridge collapsed. According to the Germans it was hit by a bomb, and according to the Hungarians it was blown up. Both versions may be correct: with German and Hungarian troops still left in Pest, the Soviets had as much interest in destroying the bridges as the Germans had in saving them. Soviet troops penetrated deep into the central districts behind Baross Street and Erzsébet Boulevard, threatening to cut

23
Shops burning in the Great Boulevard, January 1945

the southern section of the bridgehead in two. To forestall this, the defenders launched several counterattacks aimed at recapturing their original positions, but succeeded only at Erzsébet Boulevard. There was also fierce fighting for the Great Market Hall. By this time the army group had advised the IX Mountain Army Corps that their prime objective on the east bank of the Danube should be to prevent the troops being separated; this order amounted to a thinly veiled permission to evacuate. The relocation of the command posts had already begun on the previous day.

The capture of Pest being only days away, Malinovsky ordered the Romanian 7th Army Corps—which had reached the Great Boulevard after losing 23,000 dead, wounded, and missing (more than 60 percent of its strength) since October—to the front in northern Hungary. Although the real reason was that he did not want to share the victory with the Romanians, he claimed that he was responding to requests from the Romanian general staff. The Romanian commander, General Nicolae Sova, reluctantly obeyed but was nevertheless dismissed on 7 February for "insubordination" and, after the communist takeover of Romania, was sentenced to ten years' hard labor in Siberia.

On 17 January the final onslaught on Pest began, and at 7:25 P.M. Pfeffer-Wildenbruch received permission to evacuate. Now the sole objective of the Germans and Hungarians was to get to Buda across the two bridges—Erzsébet Bridge and the Chain Bridge—that were still standing, albeit badly damaged by bombs. Many Hungarian soldiers deliberately stayed behind, however, and in some units the gasoline was siphoned out of the remaining vehicles in order to sabotage the relocation. The Hungarian army corps command sent General-staff Captain Ferenc X. Kovács and Gendarmerie Captain László Kerekes to the blazing city center to oversee the execution of the evacuation order. Kovács recalls: "During the night I walked as far as Szent István Boulevard, doing the rounds of the various cellars where we suspected Hungarian units to be hiding. . . . Everywhere they were waiting for the Russians and had no desire to go to Buda. In one of the cellars an air force officer told us with an insolent grin that for him the war was over. There was nothing we could do about him." Meanwhile, several

24

Lieutenant-Colonel Nicolae Sova, commander of the Romanian 7th Army Corps
(far left), with his soldiers in central Budapest

thousand people had gathered at the two bridges in order to cross
to Buda in the drumfire. One was Lieutenant-Colonel Alajos Vajda,
quartermaster of the Hungarian 1st Armored Division:

> Coarse swearing in Hungarian and German. Total panic,
> which increased when we had to walk past a burning
> palace in a narrow street. We no longer knew where we
> were. The column swept us along, and there was no
> point in pulling out, nor was it advisable because one
> could not get back in again. Heat was pouring out of
> the blazing buildings, with window frames and other
> wooden parts showering the motor vehicles. Between
> the vehicles several infantry units were on the march.
> Motorized German field gendarmes were trying to
> maintain some order, but without much success. Every
> 10 to 20 meters we were stopped by another gridlock.
> Here and there shells and mines began to strike at steep

angles. The terrible detonations were accompanied by submachine gun salvos. Who knew who was shot and why? Of course many were hit by bullets or splinters. The wounded were moaning and screaming with pain. As if by a miracle we somehow reached the square in front of the Pest end of the Chain Bridge. There we were met by a veritable firework display. It was almost daylight in the middle of the night. . . . Through huge gaping holes in the bridge we could see the water. The rear of a German military car, which had somehow been caught up in one of the holes, pointed toward the sky. Its nose

25
German ammunition truck exploding in one of Budapest's narrowest streets

was deep in the hole, its occupants probably dead. Elsewhere a truck was on fire after a direct hit and we could
hardly get round it. Dead bodies were scattered everywhere, some having been run over many times.

In a letter to his wife, which was never posted, Benyovszky
wrote: "We were at the mercy of the fighter planes like mice in a
trap. Imagine the logjam in front of the bridge, vehicles on top of
vehicles, and then the circus started. The huge blocks of flats were
burning like torches, the streets full of wrecks, bodies, and collapsed walls. We could hardly walk." In the narrow winding streets,
close-quarter fighting with the aim of securing the evacuation was
in progress, but the defenders, lacking ammunition, were helpless
against the advancing Soviet guns. The hail of shells and bombs on
the bridges continued. The exodus lasted all night, claiming masses
of victims. One German soldier recalls:

> The infantry abandoned Pest by what was left of the two
> Danube bridges. They were running for their lives, obliv-
> ious of the heavy bombardment. The order to evacuate
> the bridges without delay created a panic. General [Kon-
> rad] Hitschler's police battalion, suffering heavy losses
> even before they reached the bridgeheads in the infernal
> heat, dwindled to 200 to 300 within a few hours. The
> units of the Feldherrnhalle Division, the 13th Panzer Divi-
> sion, and the Luftwaffe were decimated by a ferocious
> artillery barrage. The bridges remained constantly under
> massive fire, but people were surging ahead regardless.
> A tangled mass of cars and trucks, peasant carts covered
> by tarpaulins, frightened horses, civilian refugees, wailing
> women, mothers with crying children, and many, very
> many, wounded were hurrying toward Buda.

When the bridges were finally blown up at 7 A.M. there were
still evacuees on them. Another German soldier remembers:

> We ran for our lives in the intensive artillery fire. The
> order for us to withdraw to Buda before the bridges were
> blown up naturally alarmed the civilian population of

Pest, and many fled to Buda with us. In the confusion
some people (soldiers and civilians) were naturally left on
the bridges when they were blown up. But the largest
number of victims wasn't due to the blasting but to the
heavy-artillery bombardment preceding it.

Some tried to oppose the pointless destruction. One member of
the Hungarian resistance, Reserve Lieutenant Lajos Gidófalvy,
disappeared without trace, probably while trying to save Erzsébet
Bridge, which may have exploded as he was climbing the piers with
a small group to reach the fuses.

From the Buda side, Pest presented an apocalyptic picture.
A member of the University Assault Battalion writes: "At the Pest
end of Margit Bridge I saw an ocean of flames. Szent István Boulevard was closed off by the iron structure of Nyugati Station, glow-
ing red. It looked as if all life had perished over there and only the
raging fires were left to rule over the ruins. I didn't dare to think
of my loved ones who lived there." After the destruction of the
bridges it took the Soviet troops two more days to mop up the last
German and Hungarian opposition in Pest, particularly near Nyugati
Station.

The Siege of Buda: 24 December 1944–19 January 1945

In Buda between 24 and 26 December, a front line had gradually
developed between Farkasrét Cemetery and Olasz Avenue. On
25–26 December, Soviet infantry had captured Kútvölgy Valley and
the upper section of the Cogwheel Railway north of the cemetery
almost without a shot. Only at Farkasrét Cemetery, near Orbánhegy and Istenhegy Hills, and in the Szépilona quarter had the Germans and Hungarians been able to establish a defense line based on
commandeered buildings with varying distances between them. On
25 December the first Soviet troops had arrived in the Pasarét quarter. On 25 and 26 December hastily deployed defense formations in
the lower section of Hűvösvölgyi Road and Szépilona had retreated
toward János Hospital. On 25 December a Soviet rifle unit had
entrenched itself in one of the westernmost hospital buildings.

After the breach of the Margit Line on 20 December, fragments of German units had retreated to Buda, while the bulk of
what was left of the German 271st Volksgrenadier Division had
clung to the suburb of Kelenföld, and the rest to Hármashatár-hegy
Hill. The spine of the western defense, from the northern section
of the Danube across Rózsadomb Hill to the southern connecting
railway bridge, was formed by the 8th SS Cavalry Division, which
had been relocated from Pest and to which a German scratch unit,
called the Europa Flying Squad Battalion, and a number of Hungarian units—the University Assault Battalion, the Vannay Battalion, and some small gendarmerie groups—had been attached.

On 26 December, Soviet rifle units from Pomáz had occupied
the villages of Budakalász and Békásmegyer without meeting much
opposition, and on 27 December they had reached Csillaghegy Hill
and the Roman baths that had been vacated by the Germans without
a struggle. By 28 December, however, Soviet troops advancing from
Üröm Station were stopped in Bécsi Road, and others, after crossing
the Óbuda railway embankment at Aquincum, were faced with growing resistance in the Filatorigát quarter. From here the front line
extended to the old cemetery in Óbuda and Remete-hegy Hill.

The positions between the Danube and Fehérvári Road were
manned by the Budapest Guard Battalion and those between
Fehérvári Road and Kelenföld by the Kündiger Group (a remnant
of the German 271st People's Grenadier Division) before being
replaced by the Hungarian Galántai Gendarmerie Battalion and the
city-center Hungarist group. Pressure was greatest in southern
Buda, where the Soviet rifle corps soon penetrated to the inner-city
districts. Their task was made easier by the absence of any significant troop concentrations ahead of the defense line near the
Danube, and by 26 December they had captured Kelenföld Station.
Nine German tanks started a counterattack along the railway line,
where German and Hungarian cars loaded with ammunition were
parked in a long row. As they were being forced back by troops of
the Soviet 316th Rifle Division, they collided with the car, setting
off enormous explosions that demolished the neighboring houses,
and killed as many as a hundred people, although in a city under
constant bombardment it was not always possible to establish

precise figures, particularly if the bodies were lying in no-man's land or in caved-in cellars. On 27 December, however, the Budapest Guard Battalion, the Morlin Group, and a battery of the 1st Assault Artillery Division recaptured the station.

Between 24 and 28 December the University Assault Battalion, patrolling in shifts of four or five hours, sealed off the streets of the suburb of Törökvész between Látó-hegy Hill and the Bolyai Academy in Hűvösvölgy Valley. Their company commands kept in touch with each other by means of the university radio club's equipment. As the area could be seen from Svábhegy Hill, any movement in the streets had become potentially fatal, but the Soviets apparently failed to notice the weakness of the untrained forces facing them, because they avoided a gun battle and dodged the patrols until 28 December. As a result, between 26 and 28 December the students were able to carry out successful counterattacks around Kecske-hegy and Hármashatár-hegy Hill. Thirty-eight of them, though, did not survive their baptism of fire.

On 28 December the Soviets finally captured János Hospital and were less than two kilometers west of the Danube and the same distance northwest of the German and Hungarian headquarters in the Castle tunnel. A whole Soviet division, in a column measuring 200 to 300 meters across, set out toward Városmajor Grange. The grange was the most sensitive point in Buda, because a vigorous attack from there was likely to cut the cauldron in two and roll straight into the Castle District. The German command had therefore attached particular importance to fortifying it and allocated the task to the Vannay Battalion.

The fortifications were arranged in three echelons, the first at the embankment of the Cogwheel Railway and the second and third within Városmajor Grange, along Temes Street and Szamos Street, respectively. The first echelon consisted of four German MG-42 machine guns placed on the embankment, with trenches, a mine barrier, and a barbed-wire entanglement in front of them and a truck blocking the level crossing. At the foot of the embankment, more machine guns, covered by shutters torn from windows, pointed inward toward the grange. The grange buildings were mined in case any Soviet troops overran the embankment and tried to take shelter

in them. A number of smaller defense positions were set up somewhat farther back. The school in Városmajor Street was taken over
by a company with a panzerfaust. In Trombitás Road a Hungarian
antiaircraft gun was deployed as an antitank weapon, camouflaged
with a movable screen made from the Opera's Persian carpets. Several apartments in Olasz Avenue and Retek Street were turned into
machine-gun positions and ammunition dumps. All the positions
were secured by pickets, which could communicate with one another and with the command through telephone lines installed in
the municipal drains. The heavy-weapon crews waited in nearby cellars, taking up their positions only when instructed to do so by telephone, because the constant shelling made it impossible to stay long
in the open. The machine guns were moved after every few salvos to
elude the highly accurate Soviet antitank rifles. Each soldier in the
advance positions was allocated a dog to keep him warm.

The combat strength of the Vannay Battalion amounted to
some 450 men. The soldiers were initially housed in the church
within Városmajor Grange and the command in Csaba Street south
of the grange. Their heavy weaponry consisted of two 40mm automatic guns, six 81mm mortars, and two heavy antitank guns, assisted
by three guns of a Hungarian artillery battalion stationed in Széll
Kálmán Square to the east, and two additional Szálasi rocket launchers mounted in front of the church. The local knowledge of municipal employees serving in the battalion enabled them to use the
existing cable culverts as a means of providing uninterrupted contact with the Europa Flying Squad Battalion north of the grange.

On 28 December, Gyula Elischer, the founder and acting
commander of the University Assault Battalion, was ordered to
relieve a German unit at the western foot of Látó-hegy Hill. As he
recalls, he set out with 20 volunteers, hoping that he would be able,
as before, to repulse the Soviets without putting the untrained
students at risk:

> After a few hours' walk we arrived near the appointed
> place at lunch time and stepped into one of the houses.
> Everybody was in the cellar. We were given an excellent
> lentil soup. . . .

The commander of the German unit that we were to relieve was a young Waffen SS officer. He was wearing a long unbuttoned coat, and round his neck a Knight's Cross and a submachine gun. He showed me round the positions and then we entered a nice modern two-story house in a large garden on the steep slope. . . . The German officer spread out the maps on top of a black grand piano and explained the situation to me. We exchanged a few words in German. He said that he was a secondary school teacher. He was well-spoken and very likable.

Outside, between the houses, the body of a German shot through the head indicated the presence of Soviet snipers on the heights opposite. Another of the Hungarians remembers:

Our own snipers with their telescopic-sight rifles had installed themselves in the attic of one of the houses, while the others occupied a section of the makeshift positions measuring 150 to 200 meters in length. Before long our left wing was hit by shells, and about two dozen Russians were rushing toward the positions, but our machine gun opened fire on them to good effect. Only a few were able to run back. They tried to put our machine gun out of action, but it had already been moved somewhere else. The battle quieted a bit; only a few shots could be heard, and the Russians retreated.

A few minutes later Elischer was wounded. An explosive bullet shattered his shoulder and another hit him near the spine. When he had been dispatched to hospital, the command was taken over by Captain Lajos Sipeki Balás, who had already been the head of the unit in theory since 5 December 1944.

Even then many of the students failed to realize the full extent of their predicament. Olaf Szamódi, a student of mechanical engineering and an air force reserve lieutenant, started a break-out attempt in the direction of Hármashatár-hegy and Kecske-hegy Hills with members of the 2nd Company. The students, marching in closed column, were approaching the Erdei Lak restaurant at the western foot of Remete-hegy Hill when Soviet artillery stationed on the ridge above struck them from the side. Several dozen students were killed or fled, and Szamódi himself was wounded. Only a few students finally reached the restaurant, where they were eventually encircled early in January.

On 29 December the Hungarian units that had retaken Kelenföld Station on 27 December advanced 1.5 kilometers farther and occupied the industrial estates of southern Buda, but they were obliged to retreat to their original positions before evening because the German units assigned to protect their northwestern flank from a Soviet attack had been unable to keep up with them. The Soviet attack came to a standstill at the Lágymányos railway embankment, Sashegy Hill, and Farkasrét Cemetery.

On 31 December, Soviet troops crossed the railway embankment, which was, however, retaken by the Budapest Flying Squad Battalion. The battalion suffered considerable losses in the process and was replaced with two companies of the combat group led by Major Gyula Viharos, together with the 40-strong Hungarist combat group of First Lieutenant Béla Kollarits and the antitank group of Major István Déri. These were later joined by the panzer grenadiers of the Feldherrnhalle Division from Pest and some other German units. For a long time the defenders' eight machine-gun clusters, sunk into the embankment and reinforced with barbed-wire entanglements, proved impregnable. The assault battalions of the Soviet 83rd Marine Infantry Brigade launched several attacks, but the men advancing on foot across 50 to 200 meters of completely flat terrain were mowed down by the machine guns, and the tanks were unable to climb the embankment. The strength of several companies was reduced to seven. One Soviet soldier remembers:

> Fighting in this section dragged on for a long time. We were unable to advance any farther, and the term "damba" [dam or embankment] became more ominous for us every day. In the gray snow, sooty with gunpowder and churned up by projectiles, we would haul our wounded back through ravaged streets, and if we were then asked "Where from?" our only reply amid the

> ceaseless rattle of guns was: "From the damba." To all of us this word sounded threatening and sinister. . . . The brigade had long since ordered the telegraphists, cart drivers, medical orderlies, and cooks to the front line.

The dreaded "damba" was finally taken by the Soviets on 11 February, when Major Viharos raised the white flag.

On 1 January the Soviet 180th Rifle Division attempted an assault on Városmajor Grange. After a heavy artillery and mortar barrage, six to eight Soviet tanks and infantry from Kútvölgyi Road overran the Vannay Battalion's machine-gun clusters. But the Hungarians destroyed two T-34 tanks and recaptured the embankment of the Cogwheel Railway, where they created nearly indestructible machine-gun positions by building the wrecks of the tanks into the earthworks and digging foxholes underneath. The fighting abated, although Soviet snipers posted in János Hospital ensured that the defenders in the front line could be relieved only by night. This embankment was to remain in Hungarian hands until 19 January.

On the morning of 3 January, Tolbukhin withdrew the 2nd Mechanized Guard Army Corps, the 86th Guard Rifle Division, and the 49th Guard Army Division from the encirclement to ward off the relief attempts He also ordered the 46th Army to cease its attacks and concentrate on preventing any break-outs, although some of its companies and battalions continued the assault on Buda.

Ferocious battles were fought for the possession of Sashegy and Rózsadomb Hills. Mátyáshegy Hill, the extreme northwestern base of the defense, changed hands seven times on 3 January alone. This hill, with its steep southern slope, was particularly important to the defense because without it the planned break-out toward the approaching relief troops was certain to cause heavy losses. Here all Soviet attacks between 3 and 7 January were repulsed.

The loss of Sashegy Hill, which dominated the southern part of the city, would have laid Buda wide open, because with the help of observers from that vantage point the Soviets could easily have eliminated the defenders' artillery between the Citadel and Castle Hill in the southeast and the emergency airfield on Vérmező Meadow to the west of Castle Hill. The Germans had therefore developed the defense in depth. Between 300 and 600 Hungarians of the Berend Group, complemented by a gendarmerie unit, occupied the streets in the immediate neighborhood of the hill, with their command billeted in the Notre Dame de Sion Convent and the bombproof premises of the Seismological Institute. The group kept in constant touch with the corps command, and in due course with the relief armies, through a powerful radio transmitter. South and west of the hill, in front of the Károly király Barracks and in Farkasrét Cemetery, the 8th SS Cavalry Division's companies were posted in the front line, with the battery of their antiaircraft artillery immediately behind them and a Hungarian antiaircraft battery behind the cemetery. The defense was further supported by Hungarian assault guns and Hetzer antitank guns. On 12 January, southwest of the top of the hill, a Soviet battalion made a deep dent in the defense line, which was retrieved next day. On 15 January, according to a German report, Soviet troops "with heavy weapons of all calibers succeeded in storming the heights in the morning, but in a dashing counterstrike the height was recaptured and a red regimental flag seized."

One weak point of the defense was the thinly built-up territory immediately southeast and southwest of Sashegy Hill, and exceptionally heavy Soviet attacks were launched on the most vulnerable section between Sashegy Hill and the Lágymányos railway embankment to the southeast. To the west, a Soviet assault on Farkasrét Cemetery on 13 January advanced 100 to 200 meters between the headstones but was stopped by police and Hungarist combat groups, which remained in control of the cemetery's northeastern corner. On 20 January a counterattack by the Waffen SS recovered most of the cemetery. With positions set up in the burial vaults, about 80 Germans—together with some Hungarian gendarmes and Vannay men—held a defense line of about 1 kilometer against a charge of Soviet rifle divisions between 2 and 3 kilometers across. They were able to do so mainly because they had large quantities of heavy hand weapons—in particular fast MG-42 machine guns, of which one was often available to each squad of between five and seven men.

Near the northern edge of Farkasrét cemetery, the Soviets had advanced scarcely 100 meters by the end of the third week of January because the defenders compensated for their small numbers by resorting to the unconventional "chessboard" tactic well-suited to the field. At that time the slopes of Buda were only sparsely developed. The defenders took positions in the villas, which were often up to 50 meters apart, and formed a thinly manned front line with well-armed storm troops farther back. In the event of a powerful Soviet attack on one of the villas, they would withdraw, allowing the attackers to establish a deep but narrow salient. They would then suddenly emerge from other villas and open fire from two sides, cutting off the attackers' supplies and taking many of them prisoner. This method, regarded as heresy by traditional strategists, proved itself in Budapest when applied by soldiers who, while badly trained and equipped, could fall back on good local knowledge and high morale, as was the case with the university students, the volunteers of the University Assault Battalion, the Vannay Battalion, the assault-artillery men, and some German units.

In terms of equipment the University Assault Battalion was worst off. Each of its companies had to defend a section measuring 200 to 300 meters with 8 Bergmann submachine guns, 50 Mauser rifles, 5 light machine guns, 2 pistols, and 1 50mm mortar; the ammunition issued for seven to ten days consisted of 20 submachine gun magazines, 100 rounds per rifle, 10 magazines per light machine gun, 10 shells, and 775 hand grenades. None of the companies had further heavy or infantry weapons, and the ammunition was sufficient only for one or two days of heavy fighting. This constituted a great handicap in comparison with the Soviet soldiers, most of whom had a submachine gun, were supported by numerous heavy weapons, and did not need to worry about ammunition, as the label "Don't economize" on the cases indicated.

Nevertheless, the Soviets advanced slowly and suffered enormous losses, which were to leave them with hardly any infantry by mid-January. Unlike the Hungarians, the Germans were well provided with arms and ammunition. Moreover, as the front contracted and casualties mounted, the surviving defenders, spread less thinly on the ground, were able to supplement their own equipment with that of the dead. One particular fact that assisted them was that the depleted Soviet units often occupied houses at random rather than in a coherent line. The labyrinthine terrain and the presence of civilians encouraged partisan actions, in particular by soldiers in civilian clothes. Thus even when the front line of the Soviet attack had advanced as far east as Alkotás Street, enterprising Hungarian combat groups carried out raids in the west in Ráth György Street and near the school at the far edge of Várasmajor Grange. In addition, they were able to make good use of municipal installations: the Vannay Battalion, for example, blew up a Soviet ammunition dump after approaching it through the Ördög-árok culvert.

On 3 January, as a result of the German relief attempts and consequent Soviet regroupings, the pressure on Buda eased, and a two-week lull in the fighting ensued. On 10 January the defenders had begun to plan a break-out: they were to cross the Soviet line in Bécsi Road and reach their own forces at Szentendre. The plan was abandoned a few days later, however, because SS Oberführer Otto Gille's IV SS Panzer Corps had failed to reach Szentendre and had come to a halt at Pomáz.

On 16 January, Soviet units broke through on Sashegy Hill and south of Orbánhegy Hill. The original positions on Sashegy Hill were recaptured through a counterattack on the same day, but another counterattack south of Orbánhegy Hill was checked by heavy Soviet fire. The 13th Panzer Division's report states: "Throughout the day intense enemy fighter-aircraft activity with bombing and strafing of the front line and the city, in particular the Castle District, only occasionally disturbed by our fighters. Whole blocks, especially public buildings, on fire. Traffic in the city by day impossible."

Between 17 and 19 January, west of Sashegy Hill, Soviet battalions launched several attacks on Farkasrét Cemetery but were rebuffed. Above the terminus of the Cogwheel Railway, after a heavy artillery barrage, five T-34 tanks and an infantry battalion penetrated the first defense line, forcing the 1st Company of the Vannay Battalion back to the western edge of Várasmajor Grange, although three T-34 tanks were destroyed. From the gendarmerie barracks in Böszörményi Road the Billnitzer combat group attempted a counterattack toward Mártonhegyi Road, but it proved fruitless. The Soviets charged the embankment of the south Circular Railway, also without success.

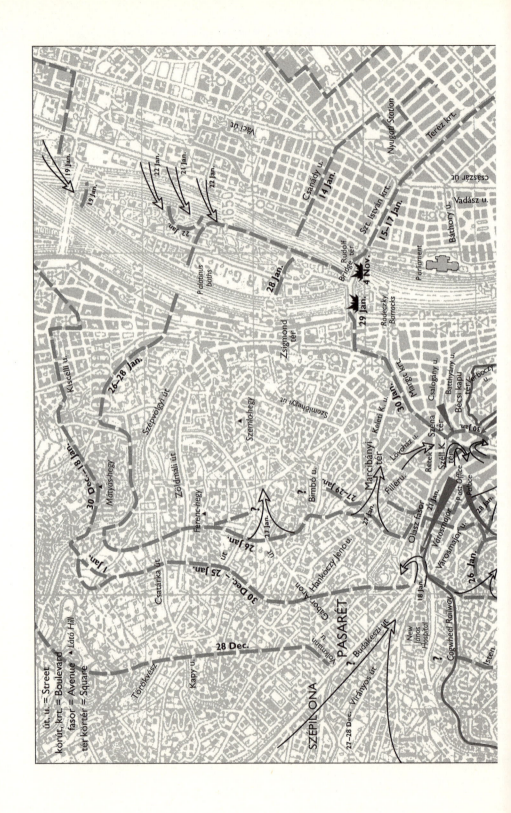

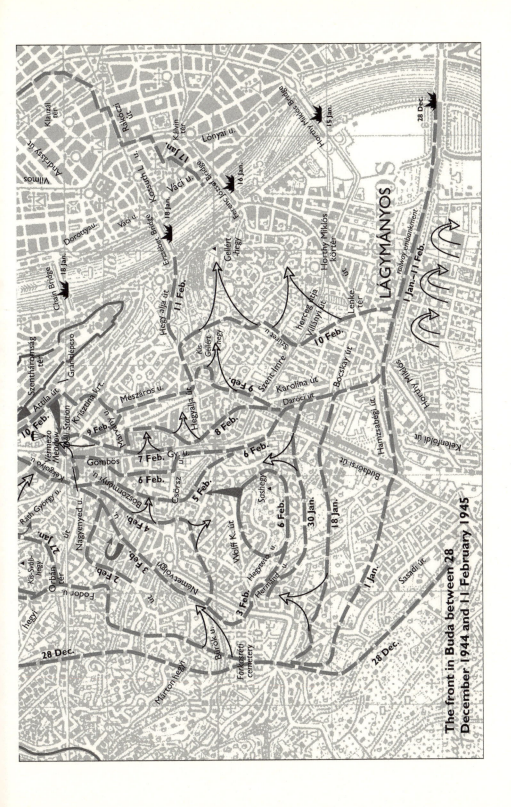

The front in Buda between 28 December 1944 and 11 February 1945

The transfer of German and Hungarian troops from Pest temporarily alleviated the tension in Buda. With no sizable Soviet attack expected across the frozen Danube, the riverside quarters of Buda were secured only by sentries from the Hungarian 1st Armored Division. To protect the traffic the streets were screened off at several points with rush matting and reed blinds.

Fighting on Margit Island

Early in January the Soviets had tried to occupy Margit Island from the north, but their rubber boats had been sunk by the defenders' machine guns. At dawn on 19 January, Soviet riflemen landed in the north corner of the island and ensconced themselves between the concrete structures of the half-built Árpád Bridge. Pfeffer-Wildenbruch sent a German battalion commanded by SS Sturmbannführer (equivalent of major) Karl Weller, together with about 100 remaining men of the Hungarian II University Assault Battalion and 36 of the Hungarian 12th Reserve Division's antitank company with four 75mm guns, to flush them out. The Soviets held their positions but were unable to continue their advance in the unforgiving terrain. During the night of 20 January "the German sentry posted in the clubhouses on the Pest side of the island fell asleep, and a Soviet infantry platoon, reaching the island across the frozen Danube, occupied one of the clubhouses and the medieval ruins." By the morning of 21 January the Soviets had established two bridgeheads near the power station on the west bank of the island. German counterattacks were thwarted by the profusion of trees and shrubs and the deep snow, in which two assault guns got stuck. Before the morning of 22 January an entire Soviet battalion had landed with mortars and antitank rifles.

On the morning of 23 December, after a heavy mortar and artillery barrage, the Soviets sliced the island in two near the Palatinus baths. The Germans in the northern half were surrounded but managed to break out after dark. First Lieutenant Litteráti-Loótz undertook an independent mission with an armored reconnaissance vehicle borrowed from the German battalion's command:

Four of my soldiers volunteered. We got in the armored vehicle and, sitting on four crates of fragmentation shells (12 in all), coupled a gun to the vehicle. At 12 noon, on the road that runs from one end of the island to the other, we drove at full speed through the line of flabbergasted Russians and, following the big bend behind the water tower, reached the medieval chapel. My four soldiers uncoupled the gun and let rip against the Soviet mortars and their crews on what used to be the open-air stage, while I covered them with my submachine gun and Sergeant Hahn turned the vehicle round. The whole thing took no more than two to three minutes. We fired our 12 shells and by the time the Russians realized what had hit them we had recoupled the gun and were rushing back to our own lines the way we had come. At the same time we were throwing hand grenades right and left, so that the Soviet antitank guns lining the road could not open fire on us. Because everything had gone so smoothly we repeated the exercise at 15:00 hours. Six of us, without the gun but with submachine guns and hand grenades, drove to the square in front of the Nagyszálló Hotel, constantly firing from the open-top truck. Having peppered the Russians posted there, we immediately turned round and withdrew. We had no casualties.

In the clubhouses on the eastern side of the island, the exhausted German soldiers were unable to repulse the constant Soviet attacks. Concerted artillery and mortar fire made all movement impossible, and those parts of the island still in the defenders' hands were hit by as many as 6,000 projectiles an hour, including several 15cm artillery grenades manufactured in Csepel, which were also used by the Soviets. Civilian men and women, press-ganged in Pest, were forced to carry ammunition to the front line across the frozen Danube before the German and Hungarian soldiers' eyes.

The university students held the premises of the Palatinus baths until 25 January, when they had to retreat. By 28 January fighting was in progress at the casino and at the edge of the polo ground, and the last clubhouse fell in the afternoon. The bridge-head had become so narrow that the Soviet troops were frequently hit by their own shells. In view of the hopeless situation, the German command gave permission for the island to be evacuated. First to leave was Litteráti-Loótz: "Because of the full moon we covered the tractors and guns with white sheets and began to withdraw at 20:00 hours. We could move only at walking speed. As the bridge surface had been wrecked by bombing, the four vehicles and three guns took more than three hours to reach the Buda shore, but they did so without any losses." A German attempt to blow up the still intact stump of the bridge failed for technical reasons. A platoon of sappers, led by a lieutenant, tried again, but when they reached the arch the bridge suddenly exploded. The only survivor, a Ukrainian volunteer, swam back to the Buda bank through the icy river.

The Siege of Buda: 20 January–11 February 1945

On the Buda side, the capture of Pest was followed by a week's lull in the fighting. The front as a whole stretched from Flórián Square in the north, via Mátyás-hegy Hill, Városmajor Grange, Orbánhegy Hill, Farkasrét Cemetery, and Sashegy Hill, to the Lágymányos railway embankment in the south.

Beginning on 20 January the effects of the German relief attempt could soon be felt, but it was only in the southern sector that Soviet shelling almost ceased and the defenders were able to readjust the battle line at some points. On 21 January, when the relief spearheads were within 35 kilometers from Buda, the IX SS Mountain Army Corps relocated the Dörner Combat Group (13th Panzer Division)—the only reserve unit of the defense—from Pest to the southwestern section of the front. According to the corps command's plans, the forces concentrated in south Buda were to recapture the Budaörs airfield as soon as preparations were completed, in order to establish an air bridge for supplies and care of the wounded. The three assault guns of the Hungarian 1st Assault Division were to break through first, followed by mine-clearing patrols and the Dörner Group. The entire reserves of the defense amounted to 800 infantry, 20 to 25 tanks, some 30 armored personnel carriers, and about 12 guns. The Soviet command, expecting relief attempts, had deployed the 1st Mechanized Guard Corps southwest of Buda and placed it under the command of the 4th Guard Army.

In north Buda, beginning on 20 December the main defense line ran from the Óbuda end of Árpád Bridge through the Kiscell quarter, Mátyás-hegy Hill, and the Csatárka quarter to upper Bimbó Road. From there on, the positions on the northeastern slopes overlooking Pasarét remained unchanged for a long time.

On 21 January the Vannay Battalion, backed up by Tibor Rátz's two Zrínyi assault guns, recaptured Városmajor Grange. The battalion paid dearly for this success, however, with 68 dead or missing and many wounded, including the dispatch runner Ervin Galántay, aged 14, who was shot through the neck. The Europa Flying Squad Battalion, reinforced with university students, suffered similar casualties: although it destroyed a Soviet flamethrowing tank and retook some buildings between Bimbó Road and Olasz Avenue—not least the villa used as headquarters by the Gestapo—54 German and 13 Hungarian soldiers were killed.

South of János Hospital, between the embankment of the Cogwheel Railway and Farkasrét Cemetery, the positions of the opposing forces in the detached houses and gardens of Istenhegy, Orbánhegy, and Mártonhegy Hills remained static. Resistance developed mainly between Farkasrét Cemetery, Sashegy Hill, Károly király Barracks, Bocskai Road, and the Lágymányos railway embankment as far as the ruins of the southern railway bridge. The bare summit of Kis-Sváb-hegy Hill became a no-man's land 400 meters across. Between Sashegy Hill and Farkasrét Cemetery the German front line lay in Hermánd Street.

On 22 January, Soviet troops began to remove the road blocks erected in the northwestern and central sections of the Buda front, which suggested that they were no longer expecting a break-out in response to the relief attempts. At the same time, reinforced with some units transferred from Pest, they renewed their attacks along the entire bridgehead. The Soviet supreme command was dissatis-

fied with the progress of the 46th Army, which in 20 days had occupied only 114 of Buda's 722 blocks.

The front in Óbuda and on Ferenc-hegy Hill livened up.
Rózsadomb Hill came under unceasing mortar and gun bombardment, and Soviet troops from Látó-hegy Hill achieved a 100-meter
breakthrough in Csatárka Street, where Sergeant Alexei Isaev died
after throwing himself in front of a machine gun that was holding
up the assault on a multistory building. In the more open spaces
between the villas, however, the attack stalled, and both sides were
able to carry out local strikes and counterstrikes in the fog. A report
of the German IX Mountain Army Corps reads: "Enemy incursions
crushed or cut off in uncommonly violent encounters. Some
encounters still in progress. Own and enemy losses high." In the
heavy fighting Lieutenant-General Afonyin, the commander of
the Soviet Budapest Group, was hit by 18 pieces of shrapnel and
replaced with Lieutenant-General Ivan M. Managorov, the commander of the 53rd Army.

26

Lieutenant-General Ivan Managorov (in major-general's uniform), commander
of the Soviet 53rd Army and subsequently of the "Budapest group"

By this time the Danube was almost completely frozen over. In the night, after hiding for five days, two German soldiers made their way to Buda across the ice near the Chain Bridge. Their example was followed, in the opposite direction, by some members of the Hungarian 1st Armored Division, mainly Transylvanian Romanians and Gypsies drafted from the division's baking company as replacements for the defense of the Buda bank.

Still on 22 January, at about 8 P.M., the seven-story Regent Building at the corner of Margit Boulevard and Mechwart Square, in whose courtyard the Germans stored large quantities of ammunition, blew up. In the supposedly bombproof air-raid shelter 300 bodies remained buried for months under the rubble.

On 23 January there was relatively little change, as the IX SS Mountain Army Corps's report indicates: "In 20 desperate raids the enemy, in company-to-battalion strength, supported by extremely intensive artillery, mortar, and antitank fire and by waves of fighter aircraft, tried to break through the front in the northwest

27
Margit Boulevard

and north today. Apart from two enemy salients, which are still the object of fierce fighting, the front line has remained firmly in our hands." However, this could not disguise the fact that the defenders' strength was rapidly declining; the losses could not be replaced.

On 24 January most of the previous day's breaches were sealed off, but according to the IX SS Mountain Army Corps, fighting continued for "every inch of ground" at Vérhalom Square and Kis-Sváb-hegy Hill, and between Sashegy Hill and the Danube: without reinforcements it would be "impossible to hold the front." Even closer to central Buda, preparations for a Soviet attack near Széna Square were observed by the Hungarian 12th Reserve Division.

During the night of 25 January the Soviets launched an assault on the Vannay Battalion's positions in Városmajor Grange. They crossed the embankment of the Cogwheel Railway and occupied the western section of the grange, but their advance was stopped by the University Assault Battalion and the 6/III Battalion in Csaba Street, Bíró Street, and Szamos Street. The defenders near Kis-Sváb-hegy Hill also came under heavy pressure.

In the southern sector, Soviet troops captured a large part of the uniform factory in Daróczi Road near the Lágymányos railway embankment. The Hungarian 1st Assault Artillery Detachment and German infantry, suffering heavy losses, tried all day to liberate the building and the soldiers trapped on its upper floor. Meanwhile Soviet soldiers with flamethrowers, forcing their way into the houses on the south side of Hermánd Street, began to encircle Sashegy Hill from the west.

On 26 January the Soviet attack that had started at Látó-hegy Hill some days before gained an increasing amount of ground along Törökvész Road. As the German and Hungarian units were completely exhausted, the defense suddenly collapsed, and total disaster was averted only because the Soviets had also sustained heavy losses. At dawn Soviet units reached the Vérhalom quarter, by which time the University Assault Battalion had lost 70 percent of its strength. In the evening fighting spread as far as the Rézmál quarter.

At the command post of the University Assault Battalion in a school in Áldás Street an exploding gasoline drum gravely wounded Captain Lajos Sipeki Balás. He was replaced by Captain Tibor Mikulich and subsequently by Gendarmerie Captain Zsombor Nagy. By then most of the students were not fit for action: those still alive were laid up in atrocious conditions in various emergency hospitals, and burying the dead was difficult because the ground was frozen. Some of the wounded had been dumped in the corridors of the command post, as Private Dénes Vass remembers:

> I stumbled unsteadily through the ruins of Áldás Street toward the commander's room to deliver the evening report. In the partly cleaned corridor only a half-meter-wide strip was free for walking. On both sides civilian and military wounded were lying on the bare floor. Somebody caught my coat. It was a girl of about 18 or 20 with fair hair and a beautiful face. She begged me in a whisper: "Take your pistol and shoot me." I looked at her more closely and realized with horror . . . both her legs were missing.

Soviet assault groups recaptured most of Városmajor Grange. The command of the Hungarian I Army Corps ordered the Szabados Group to relieve the students, but because of the rapidly worsening situation both units were obliged to continue the fight side by side. The Szabados Group, which consisted of some 300 members of the Hungarian 10th Infantry Division's supply units, had really been created to justify the existence of the divisional command and to divert attention from the fact that by late January between 1,500 and 2,000 members of the division had never seen battle. Soviet rifle units, advancing from the Törökvész and Vérhalom areas, reached the fork of Fillér Street and Hankóczy Jenő Street northeast of the grange.

In north Buda, the Soviet thrust continued toward Szemlőhegy Hill, Szépvölgyi Road, and Vérhalom Square. During the night Soviet infantry and 20 tanks also attacked south of Svábhegy Hill.

On Vérmező Meadow, members of the Budapest branch of the Deutsche Jugend (German Youth) organization aged between

13 and 16, who had been directing the gliders to the landing strip with flashlights, came under fire from the light weapons of Soviet troops in the adjoining streets. This ended the systematic delivery of supplies to the defenders, although some gliders managed to land in the southern and central sections of the meadow, which still remained outside the Soviets' range.

In Daróczi Road the Germans, assisted by the Hungarian 1st and 10th Assault Artillery Battalions, at last ejected the Soviet assault group from the uniform factory. Captain Sándor Hanák recalls:

> We rolled up with two automatic flamethrower guns and four or five assault guns. I saw the politruks [political commissars] driving their soldiers forward with submachine guns. The Russkis were jumping out near the corner of the fence. Our flamethrower licked over them three times, and then I had a fragmentation shell lobbed into them. When the smoke cleared I saw them still jumping out of that hole. Obviously they were being prodded from behind.

The trapped German and Hungarian soldiers were liberated, but the factory was soon retaken by the Soviets.

Meanwhile, south of the Buda end of Erzsébet Bridge an attack by Soviet infantry across the Danube was foiled by the defenders' fire.

In the evening, Pfeffer-Wildenbruch, after receiving news of the failure of the third relief attempt, called a war council. Colonel-General Schmidhuber and some other officers submitted a break-out proposal, which he rejected, arguing that the Führer's orders had to be awaited. The officers' response has been described by one of those present: "Leaving the room after the meeting, several commanders openly speak about Hitler's pig-headedness. Even some of the SS are beginning to doubt his qualities as a leader. One of them noisily strides out of the room saying in a loud voice, for all to hear: 'Now I know that our men are meant to be sent to the slaughter in Budapest.'" On 27 January, after the failure of SS Obergruppenführer Gille's final relief attempt, Hitler personally

28

View of Buda from the Chain Bridge, February 1945

cabled that Budapest must be held until relieved. The German Army Group South, regarding a break-out as hopeless, had written Budapest off by this time.

Soviet units overran the defense positions on Orbánhegy Hill, and in a surprise attack captured Kis-Sváb-hegy Hill through the underground passages in its northwestern slope. Having thus removed the last obstacle to their advance, they established a salient from Kis-Sváb-hegy Hill to within 150 meters east of Vérmező Meadow. A German report reads:

> The situation there has become extremely serious. The IX SS Mountain Army Corps with its currently engaged forces will not be able to stop a strong enemy thrust across the meadow toward the Danube. To prevent the defense forces splintering, it will be necessary for the northern front to be pulled back to a substantially reduced battle line during the night of 28–29 January.

Opportunities for the deployment of armored units in house-to-house and street fighting are limited. Drivers and panzer grenadiers are fighting on foot. Our own losses are extremely heavy. The number of wounded exceeds those fighting. If Vérmező Meadow, the last possible landing ground for gliders, is lost, the supply prospects are frightening. The plight of the wounded is shocking.

Pushing ahead from Kis-Sváb-hegy Hill, the Soviet units then forced the defenders still holding out in Városmajor Street and Városmajor Grange to retreat to the Déli Station and Kékgolyó Street area.

In north Buda, the German Feldherrnhalle Division and 13th Panzer Division, with the Hungarian combat groups attached to them, withdrew to Újlak Church. Soviet troops advancing from the west, encountering no significant resistance, reached the western edge of Marcibányi Square.

On 28 January the Germans continued their rearguard actions near Zsigmond Square and at the foot of Rózsadomb Hill. The Szabados Group and units of the Hungarian 10th Infantry Division that had provided cover so far began their withdrawal toward Margit Boulevard. Soviet troops, continuing their push from Kis-Sváb-hegy Hill, reached Kékgolyó Street. At 11 P.M. a counterattack led by the command of the Hungarian 12th Reserve Division failed to repulse them.

On 29 January the Hungarian 10th Infantry Division, with the Szabados and Billnitzer Groups, launched a two-pronged counter-attack from Kékgolyó Street and Istenhegyi Road to try and recapture Kis-Sváb-hegy Hill and Városmajor Grange. The Szabados Group was reinforced with 200 high school pupils, who had been armed only two days earlier; 50 bus and streetcar conductors from the Vannay Group; and 30 to 40 members of the Prónay Group, who had been caught hiding. The operation, supported by the assault guns of the 13th Panzer Division, stalled in Kis-Sváb-hegyi Road because the untrained Hungarians had sustained enormous casualties and run out of ammunition. A patched-up gendarmerie battalion attacked in the same direction and after some initial successes suffered the same fate.

It became clear that the Soviets intended to cut the bridge-head in two and encircle the German and Hungarian units still resisting on Mátyás-hegy Hill. The command of the IX SS Mountain Army Corps cabled in despair: "In order to prevent the bridge-head being split, during the night of 29–30 January the corps will move to a new battle line in the northwest and north close to Castle Hill. This is the final position. . . . Supply situation terrible. If the IV SS Panzer Corps does not arrive in the shortest possible time it will be too late. We have reached the end." As a last resort, a 200-strong scratch unit of artillery-measuring squads, baggage-train crews, signalers, and engineers was drafted into the Hungarian 10th Infantry Division to protect the remnants of some hidden formations which still existed in practice, if no longer on paper. Late in the evening, the command of the Hungarian I Army Corps, with the Germans' permission, ordered the retreat to Margit Boulevard.

On 30 January, at daybreak, the Germans and Hungarians withdrew from southern Margit Island. Pfeffer-Wildenbruch placed the commander of the 13th Panzer Division, Colonel-General Schmidhuber, in charge of the southern section of Buda and detailed the remaining units to the foot of Gellért-hegy Hill. By that time Schmidhuber had begun to contemplate organizing an independent break-out, although he knew that his chances of getting through were minimal. His initiative was foiled by the arrival the next evening of the corps command's instructions to relocate immediately to the north.

Later on 30 January the Soviet onslaught reached Széll Kálmán Square. In Városmajor Grange the defense collapsed, and only a few dogged groups continued to hold some buildings nearby. The first Soviet T-34 tank arrived from Retek Street and, sweeping a damaged antitank barrier out of its way, reached the corner of Széna Square. Artillery men of the Hungarian 12th Reserve Division stationed in the square propped up their howitzers with ammunition crates so that they could fire horizontally, and their first shot blew up the T-34. However, a second Soviet tank emerged and crushed them, together with their howitzers. In Retek Street the defenders damaged two more Soviet tanks in close-quarter fighting, but this did little to change the situation. From the northern side of Széna Square the Soviets opened fire on the Post Office Palace, the defenders' last important base before Castle Hill.

In Németvölgyi Road some Hungarian police and gendarmerie units surrendered. The remnants of the Hungarian 10th Infantry Division were transferred to Fő Street, although the majority of its baggage and administrative staff, some 900 men, remained on Rózsadomb Hill and was captured with the division's food and other supplies. The front line stabilized in Margit Boulevard, which was sealed off by the Billnitzer Group jointly with the residue of retreating combat units and Hungarian technical personnel. Pfeffer-Wildenbruch cabled:

> The battle of Castle Hill has begun. . . . Forming a main battle line in the jumble of houses on Castle Hill is an illusion. The deployment on the front of much greater forces than so far is necessary. . . . All day there have been extremely heavy air attacks on the Castle and the fighting troops. The supply situation of the troops is catastrophic, as already reported in detail. The plight of 300,000 Hungarian inhabitants cooped up in the smallest possible space is terrible. No building is intact. Losses due to enemy action are enormous. There is starvation and risk of diseases.

Soviet troops reached the western edge of Vérmező Meadow at the level of Bors Street and, storming across the open space, captured the school in Béla király Road and a base of the Budapest Flying Squad Battalion, whose members had been kept in reserve for the defense of the Castle District. With some German and Hungarian units keeping up their stubborn defense of the remaining buildings on the northern side of the meadow, the Soviets came under fire from two directions as they continued their attack toward the Castle District. Nor did their infantry weapons suffice to prevent four supply gliders landing after dark with the help of theater spotlights in the meadow's northern section.

On 31 January the fighting farther north abated and the front line solidified, for the duration of the siege, on Margit Boulevard. The Soviets raided 10 to 12 student volunteers inside the Átrium cinema and ejected them after a hand grenade battle in the dark auditorium. German troops converted the corner block near the Buda end of the Chain Bridge into a fortress, distributing sandbags and machine guns in the apartments. The Hungarian Berend Group and 201/I Antiaircraft Battery repulsed the Soviet troops that had infiltrated the northern slope of Sashegy Hill. Low-flying Soviet heavy bombers and fighter bombers relentlessly attacked the Castle District, and one building after another collapsed. Soldiers and civilians were ordered out of their houses to erect barricades in the streets leading to Castle Hill. The commander of the Hungarian antiaircraft artillery signaled: "Castle and Krisztina Boulevard in ruins. Zero fighter aircraft defense. Antiaircraft battalion engaged in infantry action. Enemy pressure heavy and overpowering. Troops tired to exhaustion. Food supplies short. Artillery equipment: 22 guns and 29 automatic guns."

On 1 February the main defense line ran from the Buda end of Margit Bridge, along Margit Boulevard to Széll Kálmán Square, and from there over a short stretch of Krisztina Boulevard at the northern corner of Vérmező Meadow to the junction of Kékgolyó Street, where the Soviets were directly threatening Déli Station. Between the station and Széll Kálmán Square the situation was confused: the Post Office Palace and the southern blocks of Krisztina Boulevard were in German hands, while two buildings at the northern edge of Vérmező Meadow were held by Soviet troops. Between Kékgolyó Street and Sashegy Hill the situation was even more chaotic. Here the main defense line bulged west, where the Germans were clinging to Farkasrét Cemetery, the streets at the eastern foot of Orbánhegy Hill (particularly Mártonhegyi Road), and Istenhegyi Road. Meanwhile the Soviets had reached Wolff Károly Street opposite the main entrance to Farkasrét Cemetery. The battle line became more coherent from

Sashegy Hill to Bocskai Road, Karolina Road, and Hamzsabégi Road.

On the same day the focus of Soviet attacks shifted to southwest Buda. There was heavy fighting in Budaörsi Road, where Soviet infantry with tank support broke into the German positions and began to threaten Sashegy Hill from the south. Elsewhere, two Soviet reconnaissance patrols advancing across the ice on the Danube were pushed back. Hindy reported to the Hungarian Ministry of Defense: "Supply situation intolerable. Menu for the next five days per head and day: five grams lard, one slice of bread, and horse meat. . . . Lice infestation of the troops constantly increasing, in particular among the wounded crammed into the tight caves. Already six cases of typhus."

A scratch unit of assorted defenders launched an attack from Orbánhegy Hill toward Kis-Sváb-hegy Hill in order to divert the Soviet threat from Vérmező Meadow, but within half an hour the action came to a bloody end. The defense line could be stabilized only from Istenhegyi Road to Királyhágó Square.

On 2 February the Germans, suffering many casualties in house-to-house fighting in Mártonhegyi Road and the lower section of Istenhegyi Road, retreated about 1 kilometer and were able to slow down the Soviet advance only through a number of holding actions along the disjointed battle line. Hungarian troops recaptured the primary school at the corner of Vérmező Meadow and Béla király Road. There was heavy fighting for the German school in the middle section of Krisztina Boulevard. According to a report of the Hungarian I Army Corps, "the Soviets made a small dent between Kis-Sváb-hegy Hill and Farkasrét Cemetery, and by evening the situation was not yet resolved. The enemy group attacking on Sashegy Hill broke into the German positions, but a Hungarian counterattack restored the old battle line." A determined platoon, led by Pioneer Lieutenant László Benkő, slipped through the battle line across Széll Kálmán Square and wiped out the Soviet battalion command billeted in the school in Városmajor Street.

On 3 February, Papal Nuncio Angelo Rotta, representing the Budapest diplomatic corps, visited Pfeffer-Wildenbruch in his bunker and asked him to urge the German supreme command to end the suffering and prevent the ultimate destruction of the civilian population. Pfeffer-Wildenbruch, realizing that the end was only days away, informed the Wehrmacht headquarters in Germany of the nuncio's intervention, inquiring whether there were still plans for the relief of Budapest and hoping to receive permission to break out. The reply was that the Führer's orders remained unchanged and Budapest must be held to the bitter end.

Fierce engagements were in progress for Sashegy Hill, and house-to-house fighting raged in Hegytető Street. Soviet troops attacking from Orbánhegy Hill reached Némavölgyi Road.

In the evening Hindy held a meeting in his bunker, attended by the few senior commanders who could be reached. All realized that defeat was likely in a matter of hours. Staff Captains Dezső Németh and Frigyes Wáczek, stressing the hopelessness of the military situation and the plight of the civilians, tried to persuade their colleagues to capitulate unilaterally. Hindy helplessly explained that he could do nothing: without the cooperation of the Germans he would not even be able to convey his commands to his units, and Pfeffer-Wildenbruch would ignore a unilateral surrender.

On 4 February, Soviet troops from Orbánhegy Hill reached Némavölgyi Road and continued their attack toward Déli Station. This marked the beginning of the encirclement of Sashegy Hill from the north. Pfeffer-Wildenbruch radioed to his superiors that he was unable to hold out and that the defense could collapse at any moment. Deliberately avoiding the word "break-out," he requested permission to "take whatever tactical step" was necessary, but permission was refused.

On 5 February the last gliders landed on Vérmező Meadow. Two touched down unscathed, three broke up in the southern part of the meadow, the sixth fell on the ruins of a restaurant, and the seventh crashed into the attic of 31 Attila Road. Paradoxically, this proved to be the most successful day for the defenders' air forces: 97 tons of ammunition, 10 tons of fuel, 28 tons of food, and four engine-oil drums and spare-part crates reached their destinations.

Soviet antitank units destroyed two German tanks and antitank guns in Királyhágó Square, and occupied the buildings to the south,

29
Crashed German gliders on Vérmező Meadow

north, and west. In the evening the 16th SS Cavalry Regiment gave
up its base at the corner of Németvölgyi Road and Farkasrét Cemetery, and Soviet troops reached the junction of Gömbös Gyula Road
and Wolff Károly Street about one kilometer east. With Sashegy Hill
essentially encircled, the annihilation of the German unit trapped in
Farkasrét Cemetery and the storm on Kis-Gellért-hegy Hill and
Déli Station began. Hungarian volunteers counterattacking in
Karolina Road suffered great losses. The Soviets took the gendarmerie barracks in Böszörményi Road and established a small
salient in Budaörsi Road. As Soviet troops had broken through to
Krisztina Boulevard near the northern corner of Vérmező Meadow,
the defenders were no longer able to hold the Post Office Palace.
They evacuated the building through an emergency exit from the
air-raid shelter, which resulted in more casualties.

Pfeffer-Wildenbruch once more requested permission to
break out, failing which the defenders would be annihilated within
days and unable to tie down the Soviet forces any longer. Even now

he dared only to make a feeble blackmail attempt by declaring that the garrison would be lost unless approval arrived by next day. Hitler again refused because prolonging the siege by a few days was obviously worth more to him than the possible success of a break-out, which would at best have meant the survival of a few thousand men, unarmed and in need of immediate hospital treatment. Since the beginning of January, the German supreme command, having written off Budapest, was interested only in deriving maximum profit from the doomed defenders. In fact, Hitler had already decided to withdraw his last effective force, the 6th SS Panzer Army, from the Ardennes and to deploy it in Hungary in an attempt to regain the initiative, regardless of what happened to the capital. Thus the defenders' endurance could only help him gain time. To make the situation even more grotesque, the Soviet tanks were only 60 kilometers from Berlin by then.

On 6 February fighting was fiercest near Déli Station and in Hegyalja Road, where the Soviet combat units included groups of officers equipped with flamethrowers. Some 20 members of the Németvölgy Arrow Cross combat group were taken prisoner and executed near Németvölgy Cemetery. A counterattack launched by the 8th SS Cavalry Division from the southeast and northwest toward Sashegy Hill was checked by strong Soviet opposition. Soviet troops attacking from Kis-Sváb-hegy Hill captured the military hospital in Királyhágó Street, while others, attacking from the west and south, drove the German defenders out of Németvölgy Cemetery. The IX SS Mountain Army Corps signaled in despair: "Given our tremendous losses and their superior equipment it will not be possible to stop the enemy in the confusing urban terrain, where whole battalions are required for the defense of small streets. All our positions have been overrun, with the exception of one artillery defense position in the process of development." On Sashegy Hill the Berend Group, with no food and ammunition left, abandoned the battle. Fighting was so fierce that in one detachment that had originally numbered 38 only 7 were still alive when the detachment surrendered. On the same day Soviet artillery began to bombard the battery positions securing the link between the defenses of Gellért-hegy Hill and Castle Hill.

On 7 February, Soviet infantry and tanks penetrated the northern and western parts of Déli Station. Farther south they reached Gömbös Gyula Road, where some buildings changed hands several times in heavy fighting. Of a volunteer detachment of 32 men engaged in Márvány Street, 30 had been killed or wounded by evening. At Villányi and Bocskai Roads the defenders succeeded in repulsing most of the Soviet advances, and from Sashegy Hill a German group of company strength fought its way back to the German defense lines. From the Post Office Palace a group of Soviet soldiers and Hungarian volunteers fighting on the Soviet side attempted an attack toward Kékgolyó Street, which foundered under intensive German fire. The last German machine-gun positions in Farkasrét Cemetery were wiped out.

During the night the Germans tried to recapture Déli Station but succeeded only in occupying its western part. A German group managed to hold a building on the corner of Krisztina Boulevard and Városmajor Street and, with its last operational tank, to foil a Soviet attack from the Post Office Palace toward the Castle District. On the northern front ferocious fighting had raged all day around a breach made by Soviet tanks with flamethrower backing, but the attackers were ultimately unable to pierce the defense positions in Margit Boulevard.

On 8th February Soviet units from Németvölgy Cemetery reached Avar Street parallel to the southern railway line. The Soviet attack from Sashegy Hill advanced to Kis-Gellért-hegy Hill. A Hungarian group reoccupied a large part of the Post Office Palace. In the night a small platoon of the Hungarian 102nd Horse-Drawn Chemical Warfare Battalion, led by Ensign Norbert Major, rescued a German detachment trapped on the upper floor of a building at the corner of Krisztina Boulevard and Városmajor Street. The Hungarians sprinted across Vérmező Meadow, burst into the building, and led those Germans still able to run back to Attila Road. Airborne supplies, weighing four tons, landed by parachute for the last time.

The IX SS Mountain Army Corps pulled the battle line back to the eastern edge of Vérmező Meadow and evacuated most of Déli Station. This time it was the commander of the German Army

Group South, Erich von Manstein, who requested Hitler's permission for a break-out, as the makeshift military hospitals in the cellars of the Castle, where the wounded were kept in appalling conditions, had reached their maximum capacity despite the growing number of deaths. When permission was again refused, the IX Mountain Army Corps began to concentrate the remnants of its units in the Castle District.

Colonel Lajos Lehoczky, the last commander of the Hungarian 10th Infantry Division, made the final entry in the division's war diary, providing a fine sample of military officialese:

> I orally reported to the Corps Commander and the Commander of the 13th Panzer Division (Colonel-General Schmidhuber) the following:
>
> In the name of martial honor I request that measures be taken, in agreement with the commander of the German Army Corps, to terminate the fighting when food or ammunition supplies are exhausted and the soldiers' nourishment becomes so inadequate (horse meat, lack of bread) as to reduce their combat value to such an extent that defection to the enemy, desertion, or robberies must be expected; nor is the possibility of the ranks turning against their superiors to be ruled out. . . . The sufferings and deprivations of the civilian population are even greater than those of the garrison and from this moment the historical responsibility will rest with the commander of the Hungarian army corps, Colonel-General Hindy. I also request that the other Hungarian corps commanders be heard.
>
> I can see no other way out of the conclusive and catastrophic disintegration than the issuing of a general order for the unified cessation of hostilities.

He then took his leave from his fellow officers and retired into the bunker.

On 9 February the German positions on Kis-Gellért-hegy Hill came under relentless Soviet drumfire. The freshly deployed Soviet 25th Guard Rifle Division and several Hungarian volunteer

30

The tunnel used as the defenders' headquarters, with a German dispatch runner
mounting his motorcycle, February 1945

companies that had changed sides advanced, backed by tanks, from
Sashegy Hill toward the Citadel. In the German battery positions
on Kis-Gellért-hegy Hill there was hand-to-hand fighting: 50 percent of the defenders' guns were destroyed on this day alone.

A small Soviet assault group from Krisztina Boulevard recaptured the school in Attila Road, making a breach in the defense system of Castle Hill. Another group, with flamethrowers, installed
itself in a house farther along Attila Road but was pulverized by the
university students with an antitank gun. From the school, 20
Hungarian volunteers who had defected to the enemy tried to
enter the neighboring building. Their commander remembers:

> Our next objective was to capture the second floor. . . .
> When we reached the bend in the staircase, a mass of
> hand grenades was thrown at us. We delivered a volley

but were thrown all over the stairs by the shock waves. There were many wounded, but we couldn't tell who and how, because the Germans had started a counterattack. . . . The walls crumbled, the ceiling fell in, there were moaning wounded and dead everywhere. Those who could would have taken cover, but there was nowhere to go. So we were shooting, and they were shooting. Soon, I don't know how much time had passed, none of us was unscathed. . . . There were broken heads and everyone bloody all over. With nobody left whole, there was nothing to be done, so I gave orders to retreat. The more gravely wounded were carried by the less. Climbing back down the ladder or jumping into the deep yard, dragging our wounded with us, we withdrew to our starting point. Meanwhile the Germans were firing at us from all sides. Three of us reached the school, the rest couldn't make it and perished.

By evening Kis-Gellért-hegy Hill had fallen. Déli Station was entirely in Soviet hands. Soviet troops and Hungarian volunteers were fighting their way from room to room in Avar Street, but their attempt to break through to Naphegy Hill failed, and between 40 and 50 volunteers lost their lives. The front line now ran along Karácsonyi Street, Győző Street, the upper reaches of Mészáros Street, Hegyalja Road, and Alsóhegy Street. Between Lágymányos railway embankment and Villányi Road the situation was chaotic: some units were trapped, while others were struggling along Karolina Road and Bocskai Road with the Soviet units pushing toward Lenke Square.

On 10 February, Soviet armored spearheads from Kis-Gellért-hegy Hill reached Döbrentei Square and began to threaten communications between the citadel, the Lágymányos quarter, and the Castle District. Parts of a Soviet battalion consisting of degraded officers reached the Danube near Erzsébet Bridge but were wiped out in a counterattack by the Schöning Group. Fighting was particularly bitter in the upper section of Kelenhegyi Road, where many Hungarian volunteers fighting on the Soviet side, who tried to storm the citadel, were killed by the Germans. Soviet troops with flamethrowers crossed Vérmező Meadow and occupied a building in the southern part of Logodi Street, which, however, was retaken by five members of the University Assault Battalion in a violent gun battle. Private Péter Noel's combat group attacked the school in Attila Road: "We went into action before sunrise. We surprised the Russians by blowing up one of the windowless walls and retook the building in ten minutes without any casualties."

During the night Soviet troops and two Hungarian volunteer companies attacked the Lágymányos defense sector. One of the volunteers, Private János Szekeres, recalls: "Here and there one of our men appeared, wounded. I was carrying the red parachute silk, because whenever a Hungarian soldier joined us we cut a ribbon for his cap from that material. The thin layer of snow on the ground smelled of gasoline and gunpowder. Burned human bodies lay beside the wrecked tanks. The Soviet soldiers softened up the territory in front of us with shells." Jenő Sulyánsky, a cadet aged 15, remembers: "During the night and morning a huge battle raged, particularly near Lenke Square. Burned-out tanks, trucks, bodies everywhere. Our battery was completely scattered. . . . Not far from us, in Horthy Miklós Road, a retreating German military truck had received a direct hit and was on fire. In and around it were bodies of German soldiers, partly or entirely charred."

On 11 February, early in the morning, the first Soviet advance guards were approaching the Gellért Hotel at the Danube end of Horthy Miklós Road. The command of the Hungarian 10th Infantry Division, billeted at 16 Horthy Miklós Road, had by then collected all weapons, and large numbers of Hungarian soldiers were crawling out of the cellars to stagger toward Budafok and be taken prisoner.

Later in the morning, the defenders along the Lágymányos railway embankment raised the white flag on the order of Major Gyula Viharos. South of Gellért-hegy Hill resistance was sporadic, and the majority of Germans withdrew to the Castle District. In the XI District the arms were almost silent by midday, although a Soviet jeep carelessly driven into Szent Imre Square was knocked out with a panzerfaust by a soldier apparently continuing a private war.

At the Gellért Hotel, Colonel József Kozma, the commander of the Hungarian antiaircraft artillery, explained to the staff of the Hungarian 102nd Antiaircraft Detachment that he regarded as pointless further resistance or a break-out attempt. At noon, after jointly disarming the majority of the Germans, the detachment raised the white flag on the building, and by evening any Germans refusing to surrender had been killed by Kozma's men and Soviet troops in hand-to-hand fighting in the underground passages. At 7 P.M. the Soviets also captured the emergency hospital in Sziklakápolna chapel. Resistance had ceased in the whole of Buda.

4

Relief Attempts

International historians generally regard the Battle of the Bulge as "Hitler's last offensive." This is wrong. Between 1 January and 15 March 1945, no fewer than five German offensives took place in Hungary—the destruction of the Garam Soviet bridgehead, the Frühlingserwachen (Spring Awakening) operation, and three attempts to relieve Budapest. The matériel thrown into these offensives and the size of the territory gained were at least of the same order as in the Ardennes offensive. As far as Hitler was concerned, by the end of 1944 Hungary had become the main theater of war, and the Wehrmacht deployed greater forces there than it had done anywhere else in an attempt to stabilize the situation.

The three major offensives designed to relieve encircled Budapest and recapture the eastern section of the Margit Line were intended, contrary to popular assumption, not to rescue the garrison but to move further forces to Hungary for Hitler's final stand. By February 1945 all available reserves—including almost half of all panzer divisions in the east—had been relocated to Hungary for this purpose, and Hitler was desperate to show some success as a result.

By now the oil fields of western Hungary were the German army's last remaining source of fuel, and this, together with the need to defend Vienna, greatly increased the importance of the Hungarian theater of war. Between autumn 1944 and April 1945—by which time the first Soviet tank was within 60 kilometers of Berlin—every briefing in the Führer's headquarters began with the

Hungarian operations. Gerhard Boldt, one of the adjutants, recalls a mistake he made in February while preparing the maps:

> [Colonel-General Heinz] Guderian began his comments on the Hungarian theater of war. In the middle of his first sentence he stopped to give me a black look. Hitler was staring up at me with an inscrutable expression before leaning back in his chair with a bored gesture. I hastily stammered something incoherent, wishing that the ground would open and swallow me up. The general-staff maps were piled up in front of Hitler exactly in reverse order, with Kurland top and Hungary bottom.

Hitler had insisted from the outset on holding Budapest and had forbidden any break-out attempt. On 24 December 1944, before the final closure of the encirclement, he had ordered the IV SS Panzer Corps and the 96th and 711th Infantry Divisions—some 200 tanks and 60,000 men—to Hungary and placed them under the command of SS Obergruppenführer Otto Gille, who had been highly decorated for breaking out of the encirclement of Cherkassy. Himmler cabled Gille that Hitler had chosen him because he had the most extensive experience of being encircled and because his corps had proved the best on the eastern front.

The cost of the relief attempts was soon to become manifest. The transfer of the IV SS Panzer Corps to Transdanubia deprived the Warsaw area of reserves, and on 12 January the Soviet offensive swept away the German front on the Vistula. The tanks of Marshals Georgi Konstantinovich Zhukov and Ivan Stepanovich Konev rolled on until they reached the Oder and even then stopped only because the Soviet command did not press the attacks any further.

The German Army Group South and Guderian disagreed about the use of the regrouped units, but there was a consensus that Budapest should be given up and the break-out approved as soon as possible. This suggestion was made to Hitler almost daily, but in vain.

The choice between two different relief routes was hard to make. An offensive from Székesfehérvár in the south (code-named

Paula), given the greater distance, would have required 900 cubic meters more fuel and delayed the arrival of the troops by five days. An offensive from the north (code-named Konrad) involved a shorter distance and offered the element of surprise but carried greater risks because of the terrain. Although Guderian preferred operation Paula, his representative, Colonel-General Walther Wenck, was persuaded by the reasoning of the German Army Group South, and the supreme command finally opted for the swifter operation Konrad.

The regrouped units began to move into Hungary on 28 December. Hoping that the Soviets had not yet built strong defense positions, the German command gave orders to attack before all the troops had arrived. At that time only 32 percent of the 5th SS Panzer Division (Wiking), 66 percent of the 3rd SS Panzer Division (Totenkopf or Death's Head), and 43 percent of the 96th Infantry Division were in place, and there was no sign of the 711th Infantry Division. The regrouping was not completed until 8 January. Guderian had arrived in Tata on 7 January to oversee the operation. Károly Beregfy, minister of defense in the Szálasi government, offered the participation of Hungarian troops. His forces, however—the 1st Hussar Division, the 2nd Armored Division, and the 23rd Reserve Division—were too exhausted to be used. Lieutenant-General Gyula Kovács, inspector general of the Honvéd army, was disappointed to find that Colonel-General Balck had no time to discuss the details of the entry parade into Budapest.

Operation Konrad I

On the evening of 1 January the IV SS Panzer Corps, only half of which had arrived at Komárom, launched a surprise attack in the Tata region, while the 96th Infantry Division, crossing the Danube from the north by assault boat, established two bridgeheads behind the Soviet troops. The two battalions of the Hungarian Ney SS Combat Group (later Brigade) were deployed for the first time, attached as antitank grenadiers to the Wiking and Totenkopf SS Panzer Divisions. The attackers captured the Gerecse Hills, but on 6 January the Soviets stopped their advance near Bicske and Zsámbék.

Two topographical factors weighed against the offensive: first, in the Gerecse and Pilis Hills it was easy for the Soviets to set up roadblocks with antitank guns; second, the long and narrow pocket that would have developed alongside the Danube after a break-through could have been cut off by the Soviets without much effort. In the event the Soviets were able to slow down the assault of the German tanks and ensure that their reserves had enough room to maneuver.

Between 26 and 31 December Tolbukhin and Malinovsky had placed the Soviet units that had so far played the key parts in reserve, leaving one armored corps, four mechanized corps, and three cavalry corps—with 500 to 600 tanks—at the front to fend off the German relief attempts. Some Soviet troops were relocated from other regions: for example, the 19th Rifle Division took up position at Adony on the Danube after covering a distance of 190 kilometers from the southern shore of Lake Balaton in a day and a half. Tolbukhin had kept so many of his units in reserve until the situation became critical because he had overestimated the strength of the Germans. As a result, his forces suffered great losses, but unlike the Germans, who had no reserves left, he had preserved his freedom of action. On New Year's Day 1945 the various Soviet units in the Carpathian Basin had about 2,130 tanks and assault guns at their disposal, compared with the German Army Group South's 1,050, more than half of which were under repair (Table 12).

On 2 January the Soviet 18th Tank Corps joined the battle, followed on 3 January by three other fast-moving units. The Bicske region was the prime target of the German offensive, and here the Wiking Division was confronted on 3 January by one heavy tank regiment, four assault-gun regiments, three rifle divisions, one mechanized brigade, and six technical battalions—two or three times the Germans' strength. The same happened else-where along the breadth of the German attack, where by 4 January the Soviet 1st Mechanized Guard Corps had also arrived from Adony. Thus no fewer than five Soviet mechanized, armored, or cavalry corps had lined up against the main thrust of the relief attempt, blocking any further advance toward Budapest. Only the group attacking in the north was able to capture Esztergom on

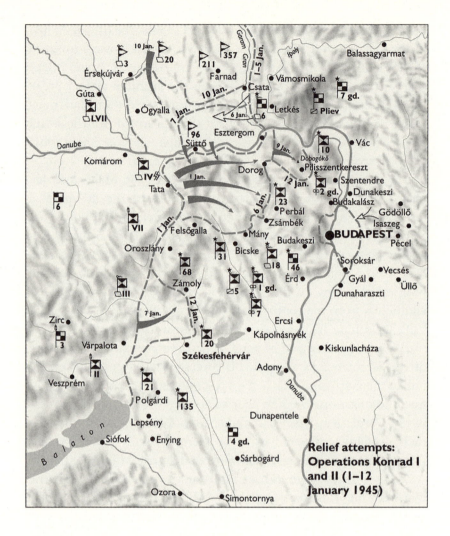

Relief attempts:
Operations Konrad I
and II (1–12
January 1945)

6 January and Pilisszentlélek on 8 January. The German and Hungarian losses between 1 and 7 January amounted to some 3,500—almost 10 percent of the IV SS Panzer Corps's strength—killed, wounded, or missing, and 39 tanks or assault guns destroyed.

Meanwhile, Tolbukhin had also made preparations to prevent a break-out from Budapest. He had erected defensive lines with antitank guns facing both the relief forces and the potential escapees, and on 3 January he ordered the cessation of attacks on Buda in order to release further forces. On 6 January seven divisions—roughly equal to the whole German and Hungarian garrison in the capital—stood in readiness between Zsámbék and Tinnye. In the event of a break-out the escapees would first have had to breach the encirclement ring round the city and then, after a long march, meet this formidable second formation. The chances of an organized break-out in any direction other than the north were therefore doubtful, and a break-out in the north could succeed only if the relief attempts in the Pilis Hills were not stopped, as they eventually were.

Guderian, unaware of the real situation, planned to include the defenders in the stalled offensive: in addition to holding the capital they were to launch an attack toward the northwest and assist the operations of the relief units. The army group, more realistically, recommended that they either abandon the eastern bridgehead on 9 January and break out northwest or, failing this, fight their way through the ring in separate small combat units. This too was rejected by Hitler.

Operation Konrad II

The setback to their northern offensive compelled the Germans to fall back on the southern option. The command of the German Army Group South decided to try to break through between Székesfehérvár and Mór with new forces (the Breith Group), the objective being not only to recapture the Margit Line but also to surround, jointly with the IV SS Panzer Corps, the Soviet units on the western slopes of the Vértes Hills. On 6 January the army group considered halting or scaling down the attack, but finally chose to go ahead on the assumption that with the newly arrived 20th Panzer Corps it would be able to hold the front. At the time of this operation, 116 tanks and assault guns, 116 guns, and a combat strength of 5,700 infantry on the German side faced approximately 70 tanks and assault guns, 260 guns, and 10,500 infantry on the Soviet side (Table 13).

Tolbukhin, aware of the German troop movements, reinforced the 20th Guard Rifle Corps in the main trajectory of the attack, which was unleashed on 7 January. The Soviets benefited from the fact that on the preceding day Malinovsky's 2nd and 3rd Ukrainian Fronts had in their turn launched an attack along the Garam River north of the Danube, so that the two enemies were moving in opposite directions on either side of the river. By 8 January, Malinovsky's units were within three kilometers of Komárom, heralding a major encirclement operation.

The attack of the Breith Group—the southern branch of Operation Konrad II—met fierce resistance, and ran out of steam as early as 9 January. On the same day the German 7th Mechanized Corps launched a strike to prevent a Soviet breakthrough, but in three days of fighting 57 of its 80 tanks were put out of action. With great losses on both sides, the Germans made no further progress, but their salients remained in place.

After their failure at Bicske, both the German Army Group South and Gille, still hoping to avoid any major relocation, made plans for the IV SS Panzer Corps to breach the Soviet defense near Esztergom and relieve Budapest across the Pilis Hills in what was to be the northern branch of Operation Konrad II. The increasingly ominous news from the capital made this appear even more urgent.

The new German attack was launched on 9 January from Esztergom, where 200 tons of supplies had been collected to be transported to Budapest immediately in the event of success. As a complementary measure, General Balck ordered a reinforced battalion under Major Philipp to smash through the Soviet obstacles near the Danube and occupy Szentendre as a refuge for the defenders after their escape. Everybody in the Wiking Division, however, including Gille and Philipp, considered the plan unworkable. As the division's staff officer put it, the Soviets were "hardly likely to open the shore road for jaunts." It is also difficult to see how Balck expected the defenders to continue their withdrawal along the road from Szentendre to Esztergom, which was within the range of the Soviet weapons across the Danube. Fortunately for the Germans, the question did not arise in practice, because the relief unit's advance soon stalled, although the 711th Infantry Division attacking southeast of it managed to capture Dobogókő.

On 10 January, with one day's delay because of Hitler's prohibition, the panzer group of the Wiking Division, including the Westland Panzer Grenadier Regiment, was deployed to fill the gap. The same staff officer writes: "Enemy weak, completely surprised. Difficult mountain terrain of pre-Alpine character. At midnight first reports of success, prisoners mainly baggage-train crews of divisions encircling Budapest. Antitank gun and mortar fire. No own losses. Westland making good progress."

By 11 January the Westland Regiment had occupied Pilisszentkereszt, 21 kilometers from Budapest. First to enter the village in his armored personnel carrier was SS Obersturmbannführer Franz Hack, who had been wounded twice during the preceding days and was awarded the Knight's Cross for the courage he had shown in this action. Many German vehicles and wounded prisoners were liberated after being held by Soviets in the village for two weeks. The German Army Group South again requested permission for a break-out, hoping to capture the airfield of Pomáz in order to remove the wounded and provide supplies for the spearheads expected from the capital.

By the evening of 12 January, the advance units of the Wiking Division had reached the Csobánka fork on the road to Pomáz, only 17 kilometers from Budapest, when they were ordered to withdraw, although no outflanking counterattack by Soviet tanks through the valleys was to be expected and Gille would have had no reason to fear that his units would be cut off in the Pilis Hills by the large Soviet force in their rear at Dorog—at least if the aim of the German offensive had been merely to rescue the defenders, rather than to relieve Budapest. The Soviet 5th Cavalry Corps between Szentendre and Pilisvörösvár, 15 kilometers from the city, would almost certainly have halted a further advance, but a coordinated break-out might still have been achieved as the short distance and the bad terrain considerably restricted the Soviets' ability to resist.

The Soviets actually hoped for a break-out. By this time the long duration of the siege had made Malinovsky nervous. He wanted the Germans to leave the capital as soon as possible, and in order to assist them, he had a one-kilometer gap in the Buda encirclement opened. His chief concern was the capture of Budapest, and to avert Stalin's anger over the delay he was prepared to spare the defenders. Ironically orders from Pfeffer-Wildenbruch and Hitler prevented a successful break-out.

From the outset Hitler and Guderian had not thought much of the chances of Operation Konrad II and had preferred an offensive from the Székesfehérvár region. On 10 January they had signaled to the German Army Group South that unless there was a radical change within hours, Gille's troops would be regrouped. On 11 January, at the request of the army group, Colonel-General Wenck had spent two hours trying to persuade Hitler to allow the break-out, but "all he achieved was the award of the Knight's Cross to SS Obergruppenführer Pfeffer-Wildenbruch." The general staff wondered whether by the end of the belated operation there would be anybody or anything to relieve, but Hitler persisted in his original plan and issued the order for Gille's forces to regroup immediately, even before their new offensive reached its full force.

A 24-hour tug-of-war began between Gille and the army supreme command. Hitler's order was delivered to Gille at 8:20 P.M. on 11 January. Three hours later Gille cabled that the offensive was making progress. Gille's superiors passed his cable to Hitler without comment. When Hitler repeated the order, Gille appealed to Himmler, but in vain. As his troops had shown no spectacular results since the capture of Pilisszentkereszt, he had lost his last trump card, and at 8 P.M. on 12 January he ordered the retreat. By the evening of 14 January the Soviets had reoccupied the Dobogókő area and Pilisszentkereszt.

The cessation of the offensive has provoked heated arguments in memoirs and historical studies. In the unanimous opinion of the combatants, Hitler's order deprived them of certain success. Several military historians argue, however, that the Soviets would have cut off the Germans if they had continued their advance. The debate is rooted in diametrically opposed interpretations of Hitler's objectives. Gille and his officers were convinced that the relief attempts were intended as a rescue mission. In their view, their offensive could have opened a corridor for the defenders to escape but could not have maintained a link over a longer period. Hitler and his generals, who were not sufficiently familiar with the situation, hoped that their limited forces would be able to restore the pre-Christmas status quo. For them, abandoning Budapest was out of the question.

By 1944–1945 there were fewer and fewer individuals in the top echelons of the Third Reich who could have confronted Hitler with the reality, and as a result more and more absurd operational objectives arose. The battles in Hungary from January to March 1945, in which new panzer units were continually being deployed while the strategic aims remained unchanged, reveal a total lack of coordination between different tactical assignments. Had these units been deployed simultaneously, their attacks would have had a real chance of success.

Time favored the Soviets, whose tanks had reached the edge of the Little Hungarian Plain on 8 January and were threatening Bratislava and Vienna. The German Army Group South would therefore have preferred to stop the relief attempts and regroup north of the Danube, which would necessarily have involved permission for the Budapest garrison to break out rather than being destroyed in a futile struggle. But Hitler preferred to gamble that the Soviet attack along the northern bank of the Danube would stall before Komárom. Events initially seemed to prove him right when the hastily regrouped tanks of the 20th Panzer Division pushed the 6th Armored Guard Army back almost 50 kilometers, but even when the Soviets launched their grand offensive of 12 January on the Polish front and no significant German forces were stationed between them and Berlin, Hitler stubbornly ignored the general staff's advice that the only possible way of preventing disaster at home was to immediately abandon the attempts to relieve Budapest and to regroup.

Operation Konrad III

On 18 January the IV SS Panzer Corps, whose relocation to the region between Lake Balaton and Székesfehérvár had been completed in utmost secrecy on the previous day, was thrown into battle. Tanks with infrared sights for nocturnal operations were used for the first time. On 18 January some 300 German tanks and assault guns faced 250 Soviet ones; by 27 January it was 250 German tanks and assault guns against 500 Soviet ones.

According to Soviet authors, "the reconnaissance section of the 4th Guard Army's staff did not have the situation under control"—in other words, the German offensive had taken the Soviet generals by surprise. Gille's tanks crushed the Soviet 7th Mechanized Corps's counterattack, separating the 133rd Rifle Corps and the 18th Tank Corps from their rear lines. Only the lack of German infantry enabled the encircled Soviet units to break out of the ring. On

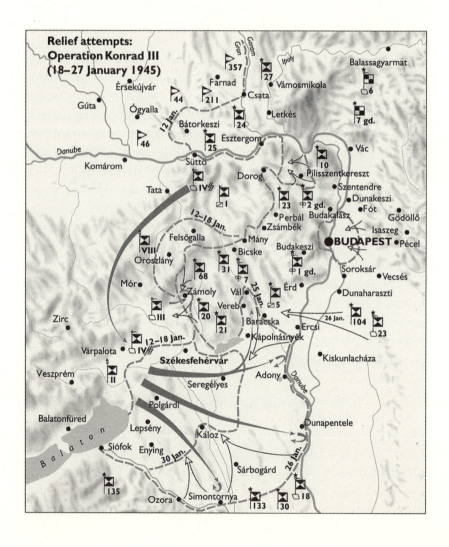

19 January the German tanks reached the Danube at Dunapentele, tearing the Soviet Transdanubian front apart. At the Danube crossings, in chaotic conditions, the Soviets moved more than 40,000 soldiers and large quantities of equipment to the east bank within a few days, although they were constantly being bombed by the Luftwaffe.

On 22 January the Soviets lost Székesfehérvár after heavy street fighting. First to enter the city was the Ney Combat Group, which had by then reached division strength, although one quarter of its members was dead, wounded, or missing. On 24 January the Totenkopf Division captured the southern section of Baracska 30 kilometers from Budapest. Tolbukhin's troops developed a firm defense along the Váli-viz River, whose icy banks the German tanks could scale only with great difficulty, but by 26 January the offensive had reached a point roughly 25 kilometers from the ring around the capital.

Toward the end of the war, Stalin was no longer inclined to take any major risks because he knew that his troops would soon be facing British and U.S. soldiers. Earlier his inflexible orders to persevere had sent millions into captivity or to death, but now he contemplated evacuating southern Transdanubia and gave Tolbukhin a free hand, even though the equipment and supplies of two armies would have had to be left behind.

On 21 January the nervous Soviet command had blown up its own pontoon bridges near Dunapentele and Dunaföldvár, halting supplies to the units still in action. Tolbukhin now chose a more courageous option: he decided to hold the bridgehead because he believed that it would be pointless to give up the occupied territories in the hope of a smooth second crossing of the Danube. On 27 January—having taken charge of the 104th Rifle Corps and the 23rd Tank Corps, which had been concentrated near south Buda to prevent a break-out, and the 30th Rifle Corps, which had been sent to southern Transdanubia as a reinforcement—he began a counterattack.

The German spearheads that had reached the Danube could at any time be cut off by Soviet divisions from Lake Velence in the north and Simontornya in the south. Recognizing this advantage, Tolbukhin attacked from both directions. Although the Germans destroyed 122 Soviet tanks on the first day, they had to abandon many of the occupied territories, with the notable exception of Székesfehérvár. Near the village of Vereb alone, the wrecks of 70 tanks and 35 assault guns bore witness to the heavy fighting. Eventually the relentlessly counterattacking Soviet forces invaded northern Székesfehérvár, and by the beginning of February the Germans were obliged to give up most of their territorial gains.

On 28 January, Hitler decided to send his last reserves— the 6th Panzer Army, in the process of replenishment after the Ardennes offensive—to Hungary to make one more relief attempt, code-named Frühlingserwachen (Spring Awakening). By 13 February, however, when this offensive began, there was nothing left to relieve because all of Buda was in Soviet hands.

5

The Break-Out

The Antecedents

I have nightmares every night because I am alive.
—Lieutenant-Colonel Helmut Wolff, one who got away

The break-out was one of the most horrific events not only of the battle for Budapest but of the Second World War as a whole. The annihilation of 75 percent of the first waves of U.S. troops landing on Omaha Beach during the invasion of Normandy is well known. The slaughter of the garrison trying to escape from the ruins of central Buda was even bloodier. In less than six hours several thousand men were killed over a three-kilometer section of the front line. Of some 28,000 less than 3 percent got through; 45 percent died, and the rest, many of them badly wounded, were captured. There had been hopeless operations bound to end in mass butchery elsewhere during the war, but in this case it all happened in the center of a city before the eyes of the civilian population. The older inhabitants of Budapest still have vivid memories of the horrors, and some of the surviving soldiers suffer from nightmares to this day.

The German command in Budapest had made repeated plans to break through the encirclement and abandon the city. This would have been possible either in early January or later in parallel with relief attempts, but Hitler persisted in refusing to give his permission. After the loss of Pest on 18 January, the "fortress" Buda could at best tie down some Russian troops, but the Führer nevertheless insisted on defending it. Pfeffer-Wildenbruch obeyed to the

31
Captain Helmut Friedrich, right, with the author

last moment. Rebuffing all Soviet attempts at negotiating, he resisted for seven weeks, until 11 February. By the time he decided to
break out it had become obvious that the few remaining parts of
Buda (the Castle District and Naphegy Hill) would be in Soviet
hands very shortly. His telegrams to the German Army Group
South are characteristic. Instead of using the word "break-out" he
only dared to write about "freedom of action."

It is by no means true that Pfeffer-Wildenbruch had no
other option. Many German, Hungarian, and Romanian commanders—notably Waffen SS Obergruppenführer Paul Hausser,
Major-General Zoltán Szügyi, and Marshal Ion Antonescu—had
had chosen to disobey orders and suffered no retributions. Between late December 1944 and mid-January 1945, Pfeffer-Wildenbruch had every chance of accomplishing a successful break-out,
but he was not willing to take a personal risk on behalf of his
subordinates until it was too late.

According to one school of thought it is a soldier's duty to
fight to the last bullet rather than try to survive. A much-cited

example is that of the French Imperial Guards in the battle of Waterloo, who refused to capitulate, despite their hopeless situation, as long as they were able to continue the struggle: this attitude became increasingly common among the German forces in the Second World War. Another approach is collective capitulation: in Budapest this would have required the German command either to take a stand against its own political system or to recognize that the situation was so hopeless that any further resistance would produce no worthwhile results and would be tantamount to helplessly submitting to slaughter. Although collective capitulation for the latter reason is legitimate in military terms, Pfeffer-Wildenbruch failed to choose this option, just as he failed to undertake an early break-out; thus he led his soldiers to their deaths.

Nor did the soldiers themselves dissent. During the whole war no German garrison surrendered to the Red Army when it had a chance of breaking out. The reason, in addition to the odium of surrender, was fear of the Soviets and of Siberia. The Germans fought to the last bullet not only out of a sense of duty and loyalty but also because, given the ideological nature of the war on the eastern front, they were afraid of what might happen to them if they surrendered or were taken prisoner. An eyewitness remembers the last hours in the Citadel:

> It was 10 February and the hill was covered in fog. A thin layer of snow had fallen, and I was shivering with the cold. The Germans were acting as if they were on an exercise. They were writing official notes and, in the rooms of the Citadel, commands brought by messengers kept everybody awake. Groups of German officers, in correct uniforms, were giving instructions to some German infantry units. They were directing the alignment of the machine guns, pointing out the enemy lines and issuing orders to fire. The men were lying in the snow and firing, with the officers standing next to them and paying no attention to the whistling bullets. It all seemed like a dream. When one officer fell, another took his place, apparently without realizing that this was the end.

Basically they were seeking death because they knew that for them there was no other solution.

It was only then that Pfeffer-Wildenbruch decided to act. With Hitler's prohibition in mind, he did not radio his intentions to the German Army Group South until the last moment, 5:50 P.M. on 11 February:

1. Our supplies are used up, the last cartridges in the barrel. In Budapest the garrison has only the choice between capitulating and being butchered without a struggle.
   I will therefore take offensive action with the last fit German troops, Honvéd soldiers, and Arrow Cross men (to secure a new combat and supply base).
2. Will break out on 11 February at nightfall. I request reception between Szomor and Máriahalom. If reception not possible, will push ahead to the Pilis Hills. Request reception there in the sector northwest of Pilisszentlélek.
3. Flares:
   Twice green: own troops etc.
4. Strengths:
   Germans 23,900, including 9,600 wounded
   Hungarians 20,000, including 2,000 wounded
   Civilians 80,000–100,000.

After transmitting these words, the radio operators began to destroy their equipment as ordered. The break-out was irreversible.

The defenders' heavy artillery, stationed between Gellért-hegy Hill and Castle Hill, had by then been lost or was engaged in close-quarter fighting. Of 120 armored vehicles and more than 450 guns originally at the defenders' disposal, only 12 Panther, nine Hetzer, and 10 to 15 unidentifiable tanks; 6 assault guns; 50 to 60 guns of various calibers; and an uncertain number of armored cars were fit for action. Most of these were blown up shortly before the break-out because they were stationed on Naphegy Hill and could not be relocated to the point of the planned break-out unnoticed.

A few tanks and armored personnel carriers stationed in the northern part of the Castle District, probably no more than 8 to 10, were spared contrary to orders so that they could be used in the break-out.

Strategic Plans and Ideas

On the morning of 11 February Pfeffer-Wildenbruch called a war council, which after a long debate decided to break out in small groups through the woods and to leave all heavy weapons behind. The use of tanks would in any case have presented problems, because road conditions would have made it difficult for them to reach the break-out point, and any significant movement, at least in daylight, would have betrayed the enterprise to the Soviets. The worst problem, however, was that in practically every street near Széll Kálmán Square and Széna Square the defenders themselves had dug deep antitank trenches which could not easily be crossed, even by infantry. The assault groups were therefore to carry ladders.

The break-out was to start at 8 P.M. the same evening. The first wave was to contain the 13th Panzer Division on the left and the Florian Geyer 8th SS Cavalry Division on the right, divided into groups of 30, each with one Hungarian who was familiar with the territory; their transport was to consist of 8 to 12 tanks or armored trucks, 10 amphibious Volkswagen cars, and 3 motorbikes for the field gendarmes who were to direct the operation. The second wave was to comprise the Feldherrnhalle Panzergrenadier Division, the 22nd SS Cavalry Division, and the Hungarian units. The third was to be formed by the walking wounded and the baggage-train crews. Tens of thousands of civilians were also expected to join.

The initial onslaught from Széll Kálmán Square and Széna Square was to wipe out the Soviet positions in Margit Boulevard over a 1-kilometer stretch. The next objective was to reach the fork of Hidegkúti Road and Budakeszi Road, about 2.5 kilometers northwest of Széna Square. The escapees were then to assemble on Remete-hegy Hill, about 2 kilometers farther north, and move west through the low hills and forests. The critical point was a strip of flat arable land, bordered by meadows and vineyards, between the western edge of the forests and the east-facing German front line (15 to 18 kilometers and about 25 kilometers, respectively, from the break-out point). A second assembly in the forest was therefore planned before launching an attack on Tinnye and the area south of it, with the aim of overrunning the Soviet front line from behind and joining the German troops positioned beyond it. This was to take place the following noon, 18 hours after the break-out—an impossible task, given the distance and the fact that the escapees had only light weapons and limited ammunition. It was hoped that the German Army Group South would start an attack in order to meet the escapees, but the army group had not been advised in time.

The plan was top secret. On the German side the divisional commanders finally received their orders at 2 P.M., the regimental commanders at 4 P.M., and the rank and file at 6 P.M. The Hungarian commanders and their units were also informed only at 6 P.M. because the Germans were afraid of being betrayed by them. The only exception was Hindy, who received word at 4 P.M.

Nevertheless, the break-out had been in the air for weeks and, by the morning of 11 February (or the evening before), many had an inkling of when the action would start. That something was about to happen could also be guessed from the fact that between 6 and 10 February a host of officers and men, particularly Hungarians, were suddenly awarded medals. First lieutenants and majors received the Knight's Cross of the Hungarian Order of Merit, second lieutenants the Signum Laudis, lieutenant-colonels and colonels the Officer's Cross, and privates the Badge of Courage. Some important members of the officer staff were also specially promoted: Hindy became a major-general, Billnitzer a lieutenant-general.

The wildest rumors were circulating about how the break-out would progress. Many soldiers expected to reach the German lines after a short walk. Others believed that after marching 15 to 20 kilometers they would be opposed only by the Soviet service corps and that the relief units were awaiting them at Pilisszentkereszt. Yet others added that the break-out point was defended only by Romanians, who would immediately run away. An Arrow Cross officer announced: "The relief units are at Budakeszi. The break-out will be child's play. The Tigers will be leading, followed by the mechanized SS units, then the Arrow Cross units, the Wehrmacht, and the Hungarian troops. In Transdanubia we'll have a rest and be given the new miracle weapons. I guarantee that in three weeks there won't be one Russian soldier in the country." Even high-ranking officers were not immune to illusions. Major-General Schmidhuber told his friends a few hours before he was killed: "We won't let them trap us. The day after tomorrow we'll be sitting together again over a drink." Many civilians, loading themselves with luggage and furniture, were preparing for the break-out with similar hopes.

Any sober observer, however, would have realized that the enterprise could not be entirely successful. It may not have been a coincidence that Pfeffer-Wildenbruch and Dörner, with 500 SS policemen, chose the route through the underground culvert leading from Ördög-árok gully to the Danube, thus avoiding the necessity of crossing the Soviet lines, which would have been the most dangerous obstacle. The Hungarian corps command was instructed to follow closely behind them.

Very little is known about the immediate operational preparations for the break-out. The attack in Széna Square at 8 P.M. was to be led by the combat groups of cavalry captain Haller, Colonel Herbert Kündiger, and Colonel László Veresváry. At 6 P.M. soldiers disguised as civilians—probably including a special unit of the Hungarian I Army Corps that operated in civilian clothes—slipped through the battle line at Margit Boulevard and elsewhere, with orders to hide in various buildings and then attack the enemy from behind, as had earlier been done by the Soviets occupying Déli Station. It has also been suggested that the action was started by a German special commando unit in Soviet uniforms, pretending to be Soviet guards accompanying German prisoners, who disarmed the real Soviet soldiers guarding Széll Kálmán Square. Although Pfeffer-Wildenbruch and other surviving officers later maintained that the front was to be opened up by the Kündiger Group, evidence that the break-out began with groups of this kind is provided both in several interviews and memoirs and in postwar Soviet studies.

The Soviets must have suspected that a break-out was in the offing, if only because they knew that the Germans generally resorted to this strategy. They set up three defensive belts: the first near Széll Kálmán Square, the second near János Hospital, and the third on the slopes of János-hegy Hill. The intention was to withdraw from the first belt at the start of the break-out and trap the escapees in a pocket formed by Bimbó Road, Törökvész Road, the southeastern slope of János-hegy Hill, the Virányos quarter, and Kis-Sváb-hegy Hill. In Széll Kálmán Square and Olasz Avenue the 180th Guard Rifle Division took up positions, supported by T-34 tanks dug in in Bimbó Road and at János Hospital. On 9–10 February—before Pfeffer-Wildenbruch had actually decided to break out—the civilians living around Széll Kálmán Square, Retek Street, and Fillér Street were evacuated and the residents of the streets farther back ordered to close all entrances and windows. One Soviet tank unit was stationed in the Dorog area to seal off the road between Tinnye and Perbál.

It has been claimed that the German plans were betrayed. There is no evidence that this was the case, however, and even if it had been, the plans would hardly have been divulged in every detail. In fact, Pfeffer-Wildenbruch had not even called his war council when, on 10 February, Hungarian volunteer companies attached to the Soviets were ordered to take up preventive positions at the edge of the woods east of Budakeszi and in the Városmajor Grange area. The direction of a possible break-out could be guessed at simply by using common sense. The Germans were bound to choose the shortest route through the woods and avoid confronting the superior Soviet armored forces in open country.

One particular story, sometimes taking the following variant form, is repeatedly told to prove that even the smallest details of the break-out had been betrayed: "At 7:30 P.M. sharp the Russians began to cover the Castle District and its neighborhood with a tremendous barrage. At the same time a mass of people began to pour out of the Castle District." This is not true. None of more than 20 survivors who have been questioned remembers such a concerted and instantaneous barrage. The one exception occurred around Bécsi Kapu gate at the northern exit of the Castle District, where between 7:30 and 8 P.M. a sudden heavy bombardment killed the assembled Arrow Cross party activists, including their leader Veresváry. Elsewhere the Soviets began by using small arms and mortars, and the artillery fire intensified only gradually, reaching its climax between 10 and 11 P.M.

In sum, the Soviets were able to make an educated guess as to the place of the expected break-out, but they were probably unaware of the exact time. This is all the more likely because since the start of the siege the garrison had carried out more than 20 counterstrikes, each of which could equally well have heralded a break-out.

The Situation of the Garrison at the Time of the Break-Out

On the afternoon of 11 February the Citadel on Gellért-hegy Hill was captured by Soviet troops and a unit of Hungarian defectors, who suffered many casualties in the process. The loss of Gellért-hegy Hill severed communications between the Hungarian troops stationed in the Kelenföld quarter and those around the Gellért Hotel, who had failed to return to their earlier quarters in the Castle District, as ordered by Pfeffer-Wildenbruch the previous evening. The Germans had evacuated the area, but, according to some reminiscences, a number of German soldiers had also stayed behind, hoping that it would prove less dangerous to be captured with the Hungarians.

In the hours preceding the break-out, the front line ran roughly along Hegyalja Road toward the saddle between Naphegy and Gellért-hegy Hills. However, the main German defense line, or what was left of it, stretched from the Danube side of Döbrentei Square—along part of Attila Street, Hegyalja Road, and Mészáros Street—to Mikó Street in the southeastern corner of Vérmező Meadow. While the undeveloped slopes in the Tabán quarter were no-man's land, Naphegy Hill was thus still in German hands. Some Germans also remained ensconced farther north in several buildings in Krisztina Boulevard, while the Soviets, leaving them behind in their advance, took Vérmező Meadow as far as opposite Déli Station.

In Széll Kálmán Square, according to former combatants, the ground floor of the Post Office Palace had been taken by Soviet troops while the upper floors still remained in German and Hungarian hands. To flush the Soviets out, the combat group of the 12th Reserve Division and the remnants of the Vannay Battalion had launched a surprise attack through the air raid shelter on 10 February. Although they had succeeded in forcing an entry, they had been unable to drive out all the Soviet troops and had therefore set fire to the palace. As this had still not resulted in the liberation of the palace, they torched it again during the break-out, and after the break-out it was found to have been completely burned out. In Fény Street and Klára Street two groups of defenders had held on and even maintained telephone contact with the palace.

The rest of the front line ran from Széna Square along Margit Boulevard as far as the Buda end of Margit Bridge. In this sector the defenders undertook only minor actions before the break-out—the condition of the boulevard would not have allowed any major troop movements in any case.

"Act One of Despair"

The break-out began at 8 P.M. on 11 February. In Battyhányi Street, Mátray Street, Várfok Street, and Ostrom Street a huge crowd had built up in the dark. Many soldiers due to attack in the first wave arrived late and were unable to push their way to the front through the crush of some 10,000 others who were supposed to follow in the second wave but had already arrived. Thus most of the initial attacks came to a bloody end because there were not enough soldiers available to carry them out. One of the participants, Captain Helmut Friedrich, recalls this "act one of despair":

> Suddenly the narrow lanes of the Víziváros quarter are under mortar fire. . . . The bombardment grows heavier. Anxiety hangs in the air. Shouts are heard. Flares light up the roofs. When they have burned themselves out, the twilight in the lanes turns into total darkness. Now from all sides foot soldiers stream toward the north. Another

mortar strike. Everybody seeks cover in doorways. More shouting, comrades have lost each other. The crush in the lanes gets worse and worse. All grope their way forward in the dark. . . . Somewhere ahead, where the narrow lanes of Víziváros reach the grand Margit Boulevard, is where the front line is supposed to be. Where the boulevard widens into a major road junction, and a Russian ready to shoot may be lying in wait at every window, is where the break-out, that desperate action, is to occur. The place is called Széna Square. . . . It is painful for a commander to watch how this break-out attempt is developing into madness, an almost animal despair, that obeys only the instinct of self-preservation, without being able to do anything about it. Through a narrow gap between the black outlines of the rows of houses on both sides, a blinding light glares like the neon signs and glittering shop windows in the boulevards of a metropolis in peacetime. It is easy to guess that all the fiery magic is made by shells, tracer bullets, and a mass of flares. So that's where the front line is, Széna Square. . . . Through that bottleneck we all must pass. Left and right people jostle madly to start the break-out as soon as possible. They elbow their way ahead, pushing and kicking, like animals.

Another, Hanns Bayer of the Waffen SS, remembers:

Then we are tearing across the open space. Bangs and crashes left, right, and center. Hand grenades exploding, machine guns rattling, submachine guns chattering, rifle bullets cracking—firing everywhere. There is no time to think. The instinct of self-preservation comes before fear or courage. In front of me a blazing tank. Somewhere ahead there must be a gun blasting into this mass of humanity. One direct hit after another. Whoever is hit is left behind. Like lemmings blindly driven to throw themselves into the sea, a mass of once-disciplined people, having abandoned all reason, now rushes down this road, headlong into disaster.

Széll Kálmán Square and Széna Square were lit up by Soviet flares, and from the surrounding buildings a hail of machine-gun bullets hit the first group. Private Péter Noel reports:

> At Széna Square we came under terrible mortar and artillery fire and suffered more casualties. . . . Then the remainder of our assault battalion attacked. Slithering across the ice in Széna Square, we took cover beside the buildings and destroyed the Soviet mortar crew positioned in the Törökbástya Restaurant. In the momentary confusion some other units also got through, and the break-out gained ground toward Új Szentjános hospital.

Lieutenant-Colonel Alajos Vajda describes events in roughly the same location: "What I saw there went beyond the wildest flights of the imagination. The squares were almost as light as day with the many tracer bullets, flare rockets, and searchlights. The tracer bullets drew horizontal streaks of light behind them. Shell after shell exploded. I am not exaggerating a bit if I write that there were mountains of dead bodies everywhere."

The attack of the Kündiger Group failed for lack of combat strength, and three further attacks, launched at short intervals, were also repulsed by Soviet fire. The bulk of the first wave, however, heading west for the Post Office Palace and Városmajor Grange, got through. They included the remnants of the Vannay Battalion, who had previously assembled in Ostrom Street next to Széna Square, having been issued snow wraps made of sheets, small bags containing chocolate, brandy, and fatty bacon, and steel helmets and hand grenades. They also had a few submachine guns, including Soviet ones, for which ammunition was readily available. Three of the men—a Bessarabian German, a Ruthenian, and a Hungarian who had been a prisoner of war for ten years—

> spoke perfect Russian. . . . They were carrying ladders they pushed horizontally across the antitank ditch to form bridges and—talking to the Russian guards in the dark—crawled across on all fours. They reported back that the second group could follow. Meanwhile all hell

32
Victims of the break-out in Széll Kálmán Square

had been let loose—heavy shelling, machine guns, sub-machine guns, and other light weapons—but many of the second group got through and also reached the post office building.

A small number of German (and possibly three Hungarian) armored vehicles broke through at Várfok Street. Some of these, carrying ammunition and dressings, covered between two and three kilometers before they were abandoned, but most were destroyed near the Soviet front line. Another group of three or four tanks and a few armored trucks tried to breach the Soviet positions in Városmajor Street. The truck leading the convoy had just climbed the barricade at the entrance to the street, when it received a direct hit: the crew was killed and the wreck blocked the group's further advance. Corporal Ernst Keller's tank was immobilized at the outset because its fuel had been contaminated with sugar. Soviet heavy weapons stationed near János Hospital caused catastrophic losses,

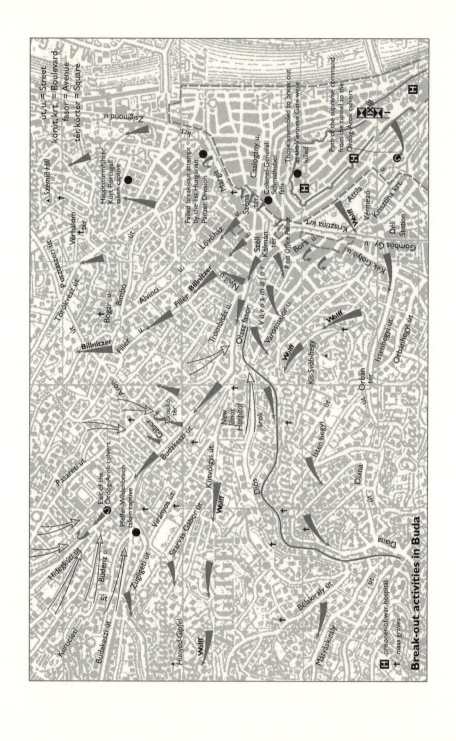

Break-out activities in Buda

| ut, u. = Street |
| körút, krt. = Boulevard |
| fasor = Avenue |
| tér, körtér = Square |

H prisoner-of-war hospital
† mass graves

Szemlő Hill

Zsigmond u.

Hauptsturmführer
Kurt Portugall
taken captive

Verhalom
tér

Failed break-out attempt
by the 1st Hungarian
Panzer Division

Csalogány u.

Colonel-General
Schmidhuber
falls

Those assembled to break out
at the Viennese Gate were
killed

Path of the supreme command
from the tunnel to the
Ördög-Árok culvert

Pusztaszeri út

Törökvész út

Margit

Lővőház

Szena
tér

Széll
Kálmán
tér

Atrila

Wolff

Vérmező

Krisztina krt.

Déli
Station

Gombos Gy. u.

Bimbó

Bogár u.

Alvinci

Fillér

Billnitzer

Nyúl u.

Trombitás u.

Várfok u.

Post Office Palace

Bors u.

Kék Golyó u.

Krisztina krt.

Billnitzer

Fillér

Olasz fasor

Várfok u.

Várfok u.

Wolff

Wolff

Kis-Sváb-hegy

Orbán
tér

Istenhegyi út

Orbánhegyi út

Áron

Torocko
tér

New
János
Hospital

Gábor

árok

Isten hegyi út

út

Diós

Diana

Pasaréti út

Exit of the
Ördög-Árok culvert

Pfeffer-Wildenbruch
taken captive

Budakeszi út

Kútvölgyi út

Wolff

Hidegkút út

Budenz u.
út

Zugligeti út

Virányos út

Szarvas Gábor út

Kurucles

Budakeszi út

Hunyad-Gáprel

Wolff

Mátyáskirály

Bélakirály út

Mátyáskirály út

making any progress in this sector impossible until a surprise strike by a rare undamaged tank destroyed them.

In Városmajor Grange, near János Hospital, and in Budagyöngye the escapees incapacitated some of the Soviet tanks—which had not gone into action until about 9 P.M.—with their panzerfausts. However, they could carry only six or seven kilograms of equipment—either a number of hand grenades, or a rifle or submachine gun with no more than seven magazines, or, occasionally, a panzerfaust—and very few had machine guns, which were heavy and required two men to lift the magazine crates. Many therefore ran out of ammunition after the first kilometer.

Captain Frigyes Wáczek, chief of staff of the Hungarian 1st Armored Division, has described one episode in detail. The divisional staff and an assault pioneer detachment numbering 30 men with submachine guns tried to break out at Mechwart Square but were stopped by heavy Soviet opposition. They returned to Batthyányi Street and cut across Széna Square into Retek Street, where two tanks were ablaze. Expecting the ammunition in the tanks to explode, they took cover in the butcher's shop at the corner. There the divisional commander, Colonel János Vértessy, fell on his face and broke his last remaining tooth. "It's not my day," he sighed. Captured on the same date 30 years earlier, after an emergency landing in the First World War, Vértessy had spent 3 years in prison camp before managing to escape. This time, he was to be taken prisoner and shot within 24 hours. The group reached the junction of Olasz Avenue between 10 and 11 P.M. From Széll Kálmán Square a large crowd was approaching, including mothers pushing baby carriages, old people, and other civilians.

> Suddenly three Soviet tanks rolled up from Pasaréti Road and from about 400 meters opened fire with grenades and tracer bullets on the tightly packed marchers. . . . Next to me the grenades wiped out eight to ten people. If one tried to move out of the way, one trod on somebody, who cried out in pain. The crowd took refuge in the buildings. When at last the panzerfausts destroyed the tanks, the people surged out, like meat squeezed

from a sausage machine, shouting hooray. But soon the next tanks appeared and the slaughter restarted. Most of those still alive escaped into Fillér Street and continued northwest from there.

The first wave, consisting of several thousand men who had broken through the positions of the Soviet 180th Guard Rifle Division, advanced about 2.5 kilometers along Olasz Avenue as far as Buda-gyöngye. But their losses were so enormous that those in the second wave—who reached the front line at Széna Square between 10 and 11 P.M.—were afraid to follow them. Ernst Schweitzer, a reserve first lieutenant in the 13th Panzer Division, describes the situation at Széna Square and Lövőház Street:

> We move about 300 or 400 meters west and reach an immense cluster of soldiers seeking cover behind a long barnlike building in front of a large open square. This is the front line. Hugging the edge of the building we see that the square is dominated from both sides by Russian machine guns and antitank guns. Farther along, the square is strewn with wounded and dead. At our feet there are more than a dozen dead who bought it when they were pushed out from the cover of the building. . . . Now we are being forced out into the firing line by those behind us. Without a moment's hesitation I grab the Ia's hand and shout: "Go!" We run for our lives across the square. Bullets whistle past us, but we are lucky. In a few seconds the death zone of about 300 meters is behind us. We are in a narrow lane flanked by buildings with four or five stories. Rifle fire rings out, shots from the upper stories and soldiers shooting upward: who knows where there is a friend or an enemy?

Many of the escapees gave up at this stage in total apathy. A medical orderly recalls the scene in Széll Kálmán Square: "Dead and wounded are lying in every doorway and in the street. Moaning, swearing and pleading everywhere. 'Shoot me, mate, shoot me, mate.' And even more urgently: 'Doesn't anyone have a heart?

Here's my pistol, by my side. Please, shoot me because I can't. Both my arms are gone.'"

The commander of the 13th Panzer Division, Colonel-General Gerhard Schmidhuber, was killed in Retek Street immediately after crossing Széna Square. His body, with those of many of his comrades, was thrown into the antitank ditch in Ostrom Street. Nearby, the commander of the 22nd SS Cavalry Division, Bridgadeführer August Zehender, had his right leg blown off by a grenade and committed suicide. In the Zugliget area, the commander of the 8th SS Cavalry Division, Brigadeführer Joachim Rumohr, and three of his officers also killed themselves. Everywhere alongside the roads out of Buda wounded men were begging to be put out of their misery. A soldier in Billnitzer's unit, which reached Széna Square about 11 P.M., remembers:

> In the dark, with the din of battle in the distance, the only people who remained with me constantly were Uncle Bill [Billnitzer] and his adjutant. It may have been about midnight. In the center of Széna Square a medium-sized tank with a clearly visible German emblem was burning. The flames lit up the whole square and one could see the traces of the fighting. The first break-out attempt toward Olasz Avenue had started from here. Everywhere we saw dead bodies and wrecked vehicles. We reached the beginning of the street leading to Olasz Avenue, where wounded German soldiers inside ground-floor windows were whimpering and asking for cigarettes to alleviate their suffering. They told me that their break-out had failed and they had seen a vast number of dead. At that time there was relative silence. One could hear the crackle of the burning vehicles and snippets of the voices of the resigned wounded.

Near Mechwart Square the Soviets stalled the break-out for a while by bombarding the area between Margit Boulevard and the Castle District with a 7.62mm antitank gun hidden in a café. However, by about 11 P.M. the Germans had advanced so far in the dark that they abandoned their gun and took refuge in the surrounding buildings together with the civilians they had forced to carry ammunition. Until dawn German and Hungarian soldiers, as well as civilians, continued to slip through the resulting gap toward Rózsadomb Hill, Fillér Street, and the woods beyond.

Soviet units also confronted the assault at Budagyöngye, Virányos Road, and Törökvész Road. Some German troops (chiefly the 22nd SS Cavalry Division) pushed west, occupying Istenhegyi Road on Kis-Sváb-hegy Hill, and Normafa, Mátyás király, and Béla király Roads in the Svábhegy Hill area. They were unable to make headway, however, on Hűvösvölgyi Road northwest of Budagyöngye. Schweitzer reports:

> We take refuge at the entrance to a courtyard. A few minutes later a bunch of divisional staff officers gather here. Most of them go down to the cellar because of the cold and pester a little old lady to show them their position on their street plan by candle light. . . . I walk up and down in the courtyard, busy with my wound and my

33
Street in Buda after the break-out

acute pain, until First Lieutenant [Hans] Lehmann, who has a large packet of bandages left, arrives and dresses my wound. . . . An SS officer staggers into the courtyard, announcing: "I'm wounded, I'm going to end it all." I ask where he has come from. He answers that he has tried one of the side streets on the left, but there too everything is sealed off. Thirty of his men had gotten that far, but more had been wounded or killed since. He shoots himself.

At Széll Kálmán Square and Széna Square it became relatively calm around midnight. Billnitzer's soldier recalls:

A few hours later, when I got back to Széna Square with Uncle Bill, a new crowd instinctively set out again toward Olasz Avenue. . . . We joined some groups. The movement was not all of a piece, some smaller or larger groups were also meandering back toward the city. In the silence of the night all were stubbornly, doggedly heading for somewhere or other, apparently without any organization whatsoever. I clearly remember how we, including Uncle Bill and his adjutant, reached Bimbó Road and drifted uphill with the crowd. Suddenly we heard the sound of caterpillar tracks. We were dead silent and immediately threw ourselves on the ground beside the houses and fences, so that none of us could be seen. It was pitch dark.

Billnitzer himself adds: "The noise of the tracks became louder and louder, till the tanks passed us with a tremendous rattle. . . . Our experience that tanks are totally blind in the dark was confirmed once more."

A few officers still had some grasp of the situation. Lieutenant-Colonel Helmut Wolff of the Feldherrnhalle Panzergrenadier Division realized that no progress could be made toward Olasz Avenue. He ordered one of his battalions to attempt a breakthrough across Vérmező Meadow and Kékgolyó Street, and the action at this unexpected point proved successful. The soldiers crossed the Soviet positions without encountering any resistance. By dawn they were on the summit of Nagy-Svábhegy Hill above the road to Budakeszi. During the day they were joined by some 2,000 more troops, bringing their total to nearly 3,200.

At the sight of the frenzied escapees throwing themselves into enemy fire regardless of casualties, panic began to spread among the Soviet soldiers. Judit Lichtenberg, a captive of the NKGB (the Soviet People's Commissariat for State Security), who was being marched from the Lipótmező quarter toward János Hospital late on 11 February, observed the events:

> In Kútvölgyi Road . . . we had to wait for a long time at the stone wall of one of the most beautiful villas. . . . Horses, startled by hooting cars, neighed and reared. Soldiers, shouting, tried to move cars stuck in the snow with wheels spinning. In the teeming crowd trucks lumbered like clumsy elephants. The many foreign men, animals, and machines formed an inextricable knot on the narrow uphill road. It all bore the marks of anxiety, alarm and agitation. . . . After a great deal of shunting and regrouping we reached Béla király Road and . . . the underpass beneath the Cogwheel Railway.
>
> Here and there a ghostly light would flare up from the weapon of an unknown soldier, but I didn't care. I had gotten used to it as part and parcel of the scene, just like the endless motley column now passively waiting. Then I heard, rather than saw, rifle fire, and suddenly somebody was shouting so close by that I could clearly recognize the German words "Hier, hier, herbei" [here, here, come here]. . . . The crackle of rifles had unmistakably turned into concerted machine-gun fire, and the Russkis, who had so far been trampling the snow together with us, plunged into the ditch or between and behind the vehicles. Half a minute later most of them turned about face and scampered away. I realized that they knew the ropes better than I did, and so I also decided to clear out. . . . I bumped into a sergeant, who grabbed my arm and, shouting "Devochka

poshli" [Come on, girl], began to retreat with me at the double, stopping at each villa we reached. At one point we met a man who was probably some kind of inspecting officer, because I could understand the sergeant explaining what I was doing there, a civilian woman alone in the middle of the battle. . . . I shouted, "Bang-bang Germanski!" The man knew perfectly well that I was telling him to fight back. Me, the prisoner. "Ne commandant," he answered. I became furious. I felt like organizing the defense myself. . . . But the sergeant dragged me along, saying: "Panic."

Panic. Thank you very much. I could see that myself. Next to me a character in a fur hat was wailing: he had been hit by a bullet. The Germans were advancing behind us, step by step. The column, swearing about the obstruction caused by stalling vehicles, was clearing out and drawing back as fast as it could. I got separated from the sergeant, but soon a cook took my hand and we ran together until the loose sole of my boot got caught in a heap of snow and I fell. The right-hand front wheel of a car immediately behind me caught my left knee. Hearing my screams, the officer in the car opened the door. A discussion followed between him and the cook, who pulled me across the snow to the nearest tree alongside the road, as he was ordered. He leaned me against the tree and, calling out the familiar "poshli," disappeared in the terrified mass. . . .

When we reached Budakeszi Road . . . an incredible sight opened before my eyes. In rows of three, getting stuck again and again, pushing and shoving to gain a meter on each other, the Red Army was speeding hotfoot toward Budakeszi. It was a breakneck, every-man-for-himself flight, a panic that can only overwhelm a frightened, beaten army.

On the morning of 12 February a dense fog descended into the valleys around Buda. Several groups of between 2,000 and

3,000, including civilians, took advantage of this to make their way toward Svábhegy, Remete-hegy, and Hármashatár-hegy Hills. Thus some 16,000 people escaped from the city into the hills.

The Journey Through the Ördög-árok Culvert

According to plans, the German and Hungarian commands, SS Oberführer Dörner's 500 assault troopers, the antiaircraft crews, the glider pilots, and a few other units were to escape through the culvert between Ördög-árok gully and the Danube. They were to start near the tunnel under Castle Hill about two kilometers in front of the Soviet lines and resurface about two kilometers behind them, covering about four kilometers under ground.

The Hungarian commander Iván Hindy was not informed of this until after 3 P.M. In his trial after the war he stated:

> On 11 February I heard that all food supplies had been used up and decided to negotiate with Pfeffer-Wildenbruch. As agreed by our adjutants, I called on him in his office at about 3 o'clock. Before I could speak he said that he also wished to speak to me as he had two orders to give me. The orders were that the garrison was to break out at 7 o'clock that same evening. I told him that I thought it strange that he had not discussed this with me beforehand, and asked how he had come to this decision. He said that our divisions were subordinate to his divisions that had received the orders; moreover, he had discussed the matter with his divisional commanders on the previous evening, and as the food supplies had run out in the meantime he had had no other option. I remarked again that if he had not discussed the matter with me, I would at least have expected to be informed in advance, because now I had only three hours left to prepare my staff and could not guarantee that everybody would receive the order in good time.

As Captain Ferenc X. Kovács, the head of the Hungarian I Army Corps's operative section, remembers, Hindy then "summoned the

officers to my office and . . . told us that he would not force anybody to take part in the break-out. He said that we would have to
start at 11 P.M. He would join the Germans, and if nobody had any
objections or comments, his wife would go with him. (Nobody had
any comments.)"

Lieutenant-General Billnitzer was also due to go through the
culvert, while his soldiers were to escape on the surface across Széll
Kálmán Square. When he heard Hindy's instructions, he decided to
join the soldiers.

József Paulics, an officer cadet in the Hungarian I Army
Corps, remembers the cocksure optimism shared by many at that
time:

> At the exit of the sewer [in reality the culvert carried only
> water] near the Bolyai Academy the corps command, the
> Hungarian and German general staffs, and the office per-
> sonnel will be received by combat groups, who will assist
> us in continuing our escape from our fortress, which has
> by now become indefensible. If we succeed, we guaran-
> tee that the heroic defenders of Buda Castle, from the
> lowest ranks to the highest, will be promoted and deco-
> rated and given three weeks' leave somewhere at the
> German seaside.

While many would not face facts even then, Hindy anticipated the
end of the enterprise and looked on lethargically, as Károly Borbás,
an officer in the army corps, records: "I last saw him before the
break-out at a quarter to eight in the evening, when the groups
were being assembled. The Arrow Cross men climbing into a Hungarian armored truck wrapped in red blankets looked funny. Hindy
was watching them silently. I asked him whether he thought this
right, but instead of answering he was saying farewell to everybody." The German and Hungarian commands left their headquarters at about 11 P.M. They were preceded by some of Dörner's
assault troopers. Kovács specifies: "The Hungarian corps command
came immediately behind Pfeffer-Wildenbruch. Ahead of them the
assault group was carrying panzerfausts, mortars, machine guns,
and other heavy weapons." One of the soldiers recalls:

I was given a smoked chop, two kilos of sugar, two loaves of bread, some rice, salami, margarine, and a flask of brandy. Unfortunately, I could take only a small part of this with me because I also had to pack other things. . . . The entrance to the sewer was about 200 to 300 meters from the exit of the tunnel in Krisztina Boulevard, I think at number 97. We walked this short distance amid shells, artillery fire, and signal rockets. . . . At last we got to the cellar of that building, from where, through a sloping barrel-shaped opening 1 meter in diameter and several meters in length, we reached the sewer . . . a circular passage about 3 by 3 meters with a ditch about 40 centimeters in depth along the bottom. . . . Luckily we had a few candles to bring some light into this otherwise completely dark underworld. I don't believe that mountaineers in the Alps advance more slowly than we did. . . . From time to time we found ourselves under manholes with spiral staircases closed off by iron plates, where we could hear the din of the desperate battle above ground.

Various other groups entered the culvert without permission. Staff medical officer Werner Hübner remembers the chaos after the departure of the commands: "In the large tunnel, where the corps's communication vehicles were stationed, people were beginning to realize that they were trapped. A drunken staff doctor had taken charge and decided to escape with some soldiers through an underground culvert which was supposed to lead from the Danube to Budakeszi. Roaring insanely, they started to look for the culvert. I never saw them again." With so many men squeezing into the culvert, the water level slowly rose, and making headway became increasingly difficult. A German participant remembers: "For many their luggage grew too heavy, and knapsacks were soon abandoned right and left." A Hungarian recalls:

The current brought every conceivable object with it—combat equipment, helmets, flasks, hand grenades, panzerfausts—which obstructed our progress. And among

other things the body of a woman. I don't know how she
had gotten there, but she probably belonged to the so-
called better classes, about 40, fair, plump, wearing a foal-
skin coat, silk stockings, and light colored shoes with high
heels, and gripping her handbag like grim death.

Many left the culvert before reaching its end. Lieutenant-Colonel
Usdau Lindenau, chief of staff of the IX SS Mountain Army Corps,
surfaced near Olasz Avenue and was soon wounded and captured.
First Lieutenant Wolfgang Betzler, the corps's war diarist, did likewise and reached Labanc Road, where he burned the diary in a
cellar before surrendering.

Some Germans tried to follow a side culvert that branched off
under Hűvösvölgyi Road toward Budakeszi. Pfeffer-Wildenbruch
also chose this route, probably after discovering that Dörner's
men could not advance beyond the exit near the Bolyai Academy.
Ferenc X. Kovács recounts:

> The Russians launched a counterstrike with artillery and
> mortars, gradually pushing the Dörner group back into
> Ördög-árok. . . . . The artillery and mortar fire grew
> heavier and could be heard by those in the underground
> section of the culvert, including us. Then the following
> command was issued by Pfeffer-Wildenbruch: "All SS
> officers join the Obergruppenführer in front! At once!
> Pass the message on!"—whereupon SS officers of all
> ranks rushed forward to join Pfeffer-Wildenbruch.

Pfeffer-Wildenbruch waited neither for his Hungarian partner
nor for his own officers, who were unable to follow him in any case,
because the rising water level in the side culvert made any further
advance impossible. He and his staff were the only ones to reach
the surface after a few hundred meters. Between 10 and 15 of them
hid in a villa in Budakeszi Road, where they were discovered by the
Soviets in the morning. The political officer of the Soviet 297th
Rifle Division writes:

> During the struggle for that building we sent a Hungarian
> civilian who spoke German to the enemy to demand

34
Pfeffer-Wildenbruch and Lindenau in Soviet captivity

their surrender. To underline the ultimatum we positioned a 45mm gun, commanded by First Lieutenant M. U. Zagorian, opposite the building. Those inside replied that they would surrender on condition that

a) we guaranteed that their lives would be spared,
b) the Soviet officer receiving them will hold at least the rank of major.

Major Skripkin, the commander of the division's chemical defense detachment, dipped his finger in ink and wrote on a piece of paper that he was a major in the Red Army, ready to receive them.

Dörner, after being wounded, was probably captured in similar fashion.

As the Soviets were not keeping the entire culvert under constant surveillance, some escapees succeeded in climbing out near the Bolyai Academy unnoticed. A group of ten men, led by a medical corps lieutenant, ended up in local resident Iván Boldizsár's house in such a state of exhaustion that they immediately fell asleep. Others came out at Budagyöngye:

> The coast was clear. The enemy must have been everywhere but probably didn't suspect anything. "Officers forward!" Nobody moved. The few determined officers were already in front, while the others, who had cold feet, were plodding on behind. . . . One by one, we climbed the iron steps, wriggled through the tight manhole, and took cover behind the snow piles in the suburban street. We must have been on the outskirts of Buda. In the east dawn was breaking.

Approaching lights caused panic among the escapees, as it was impossible to tell whether they came from the torches of their own comrades or from Soviet flamethrowers:

> The only way to escape from this mousetrap was by climbing into the street through one of the gratings that normally let water drain into the culvert. It was not hard to remove the gratings, but much harder to work one's way up. The first man would get through, and the second too, most of the time, but by then the Russians seemed to have discovered our escape holes. When the next man stuck out his head he would fall back lifeless, hit by a Russian sniper. What could we do when an escape hole had been discovered? We walked on; the Russians could not keep all the gratings under fire. We had to make another attempt; our only thought was: out of this prison! Carefully my friend stuck his head out, a centimeter at a time. No Russian was to be seen, no shot to be heard. He pushed his whole body out and lay flat on the ground. Had they discovered him? Would they be taking aim at my head when I followed him? With my heart pounding I worked my way out centimeter by centimeter. It was still quiet. In one bound I was outside and we were running toward the nearby [Szépilona] streetcar depot.

Such groups were soon discovered by Soviet tanks patrolling the streets and chased into the surrounding buildings, where the round-up began on the morning of 12 February:

> About noon a Russian delegate approached waving a white flag. He was received at the front door and taken to our "leader." He told us that antitank guns and mortars had just arrived and assumed firing positions against us. If we surrendered, nothing would happen to us; otherwise, if we didn't raise a white flag within half an hour, our building would be reduced to rubble in a matter of minutes. Death or captivity. With heavy hearts we chose the latter.

Many Germans committed suicide—for example, 26 SS soldiers who had taken refuge in the garden of 2 Diósárok Street. Some panicked right at the outset and killed themselves even before the Soviets were anywhere near them.

Among the Hungarians there were hardly any suicides. Of the 60 staff members about 40 returned to the cellar of the building from which they had entered the culvert. The sole survivors of the 4th Hussar Regiment—two lieutenant-colonels and a major, who had undertaken an unarmed reconnaissance mission alongside the Cogwheel Railway—surrendered in a nearby villa. This outcome was typical.

The Ördög-árok break-out proved a dismal failure. None of those who took this route are known to have reached friendly lines or even to have gotten beyond the suburb of Hidegkút. A Hungarian participant writes:

> The atmosphere was thick with confusion, shouting, tussles, and desperate fear. . . . By then the German corps commander and his officers were no longer in the culvert. Who knows where they were. There were only the few hundred desperate German soldiers and us. Climbing up the spiral staircase was tantamount to death. The men nearby said that those who had gotten that far were lying shot in a pile around the opening. . . . About

20 meters or more from the manhole there was a side passage, a service pipe. It was one and a half meters in diameter, also barrel-shaped, with water about 20 centimeters deep running out of it. . . . The German soldiers attempted the impossible feat of escaping through this pipe. As there was room for only one at a time, they crawled away on their knees, one after the other. The more that entered the pipe, the higher the water rose. When there were about 100 inside, the pipe was almost half full of water, and all those bodies crawling on their knees had swelled it to such an extent that it was pouring out like a waterfall. . . . When almost all the Germans had gotten into the narrow pipe, they suddenly started to crawl back, screaming horribly and drenched to the skin. They had seen a light in the distance and concluded that Soviet soldiers with flamethrowers were coming toward them. . . . Those of the wounded who could, fled. One, who had been hit in the thigh, was dragging himself along with his hands as if he were swimming; another was trying to save his wretched life sliding on his bottom, each as he was able.

In the afternoon Hindy and his entourage realized that the Germans were being pushed back from both the Ördög-árok exit and the Budakeszi side section of the culvert. Kovács took the initiative:

Behind us was a group of Germans with various weapons, and from the end of the underground section a Soviet assault could be expected. We would have been the target between two fires. I suggested to Colonel-General Hindy and Staff Colonel Sándor Horváth that we separate from Pfeffer-Wildenbruch's party, turn back, and try to reach the surface somewhere. . . . Wading through water up to our waists, we pushed aside the many discarded objects obstructing us. Iván Hindy's wife followed us in a long skirt, and we were clearing the way for her.

Another participant continues:

> At last we reached the point where . . . the culvert was built like a waterfall. But this time we were going in the same direction as the water. We had to get down into the lower culvert, but it was full of water, about one to one and a half meters deep, up to our waists or armpits, depending on how tall we were. The slow movement of the water indicated a blockage somewhere. We remembered that at one point there was a floodgate, which might have been closed in order to drown us. Something had to be done because having reached the end of this terrible war we were not willing to be drowned, and even preferred the risk of being shot dead.
>
> Two staff captains [Ferenc X. Kovács and László Kerekes] volunteered to open or smash the floodgate. A quarter or half an hour later—who knows how long the painful wait lasted—we at last heard the floodgate being smashed. . . . The two captains returned and sat Hindy's wife on their arms to carry her toward apparent liberation. The poor old lady's heroic behavior put the courage of many men to shame: not one word of complaint was heard from her.

In Széll Kálmán Square there was an exit covered by a small building, where the group stopped at about 5 P.M. Climbing the spiral staircase, Kovács heard Russian voices, and the escapees continued their march. As they were unable to leave the culvert either at its Danube outlet or at Döbrentei Square, where the ceiling had caved in, they finally decided to return to their original starting point.

> An hour and a half later we saw the "ladder reaching up to heaven." . . . Captain Kovács again volunteered to climb out of the culvert first. . . . We arrived safely. The cellar door was open and above us we heard the clatter of hooves and Russian voices. Apparently they had also noticed us, because two came downstairs. They were so surprised to see so many high-ranking officers [Hindy,

Major-General Gyula Sédely, a staff colonel, a lieutenant-colonel, and three captains] together that they even forgot to use their weapons.

The Escapees' Further Progress

The closed units that had broken out above ground soon dissolved into several large groups, with the majority reaching the woods near Buda at various points and heading toward Hármashatár-hegy Hill. Assault Artillery Lieutenant Róbert Garád reports how one group came into being:

Uncle Bill [Billnitzer] and I . . . instinctively headed toward the hills. In some places the snow was up to 20 centimeters deep and clearly showed our tracks. I tramped through the snow and Uncle Bill slowly followed me. The fences were either missing or flattened. We got to an unpaved road leading uphill. On a rough wooden board I could read "Törökvész Road." By now we had reached a wooded area. We climbed higher and rested among the trees. Then the surprise came. Day was slowly breaking. In the valleys the battle noises became more intense, and fog spread everywhere. Behind us, along our tracks in the snow, an endless line of people was approaching. . . . We were surrounded by civilians, soldiers, children, women, and unshaven SS assault troopers with machine guns, who were asking Uncle Bill in Hungarian and German where we should now be going. Quite involuntarily Uncle Bill had become the center of the murmuring crowd. The fog grew even thicker and Uncle Bill dispatched the group with the machine guns toward the spine of the hill as a vanguard. . . . The German SS soldiers with the machine guns were in front. There may have been about seven of them. After a sleepless night they were forging ahead through the snow and between the bushes, crumpled, unshaven, and impassive. Uncle Bill and I were next, and behind us the endless winding file of the others, all mixed together. A young German major, wounded and encased in plaster, was sitting on a small shaggy horse led by an orderly. Wailing women with children were trudging through the snow dragging their bundles behind them.

Cadet Gyula Kokovay, coming from Svábhegy Hill on his way to Hármashatár-hegy Hill with probably the largest group, passed the site of the panic witnessed earlier by Judit Lichtenberg:

> About two o'clock we reached Béla király Road. Here we saw many abandoned cars, guns, horses, and trucks loaded with ammunition. Next to a column of assorted trucks we saw many civilians who had been shot dead. . . . It was already growing light when we reached a cluster of buildings where many German soldiers and eight university students, survivors of the Winter group, were resting. There must have been at least six hundred of us.
>
> I accompanied the captain on his search for a senior officer and we found a German major. After a brief consultation the whole group set out toward the Kossuth Monument, led by the German major and Captain [Zsombor] Nagy. Leaving this behind on our right, we passed through a valley with steep banks, with Russians firing at us from the villas above. We fired back.
>
> By this time there were some dead and wounded among the Germans, but we Hungarians were still unscathed. . . .
>
> As there were Russians in Budakeszi we continued north across the wood. At about three o'clock word came from the end of the long column that we were being followed by Russian troops. . . . We marched faster and on top of a wooded hill came under fire from all sides. Among the crowd on the hill we met Artillery Colonel [Lajos] Lénárd, and infantry captain and Arrow Cross member Áron Vajna.
>
> After a discussion between Captain Nagy and the commanders of a few relatively well-organized German

groups, we Hungarians, together with the Germans, waded north through the nasty deep snow and attacked a group of Russians, who ran away after a lot of shooting, leaving a mortar behind. After this breakthrough the whole crowd from the hill followed us. None of the attackers was hurt, but while we were fighting in the wood, the Russians had opened fire on the people on the hilltop with heavy mortars, infantry weapons, and the machine guns of two Stormovik planes. Many had been wounded or killed. The wounded included a German major-general, Colonel Lénárd, and the infantry captain. . . .

After dark we rested about six hours, and those who had some food ate. Then we marched on until late into the night, leaving the wounded near a village (maybe Páty) with a few companions to look after them.

About midnight we stopped between some logs in a clearing. As we had no blankets, we huddled together like bundles of firewood but were constantly shivering in the strengthening wind and sleet. About two hours later our clothes, soaked with the sleet, began to freeze, and we moved on.

From Hármashatár-hegy Hill some continued north toward Csobánka and the Pilis Hills, while the majority turned west through the woods above Nagykovácsi. Ernst Schweitzer remembers:

On a forest path several groups of privates are marching northwest. Now we recognize them, they are Germans from Budapest. There are many Hungarian civilians with them. . . . In our column there are civilians carrying all their possessions on their heads. A wounded soldier, whose foot has been blown off above the ankle, is sitting without a dressing on a horse without a saddle. . . . Now Russian reconnaissance aircraft circle above. At 2:30 the first bombers spot us. There are dead and wounded. In a clearing a Russian outpost spots us. At almost regular intervals individual members of the column are picked off with rifles, until a captain persuades ten soldiers to open fire on the outpost and cover our side. About 4 o'clock we reach the Pesthidegkút-Solymár road. Here Russian tanks are stationed and it is impossible to cross the road. The hill east of the road looks like a huge army camp. Now the Russians are shelling us. More casualties.

Suffering heavy casualties, one group, consisting mainly of SS, reached the western edge of the forest near Tinnye and Perbál, and another, led by Lieutenant-Colonel Helmut Wolff of the Feldherrnhalle Division, near Budajenő and Perbál. A third group ran into a Soviet ambush in Nagykovácsi. Billnitzer with his followers swerved south and was taken prisoner near Perbál. Lieutenant József Bíró watched "Germans in flight toward Solymár along the tourist path on the slope of Hármashatár-hegy Hill for two hours. They were carrying their wounded on stretchers. Only their rearguard was firing backward, running from tree to tree." They tried to make headway along the Vienna road but, rapidly running out of ammunition, were harassed at every clearing by Soviet crossfire and raids.

A large group, including many soldiers of the Maria Theresia SS Cavalry Division and the Hungarian contingent of First Lieutenant Litteráti-Loótz, had chosen a southwesterly route along the Cogwheel Railway. Some managed to scale Svábhegy Hill but were ambushed by Soviet troops, who slaughtered the Germans but spared the Hungarians. Others took Kis-Sváb-hegy Hill before they were stopped by the Soviets. Several mass graves were later found in this district, four alongside the Cogwheel Railway and two between Orbánhegy and Kis-Sváb-hegy Hills.

On their way west, the escapees frequently came up against Soviet baggage trains. Such an encounter took place on the road to Budakeszi:

At the head of the column somebody starts shooting. A lieutenant and some machine gunners go to investigate, while the crowd surges back. Nobody wants to be wounded—anything but being left lying there. Some other courageous guys go forward with the ammunition

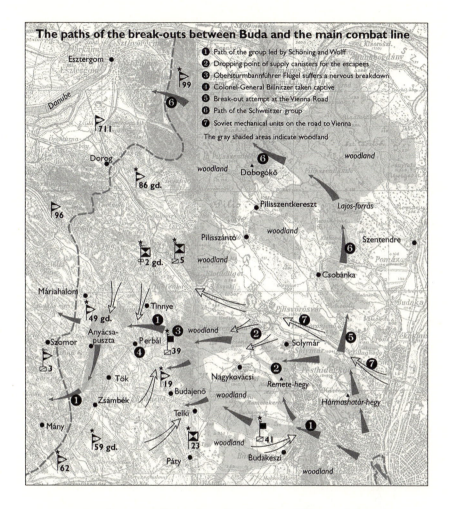

The paths of the break-outs between Buda and the main combat line

① Path of the group led by Schöning and Wolff
② Dropping point of supply canisters for the escapees
③ Obersturmbannführer Flügel suffers a nervous breakdown
④ Colonel-General Billnitzer taken captive
⑤ Break-out attempt at the Vienna Road
⑥ Path of the Schweitzer group
⑦ Soviet mechanical units on the road to Vienna

The gray shaded areas indicate woodland

crate and are swallowed up by the fog. We can hear our
MG 42s, and Russian machine guns rattle in reply, but
they are soon silent; the episode closes with the dull
thuds of hand grenades. Now we can continue our
march. A few dead Russians are lying around, and nearly
a dozen wounded Germans.

The starving men were frantic, and there was no discipline left:

As we were dragging ourselves along, we saw some
Soviet carts containing bread, captured by those ahead
of us. A small crowd of people were fighting over the

loaves. It was horrible to see these fugitives firing their pistols at each other. We stood helplessly a little distance away. The most savage of them soon disappeared, laden with loaves. The dead and wounded were left among the silent horses and the carts.

By now fewer and fewer were willing or able to continue the struggle: "There is not much fighting spirit left among us. Privates are constantly throwing their weapons and ammunition away. Partly because the stuff is becoming very heavy and even more because nobody wants to be around when the call 'Machine gunners and riflemen to the front' comes again." Some were lucky:

> Silent march through the forest in the night. Smoking forbidden. Suddenly loud voices, pistol shots ahead. Then a delighted "Don't shoot, comrades." In the middle of the forest those at the head of the line had reached a road where some German prisoners were being taken away on Russian horse carts. . . . The Russians had bolted and our mates were free. What they told us gave us a foretaste of what could happen to us. . . . Pillaged down to their handkerchiefs and spoons, nothing to eat since last night. Those badly wounded had been shot immediately.

But many gave up: "The Germans ahead of us suddenly stopped and we stopped too. We didn't know what was up, so I walked on with the lieutenant. The most senior German, Obersturmbann-führer [Hans] Flügel, was lying in the snow, shouting that he had had enough of this madness, there was no point in anything any more, he wasn't going one step farther, etc. His soldiers just stood there."

Schweitzer's group had set up camp north of Pilisvörösvár when the Soviets struck:

> A moment's respite with a cigarette. . . . Then suddenly, below us, Russians shouting hurrah. They fire on us. Like startled animals we leap up the steep hill toward the north. We soon run out of breath. Some more are killed

with carefully aimed fire. An NCO walking directly in front of me is suddenly hit in the head and falls down like a tree. I can't bear it. I clutch a low shrub to avoid sliding down, wondering if I should end it all. . . . Up and on again, until we have climbed the 537-meter Kevély Hill under constant fire. . . . We slither down the other side of the hill, sinking up to our elbows in the deep snow and aware that the Russians need only to follow our tracks to catch us. At the foot of the hill we seek shelter in a thicket. There are 13 of us left. Today's rations are a piece of chocolate, a sweet, and a small cube of bread.

After two or three days, most of the escapees began to hallucinate. Some saw houses, kitchens, and food in the snow fields; others imagined that they were at Déli Station. Many were teetering on the edge of madness. However, the worst was still to come. To reach the German lines near Mány, Zsámbék, and Szomor, they had to leave the forests and cross the bare Zsámbék Basin, where a tight Soviet tank barricade awaited them.

Arrivals

Of about 28,000 soldiers who took part in the break-out, some 700 reached the German front in the west. The first group, comprising a Hungarian officer, three German officers, and 23 privates, crossed the German lines in Szomor Catholic Cemetery during the night of 13 February. They owed their success mainly to the local knowledge of their leader, First Lieutenant László Szilasi Szabó.

SS Hauptsturmführer Joachim Boosfeld and one of his men, running hand in hand, had dodged the hail of bullets in Lövőház Street and slipped past some buildings where Soviet soldiers who had not heard of the break-out were making merry. Early next morning they caught up with a large group, mainly Germans, on Remete-hegy Hill. They set out north, lacking the energy to defend themselves against repeated Soviet attacks or to look for supplies dropped from the air. In the morning of 13 February, after spending the night on a thinly wooded hill and encountering no further obstacles, about 100 of them had reached the front line, where the Soviets had established positions on a height beyond a small stream. Boosfeld recalls: "On the rising meadow leading to the German positions we could clearly observe small gray dots— German soldiers—working their way forward. From the German side we received no fire assistance, while the Soviet snipers shot down one escapee after the other." Only 10 to 20 of them finally reached their destination.

The largest single group, 300 to 400 men led by Helmut Wolff and Wilhelm Schöning, reached the western edge of the forest above Nagykovácsi on 13 February. After dark they broke through the Soviet defense ring at Budajenő and, fighting a series of gun battles, reached the positions of the German 3rd Cavalry Brigade. To facilitate their progress they had split up into parties of 15 to 24 men. Sergeant Otto Kutscher was in one of these:

> Suddenly two green flares rose in the air. That had to be our own troops and the front line. Every 500 to 1,000 meters along the German line two more green flares went up. We had reached the Russian trench when we were challenged. We immediately opened fire on the Russians with our light weapons, and those who still had hand grenades threw them into the trench. We jumped across the trench as fast as we could, and then the Russians started shooting. A hand grenade landed exactly midway between Schöning and me. Schöning was badly wounded in his right foot and I caught a large splinter in my left thigh. After crawling and limping a short stretch, I was picked up by two soldiers who were positioned there, and carried to our own lines.

Schöning remembers:

> Suddenly I felt as if my legs had been torn off. The divisional staff's medical officer Seeger, who was lying beside me, tried to help me. While he was leaning over me, he was also wounded. His Achilles tendon had already been exposed by a hit at the start of the break-out, and now

his whole bottom was ripped open. As my magazine was empty, I ordered my lieutenant, who was himself wounded in the arm, to shoot me so that I would not be captured. He shouted: "Only another 2,000 meters, Sir. We've got to make it." I crawled up a slope through the snow, with the medical officer next to me. . . . Under extremely heavy fire, two wounded grenadiers of my combat group pulled us up by the arms, and with several wounds in my feet I dragged myself the two kilometers to the German position.

The Hungarian ensign Gyula Kokovay and some of his companions reached Anyácska-puszta after breaking through several Soviet positions, despite attacks from ground troops on skis and fighter aircraft:

It was growing light when we came under rifle fire after 500 or 600 meters. I was going to fire back, but my submachine gun had suddenly jammed. As there was no time in the middle of the assault to see what was wrong, I threw it on my back and, running along, put my bayonet under the buckle of my waist belt to be handy.

When we were near the positions of the Russians, they threw hand grenades at us. One grenade hit me on the head and I fell, but because it landed in the snow in front of me, I lay there until it exploded, filling my eyes and mouth with snow and blowing my cap away. I picked up my cap and ran after the others, who had just reached the Russians' shelter. Eight or ten paces from me a Russian, stepping out from behind a tree, pointed his rifle at me. I could distinctly hear it click, but it didn't go off. He raised it above his head to knock me down, but he was too late because I rushed at him and sank my bayonet in his flank. He doubled up and fell to one side, while I caught up with the others, who had gotten beyond the shelter and to the edge of the forest. We dispersed and bounded toward the line of trees, hoping that our men were in there. Under heavy fire, crawling and sprinting for about half a kilometer, I reached the line of trees and took cover in the ditch behind it. . . .

When we started again, Áron Vajna was first to jump out of the river bed, but he was dead after less than ten steps. A bullet had hit him in the neck. About 10 o'clock those who had gotten through began to trickle in, 36 Germans and 9 Hungarians of whom only 3—József Jász, Béla Hidvégi and I—were unscathed; the other six were carried away on stretchers.

By 16 February a total of 624 had reached the German lines. Schweitzer and three of his men were among the 80 to 100 who arrived later. Trekking toward Esztergom through the Pilis Hills, on 15 February they found themselves at Lajos-forrás Source. Schweitzer recounts:

The sight of a house is enormously attractive because we are exhausted and starved. But first we must see whether there are any Russians there. We cautiously advance in pairs. . . . The house is deserted, all the rooms looted, with the exception of the kitchen, where the utensils are lying around in a muddle. In the corner on the left there is a couch, but no food. All we want is sleep . . . while an old lance-corporal searches the house for something edible. He comes back with a shapeless mass that turns out to have been German army bread. So it is at least seven weeks old. . . . We cut the rotten bits out and are left with a handful of crumbs interspersed with mould, whose origin can just be recognized. These are fairly distributed. . . .

The sun is high in the sky when my comrades wake me. I jump. We must disappear at once. It's uncanny. Suddenly some footsteps in the house. We stand rooted to the spot, staring at the door. Gingerly a head is pushed in. A Hungarian civilian. He is even more frightened than we. What are you doing here? Behind him two young people. One of them speaks German. They implore us to leave immediately. If the Russians came, as they do daily to collect hay or something, they would also be lost because they had not reported us. They have been robbed of everything down to their shoelaces. We prepare to leave and beg for something to eat. . . . At half past three in the afternoon our morale is so low that we decide to return to the house, come what may, even though the Russians have not shown. Our three Hungarian friends turn pale with fright when we turn up. For their own safety they demand our weapons and ammunition, which we hand over on condition that they return them before dawn next day. Then they would at least be able to say that they had disarmed and captured us, if a Russian came along. We peel and boil the potatoes we found. . . . I lie down and fall into a deep sleep. When the potatoes are ready, my comrades try to wake me but without much success. Half asleep I eat two spoonfuls of potato and drop off again. At six in the morning we are up. The Hungarians give us some tea and a bite of bread. Now I feel fresh again.

The four men continued their journey past the tourist hostel on Dobogókő, the highest peak in the Pilis Hills. As the hostel was occupied by Soviet guards, they had to follow the steep northern slope, which took a whole day in the deep snow, although the distance was only four kilometers. On 20 February, early in the morning, they were finally near Esztergom:

My feet hurt so badly that I have to take off my boots. I manage this with some help, but when we try to continue I am unable to get into them again and stand on my feet. I tell my comrades to go on, I would drag myself to the nearest hut I could find during the day and take a chance on whether it was in Russian territory or our own. My comrades decide to stay with me. . . . At daybreak, from the top of a hill, we see a town only a few hundred meters away. According to the map it is Esztergom. Ten days ago it was still in German hands. On all fours, on my knees and elbows, I crawl toward the first houses. One of us goes on ahead and reports back happily that the first house is a German billet. We have made it.

For a number of Germans the break-out lasted longer. Afraid of being captured, some took refuge in the forests until the spring or even summer, while others went underground in the capital and escaped in civilian clothes weeks or months later. SS Untersturm-führer Fritz Vogel was hidden by members of the University Assault Battalion until April 1945. He emerged from his hiding place pretending to be a deaf-mute, before making his way home to Vienna. Another escapee was observed, freshly shaven and wearing a smart raincoat, asking his way, in German, to Budakeszi.

Events in the Castle District and the Military Hospitals

Up to 5,000 soldiers, mostly Hungarians, had remained in the Castle District, either because they had never received the break-out order or because they regarded the enterprise as pointless. Several thousand badly wounded—in the military hospitals in the tunnel, in the vaults of the National Bank, and elsewhere—had also been left behind. The chief medical officer and his personnel had fled, abandoning their patients to their fate. After the failure of the break-out only medical officer Hübner returned to care for some 2,000 wounded who lay deserted in the cellars of the Royal Palace:

> In the Castle sheer madness ruled. The weeks of encir-clement had driven everybody to the brink of insanity. Deprivation, misery, and worry about the future pro-voked actions for which the individual could no longer be held responsible. . . . Pistols were going off in every corner of the huge underground infirmary: nobody wanted to be captured by the Russians in a wounded state. I quickly lined up some sensible, only slightly injured officers, a staff paymaster, and a group of eight NCOs and sergeants, whom I deployed at key points. We announced to the wounded by radio-telephone that we were immediately taking responsibility for their care. . . . The Hungarians contented themselves with collecting

the remaining weapons of the wounded and spreading horror stories. Only two doctors volunteered immediately and then remained good comrades and friends to the end. . . .

There had been no need to starve the soldiers for weeks in the city's cellars and in the trenches. The soldiers stormed the supply stores in a frenzy. They gave vent to their fury over the deceit in pointless destruction. A young NCO had discovered the evacuated bunker of General Pfeffer-Wildenbruch and put on his abandoned uniform. One of the maniacs, taking him for the general, shot him dead before we could intervene. . . .

Toward eight o'clock in the morning I started to amputate the arm of a badly wounded first lieutenant who had dragged himself back to the Castle. The operating room was in the deepest catacomb. . . . Suddenly a Russian was standing in our operating theater, pointing his submachine gun at us. With an immense calm replacing my earlier excitement, I continued, taking no notice of the visitor. After the operation we swigged a big gulp from the bottle. "Ivan" did the same, and then we went up to surrender. . . . Meanwhile Russians of all ranks had made themselves at home in the empty rooms, and the vodka was flowing profusely. . . . By evening nobody had attended to us and we went back to our work. . . .

Suddenly the infirmary was in total darkness. When we looked for our generator, we saw it being towed away by a jeep and disappearing in the distance. Apparently it had interfered with the Russians' radio signal, but we would definitely be given a new one with a suppressor. I never saw it delivered. With the generator gone, the water supply also ended. The latrines overflowed and excreta floated between the straw beds of the wounded. In the darkness we could not find any candles. The Russians showed us how to make lights out of lard and rags, and these contraptions were smoldering everywhere. . . . In every nook and cranny the wounded were doing their business, all discipline gone. In the dark we were continually treading on filth and excrement. The stench was unbearable. There was no question of nursing the wounded.

The number of dead was frightening. The bodies were piled up in the former kitchen in the deepest catacomb, where they stiffened into gnarled shapes. Between them, medicines, tin cans, slashed paintings, precious china, laundry, etc., were lying all over the place.

The Soviets decided to leave the hospital and sought doctors among their prisoners to look after the wounded. One of these, Ensign Aladár Konkoly-Thege, describes his first encounter with Hübner and the hospital:

On the south side a dark entrance leads to the German military hospital in the cellars under the Castle. A German doctor, looking thin and tired, comes out with two medical orderlies. He says that he and his men can manage only the removal of the dead, and there is no other treatment. We are divided into three groups with orders to ascertain how many people are needed on each floor and what we can do for the wounded.

I am sent to the second basement. We make slow progress, with only a few candles flickering in the dark. The air is thick and stifling. Pus, blood, gangrene, excrement, sweat, urine, tobacco smoke, and the smell of gunpowder mingle in a dense stench, which fills the passage. . . . On both sides of the passages the wounded are lying in long rows, some on plank beds or in bunks, many on the bare concrete . . . almost motionless, feverish, weakened, and helpless. For days there has been no treatment, change of dressings, or cleaning, nor any food. As the doctor said, only the dead have been taken away. Groans, sighs, barely intelligible German laments, prayer, fragments of swearwords. . . . The lowest level contained the men who were wounded in the head, paralyzed or blind, including some Hungarians. Those brought here were given a few painkillers as a farewell.

Several fires broke out, probably as a result of smoking, although some sources claim that in one ward Soviet soldiers poured gasoline over the patients and set them afire. Some of the wounded were demonstrably burned alive in the emergency stations in the tunnel and underneath today's Institute of Military History. Hübner tells about events at his post:

On 18 February there was another fire on the upper floor. It came from a side wing under . . . our hospital, where there was an ammunition store. I had just recovered from a very uncomfortable situation. We were removing a splinter from the stomach of a young Hungarian when the door of the operating room was torn open and two savage-looking fellows burst in, furiously shooting at each other. One of them crouched at the foot of the operating table, shooting at his opponent, who in turn was shooting back across the open stomach of the anesthetized patient. We took cover, trembling, until the marksman at the foot of the table lay on the floor with a hole in his head. Without saying a word, the champion swaggered out, leaving us with an unknown body. We had earned a large brandy but had no time to look for any because by then the whole place was blazing fiercely.

The fire found ready fodder in the wall coverings, the wooden paneling and the patients' beds of straw. The ominous crackle of the fire merged with the sound of shells and grenades exploding in the ammunition store, and the desperate screams of people being burned to death. The only way out was a door about two meters wide in the upper catacomb. There could be no question of rescuing the many wounded. We managed to pull about 100 people out of the fire, but most of them were going to freeze to death outside because all we could do was to lay them down in the snow as they were.

Konkoly-Thege continues:

> Smoke billows from the exit and explosions are heard. Some wounded drag themselves into the courtyard. Others appear after them. They crawl along painfully, some on their knees and elbows inch by inch, pulling the stumps of their amputated legs behind them. Those who can, support each other. They are trying to escape from the blazing hell because the hospital in the cellar is burning. The German doctor cries in despair: "Comrades . . . my comrades are being burned alive inside and I can't help them."

According to some sources the fire claimed 300 lives, although others cite as many as 800. But there were also a number of survivors:

> In a side room separated from the catacomb by a heavy iron door, we had accommodated some badly wounded Hungarian and German officers. The door was completely warped, but from behind it I heard knocking. With our combined strength we broke it open. The officers were sitting in what seemed like a revolting stinking oven. They had undressed and watered the scorching walls with the content of their urine drum.
>
> It was summer before the few survivors were able to return home.

The German Army Group South's Reaction to the Break-Out

The high command of the German Army Group South received Pfeffer-Wildenbruch's radio message about the impending break-out at 7:45 P.M. but did not forward it until 10:30 P.M. General Balck, the commander of the 6th Army, immediately informed the army supreme command: "I will try to meet the IX Mountain Army Corps via Zsámbék or Pilisszentlélek. We are honor bound to do this for the Budapest garrison. I envisage a joint strike of all available forces of the cavalry corps and such tanks of the panzer units behind them as may be placed at our disposal."

The Red Army's 2nd Mechanized Guard Army Corps and 5th Cavalry Corps, however, were assembling in precisely the same area. Moreover, the preparations for a German attack, even if immediately approved by the supreme command, would have taken at least one or two days, and in any case there were not enough fast-moving units available. For want of anything better, Lieutenant-General Otto Wöhler, the commander of the German Army Group South, ordered farewell telegrams—printed days if not weeks earlier—to be dropped to the garrison from the air, and Pfeffer-Wildenbruch was awarded the Oak Leaves in addition to his Knight's Cross.

Thus the commands of the German Army Group South and the 6th Army were obliged to watch the tragedy unfolding in front of them without being able to intervene. The initial plans soon evaporated, along with the optimistic mood. The war diary of the army group, not without errors, narrates the situation as follows:

Monday, 12 February 1945.
. . . No detailed reports available from the garrison, which broke out of the western part of Budapest last night. According to aerial reconnaissance, they seem to be fighting their way northwest through the Pilis Hills in several combat groups. A group of our own forces is being assembled southeast of Esztergom to launch a counterstrike. . . .
Army Group Balck:
   According to reconnaissance reports—in the absence of current radio contact with the corps—the main thrust is developing along the Pesthidegkút-Solymár-Pilisvörösvár-Pilisszántó-Pilisszentkereszt-Pilisszentlélek road. The head seems to have reached the Pilisszentkereszt area. Two grenadier regiments and an assault-gun brigade have therefore been ordered to assemble southeast of Esztergom. . . .

Incomplete air reconnaissance since midday suggests that the Budapest garrison, counter to the original plan, is moving northwest—that is, toward the Pilis Hills. At 17:50 hours the 1st general-staff officer reported . . . that some groups had been seen near Pesthidegkút and Solymár. . . . German groups had also been seen at the southern entrance to Szentendre, in the woods west of Szentendre, and even at the western entrance to Pilisszentkereszt. . . . A short while ago German groups were apparently also observed near Pilisvörösvár. . . .

At 23:25 hours the Army Group Balck's chief of staff reported . . . that since the Pilis Hills were clearly becoming a break-out destination, the army group had relocated its combat group to that area in order to open a gateway at the approach of the IX SS Mountain Army Corps. A forward squad was ready to provide initial assistance and medical care. The army group hoped that the first escapees would be arriving during the second half of the night. The left wing of the 3rd Cavalry Brigade and the right wing of the 96th Infantry Division are reporting battle sounds and flares five kilometers east of their front line.

Tuesday, 13 February 1945

Army Group Balck:

. . . IX SS Mountain Army Corps: In the Szomor sector (3rd Cavalry Brigade) 3 German officers and 1 Hungarian officer with 23 NCOs and privates of the garrison have fought their way through to our own front line. These soldiers had not formed a closed combat group since the beginning of the break-out but met after being scattered from several different groups. . . . The 30 escapees followed a route from Budapest via Budakeszi and then through the forest between Perbál and Tinnye, where several more groups seem to be present. The roads are said to be heavily barricaded and partly impassable because of ruined buildings, motor vehicles, and dead horses. . . . The break-out was due to be carried out in three groups, north, west, and south, with Nagykovácsi as the assembly point. The escaping groups are reported to have run into a very strong defensive barrier, suffering many casualties and promptly falling into disarray. The second barrier, made of baggage trains, is reported to have been easier to penetrate.

The same day German troops recaptured the village of Mány, probably in order to assist the escapees, although the diary continues without mentioning this action:

Wednesday, 14 February 1945
Army Group Balck:
    On both sides of Szomor several small groups of the Budapest garrison have fought their way through to our own lines. According to the escapees the main thrust of the break-out was directed west and northwest. Unified command of the escaping combat groups of the garrison has apparently been lost. We can still expect only small groups or individuals to arrive. . . . Air reconnaissance has sighted parts of German units in the hilly region south of Pilisvörösvár and Pilisszentiván. This is where some groups were also observed yesterday. Likewise, according to air reconnaissance, the village of Telki, nine kilometers south and southwest of Pilisvörösvár, is being attacked from all sides. It is not known whether the attackers are German or Russian, but some German troops are likely to be enclosed in Telki. Another German group is assumed to be three kilometers east of Zsámbék. According to the morning report some groups, 100 men in total, have gotten through near Szomor.
    This confirms yesterday's impression that most of the escaping groups have not chosen the longer and more arduous but perhaps more promising route through the Pilis Hills, but the shorter one toward the west, despite the strong enemy presence. . . .

According to further air reconnaissance, battle noises, artillery fire, and blazes have been observed in the western part of Budapest. This suggests that some of our troops are still holding out in that sector. At 21:48 P.M. the command of the Army Group Balck reported to the high command that a total of some 600 men had gotten through so far. The command expected the escapes to continue for about three more days. . . .

Thursday, 15 February 1945

Yesterday it was reported that a group of escapees had gathered at Perbál. One of them had asserted that the entire enemy contingent had turned about face to confront them. The cavalry corps had therefore decided to launch an attack from the sector of the 3rd Cavalry Brigade. However, the enemy had been fully prepared for the attack, so that 50 escapees and 100 soldiers of the corps were lost. Therefore [the commander in chief] was unwilling to start an attack toward the Pilis Hills in order to rescue the groups of escapees allegedly located near Kesztölc. Moreover, he considered an attack across the Danube, in concert with the Südwind [South Wind] enterprise, more important and did not wish to jeopardize it through casualties or delays. . . .

However, in the evening report at 17:40 P.M. the Army Group Balck's 1st general-staff officer stated that air reconnaissance had observed no more German groups in the Pilis Hills. . . . No further escapees had arrived today. The commander of the Army Group Balck believed that any actions on the part of the army group would only put the trickle of small groups at risk.

Friday, 16 February 1945

Nocturnal air reconnaissance has produced no new information on the Budapest garrison. The Luftwaffe is continuing its search, but it is unlikely that any significant groups of escapees are left between Budapest and our own front lines. The number of escapees arriving at our lines has significantly decreased since the day before yesterday. Today only 14 arrived, and the total so far is 624.

Wöhler transmitted his closing message to the army supreme command at 11 P.M. on 16 February 1945. The Budapest garrison was not mentioned again in the daily reports.

Soviet Views on the Break-Out

Soviet studies contain surprisingly few details of these events, although Soviet historians have had some access to Soviet archives. The break-out certainly did not come as a surprise: the Germans had always resorted to this tactic, and as we have seen the Soviet command took measures in response. In contrast to the situation in early January, it was no longer in Tolbukhin's interest to allow the garrison to leave, because the defense was in any case about to collapse, within days if not hours. Some Soviet recollections give a powerful impression of the fighting.

An officer of the Soviet 297th Rifle Division, who had been stationed at 38/b Virányos Road, in the main trajectory of the break-out, remembers:

At about 23:00 P.M. the Hungarians [fighting on the Soviet side] brought in a German soldier, who was subsequently discovered to have escaped from the encirclement. He had been separated from his group, and when he saw some Hungarians warming bath water (some in uniform) he took them to be from his side. . . . We tried to discover how he had gotten behind our rear, but his replies were incomprehensible, and we sent him to the divisional staff.

An hour and a half or two hours later massive rifle and machine-gun fire erupted at various points of the city, but above all north of us, and we could also hear grenades exploding and artillery fire.

During the night, at about 3 o'clock, reconnaissance and signal troops in the corps's sector stopped a group of seven German soldiers headed by a first lieutenant, who in the dark had reached the vacant plot behind the villa. The lieutenant said that they had received orders to escape from the encirclement at all costs during that night. . . .

Early the next morning a large enemy column appeared, numbering 1,500 to 2,000 and taking up the whole width of the street. They were escaping at the double, firing into windows and throwing hand grenades. In the neighboring street (Szarvas Gábor Street) a German light tank was clanking along and had almost found cover when a shot from a bazooka paralyzed it. The mortar detachment next to us immediately set up a 120cm mortar produced from somewhere in a hurry. The open plot made accurate firing possible, and we showered the dense enemy crowd with shells. We barricaded the entrances and—almost without aiming—fired our rifles from the windows into the frightened mass swirling past us. . . .

The Hitlerists continued their advance toward the city exit despite their huge casualties, but soon ran into our multiple rocket launchers firing salvos at them from point-blank range. It was a terrible sight.

The experience of the Soviet 37th Rifle Corps exemplifies the violence of the encounters:

It was a cruel night. The thunder of guns and the whistle of shells mingled with the frightened yells of the escapees and the death rattle of the wounded, as muzzle flashes lit up groups of people dementedly running to and fro in the deep darkness.

To prevent the break-out, every able-bodied Soviet soldier took up arms. Positioned in the ditches alongside the road and behind the trees, commanders of every rank, together with all the men from the staffs and the workshops, were decimating the rows of escapees with their submachine guns or rifles.

A staff officer of the Soviet 23rd Rifle Corps recalls that the route of the escapees toward the western end of the Buda hills was blocked:

On the night of 11 to 12 February the Hitlerists made a desperate break-out attempt through the positions of the 37th Rifle Corps. Over the dead bodies of their soldiers and officers they blindly charged west and northwest toward Zugliget and Nagykovácsi. Finally 16,000 fascists managed to break through the inner encirclement ring and hide in the nearby woods.

On 12 February the corps commander withdrew the 19th Rifle Division from its positions and ordered it to organize the defense along heights number 262 and 544 and the eastern edge of Nagykovácsi, facing southeast, to prevent the enemy filtering out of the woods toward the west. At the same time the 11th Cavalry Division was attached to our corps. The task of this division was to comb the woods and destroy the scattered enemy groups. . . .

During the night of 13 to 14 February the telephone connection between the corps and the staff of the 49th Guard Division in Perbál . . . was unexpectedly cut off. About an hour later the calm and confident voice of Vasili Filippovich Margelov was suddenly heard on the receiver, saying that in the section of the divisional command in Perbál no fascist had succeeded in breaking through to the west.

It was later discovered, however, that an enemy group with a submachine gun had slipped through the wood to the northeastern part of Perbál. The divisional commander alerted the staff and personally led the fight against the German enemy. The majority of the Hitlerists were destroyed and the rest taken prisoner. . . .

The army corps's battles against the isolated enemy groups, who numbered about 400 to 600 and tried to escape through wooded territory far from roads and human habitation, lasted until 17 February. They were fought against enemy groups determined to break through toward the west, regardless of the cost; leaderless and having lost all military bearing, they prowled only at night like a pack of wolves mad with hunger. By 17 February we had annihilated or captured the largest enemy groups that had tried to break through toward our positions. Our six units annihilated 400 to 700 Hitlerists and captured 1,376, including many officers and two generals.

The Soviet troops had begun to advance cautiously into the capital soon after the break-out. By the afternoon of 12 February, Széll Kálmán Square, Széna Square, and parts of the Castle District were in their hands, although they took until noon on 13 February to advance along Olasz Avenue as far as János Hospital. On 15 February the Soviet command decided that the break-out as a strategic operation had ended, and the daily reports stopped mentioning it. The Hungarian Buda Volunteer Regiment, siding with the Soviets, had taken a significant part in the encounters, occupying the Royal Palace, rounding up German prisoners, and fighting on Remetehegy Hill and in the forests.

The failure of the break-out can be regarded as a success of the Soviet command in that only a small proportion of the escapees finally managed to get through the Soviet positions. But the tactic of evacuating the front line after holding it for a while may have been mistaken. The outcome of a break-out generally depends on timing. If the escape can be held up for long enough, panic ensues, ammunition runs out, the command loses control, and the whole enterprise disintegrates. This happened in Buda, but if the Soviets had set up several defense lines within the city, they would have saved effort in pursuing the escapees on the outskirts, taken more prisoners, and suffered fewer casualties.

The Outcome

The break-out of the Buda garrison was one of the most futile enterprises of the Second World War. On 11 February Pfeffer-Wildenbruch had about 44,000 soldiers. By 15 February 22,350 were prisoners and some 17,000 had been killed, mainly between Széll Kálmán Square and Hűvösvölgy Valley in the first six hours. As many as 3,000 were hiding in the hills, but by 17 February most of these had also been rounded up. About 700 reached the German lines, and a similar number managed to hide in the city (Table 14).

After the break-out, the escape routes showed an apocalyptic picture, with mountains of bodies, human remains carved up by Soviet tanks, and paving stones covered in blood and pieces of flesh. In Széll Kálmán Square, Vérhalom Square, and elsewhere bodies were piled up in pyres several meters high. Others were buried in mass graves near the spots where they had been found. Most of these graves have not been exhumed to this day, although 28 have been identified in the city and many more in 29 villages, holding an estimated total of 5,000 bodies. At the time of writing, traces of the fighting can still be seen, for example, on the walls of the former Ministry of Defense in the Castle District and some buildings in Széll Kálmán Square and Batthyányi Street.

The history of the siege and the break-out can be appreciated only against the background of total-war psychosis. Pfeffer-Wildenbruch deferred to Hitler's order to fight to the last bullet, when the Soviets would have welcomed an offer of capitulation, and he authorized the break-out only after the failure of the relief attempts, by which time it could no longer succeed. He regarded the hopeless escape bid as a better alternative than the dreaded capture, although when confronted with the reality he immediately surrendered to save his own life. The German command covered up for him. Oblivious of Hitler's earlier orders to the contrary, the war reports speak of the "break-out as ordered," and the tributes and obituaries in German newspapers preserve the same fiction. But this does not alter the fact that Pfeffer-Wildenbruch and his officers, dominated by fear of the Russians, remained incapable of making the right decision to the very end: instead of jointly capitulating at the last moment, they drove their soldiers blindly to destruction.

6

The Siege and the Population

The Plight of the Hungarian Population

Therefore nobody needs to worry that the Hungarian
capital will become the scene of street fighting.
—*Magyarság,* six weeks before the start of street fighting

During the Second World War several capitals suffered sieges, but
the tragedy of the siege of Budapest was second only to those of
Warsaw and Stalingrad. In Warsaw, though, the greatest devastation was caused by the 1944 Polish uprising and the 1943 uprising of the Jewish ghetto; in Stalingrad the Soviets had been able to
evacuate the majority of the civilian population. Later, in Berlin and
Vienna, the civilians were not evacuated, but the fighting was brief.
In contrast, the inhabitants of the encircled Hungarian capital had
to endure one of the longest and bloodiest sieges of the war. The
experience was shared by several generations, and almost every
family living there at the time can tell stories connected with it. Just
how alive the events are in the memories of eyewitnesses is demonstrated by the almost weekly letters I have been receiving since this
book was first published in Hungarian in 1998, not only from people who remained in Budapest but also from some of the thousands
who escaped to the West from the Hungarian communist dictatorship after the war or during the 1956 revolution. Although the damage caused by the siege is rarely visible today, the broken marble
staircases of some houses in central Buda, the bullet holes in the

wooden paneling inside others, and the regular discovery of infantry and artillery ammunition on building sites still bear witness to what happened in Budapest.

As the front drew closer to the city in the autumn of 1944, no political decision was taken about the fate of the population. The Hungarians would not have been able to carry out an evacuation, and the Germans were not interested in helping. The million inhabitants were therefore initially invited to leave voluntarily. Posters to that effect were appearing by 7 November 1944. At the same time the evacuation of schools began but made slow progress. Arrow Cross leader Ferenc Szálasi originally intended to leave the capital with his entire government, changing his mind only when Edmund Veesenmeyer, the German envoy, informed him on 8 November that the German embassy would stay in Budapest even if the Hungarian leaders departed.

As an "overture" to the siege, at 2 P.M. on 4 November, a section of Margit Bridge, between Pest and Margit Island, was blown up. Although the guns could not yet be heard in the city, the explosion stunned the inhabitants. Miklós Kovalovszky writes in his diary:

> When we arrived in front of the Comedy Theater, we were shaken by a tremendous explosion. . . . I ran back to the Danube embankment, where a huge crowd had gathered. It was a terrible sight. On the Pest side two arches of the bridge had collapsed. Streetcars, cars, and hundreds of people had fallen into the river. Two shattered number 6 streetcars jutted out of the water, and the moans of the injured could be heard. Bodies were hanging from the railings, and in the swirling water there were dead and wounded. Ships, boats, and police craft were trying to save whomever they could. About 800 people had been on the bridge at the time of the explosion.

The exact number of victims is still unknown: a contemporary inquiry cites some 600. According to the same inquiry, the blast occurred because the Germans had been installing primed charges

35

Colonel-General Hans Friessner surveying the wreck of Margit Bridge,
4 November 1944

on the bridge as an exercise and the fuse had been ignited by a spark from a passing vessel. The dead included 40 German pioneers fitting the charge.

Various directives to evacuate the suburbs of Pest appeared in succession. On 10 November orders were given for the evacuation of the most sensitive areas—Kispest, Pestszenterzsébet, Pestszentlőrinc, and Soroksár—but only a few inhabitants moved to the central districts of the city. Ten days later the order was rescinded, because no accommodation for the evacuees could be found. On 4 December the evacuation of Csepel was decreed, but protests of the population undermined the effort. By the time the encirclement was completed on 27 December, some 100,000 people had fled from the capital, but the majority preferred to stay behind. Sándor Magyarossy, the government's commissioner for evacuation, notes: "The evacuation ordered on 26 November was mainly obstructed by the sabotage of MÁV [Hungarian State Railways], as only 35 passenger cars out of 353 earmarked for the evacuation were delivered. . . . Neither the boilermen nor the engineers showed up at the station. . . . The overwhelming majority of the city's population, rather than fleeing, chose the horrors of occupation by the Bolshevik horde." The Russian colony in Budapest continued to function even during the siege. Its members included a number of historic figures: Count Michael Kutuzov-Tolstoy; General Boris V. Shulgin, the last adjutant of the Czar; and Count Pushkin, the pastor of the Pravoslav parish. Kutuzov-Tolstoy, as representative of the Swedish embassy, remained in charge of a hospital for severely injured Soviet prisoners of war, manned mainly by Polish doctors, who were allowed to work undisturbed during the siege. A niece of Winston Churchill's also stayed in Budapest and was most distressed by the temporary loss of her favorite dog.

Civilians were first drafted to build defenses on 7 November. Fifteen thousand people assembled in Kispest, but—as a result of air raids, artillery fire, and lack of organization—dispersed even before they started work. No further action of this kind was undertaken in earnest. On 19 November only a few hundred reported for duty, despite the statutory obligation to do so.

The Arrow Cross Lord Mayor of Budapest, Gyula Mohay, was inaugurated on 14 November. On the next day, he ordered all men born between 1912 and 1923 to the earthworks. Only some 500 turned up because, as was discovered later, those drafted early in November had been "informed after walking several kilometers to the assembly point that the order had been rescinded." On 20 November in Csepel, only 200 people could be recruited. Many police and gendarmerie officers had either been transferred to the fighting units or decided to sabotage the pointless orders, and without their participation the civilians could not be forced to work. From the beginning of December, Arrow Cross Party activists appeared in all private and public offices and demanded from each employee a day's voluntary labor. But the population remained totally passive.

By winter 1944 Budapest was being described as a "second Stalingrad," both in Hungarian military reports and in Soviet propaganda leaflets dropped from the air. It is no coincidence that on 23 December the command of the Hungarian I Army Corps ordered the introduction of a special badge for the defenders along the lines of the Crete, Africa, Crimea, and other combat badges of the German army. The Germans planned a similar badge for Budapest, of which a prototype was found during the break-out: it shows the Imperial Eagle enthroned above the burning Royal Castle and a sky full of aircraft and parachutes carrying canisters. The Arrow Cross government further intended to create a decoration called Cross of the Heroes of Budapest, but by February 1945 there was hardly anybody left to whom it could have been awarded. Thanks to bureaucratic delays, even those few Hungarian soldiers who had escaped from the city failed to receive it.

In November the food situation began to worsen. Some items were available only at irregular intervals, and fresh meat became a rarity. Because of administrative deficiencies even existing stocks could not be used effectively. The large pig farm in Tétény was suddenly evacuated on 10 December, and many animals escaped to nearby Kamara-erdő Forest. One shocked eyewitness recalls:

> People were sawing at the throats of the poor animals with penknives and dragging them away half dead. Those pigs still alive were licking the blood of the others in their hunger, while their heads were being bashed in with rocks. A soldier also took part in this terrible hunt. People were asking him to shoot the pigs, and he bumped them off for 50 to 100 pengős. It was like one of those summer restaurants where people choose the poultry scratching about in the courtyard before it ends up on their plate as roast chicken.

On 23 December Szálasi asked the German Army Group South for help. This is how he described the plight of the population: "I have been informed by Minister Kovarcz that it is not possible to guarantee supplies to the capital from the capital's own stocks, which are, in fact, catastrophic. The number of deaths by starvation is already alarmingly high, particularly among children. In addition, hunger riots must also be expected." On 24 December Endre Rajk, the Arrow Cross secretary of state, reported that food supplies would last only 12 days. The rations had been reduced several times since the Arrow Cross had come to power: by mid-December people were receiving 150 grams of bread a day and, at Christmas, 120 grams of meat. The International Red Cross's offer of food aid worth 50 million pengős was rejected by Szálasi because of the condition that part of it be delivered to the ghetto.

In that year, many families in Budapest decorated their Christmas trees with antiradar aluminum strips dropped by British and U.S. aircraft to interfere with radar, while others, lacking firs, decorated fig trees. Midnight mass was held in the afternoon. Instead of visiting each other, people telephoned:

> The evening's sensation came over the phone. We called the family we had spent 15 October with in Pasarét. . . . They said that some strangers had arrived in front of their villa. We understood from this hint that the strangers could only be Russians. . . . Half an hour later

36
Siege food: civilians carving up a dead horse

three or four others called us, asking if we had heard. Naturally each time the reports became more and more sensational. Some thought that the Russians were at Széll Kálmán Square, others even believed that Russian advance guards had reached the Buda end of Margit Bridge.

Similar news arrived from Széher Road in the Kurucles quarter: "They are here. So far there are no problems. I must stop because they are coming again. In a day or two it'll also be over for you, and then we can talk." The majority of the population had no idea what the siege of a capital city meant as they watched events naively and passively. Ensign István Szalay remembers the bizarre mood: "On 25 December people brought Christmas pastry with nuts and poppy seeds on dishes and baking trays and distributed it indiscriminately among us soldiers. They brought something from every house and apartment and asked us what we knew about the military situation. I am sure they were not expecting defeat." On the same day, during mass, Bishop István Zadravetz reprimanded his congregation as if they themselves had invited the Soviets in: "You, you are to blame for this terrible Christmas we are having." The last streetcars started from Széll Kálmán Square in the morning, but during the day most were hit by shells, and public transport ceased entirely. Nevertheless, some people still did not want to face facts. Ervin Galántay, the 14-year-old dispatch runner of the Vannay Assault Battalion, tried to arrest a conductor, who had told him that the Russians were already at Budagyöngye, for scaremongering.

After Christmas organized food supplies ceased almost completely. As the population had not been prepared for a prolonged siege, most people began to starve after a few days. Many survived only thanks to the 30,000 or more horses that had been brought to the city by the Hungarian and German cavalry and artillery units. The fodder had run out by early January, and the starving animals—reduced to nibbling the woodwork in the churches and shops serving as stables—had to be put out of their misery in any case. By the end of January, with only horse meat and carrots or peas available, the soldiers were also starving. The greatest problem, however, was the distribution of what food there was. Some people were positively feasting, while others had hardly anything to eat. Reinhard Noll, an NCO of the 22nd SS Cavalry Division, writes:

> Our life was full of contradictions. There was barely enough water for a soup a day, but the best spirits were available in huge quantities. We got only one slice of army bread a day, but were fully supplied with lard, jam, and the like. . . . The most expensive Hungarian cigars we had never even heard of surrounded us in our cellars by the case. I became a chain smoker, otherwise I couldn't have survived this last great nervous strain.

Some bureaucrats were not prepared to open their stores without orders, even as the Soviets were approaching. Officer Cadet Norbert Major's requests, for example, were refused at the food store in Lehel Street, although enemy machine guns were already firing in the neighboring streets: "Leave me alone with such defeatist talk. Who do you think you are? In three months the siege will still be on, and what am I going to give the people then," the store commander told Major, who nevertheless succeeded in "liberating" a few cases of supplies behind the commander's back.

Civilians were forbidden on pain of death to touch the contents of the canisters dropped by parachute, and the penalty was actually carried out by some of the German units. Often the water shortage could be alleviated only by melting snow, but this could also be fatal because soldiers of both sides would open fire indiscriminately on any civilians who ventured out of doors. Many civilians were killed by hand grenades or phosphorus thrown through cellar windows.

On 26 December, Hindy addressed the population over the radio, describing the seriousness of the situation but promising that the capital would be relieved shortly. On 30 December he sent the following dispatch to the minister of defense and the Honvéd army's chief of staff:

> Food supplies to the army and the civilian population in the first week of January will be catastrophic. Today

I have been informed that supplies to the ghetto, which is said to contain 40,000–60,000 Jews, have ceased completely and as a consequence the Jews are restless. If these Jews were driven by hunger to break out of the ghetto, the consequences could be very unpleasant. For the time being I have ordered some corn flour to be delivered to the ghetto. . . . The population of the capital, according to information received, regards the situation as desperate. . . . In the city the wildest rumors are circulating. Several days ago I and my staff officers, as well as the German general staff, were said to have left Budapest by air. . . . The masses, while not expecting the Russians to come as liberators, have been reduced by the barrage to such a state that they are at least resigned to Soviet occupation. The local patriotism of the citizens of Budapest is so great that they are not crying about their own fate but are desperate about the destruction of the city. . . .

Neither the officers nor the privates expect to be relieved any longer. . . . The majority of the officers are carrying out their tasks dutifully. Some would like to save their own skin unnoticed, but the serious and disciplined officers have been talking about the possibility of a break-out and have submitted serious and thoughtful proposals to me.

Naturally I am unable to express an opinion on these proposals, particularly as I am not in charge of the defense of Budapest and can only suggest possibilities to the commander of the German IX SS Army Corps, who, in response to my request, has informed me today that there are no plans for a break-out.

The Hungarian command was rarely kept informed about events by the Germans. On 31 December, Hindy did not even know whether the purpose of the promised German counteroffensive was to free the capital or to rescue the garrison. In an attempt to clarify matters he cabled the minister of defense: "The strength of the people of Budapest is rapidly declining. To inspire them psychologically with the will to persevere, I consider it necessary to issue a proclamation. For this proclamation I request an appropriate situation report based on concrete facts."

During the relief attempts in January, the Hungarian command set up the Henkei Group as a crisis-management unit which was due to deliver "food supplies in the event of the liberation of Budapest." The supplies would have been transported by train to Bicske and Dorog and then by road to the capital. Within six hours of the relief it would have been possible to dispatch three consignments, weighing in total about 1,000 tons, which would easily have satisfied the needs of the population, and the trucks would also have been used to evacuate civilians. On 14 February, the day after the capture of Buda, the group was dissolved.

Hindy received visits from representatives of various embassies and the International Red Cross, and from Angelo Rotta, the Papal Nuncio. Rotta had sent the Arrow Cross foreign minister, Gábor Kemény, sharp notes on 13 November and 23 December condemning the deportations of Jews. On 27 December, jointly with the Swedish ambassador, he tried to persuade Hindy to stop the fighting, but Hindy sent him away, saying that he did not have the power to do so.

The International Red Cross, in a cable of 6 January, requested the German and Soviet commands to permit the evacuation of the civilian population and suggested a ceasefire of limited duration for that purpose. Hitler agreed in principle but asked his military leaders for their opinion. The German command, afraid of unauthorized actions by the Hungarians, advised the Hungarian minister of war, Károly Beregfy, that there could be no negotiations until orders were given from above. The Soviets in turn may have balked at the prospect of dividing the garrison's scarce supplies among smaller numbers after the evacuation of the civilians. In any case the Red Cross's proposal came to nothing.

On 3 February, Rotta and his secretary, Archbishop Gennaro Verolino, called on Pfeffer-Wildenbruch. Verolino recalls:

Wherever we went, wounded were lying in every room and in every corridor, and operations were in progress on ordinary tables. We heard moaning and whimpering everywhere. It was hell. Eventually we reached the German general somewhere in the depths of his bunker, and he said: "If anybody wants to defect to the Russians, he can. The Danube is frozen, one can walk across the ice."

When the shocked Rotta asked him why he would not agree to a ceasefire, Pfeffer-Wildenbruch said that he was not authorized to do so, but promised to apply to his superiors, although he must have known that this would not produce any results.

Relations between the Hungarian and German commands became more and more strained. Initially Hindy tolerated the insults of the Germans, noting only the most blatant cases in his reports, as, for example, on 30 December:

> A German pioneer captain blithely blew up a barricade in Ostrom Street, regardless of the fact that he was also blowing sky high a water pipe 800mm in diameter. Consequently there has been no water in the Castle for three days. . . . I have reported this to the commander of the IX SS Mountain Army Corps. . . . But, given my experiences so far, I do not expect my protest to bear any fruit. . . . As a rule the Germans not only behave aggressively, but they also flatly refuse to give the names of their units and threaten the employees of industrial installations with their weapons; any vehicles and fuel they commandeer by armed force are of course lost forever. . . .
>
> I myself get on well with the commander of the German army corps and his chief of staff. We have never had any differences of opinion that could have interfered with our cooperation. As it is he who has been given the task of defending Budapest, I consider it natural that I should comply with all his wishes and lend him a helping hand with everything. . . . Nevertheless, I must also report that by now the commanders of all the Hungarian units have appeared in front of me and asked me to take over the tactical command.

In reality, the two commands were hardly on speaking terms. Pfeffer-Wildenbruch never consulted the Hungarians and informed them of his plans and orders only after the event. Hindy's growing bitterness shows in his daily reports, submitted in mid-January, about the plight of the capital:

The lack of fighter aircraft protection was decisive in the destruction of Budapest.

Among the civilian inhabitants fear of death is relegating all other questions to the background; their fate and plight are desperate. In many places the city center is now only a pile of burning ruins.

1. In the southern parts of the Pest bridgehead only the strong points are still holding on. With enemy pressure increasing further, Buda can soon expect a similar fate. 2. The constant air raids and bombardment by mortars and artillery are causing immeasurable losses to the massed troops and matériel. 3. The streets are blocked by huge heaps of rubble. There is no hope of clearing them. 4. The water supply is exhausted. At the few wells there are huge queues. 5. Infestation by lice is spreading rapidly. 6. Many German soldiers have acquired civilian clothes. 7. Lieutenant-General [Imre] Kalándy has been badly wounded. 8. The combat value of the troops is deteriorating by the hour, most noticeably among the German troops.

Hindy finally lost his patience on 30 January, when the Germans reported that the majority of the Hungarian army and gendarmerie had defected to the Soviets. Beregfy had sent the text to Hindy, demanding an investigation. Hindy's reply includes the following:

Civilians, bombed out of their homes and shelters, stripped of their possessions, and tormented by hunger, lack of water, and both friendly and enemy fire, are increasingly expressing their hatred of the Germans and the Arrow Cross through an unstoppable whispering campaign, because they regard their own suffering and the destruction of the capital as pointless. They hate the appearance of our own soldiers in the shelters, where Russians have distributed cigarettes and brought water to civilians on some occasions. Therefore the Russians are awaited as liberators by many. The Russians respond to every military movement by shelling, but they do not fire on civilians. The concerted Russian propaganda is also confirmed by the behavior of the Germans toward the Hungarian civilians and soldiers.

More than once Hungarian civilians and soldiers have been arrested by the SS for no apparent reason and kept in the most terrible conditions until they were freed by the Hungarian I Army Corps. . . . Officers have been insulted and beaten without cause. During attacks the Germans lag behind, goading the Hungarian soldiers ahead with their arms, while German units rob the Hungarians' barracks. Unarmed workers have been forced to take part in attacks simply in order to create a commotion and have suffered bloody losses in consequence.

After citing further examples of German brutality and emphasizing the daring of various Hungarian units, he declares that the defending army is at the end of its tether and that even the best officers' nerves can no longer bear the siege. His reports in early February are equally explicit:

The Germans have turned the Capuchin Church in Corvin Square into stables. Relatives of soldiers and other civilians, tormented by hunger, setting aside all modesty and shame, are calling at the command posts and the kitchens of the Hungarian units to beg.

The Germans are taking the civilians drafted for labor to the front line. Enemy fire is causing casualties and obstructing their work. In most cases they return home under mortar and infantry fire without having done any work. Looting of private homes is on the increase.

According to the Germans only minimal food supplies are arriving by air. They do not pass any of these on,
but where possible even seize the scarce supplies issued
for the civilians or made available, under inadequate
surveillance, by the Hungarian army's collecting agencies. . . . It is impossible to resist the more and more frequent requisitions and robberies by numerous armed
Germans behind the front line.

The mood of the civilians is desperate. Their relations
with the Hungarian soldiers are good, but they dislike
the Germans because of their aggressive behavior. The
civilians no longer see the Germans as a liberating army.
They say that was a fairy tale.

Hindy's reports were somewhat one-sided—the morale of the
Hungarian units was worse than that of the Germans, and military
cooperation as a rule presented no problems at the lower level.
What the reports reveal is that the Hungarian general regarded the
continuing defense of Budapest as senseless and even culpable,
although he still failed to break ranks with the Germans.

Work at the metropolitan public utilities ceased comparatively late, because most of the plants (water, gas, and electricity)
fell into Soviet hands gradually. Gas supplies broke down on
28 December, water supplies on 3 January. Telephone connections
continued to function until the end of December, and in some
places—particularly near the Buda telephone exchanges—even
until the beginning of the break-out in February. Electricity supplies finally failed on 30 December. During the artillery bombardments, gas pipes were frequently damaged: the main under
Vérmező Meadow, for example, caught fire and the flames shooting out of the ground presented a ghostly spectacle for days.

Despite the breakdown of telephone links the population continued to receive information about events in the city. News about
the death of the Soviet parley delegates or the capture of the notorious Arrow Cross leader Father Alfréd Kun, for example, reached the
deepest cellars in Buda. When a red German parachute got caught

on the dome of the Parliament building, rumors spread like wildfire. Most took it for a Soviet flag, while some embroidered the narrative further, claiming that the Hungarian standard with the Virgin Mary—the national patron saint—was hanging next to the Soviet.

For weeks, the cellars of the large apartment blocks sheltered hundreds of thousands, although many people on the run did not go there even during the bombardments because they had reason to fear that some of the others would denounce them.

> The worst thing about the shelters was that they had been designed only for short air raids and not for large crowds staying there day and night for weeks on end. Therefore most only held a few benches, some firefighting equipment, and a first-aid cabinet. Sometimes a wireless was later added to this primitive equipment. . . . People moved into the shelters in stages. The first were usually families with small children, who would have had difficulty running down to the cellar from the third or fourth floor when the air raids began, and then back up again. The lifts in most apartment blocks had not been working since December. . . . The better shelters were tiled or plastered. Almost everywhere the breath of so many people condensed on the walls, and the ceilings were constantly dripping.

The greatest conflicts among the occupants erupted over cooking, water carrying, and washing. Only a few buildings had wells of their own, so drinking water had to be brought mostly from far away and in life-threatening conditions. In Pest, by the end of December, water could be obtained only from the wells near the Parliament Building and on Margit Island. First Lieutenant Vladimir Oldner claims that the Soviet troops did not prevent supplies reaching the unoccupied parts of the city even after the capture of the water works, but this is contradicted by many other recollections. The population of Buda obtained water from the medicinal springs near Gellért-hegy Hill and from wells drilled under residential buildings, which were more numerous than today and which increased substantially in number during the siege. In some places, however—for example in the Castle District—the shortage became catastrophic. Normally, between 15 and 20 families had to share a cooker for cooking and heating water. Those with foresight organized communal cooking, which not only reduced the preparation time but was also more economical and had the further advantage that meals did not create a sense of inequality. Conflicts were more common in the absence of communal cooking. People eating in secret to avoid provoking others sometimes gave themselves away by the sound of chewing in the night.

Following the breakdown of water supplies, the lavatories also stopped working. Where people tried to use them regardless, the dried-out drains soon discharged a suffocating stench. "The toilets are full, now it's the turn of the baths, but some guys wrap it in paper and burn it in the stove," writes Blanka Péchy in her diary. By January, the ubiquity of excrement in the streets created a risk of epidemics in the shelters.

The ever-growing quantities of refuse caused similar problems. After the collapse of the public disposal system, the inhabitants began to carry their accumulated household waste to the streets and parks. It was not until summer 1945 that the mountains of rubbish began to be cleared away.

On 26 December the Arrow Cross mayor of Budapest had broadcast instructions for the party leaders in the various districts and their families to report to the Danube side of Gellért-hegy Hill on the following morning in order to attempt a break-out in the city's buses, for which Hindy had promised the assistance of the Hungarian army. However, Pfeffer-Wildenbruch had forbidden the action.

In fact, the majority of Arrow Cross members had already tried to leave earlier. Wilhelm Höttl, the representative in Hungary of the Reichssicherheitshauptamt, and Norbert Orendy, commander of the Arrow Cross secret police, had departed on 24 December, together with the majority of the German security service and the Gestapo. Adolf Eichmann, head of the Reichssicherheitshauptamt's section in charge of Jewish affairs, had flown out on 23 December after visiting the office of the Jewish Council in the ghetto for unknown reasons. By the time the encircle-

37
Bombed-out residents escaping along the Great Boulevard, c. 18 January 1945

ment was completed on 27 December, only a few district leaders had been left behind. Lieutenant-Colonel Béla Almay, one of the last to leave Budapest by air, recalls: "I had orders to report to the minister for total mobilization [Emil Kovarcz] in the Castle at 8 o'clock every morning. . . . It was shocking—Nobody there— The strongboxes open—A complete mess—Some drunk Arrow Cross men said: 'They all scrammed during the night.'"

The Arrow Cross Party had split into several armed factions. Two of these, the Armed National Service and the Party Service, had actually been fighting each other, and on 24 December members of the latter had kidnapped the commander in chief of the former. After the flight of the Arrow Cross potentates, the power of the uncontrolled party militia, restrained neither by the police nor by the military, had become almost absolute.

The post of chief district commander had been temporarily taken by Kurt Rechmann before Szálasi tried to end the chaos by appointing as head of the capital's party organization Imre Nidosi (who proceeded to call himself Budapest Arrow Cross Party police chief in his edicts) and as military commander of Budapest the chemistry student Erich Csiky, although neither was given any practical function. On 9 January, Ernő Vajna (brother of Interior Minister Gábor Vajna), who had arrived in Budapest on 1 January as Szálasi's personal representative, made both of them lieutenant-colonels, while styling himself party representative for the defense of Budapest. The party saw fit to announce these appointments by posters in the deserted streets.

The organs responsible for internal security, apart from those Gestapo sections left in the city, were the Armed National Service, the Party Service, and a detachment of the Arrow Cross secret police. Almost 25 percent of the Party Service consisted of convicted criminals. Vilmos Kröszl, party chief of the XIV District, for example, had stolen the car of a Wehrmacht unit. The Arrow Cross secret police not only spied on, arrested, and tortured real and supposed enemies of the system but also investigated various right-wing individuals, even opening a file on SS Obergruppen-führer Winkelmann, which was closed only after his vigorous protests.

Relations between the Arrow Cross Party and the Germans were neutral, but those between the Arrow Cross and the Hungarian military were extremely tense. Honvéd officers despised the Arrow Cross "proles," who missed no opportunity to demonstrate that they were now in charge. The Arrow Cross mob loathed both the semifeudal Hungarian social system and the officer class. It was no coincidence that some of the first measures of the Arrow Cross regime were to abolish the exalted status of officers and to enable NCOs to be promoted.

Some gendarmes, previously regarded as reliable, had also joined the party. Sergeant Fehér of the Galántai Gendarmerie Battalion, for example, let slip that the Arrow Cross was using him to do the "rough work" during interrogations, and defended his actions by saying that he had been promised an officer's rank as a reward. Another sergeant, blameless before he joined the Arrow Cross, dragged a Jew whose boots he had coveted out of a group of prospective deportees and chained him to his bed until finding time to kill him on the following morning. The same sergeant participated daily in the ill-treatment of Jewish prisoners.

The Arrow Cross gangs did not even spare the Hungarian military from their excesses. Lieutenant-Colonel Erich Kern, for example, was killed at his combat post in the Ludovika Academy because he had refused to hand over his car. "Burn him, boy," one of the Arrow Cross men said to his adjutant, who took his submachine gun from his shoulder and emptied the magazine into the lieutenant-colonel. Finally, the lieutenant-colonel's adjutant shot the "boy" dead and wounded his companion with his own submachine gun.

The Arrow Cross terror also threatened diplomats and others who issued protective documents. On 17 November 1944, for example, Arrow Cross militiamen grievously injured József Cavallier, the president of the Hungarian Holy Cross Association, by pushing his head through a window pane as a punishment for distributing passes from "Stalin's friend, the Pope" to persecution victims. On 29 December the party activist Father Kun robbed the Swiss chargé d'affaires Harald Feller, after having him stripped to establish that he was not circumcised. Feller lodged a complaint with Csiky, who had earlier been employed by a Swiss firm, and Hindy returned his 100 Napoleon gold coins with apologies.

All the licensed newspapers of the Arrow Cross and other right-wing groups continued to appear until Christmas Day. In the early part of January the dailies *Új Magyarság* and *Összetartás* were printed. Later on, the daily *Budai Összetartás* published from 22 January to 11 February, and *Budapester Kesselnachrichten*, published since the beginning of the encirclement, served as the official "fortress press." The few incomplete copies of these papers still in existence are regarded as rarities of press history. The following extracts are from *Budai Összetartás*, published by the Arrow Cross in the XI district:

[22 January:] Apartment-block commanders must collect rents and pay outstanding property taxes to the district tax office immediately, as war relief can be disbursed only if the corresponding funds are at the tax office's disposal.

[24 January:] The owners of shops selling horse meat are informed that slaughter may be carried out only in the Bicskei Street garage, under supervision of the medical officer. Slaughter time is 8 A.M. A well-digging team commanded by technical director Ferenc Fancsaly has been formed and will begin digging wells in successive groups of buildings in the district.

[27 January:] A maternity clinic has been opened. . . . Sign writers are to report to the party.

[5 February:] Life was beautiful, but is still beautiful with all its sufferings, sacrifices, and tribulations. If you lose heart, brother, think of the words of Ferenc Szálasi: "Without Good Friday there is no resurrection." This is Budapest's Good Friday.

[7 February:] Pumping the water of the Gellért Baths up into the water-supply network and repairs to the network have enabled water supplies to resume on both sides of Horthy Miklós Road. . . . In Budapest under siege a new type of woman is being born: her face is no longer covered in lipstick and powder, but in soot and lime dust. It is the soot of burning houses and the lime dust of collapsing walls, but it becomes her better than any cosmetics, for it bears witness to her heroic soul.

[9 February:] Deputy Prime Minister Jenő Szöllősy published a message to the people of the capital in the *Budai Összetartás* newspaper. Subsequently the paper repeatedly and emphatically reminded block administrators to remit rents immediately to the City Council. State employees could collect their salary at the same location.

Today it is almost unimaginable that the activities mentioned in the paper could be kept up under the daily barrage and air raids. It seems grotesque that people were required to pay property tax when 80 percent of the buildings had suffered damage of some sort.

Béla Almay, as we have seen, was one of the last to be flown out of Budapest. This is what he observed:

> The streets are deserted, the shops closed, the people in unheated cellars. Gas is not available and electricity only in a few places in Pest. Demolitions by nonexperts often make the water pipes unusable for days. Since 1 January the population has been receiving 50 grams of bread a day. As from 31 December all the horses are being slaughtered. Food supplies cannot last longer than 10 to 14 days, even if systematically collected. The hospitals are unheated. There is not even enough fuel for the operating theaters. The deprivations of the population are beyond imagination.

Conditions were worst in the sick bays. Thousands of civilian and military wounded were lying in the cellars of the Parliament Building, the Museum of Military History, the State Printing Press, and the Castle District. Klára Ney, a local resident whose brother Gyurka had been hit by a shell splinter while fetching water, reports:

> On the top step, we are overpowered by the rising heat and stench. No wonder, for on the stairs leading two floors down into the cellar dead bodies are lying on stretchers. . . . On the floor the patients are lying on both sides, with only a narrow passage between them. It takes my breath away. I can't see Gyurka anywhere, although we are almost beside his bed. We didn't recognize him! Like all the patients here, he is lying in the infernal heat stark naked. In nine days he hasn't been washed once. If he finally gets his cup of soup or vegetable it's after several hours' delay. . . . Nobody cares. Some people practically starve to death. . . .
>
> The inner section of the public shelter . . . was appropriated by the Germans as a "military hospital" during the second week of the siege. The sick bay in the rock, a scene of terrible suffering, is a paradise of

civilization and hygiene compared with this "military hospital." There is some electric light here, but nothing else. Gloomy passages, branching out in all directions. People crammed together in indescribable filth and misery. Under the bare rock faces on the black soil, human wrecks, with only one arm or one leg, disfigured by wounds, are lying literally one on top of the other on makeshift pallets contrived from planks, doors and stretchers. . . . In addition, everything is positively crawling with millions of lice.

After Christmas a number of motherless babies were left in the maternity ward of a hospital, where it was becoming impossible to feed them for lack of mother's milk and other nutrients. In despair the nurses clutched the babies to their breasts so that they might at least enjoy the comfort of a warm human body before fading away. After a while the nurses found themselves producing milk, and the babies were saved from starving to death.

The civilians were obliged to watch the killing and the destruction of their city for weeks without being able to intervene. On 2 January a Soviet incendiary bomb set the roof of the Parliament Building alight, with flames tinted an unearthly shade of blue and green by the melting lead covering. The explosions of German and Hungarian ammunition stores caused a great deal of damage: a six-story building in Klotild Street blew up on 13 January, a building used by Germans in Rothermere Street on 15 January, and the Regent Building in Margit Boulevard on 22 January. These disasters alone claimed about 1,200 lives.

Many residents were obliged to watch all their property being destroyed. Between 14 and 15 January a Soviet platoon became involved in an exchange of fire with a German unit in the cellar of an elegant apartment block at Kálvin Square. Many civilians, used by both parties as shields, were killed. The Soviet soldiers retreated, and the Germans charged through the building after them with their flamethrowers. When the Soviets finally took the building on the next day, it was entirely burned out behind its marble façade.

On 30 January, Hungarian gendarmes and German troops stationed in an apartment block in Várfok Street became aware of a group of Soviet soldiers who had managed to occupy a nearby school and advance from there unobserved. In the ensuing exchange of fire, a German soldier with a submachine gun killed four of the civilian residents, while the Soviet intruders remained in the building until German flamethrowers set it on fire on 2 February. The Soviets withdrew, and the burned-out apartment block remained in German hands until the end of the siege. The surviving residents, who had taken refuge in the cellar of a neighboring building, lost everything they had.

In an area near the front line László Deseő, aged 15, recorded the progress of the tragedy, hour by hour, in his diary:

> 7 February. . . . The front has arrived. They are installing machine guns on both balconies of the upper floor. In my room they wanted to set up an automatic cannon. I was talking with one of the Germans in the hall when a mine exploded in front of the door and the German collapsed. A splinter had neatly shaved his fingers off down to the roots. The poor devil is screaming.
>
> They are carrying firewood from the garden to build barricades in the windows. They are also putting furniture into the windows. While they build a barricade in one room I pull it down in the other. . . .
>
> 8 February. . . . The wounded are innumerable. In the house opposite there are Russian snipers; if anyone appears at the window he is shot at. . . . Wagner [a press-ganged ethnic German private] is badly wounded. Only two hours ago he admitted, laughing, that he had been responsible for the destruction of the whole house, because he could just as well have led the horses into the empty cellar next door. There is heavy firing throughout the evening.
>
> 9 February. . . . Half past eight in the morning. I am standing near the stairs to the cellar. A little while ago 17 Germans arrived to defend the house, among them an

SS man of English origin. Five of them are standing next to me. We are not talking. They are very nervous. They smoke one cigarette after the other. Their hands are shaking. They load their submachine guns. One is a pilot. His plane was shot down and now he is one of the defenders. A large signal pistol is dangling at his side. . . . So far two have asked us for permission to put on civilian clothes. On the upper floor it's OK, but down here in the shelter we don't allow them to change. . . .

10 February. . . . At 10:05 they are bandaging a German wounded by a grenade. He has thigh and hand wounds. I've had a look at them. The blood doesn't bother me any more. A splinter has torn off his fingernail down to the bone. You can see the bone. . . .

At half past five they sit down in the big cellar. They won't negotiate. The cellar must now be constantly guarded.

At six they demand a kilo of potatoes and they get it. It's impossible to refuse them. One of the German wounded told me that the wounded are dying like abandoned dogs; nobody takes care of them. A man called János Schreiber who was wounded some time ago can't walk yet and says that he has to hide from the Germans because with his leg he wouldn't be able to escape from the Russians and so the Germans would probably shoot him. The man wounded last night . . . didn't get any supper because his mates gave him nothing, saying they too were getting food only once a day. They gave the poor devil a few spoonfuls of bean soup, but only because my father asked them several times. He is very afraid that his mates will shoot him when the Russians get close. The situation of the wounded is indescribably bad. In the apartment there are already six dead horses. Apparently six are still alive.

10 February. . . . A quarter to ten. One of the soldiers looked out of the lounge window (curiosity killed the cat), bang, shot in the head. When I was trying to

crawl through the lounge underneath that window (I didn't fancy showing myself), I accidentally put my hand in the bloody brain matter that had spilled on the floor. At lunch I remembered I hadn't washed my hands, but went on eating calmly. Washing hands is a luxury. . . . They are shooting from the shelter stairs. This is how I imagined war to be. But now I'm pretty fed up with it.

The mortar fire is intense. In the caretaker's flat there are already four dead bodies. In the shelter you sometimes can't see anything because of the lime dust. The lamp swings for a long time. The light is refracted by the specks on the plaster. Deathly silence. Then again the rattle of machine guns, mines exploding. Today we didn't even light a fire because the chimney is so shot up that we wouldn't be able to stand the smoke.

Krisztina Church is in Soviet hands, the house at number 50 also. I looked out on the street through the one remaining window. One can already see the Russian dead with one's naked eye.

11 February. The Russians have reached the Prei-singers' house, the third down the street. . . . In the apartment there are still Germans. Dead horses every-where. The smell of blood with a whiff of cadaver smell, nicely mixed with smoke. It's cold. In the rooms the muck is knee high. . . . The Germans look rather frozen. They have become tame. They even inform me in a friendly manner that they will shoot me if I don't go back to the cellar, as civilians have no business to be in the front line. I assure them that it won't stay the front line long, and they calm down. Apparently the station has been set on fire.

11 February. The Germans finally leave the house.

12 February. At a quarter to three in the morning the first two Russians arrive. They look smart. They have machine guns. They are jolly. . . . I go up into the apart-ment. One could howl, walking through the rooms. There are eight dead horses in the apartment. The walls

are red with blood as high as a man, everything is full of muck and debris. A room-sized section of the loft cover has fallen down. All doors, cupboards, furniture, and windows are broken. Nothing is undamaged. The plaster is almost all gone. In front of the house there are abandoned German supply vehicles. . . . From the bedroom window to the window in Katica's room the wall is missing. One steps over dead horses. The horses are soft and springy. If you jump up and down on them, small bubbles, hissing and bloody, rise near the bullet wounds.

13 February. When I was in the street a Russian handed me a wicker bottle and tried to make me go with him. Then the caretaker of the house next door came along, I gave the bottle to him and so the Russian led him away. I'd be interested to know where he took him.

Today the girls went to see Uncle Zoltán. Their house had been hit by eight bombs. They live in the Térffy villa. The Russians have robbed them massively. During the robbery they had been locked in a closet. The Russians took 35,000 pengő, watches, food, clothes, simply everything.

14 February. In the morning four Russians came twice and robbed us. They broke open whatever was locked and took away an incredible amount of stuff. The horses are worrying us a lot. The cadavers are beginning to swell up because of the warmth.

15 February. I have heard from several sources that free looting is at an end. If you call an officer he will tell the looting Russki to get lost.

I have seen a Jew in Russian uniform. He looked really good in the Russian clothes.

In many places they are raping women. Women are being hidden everywhere.

On Rókus-hegy Hill almost all the villas had been destroyed. Böszörményi Road, Déli Station, Széll Kálmán Square, and Margit

Boulevard had been reduced to rubble. The villa in Olasz Avenue, where the Gestapo hoarded silver, gold, china, tapestry, and carpets stolen from Jews, had been blown up and all the valuable objects ruined. The streets of the Castle District could hardly be found and people were often walking on the roofs of the razed buildings. The author Sándor Márai describes the apocalyptic picture:

> What I see in Óbuda is at first sight horrifying, but after every hundred meters becomes more and more gro-tesque and improbable. The mind boggles. It is as if the wanderer were passing not through city districts but through excavations. Some streets must be guessed at: this was the corner house with the Flórián Café, this is the street where I once lived—no trace of the building—this pile of rubble at the corner of Statisztika Street and Mar-git Boulevard was a five-story block with many apart-ments and a café a few days ago. . . . Here is a wall of a building where friends used to live, there the remnants of a street, in Széll Kálmán Square the wrecks of streetcars, and then the devastation of Vérmező Meadow, the Krisztinaváros quarter, Naphegy Hill, and the Castle.

The zoo also suffered heavy damage. Of the 2,500 animals only 14 survived. In the final week of the siege, when the hail of bullets had killed three attendants, all attempts at feeding ceased. Many animals were slaughtered by local residents for their meat. The glass walls of the palm garden were shattered by the shock waves of explosions, and in the pool behind it the crocodiles died when the heating system received a direct hit, although the hippos lying in the warm water of an intact artesian well were saved by their fat reserves. Several large carnivores escaped from their bro-ken cages and devoured each other or were shot by soldiers in nearby gardens. A few birds of prey flew away and kept alive by scavenging carrion. One lion hid for weeks in the tunnels of the underground railway, eating stray horses, until a task force set up by the Soviet city commander, Lieutenant-General Ivan Terente-vich Zamertsev, caught him. Two Shetland ponies disappeared in January but returned to their stable in March after spending two months unscathed in the starving city. According to one source they had been abducted by a cart driver, who brought them back after the siege because he was afraid of punishment.

All the sculptures in the capital's squares were disfigured by shrapnel and bullets, and many were destroyed. Some were demolished by Communist Party activists after the fall of the city. Others, including the bronze lions in front of the Parliament Building, were taken away by Soviet plunderers. The metal of an equestrian statue of the 1848 revolutionary Artur Görgey was used to cast a statue of Stalin: half a century later it was recast and placed on the plinth of a former statue of Lenin in Felvonulás Square.

In the last tragicomic episode of the siege, on 1 March 1945, Parliament adopted Szálasi's recommendation to confer the title City of Heroic Resistance on Budapest by analogy with the Soviet title of Heroic City bestowed on Leningrad, Stalingrad, and Moscow. After the fall of Budapest, Károly Beregfy, as commander in chief of the Honvéd army, prepared a radio speech in tribute to the defenders, which was recorded by the security and propaganda section of the supreme command. A group of soldiers, on their way to deliver the recording to the radio station, stopped at a bar, where one of them, no doubt after a few drinks, sat on the disk and shattered it. The soldiers were probably saved from severe punishment by a first lieutenant of the propaganda section who was famous for his imitations of other people's voices and who happened to be there. He re-recorded the speech, and even Beregfy was unable to tell the difference.

Persecution of the Jews

I would not wish any of you gentlemen to live in one of those houses.
—Gábor Vajna, report to the Hungarian parliament on the establishment of the International Ghetto

During the siege of Budapest crimes unparalleled anywhere else in Europe under Nazi rule were perpetrated—with the approval or at least tolerance of the state—against Jews. After the failure of Horthy's ceasefire attempt of 15 October 1944 the Arrow Cross regime immediately embarked on the "final solution of the Jewish question." By this time the only Hungarian Jews not deported to German concentration camps were those in the capital and in the forced Labor Service. The deportations had been organized by Adolf Eichmann—who had come to Hungary in the wake of the German invasion of 19 March for that purpose—with the assistance of the Jewish Council that had been set up on German orders one day later.

On 18 October, Eichmann reappeared in Budapest. The SD and the Gestapo took up quarters in the Royal Hotel in the Great Boulevard and a number of boarding houses on Svábhegy Hill near the terminus of the Cogwheel Railway. Gestapo official Hans Geschke, who had already proved his "expertise" by murdering the population of Lidice, was appointed head of the SD in Hungary, and his colleague Alfred Trenker head of the SD in Budapest.

38
"Jewry and Soviets, the death of Hungary," contemporary poster

For Szálasi and his gang, making Hungary "Jew-free" seemed to be more important than anything—perhaps even winning the war. There can be no other explanation for their totally irrational behavior, the sole purpose of which was to humiliate, eliminate, and annihilate the Jews. This must have struck even some of the Arrow Cross leaders who, while failing to examine the ideological justifications of the inhuman measures taken, questioned their usefulness in the existing circumstances. Gábor Kemény, the Arrow Cross foreign minister, for example, asked whether "we are rich enough to lose four million working hours a day." His fellow ministers shouted him down, however, and later the Hungarian government actually lodged a complaint with the Germans for allowing Jewish forced laborers digging entrenchments along the German border to work on Hungarian soil, demanding their immediate removal.

The German leadership also insisted on deportation and constantly pressed the Hungarians to take action. On 21 November, for example, Foreign Minister Joachim Ribbentrop sent a first-class telegram to Edmund Veesenmayer, the Reich's representative in Hungary, urging him to explain to Szálasi that the speedy elimination of the Jews was essential for the defense of the capital. In reality, Jews—with the exception of those in the Warsaw ghetto—hardly ever offered any organized resistance even when they were on the verge of annihilation.

On 17 October, as a prelude to the deportation, the residents of buildings marked with stars in the VIII District received orders to assemble in the courtyards next morning. On 18 October they were marched, hands above their heads, along Rákóczi Road to the Tattersaal Racecourse north of Kerepesi Cemetery, and on 19 October to the Danube embankment. When they were lined up facing the river, a German officer stopped the imminent execution and the Jews were sent home. In some buildings the assembly order had been delivered in surprise raids by police and Arrow Cross militia, who beat up the residents and even killed some who would not go at once. An old man at 6 Teleki Square, who was unable to walk, was dragged down the stairs from the fifth floor by his feet, with a long trail of blood pouring from his broken skull, and left dead in the street.

The deportation marches to Germany began soon after. After a first stop at the Óbuda brick works, some 6,000 Jews a day were made to set out on foot by three different routes and cover on average 30 kilometers, driven by Arrow Cross militia who openly killed and tortured many of them along the way. Beginning on 20 October the residents of marked buildings were rounded up to dig defense works regardless of their physical condition: among the forced laborers was a man of 81. Most of the antitank ditches were made by these workers.

The first Jewish suicide was registered by the police at 7:32 P.M. on 15 October. The first shooting beside the Danube was noted in the diary of the ambulance service on 23 November, although Jews had been shot there daily since 15 October. After 25 November police reports like the following multiplied:

> Labor-service man András Pitschoff, 22, was recovered by police officers numbers 2017 and 2048 from the Danube with a gunshot wound.
>
> Jews were shot at Széchenyi Quay on the Danube and several got stuck in the canal.

A favorite place for mass executions was the Danube embankment, although at night the Arrow Cross killers aimed badly, so that their captives were often able to jump into the icy Danube and clamber out at bridge ends or drain outlets. The following report of the Hungarian I Army Corps command describes such an incident in a characteristically roundabout way: "In the early morning of 30 December a police officer on duty stopped five Jewish-looking men, running and soaked to the skin, who were so confused that they were unable to say who they were or how they had fallen into the Danube."

In retrospect one wonders how such inhuman conditions could have developed. Before the end of the siege a government official told the Swiss diplomat Carl Lutz that in the whole city there had been only 4,000 armed Arrow Cross militiamen. Under normal circumstances, 4,000 could not have terrorized a million. Nowhere in Nazi-occupied western Europe were people publicly killed in large numbers merely because of their origins, and in the

39

Arrow Cross militiamen putting up a poster; in the background Father Kun with
a pistol holster across his monk's habit

Soviet Union such events ceased after the early phases of the German occupation. In Hungary nobody would have been called to
account by the Germans for trying to prevent the slaughters, and
the authorities would only have needed to abide by existing regulations. Nevertheless, the police, the gendarmerie, and the military
idly watched the Arrow Cross atrocities. This could not have happened without a deep and far-reaching moral crisis among the population, which may be illustrated here by a few contemporary
notes:

> The officer told us that the Jews had been stripped to
> their shirts, shot at the Danube embankment, and
> thrown into the water. "The trouble is not that this was
> done," he said, "but that some were left alive, because so
> long as they aren't completely exterminated, they'll all
> turn into vindictive swine."

Two deaconesses are having a conversation. One says: "It's certain that the Arrow Cross are preparing something dreadful against the ghetto." The other: "I'm sorry for the poor people, but maybe it's just as well, because then they won't get a chance to take revenge."

On the road a man joins me. He has fled from Lajosmizse and regrets it. "I fell for the propaganda," he says. I assure him that he will soon be able to go home. He mumbles with embarrassment: "I've got two acres of Jewish land. Do you think I'll be allowed to keep it?"

The Arrow Cross rulers' concern that the excesses of the militia might induce the population to pity the Jews is reflected in parliamentary deputy Károly Maróthy's rider to his speech advocating executions: "We must not allow individual cases to create compassion for them. . . . Something must also be done to stop the death rattle going on in the ditches all day, and the population must not be allowed to see the masses dying. . . . The deaths should not be recorded in the Hungarian death register." A statement by the national Police Commissioner Pál Hódosy was in the same vein: "The problem is not that Jews are being murdered; the only trouble is the method. The bodies must be made to disappear, not put out in the streets."

The behavior of the Arrow Cross militia may be exemplified through two eyewitness accounts:

In one of the streets leading to the Danube I saw a column of 30 to 40 people, all in white. As they approached I saw men and women in shirts, underpants, and petticoats, with the snow and broken glass crunching under their bare feet. Appalled, I stopped in my tracks, and when they reached me asked one of the Arrow Cross men who they were. I shall never forget his cynical reply: "The holy family." I stood petrified for a long time, until the sound of submachine gun salvos from the Danube embankment made me realize that it had been these people's last journey.

They were herding Jews along the Great Boulevard. Four or five Arrow Cross boys aged 14 to 16 were escorting them in Kecskeméti Street toward Erzsébet Bridge. An old woman collapsed. Understandably, she couldn't cope with the march. One of the boys started to beat her with his rifle butt. I went up to him in my uniform: "Haven't you got a mother, son? How can you do this?"—"She's only a Jew, uncle," he said.

Many Arrow Cross men had a "token Jew" they treated well and whom they later, when tried for war crimes, tried to use as proof of their sympathy toward Jews. The law student István Kelecsényi, head of the Arrow Cross Department for the Elimination of Jews and deputy director of the Anthropological Department in Charge of Racial Screening, was prepared to certify the Aryan descent of wealthy Jews, at a price. The wife of Gábor Vajna, the interior minister, became the party's national social organizer,

40
Body on the Danube embankment

although she had some Jewish ancestry, resigning only when her background was discovered and her husband divorced her.

Occasionally the viciousness of the Arrow Cross militia revolted not only the generally indifferent Hungarian population but also some Germans. Pfeffer-Wildenbruch, for one, forbade his soldiers to take part in anti-Semitic actions. The German political leadership, however, found it convenient that somebody else was solving the "Jewish question" even more brutally than they. Veesenmeyer received instructions from Berlin to assist the Arrow Cross "in every way" because it was "in our particular interest that the Hungarians should now proceed against the Jews in the harshest possible manner."

As a result of the Arrow Cross terror the number of Jews in Budapest declined by 105,453 between 15 October 1944 and 13 February 1945. Of some 50,000 "loan-Jews," who had been handed over to the Germans before the closure of the encirclement to build fortifications, about 7,000 became Soviet prisoners and

41
Bodies in the garden of Dohány Street synagogue

6,000 died outside the city. Forced laborers in uniform falling into Soviet hands had little chance of being spared prison camp, and even after the siege the Soviets captured people regardless of whether or not they had been persecuted.

Most police and gendarmerie officers had disliked collaborating with the Arrow Cross from the outset. When party militiamen in Zugló, for example, noticed that they were recapturing more and more individuals whom they had earlier delivered to the police station, the party leaders in the area decided that any undesirable elements should be liquidated by their own men. The first multiple murder of this kind took place on 12 November after the opening ceremony of the party headquarters, when about a dozen prisoners were executed on the bank of the Rákos stream.

The only protest against these actions, which were theoretically illegal, came from the Angyalföld branch of the party, whose leader angrily objected to others leaving "carcasses" in his district, where it was "hard enough to justify their own to the population." Among the murderers was a boy aged 15, who became an officer in the Hungarian air force after the war and was arrested in 1966, together with other members of his group, as a result of investigations into former Arrow Cross activists. He and his companions carried out continuous executions, preceded by savage torture and perversions. On Christmas Day alone they shot more than 50 people, and in total killed at least 1,000, perhaps as many as 1,200. The murders took place on the Danube embankment, in Városliget Park, alongside the Rákos stream, on the backs of trucks circulating in the city, and in the laundry room of the party headquarters, where interrogations continued until the drain was blocked by clotted blood. The bodies were usually left at the scene to create a continuous atmosphere of terror. On the benches in Városliget Park and Stefánia Road so many had piled up in November that it took several days to remove them.

Practically all party activists were obliged to take part in tortures and executions, which served as a so-called loyalty test. Boys aged 14 to 15 and women also participated in the bloodshed, the most notorious of the women being Mrs. Vilmos Salzer, 23, and the former nurse Piroska Deli. Party militiaman Péter Pál

Katona, conducting a group of 1,100 from the Óbuda brick works to the ghetto, personally shot 62 stragglers. Father Kun, who directed several bloodbaths, admitted after the siege to 500 murders. His order usually ran: "In the name of Christ—fire!"

Some 8,000 Jews had been exempt from persecution by special legislation. The Arrow Cross government reduced this number drastically. Seventy-one, who had received the golden Hero's Medal in the First World War, were awarded exceptional status by Szálasi, while 500 others were granted immunity by the Interior Ministry.

Commissioned by the International Red Cross, the Swedish embassy, under Ambassador Carl Ivan Danielsson, was the first to issue letters of safe conduct to Jews after the German invasion of 19 March. Subsequently, Raoul Wallenberg, who had been sent to Hungary by the Swedish government and the U.S. War Refugee Board, introduced special passes on his own initiative. These documents—which had come into being without any legal foundation and were retroactively approved by the Swedish government—stated that the Swedish Red Cross or the Swedish state had a particular interest in their holder, who was therefore under Swedish protection.

The various protection papers were honored by the Sztójay government and also accepted by the new Foreign Ministry after Szálasi had come to power. Although Foreign Minister Gábor Vajna had declared on 18 October that he "did not recognize any letter of safe conduct or foreign passports received by a Jew of Hungarian nationality from anyone or anywhere," the Arrow Cross government, under pressure from the countries concerned, eventually recognized 34,800. In reality more than 100,000, either genuine or forged, were in circulation, and the embassies themselves significantly exceeded the permitted quotas. Various other methods of saving lives were developed by Wallenberg, who was among the first to establish "protected houses" and organize supplies for their occupants, often risking his own life. Jews of military age were drafted into "protected" labor-service companies, although on 29 November they were loaded into cattle trucks and handed over to the Germans.

Like the Swedes, the Swiss diplomat Carl Lutz, the Portuguese diplomat Carlos Branquinho, and the Papal nunciature supplied protection papers. Friedrich Born, chief delegate of the International Red Cross, issued 1,300 identity cards serving as letters of safe conduct. The B section of the Red Cross, directed by the evangelical pastor Gábor Sztehlo, under the Good Shepherd Children's Action, set up 32 homes for children who had lost their parents, saving 1,540 from deportation or death by starvation. In addition, the Red Cross ran 18 hospitals and emergency clinics. The El Salvador Embassy distributed 800 special certificates of citizenship, and the Nicaraguan Embassy distributed 500.

The most daring rescues, perhaps, were accomplished by Giorgio Perlasca, the "Spanish chargé d'affaires." Perlasca was actually an Italian citizen who had been interned on 19 March 1944 because of his anti-German views. After escaping he took refuge in the Spanish embassy, where he joined the lifesaving missions. The Arrow Cross tolerated the actions of the embassy, hoping that the Szálasi regime would be recognized by the Spanish dictator Francisco Franco. The Spanish chargé d'affaires Angel Sanz-Briz had firm instructions to the contrary. He sent enthusiastic but meaningless statements to the Arrow Cross Foreign Ministry, where the truth remained unrecognized for a long time. The embassy was thus able to adopt a more aggressive approach than its Swedish and Swiss counterparts. It called the Arrow Cross to account for every single atrocity and demanded a special train for protected Jews, calculating that the regime, unable to meet these demands, would be prepared to make other concessions. On 29 November, Sanz-Briz left for Spain, as the Arrow Cross's pressure for an unequivocal answer on recognition was beginning to make his position untenable. Before leaving he gave Perlasca a German visa and promised to help him escape through Switzerland. Perlasca, however, would not desert his charges. He told the Arrow Cross that Sanz-Briz had gone to complete the recognition formalities and left him behind as chargé d'affaires designate. He was thus able to save the occupants of the Spanish protected houses, as they were about to be taken to the ghetto. Until the closure of the encirclement he constantly supplied the Foreign Ministry with misleading information and even resorted to blackmail, claiming that several thousand Hungarian hostages could be found in Spain if anything happened to his protégés. By the time his activities came to an end the number of Jews under his protection had grown from 300 to 5,000.

When Perlasca confessed his lies to Angelo Rotta, the papal nuncio, he was only cautioned not to mention them to Archbishop Verolino, who was "so punctilious that he wouldn't be able to sleep afterward." But when Perlasca later asked Rotta to threaten the Arrow Cross regime with breaking off diplomatic relations, he recalled, the nuncio replied that "'he couldn't do it without asking the Vatican.' Unable to bear this, I said a few sharp things about diplomats and ran away. I was so upset that I even forgot to kiss his ring."

The case of Miksa Domonkos, a member of the Jewish Council, was equally bizarre. When an Arrow Cross gang tried to loot the council's headquarters immediately after Szálasi's coup of 16 October, Domonkos phoned gendarmerie Superintendent László Ferenczy to ask for help. The superintendent, who was in charge of the deportations, merely replied: "Everything is fine. Now the Jews have gotten what they wanted." Nevertheless, Domonkos advised the Arrow Cross thugs to leave because Ferenczy was sending patrol cars, and they obeyed. Later on, Domonkos, in captain's uniform, began to distribute "official certificates" in Ferenczy's name, saving many Jews from deportation and liberating several members of the Jewish Council from Arrow Cross captivity. He carried such authority that he was eventually appointed police chief of the ghetto, as he was thought to represent the Ministry of Defense and nobody realized that he was himself Jewish. When Arrow Cross militia operating in the neighborhood captured Jews outside the ghetto, they would deliver them to his "command post"—if they did not shoot them on the Danube embankment.

The anti-Jewish laws of 1942 had been supported in Parliament by the representatives of Hungary's three principal churches. By 1944, having witnessed the inhumanity of the deportations, many church organizations began to save Jews. In early summer the Reformed and Evangelical churches submitted a joint Protestant Memorandum to Prime Minister Sztójay, and on 29 June,

Cardinal Jusztinián Serédi wrote a circular condemning the persecutions. Sztójay responded by banning the publication of the memorandum and the reading in church of the circular. In the course of the summer—again without much public response—Bishop László Ravasz of the Reformed church, followed by Serédi, repeatedly spoke out against the deportations. In a letter written five days after the Arrow Cross seizure of power, the bishop asked Szálasi to declare Budapest an open city, and in another, written on 1 December, he demanded a halt to the persecutions. Smaller church organizations joined in rescue missions with the knowledge of church leaders. In many instances, however, only selected groups—converts in particular—received assistance.

The police chief constable of Budapest, Gyula Sédey, and his deputy, Gyula Gyulai, also tried to help the inmates of the ghettos. There were even a few humane Arrow Cross Party members who took part in rescue missions. Best known among these was Pál Szalai, who had left the party in 1942 and rejoined it after Horthy's ceasefire attempt, becoming its police-liaison officer. In this post he was able to do even more good than before. He banned the removal without official warrant of possessions from apartments vacated by Jews, thus preserving 50 to 60 percent of movable property. He persuaded party organizer József Gera to protest against the atrocities and managed to set some police investigations in motion. He informed Wallenberg about a planned pogrom in the ghetto, and his deputy, Ferenc Perjési, actually moved into the ghetto in an attempt to improve conditions.

Ara Jerezian, a doctor of Armenian origin, had been the Arrow Cross's deputy youth leader until his expulsion in 1939. After Horthy's ceasefire attempt he rejoined the party and became its second deputy leader in the VI District. As the only functionary with legible handwriting, he was assigned the task of completing all the official warrants, which enabled him to save several lives—particularly at 1 Zichy Jenő Street. He obtained a protection certificate for this building from the Swiss embassy and then procured orders from the Interior Ministry to convert it into a Jewish hospital, although officially it was supposed to be a free Arrow Cross clinic. More than 400 Jews, including 40 doctors, survived here.

On several occasions Jerezian avoided discovery thanks only to his presence of mind. In January 1945 an Arrow Cross commander with 30 armed men surrounded the building and arrested him, announcing that everybody inside would be massacred according to regulations. After invoking the Interior Ministry order in vain, Jerezian invited the commander to carry out an inspection. A group of people wounded by an exploding shell had just arrived, and the visitors were obliged to make their way past the beds of groaning and dying patients. Jerezian's report paints a somewhat romanticized picture of the outcome:

> The nerve-racking inspection lasted almost an hour and a half, after which he returned my pistol and asked me to summon the doctors. . . . Some women began to feel sick; one unfortunate soul, unable to bear the uncertainty, jumped out of a third-floor window, and the . . . orderlies could only recover her dead body.
>
> When the doctors had assembled in one of the rooms, the commander positioned himself in the center and began:
>
> "I was sent here today with orders to massacre 400 Jews said to be hiding in this place together with their leader Jerezian. I came with that intention, but what I have seen and experienced here goes beyond imagination. I wouldn't have believed, and I don't think anybody could have thought, that such a perfectly functioning institution could have been created in the heart of the city within a few short weeks. What you have done and are doing here is such an achievement that I must bow to it even though I know that it is being performed by Jews. From now on your magnificent work won't be disturbed by anybody, I will see to that. Hold out a few more days. The liberating troops are on their way.
>
> As far as a reward for your extraordinary achievement and heroism is concerned, rest assured I will see to it . . . that in the new Hungarist state you will not be classified as Jews."

The Jewish hospital survived unscathed, although Jerezian was arrested and deported by the Soviets on trumped-up charges made by a doctor, and was released only months later. In 1981 he received the Yad Vashem order, the highest distinction in Israel awarded to those who had saved Jewish lives.

The embassies of the neutral states lodged continuous protests against the persecution of the Jews. On 21 October Papal Nuncio Rotta negotiated for more than two hours with Szálasi. On 17 November, jointly with the neutral embassies, he addressed a note to the Arrow Cross government, demanding the immediate cessation of the deportations and humane treatment for the Jews. On 23 December the neutral powers sent another note to the government, which had fled in the meantime. The suggested evacuation of the embassies was rejected by all. On 5 January 1945 Wallenberg addressed a comprehensive final note to Pfeffer-Wildenbruch.

On 12 November, 72 buildings near Szent István Square in the VI District in Pest had been placed under Swiss protection, and after 15 November this area became officially known as the International Ghetto. It was intended to concentrate all Jews with foreign passes in these protected houses, which had been designed to hold 3,969 people, but which began by taking in 15,600 and ended with nearly 40,000. In theory the houses were extraterritorial and each should have been guarded by two police officers, but Arrow Cross hit squads regularly raided them regardless.

The International Ghetto was far more dangerous than the "ordinary" ghetto—which was created a little later in the VII District—because the proximity of the Danube embankment and easy access to the houses encouraged the Arrow Cross to perpetrate bloodbaths. By the end of November, when only 32,000 Jews instead of the expected 100,000 had moved into the "ordinary" ghetto, the Arrow Cross grew suspicious, and when tens of thousands—instead of 7,800—sought refuge in the "Swiss houses" of the International Ghetto, it became clear that many protection papers were forged. These houses were searched as a priority, and because it was difficult to distinguish between genuine and forged documents many people were deported indiscriminately.

The creation of a segregated quarter for Jews without protection papers in the VII District had begun on 18 November 1944. The formal order for the conversion of this quarter into the "ordinary" ghetto was issued by Interior Minister Gábor Vajna on 21 November, and all Jews without protection papers were ordered to move here by 2 December. On 10 December the area was closed off with wooden boards, leaving only four exit gates. About 60,000 people were packed into 4,513 apartments, sometimes 14 to a room. According to plans, all the Jews—with or without protection papers—were eventually to be brought here. Officially the daily food ration was 900 calories plus any supplies available from the Jewish Council and the neutral embassies. In reality five soup kitchens provided barely 790 calories. Occasionally food carriers were robbed or hit by shells, and then the occupants of the houses concerned starved all day. The one police station within the ghetto had been closed on Vajna's orders, and internal security was provided by unarmed Jewish policemen, of whom Arrow Cross raiders bent on robbery took no notice. An eyewitness recalls conditions in late December:

> In narrow Kazinczy Street enfeebled men, drooping their heads, were pushing a wheelbarrow. On the rattling contraption naked human bodies as yellow as wax were jolted along, and a stiff arm with black patches was dangling and knocking against the spokes of the wheel. They stopped in front of the Kazinczy baths and awkwardly turned into the lattice gate. In the courtyard of the baths behind the weatherbeaten façade bodies were piled up, frozen stiff like pieces of wood. . . . I crossed Klauzál Square. In the middle people were squatting or kneeling around a dead horse and hacking the meat off it with knives. The animal's head was lying a few meters away. The yellow and blue intestines, jellylike and with a cold sheen, were bursting out of the opened and mutilated body.

The Arrow Cross committed innumerable atrocities against the inmates of each ghetto and even invaded neutral diplomatic missions elsewhere in the city: members of the Swedish embassy were murdered on 7 January, and blood was also shed at the Swiss embassy. The Germans were relatively humane: although they frequently rounded up Jews for work on fortifications, they always sent them back to the ghetto alive.

Between 14 November 1944 and 18 January 1945, the average daily number of deaths in the ghetto was 80: the comparable number in peacetime would have been 8. For a while, between 50 and 60 Jews shot through the base of the skull were brought every day to the Forensic Institute. In one incident on 28 December, Arrow Cross activists, joined by some Germans counter to their orders, dragged a sizable group of men from the hospital in Bethlen Gábor Square to the Danube embankment and executed them. The number of Jewish suicides in one week exceeded the total of all suicides in Hungary in 1943. "Old men, young girls, pregnant women killed themselves. Some mothers knocked their reluctant daughters unconscious with rolling pins and laid them under the open gas taps." On 3 January, Inspector General István Lőcsei, the ministerial commissioner for the concentration of the Jews, ordered the immediate formation of 12 Jewish labor regiments. The order could not be carried out because by that time the starving inmates were hardly able to walk.

On 1 January 1945 Szálasi's special representative, Ernő Vajna, had issued his first order for all the occupants of the International Ghetto to be transferred to the "ordinary" ghetto, purportedly "for military reasons" but in reality to facilitate the murders. On 4 January he repeated the order, and this time even Wallenberg found it impossible to prevaricate. On 5 and 6 January, 5,000 occupants of the "Swedish houses" were marched, under fire from Soviet fighter aircraft, to the "ordinary" ghetto. The Arrow Cross declared that if foreign states did not recognize their government, they in turn were not obliged to honor any agreements. On 7 January the evacuation was stopped, after Wallenberg's offer to give any surplus food in the protected houses to the Arrow Cross, but on the same day Arrow Cross men attacked one of the "Swedish houses" and, having herded some 130 people from there to the

Danube embankment, machine-gunned them down. A survivor remembers:

After me they interrogated my mother, a woman of 67. They stripped her naked, and three of them beat her up with rubber truncheons. When she fell they trampled on her and tore her hair out. Then I was . . . beaten up again by three men. . . . At midnight I had to go to the cellar, where about 30 torturers stood in line. All 30 of them had clubs, straps, and cudgels, and all set about me. From the cellar I was pushed into the laundry room, where there were already about 30 people with blood pouring from them. In the cellar the younger women were stripped and beaten with rubber truncheons. In the hall Arrow Cross man [Dénes] Bokor then told me to ask for a Hungarist blow in the face. Afterward I had to stand in the doorway, where they started kicking me. They did the same to women of 60; they hit us till we fell. At three o'clock we were tied together in pairs with leather belts and sent off, allegedly to the ghetto. I was constantly watching how they were carrying their rifles and machine guns. At the Chain Bridge there was a German guard, who let our group of 45 or 50 pass. On the Chain Bridge the weapons were leveled, which looked ominous. I began to loosen the belt. I was tied together with a man called Guttmann, who was only wearing a pair of underpants and a shirt. When we turned off from the Chain Bridge to the Danube embankment, the situation had become totally hopeless. I let go of my mother and released the belt completely. After 20 meters they stopped and ordered us to line up on the embankment and face the Danube, saying that they were going to shoot us. I had gotten to the embankment first with Mr. Guttmann. The torturers' leader, a stocky fellow with a small moustache, ordered me to go a bit farther. I pretended to obey and dived into the Danube, with the machine guns firing at me. From the water I could hear them execute the 50 people.

First Lieutenant Iván Hermándy describes a similar execution on the embankment:

> I peeped round the corner of the Vigadó Concert Hall and saw the victims standing on the track of the number 2 streetcar line in a long row, completely resigned to their fate. Those close to the Danube were already naked; the others were slowly walking down and undressing. It all happened in total silence, with only the occasional sound of a gun shot or machine-gun salvo. In the afternoon, when there was nobody left, we took another look. The dead were lying in their blood on the ice slabs or floating in the Danube. Among them were women, children, Jews, Gentiles, soldiers, and officers.

To stop the constant massacres 100 police officers were ordered into the ghetto on 10 January, but the next day 45 Jews were murdered in Wesselényi Street only a few steps from the police shelter. Their bodies were deposited in the garden of the Kazinczy Street synagogue and in Klauzál Square, as nobody had the time or the inclination to follow the cynical advice of Ferenc Orsós, the professor of medicine and former member of the international commission investigating the massacre of Polish officers: "Throw the dead Jews into the Danube; we don't want another Katyn."

On 16 January, when the Soviet troops had reached the Great Boulevard near the ghetto, the Arrow Cross decided to mount a pogrom. The plan was betrayed by a police officer to Pál Szalai, the Arrow Cross police-liaison officer. Szalai called on Ernő Vajna, who told him that he knew about the plan and had no intention of stopping it. With Wallenberg's agreement Szalai warned Major-General Schmidhuber, the German commander of Pest, that he would be held responsible for the actions of his subordinates. Schmidhuber promptly summoned Vajna and the German and Hungarian initiators of the plan, arrested an SS sergeant, and forbade the pogrom.

To ensure that his order was obeyed he sent his Wehrmacht soldiers into the ghetto.

On 17 January, Soviet troops reached the edge of the ghetto in Wesselényi Street. László Benedek, a doctor in the temporary Jewish hospital at number 44, persuaded a Hungarian antiaircraft battery stationed there to abandon the struggle. He admitted the soldiers as patients, having their uniforms burned in the hospital's ovens. The next day, after a short street battle, the ghetto was liberated.

In Buda, however, the persecution continued. On 14 January a gang from the Arrow Cross headquarters in Némétvölgyi Road, led by Father Kun, murdered 170 patients and others hiding in the Jewish hospital in Maros Street. On 19 January they slaughtered 90 people in the Jewish almshouse in Alma Street and on 21 January another 149 in the Jewish hospital in Városmajor Street. At the Városmajor Street hospital they ordered any occupants who could prove their Christian origin to come forward. When some produced their forged documents, they were shot. The rest were told to line up in the street to be "taken to the ghetto" in Pest—which was already in Soviet hands and in any case unreachable as the Danube bridges had been blown up—and were gunned down as they waited. Patients unable to walk were killed in the wards, along with their nurses, and their dying screams could be heard for two hours. Only one woman survived, by hiding among the dead bodies in the street.

The same gang also attacked the high-ranking police officers responsible for the security of Chief Constable Gyula Sédey. They forced the officers to hand over their arms and left. At midnight, however, they returned with Father Kun. The officers were stood against a wall and abused by Kun for "hiding while others are suffering for victory in the front line." The six officers present were taken to the Arrow Cross headquarters. The seventh, Chief Inspector László Beliczky, who had hidden in the lavatory, alerted Sédey, but a police detachment sent to free the officers was disarmed by the Arrow Cross men. "Brothers, here's Dr. [Imre] Marosvölgyi of the detention center," one of them, a former convict, shouted when he saw the captives—who were already well known to the

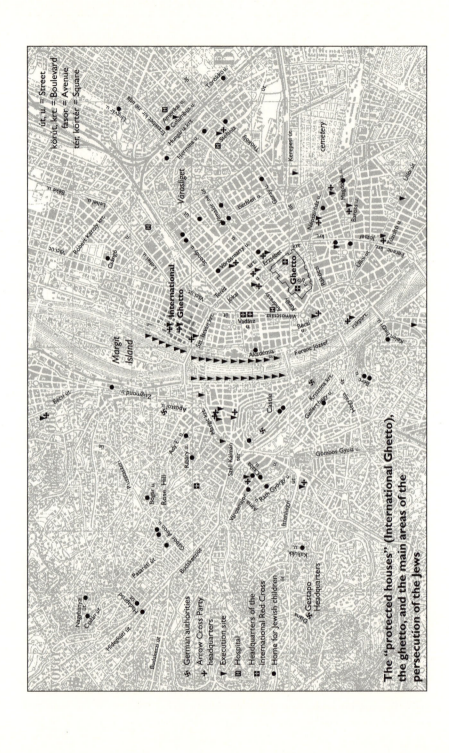

The "protected houses" (International Ghetto), the ghetto, and the main areas of the persecution of the Jews

party membership, as their duties had included interrogating dangerous criminals. Now the moment of revenge had come: "The door burst open. Father Kun was first to rush out and to make a start. He rammed his fist into the face of one captive and then, for good measure, added a hard slap with his open hand. 'Well, you bastard, we've got you at last,' he said and pushed the man into the room he himself had come from." The captives could be freed only by a second, reinforced, police detachment. Father Kun and his accomplices were arrested, although Kun managed to escape during the break-out. Péter Szabó, the leader of the gang, had kept a detailed diary, which he buried together with his identification papers and photos, but which were later found by chance and handed over to the police. The exact record of the crimes, including the rape of nuns, also made it possible to bring to trial other members of the group, who had been in hiding. Kun was finally sentenced to death by the People's Court and executed.

The Resistance

Internal resistance in Budapest features in many Hungarian studies published after 1945, primarily because the communist state had an interest in recording antifascist activities in detail. It is hardly mentioned in contemporary German and Hungarian military documents, possibly because its strategic significance was minimal.

Military units fighting the Soviets seldom came under attack from resistance groups. Germans, whom Hungarians did not generally regard as enemies, were rarely targeted, so that Alfred Trenker, the Gestapo commander in Budapest, declared that for Germans a year in Hungary was less dangerous than a day in Yugoslavia. The Arrow Cross, however, was feared and hated. According to German reports, even among Hungarian army officers only 3 to 5 percent were in favor of the regime, and many rejected the propaganda of the extreme right. Consequently, the resistance engaged mainly in saving lives, sabotaging deportations, and increasingly undertaking armed operations against Arrow Cross units and party buildings.

After the Arrow Cross coup several politicians who had been forced to go underground began to develop the rudimentary resistance movement. Based on the illegal Hungarian Front, which had been operating since the German invasion, the Liberation Committee of the Hungarian National Uprising (MNFFB) was founded on 9 November, with Endre Bajcsy-Zsilinsky as president and János Csorba as deputy president. Its military arm was set up on 11 November, under Lieutenant-General János Kiss as chief of staff and Major Jenő Nagy as his deputy, assisted by staff officers Vilmos Tartsay, Pál Németh, and István Beleznay, technical officers József Kővágó, Pál Almásy, and Imre Radványi, Hussar Captain Kálmán Révay, and many others. The MNFFB was joined by various illegal organizations, formerly of the Hungarian Front: the Independent Smallholders' Party, the Social-Democratic Party, the Legitimist Dual Cross Association, the Hungarian Communist Party, and the National Peasants' Party.

Hoping to prevent the siege and destruction of Budapest, the MNFFB planned to open the front line to the Soviets and trigger a simultaneous uprising: it even approached the Hungarian 10th Infantry Division, commanded by Sándor András, and several KISKA auxiliary units with this suggestion. On 13 November, Major Ernő Simonffy-Tóth, the Hungarian VI Army's chief of operations, flew to the Soviets as the Hungarian Front's representative. He had spent the preceding days dictating to his secretary behind closed doors and was later discovered to have been describing the air-raid protection and fortification system of the capital. Eventually he became a Red Army propagandist, urging the Hungarian defenders to change sides.

On 22 November, having been betrayed by Captain Tibor Mikulich, the military staff of the MNFFB was arrested during a meeting. Imre Kovács, a leader of the Peasant Party, owed his life to his late arrival:

> I heard shots being fired near the Opera. I walked faster and could hardly believe my eyes: the neighborhood of the Opera looked like a battlefield. From gateways and from behind trees and advertising pillars, field gendarmes

and party militiamen were firing like mad on a car, which was returning their fire. The bodies of four gendarmes were lying on the road covered by soldiers' coats.

The fray had been unleashed by Ensign Pál Széchenyi and Lieutenant János Messik, who had also arrived late. Both were killed and more than 30 people arrested. Subsequently the majority of the organization, numbering several hundred, were rounded up. János Kiss, Jenő Nagy, and Vilmos Tartsay were sentenced to death by a special court of the Hungarian army and executed in the military prison on Margit Boulevard on 8 December. Endre Bajcsy-Zsilinszky was hanged in Sopronkőhida on 24 December. Most of the remainder received prison sentences of between 10 and 15 years.

A resistance group of university students, KISKA units, and others was organized by staff Captain Zoltán Mikó, head of the supreme command's defense section, who belonged to the MNFFB but had evaded arrest. In the supreme command Mikó had supervised the KISKA auxiliaries, and toward the end of November was entrusted with organizing subversion and espionage units; he had also been placed in charge of the Prónay commandos and a gendarmerie investigation detachment. Early in November he had set up the Görgey Battalion, a sabotage unit designed to procure legitimate identity papers for people in hiding and members of the resistance, which consisted entirely of deserters, left-wing activists, outlawed politicians, and resistance fighters, although it was officially part of the Prónay commandos and the Arrow Cross. Through Wallenberg, he continuously sent food from the battalion's supplies to the "protected houses." Thanks to his connections with the head of the State Security Center, Chief Superintendent Lajos Kudar, a gendarmerie unit was sent in November to the International Ghetto, where it fought several gun battles with Arrow Cross marauders.

For a month the Görgey Battalion took part in exercises alongside the Prónay commandos while surreptitiously carrying out acts of sabotage and attacking Arrow Cross men. On 21 November one of its members, a Jewish deserter from the labor service, was recognized by a sergeant on duty in the Prónay food stores and arrested with his yellow star in his pocket. Ten more labor-service deserters in the battalion were seized by the Arrow Cross secret police, and all executed in the prison on Margit Boulevard on 4 December. Mikó transferred the battalion to the Börzsöny Hills north of the Danube, using as pretexts the need for "training" and a request from Germans for the deployment of Arrow Cross partisans.

Mikó had recruited some 800 armed resistance fighters, comprising 250 members of the Görgey Battalion, 500 members of various KISKA units, and 50 members of his own staff stationed at 54 Bimbó Road. A contingent of this size seemed capable of undertaking serious operations. On 20 December, Imre Kovács and three other representatives of the MNFFB visited the Soviets in the Börzsöny Hills to discuss the possibility of changing sides. But Kovács was arrested by suspicious Soviet counterespionage officers and did not escape until the end of February.

As the encirclement was about to be completed, Mikó made plans to defect and open the front line to the Soviets in Zugló and on Rózsadomb Hill. On 25 December the University Assault Battalion delivered a Russian prisoner called Krylov to his unit; Krylov had lived in Hungary since the First World War and had been returned to Budapest as a scout after being captured by the Soviets at Szentendre. Mikó sent Krylov back to the Soviets as an intermediary. After obtaining the German commander's permission to take over part of the defense on Rózsadomb Hill, he alerted his men, but instead of the expected 300 to 400, only 70 turned up: the majority had been either unwilling to risk their lives or unable to cross the Danube from Pest to Buda.

In despair Mikó approached the commander of the University Assault Battalion, Captain Sipeki Balás, a former fellow student at the military academy, whom he hoped to persuade to defect with him. Sipeki Balás took Mikó—who had arrived with eight armed companions, including First Lieutenant Vilmos Bondor, wearing a large number of medals—for an agent provocateur, and prevaricated. Finally, Mikó made his final argument: "So far I haven't told you the whole confidential truth. The differences between the German and Hungarian commands have become so acute that tonight there will be a complete volte-face. At 8 P.M. in four important sections of the front line the Hungarian troops will lay their arms down and let the Soviet forces pass." When Sipeki Balás replied that he was going to make inquiries at the army corps command, Mikó knew that his bluff had been called. Some members of the group decided to call off the defection and disappear as fast as possible. Mikó fled with his secretary to the Turkish embassy, where he survived the siege. Others decided not to disband, hoping that something would turn up, although it should have been clear that Sipeki Balás would not defect on his own initiative.

There are two versions of what happened next. According to Bondor and his companions, Sipeki Balás deliberately betrayed them. Sipeki Balás himself claims that he had every reason to distrust Mikó, as nobody at the corps command had mentioned any intention to defect, and he could not ask because he was not sure who else was involved. He maintains that he was about to leave when a gendarmerie chief inspector approached him:

> He asked me who I was and whether I had reported that Mikó had come to see me about defecting. I said that I had not. He took me to a colonel, whom I did not know but who could have been the head of the corps's 1.b section. The colonel received me by saying it was a pity that I had not reported of my own free will that I had been invited to defect. I was to tell everything exactly as it had happened if I did not want to find myself in an even more awkward position.

The Arrow Cross secret police had kept Mikó's group under surveillance since 26 December, when the University Assault Battalion had apprehended some Russian soldiers in civilian clothes, carrying identity papers issued by Mikó. Bondor was summoned to Bimbó Street, ostensibly for a meeting, and arrested together with his companions. After the siege it was the Russians who arrested Mikó and Bondor and sentenced them to death for espionage. Bondor's sentence was commuted to 25 years in prison. Mikó was executed in Odessa on 15 August 1945, even though he had voluntarily cooperated with the Soviets—for instance, in identifying Arrow Cross members among prisoners of war.

After the failure of Horthy's ceasefire attempt, many Hungarian officers had defected to the Soviets. They included Colonel Sándor András, commander of the 10th Infantry Division, who was aided by the antiespionage and intelligence section of his unit, and Colonel Ottó Hátszeghi-Hatz, the VII Army Corps's chief of staff, who had taken part in the ceasefire negotiations as a military diplomat. On 7 November 1944 Hátszeghy-Hatz flew to Szeged, where he delivered detailed sketches of the Margit Line to the Soviets. Subsequently he performed propaganda missions for the Soviets and from February to 5 April 1945 held the appointment of liaison officer at the Soviet military command in Budapest. Having been arrested by the NKVD (People's Commissariat for Internal Affairs) on false charges and sentenced to 15 years in a labor camp after seven years on remand, he was acquitted on 30 June 1955.

Dezső Németh, chief quartermaster of the I Army Corps, played a particularly important part in the resistance, issuing false papers to persecution victims, assisting in the defection of Simonffy-Tóth, hiding Soviet soldiers, and sabotaging the capital's defense. When the closure of the encirclement was imminent, it was Németh who deliberately moved the food stores to the outer suburbs where they could be reached sooner by the Soviets. He kept most of the corps's ammunition in railway wagons on Margit Quay, hoping that the Soviets would destroy it. This indeed happened, but the enormous explosions also destroyed the adjacent buildings, killing all the occupants. Together with his staff, Németh defected to the Soviets on 7 February 1945 and subsequently fought against the German and Hungarian garrison as a company commander, being wounded in the process. In 1949 he was sentenced to death in a show trial and executed.

The Hungarian Students' Freedom Front (MDSZF) was formed on 7 November by amalgamating seven illegal university organizations. Led by László Kardos, Sándor Kiss, and Tibor Zimányi, the front represented the radical wing of the people's movement. Many of its members enlisted in the University Assault Battalion, the Görgey Battalion, and the Táncsics Mihály Battalion.

An illegal newsletter published by the MDSZF brought the front to the attention of the Arrow Cross secret police, who on 12 December raided its headquarters and arrested many of its members.

The Táncsics Mihály Battalion, camouflaged by the official name I Hungarist University Reconnaissance Battalion, was recruited mostly from the National Guard at the Budapest universities. It had between 350 and 400 members, who issued hundreds of false identity papers and carried out several armed attacks on the Germans and the Arrow Cross. When their attempt to defect was foiled by Arrow Cross militia and German troops, they dispersed to await the arrival of the Soviets in Budapest.

In various offices of the City Hall of Budapest, resistance groups were formed after the German invasion. These concentrated mainly on providing certificates of immunity from persecution and other protective documents. Their military nucleus was the KISKA company in the VI District, with whose help they intended but failed to take over the City Hall and various public utilities. They were also in touch with resistance fighters in the MÁVAG arms factory, led by Endre Mistéth and Ferenc Koczkás, who sequestered some antitank guns for the MNFFB. On 19 November a number of their members were uncovered together with the MÁVAG group.

The Hungarian Freedom Movement, led by Frigyes Pisky-Schmidt, was close to the Social Democratic Party and primarily engaged in intellectual resistance. Beginning in 1943, with the tacit support of the government of Miklós Kállay, it had run a clandestine radio station and published a newspaper entitled *Feltámadás*. After the German invasion it became more active, and after the Arrow Cross coup it published an illegal newspaper entitled *Szabadságharc*. By agreement with Árpád Szakasits, executive president of the MNFFB, it also deployed an armed group to protect the illegal Légrády print works from being dismantled. In a gun battle on 25 December the group's leader, Béla Stollár, and 23 of his companions were killed, but the works were saved because the workers had taken the bulk of the equipment to their homes.

The Future in the East Group consisted of civilians and cadets of the Security Battalion. They were preparing to save some public buildings and factories mined by the garrison, but on 10 November, 27 of them, including their leader, Captain Sándor Fürjes, the commander of the Security Battalion's 2nd Company, were arrested, and the group disintegrated.

The Congregation of Marist School Brothers hid Jewish children, French and Alsatian SS soldiers on the run, and escaped French and Belgian prisoners of war. The Wehrmacht arrested them on 19 December, but their protégés were saved.

The poet Zseni Várnay, together with the Nobel Prize–winning biochemist Albert Szent-Györgyi, had begun to organize a resistance group on the day of the German invasion, recruiting several officers of the river guard and the manager of the Taurus factory. After Horthy's ceasefire attempt, Szent-Györgyi took refuge in the Swedish embassy, while the group developed a base in a cave on Ferenc-hegy Hill. Early in December the Germans raided the cave and arrested its occupants.

Since September 1944 two rival factions of the Communist Party—one led by Pál Demény, the other following the Moscow party line—had been setting up small resistance groups. The leaders of the Moscow faction weathered the siege in an apartment in Hungária Boulevard and a cellar in Francia Road, fed by György Aczél, who was to become an active cultural politician in the Kádár era. The military committee of this faction included György Pálffy-Österreicher, Lajos Fehér, and László Sólyom, with János Kádár as liaison officer. Their task was to organize, arm, and direct the operations of the Szír, Laci, Marót, and other "action groups." In Csepel, where Demény's cooperation was indispensable, the two factions, together with the Social Democrats, set up a committee of 13 to coordinate the resistance, which most notably prevented the dismantling of factories and sabotaged the production of armaments, including the rocket commonly known as the Szálasi popper.

The most important operation of the resistance in Csepel was the prevention of the evacuation. On 4 December posters appeared ordering the civilians to leave within 24 hours. This caused enormous anger, and several thousand people gathered at the town hall, where windows were broken in a spontaneous demonstration against the Germans and the Arrow Cross. Hungarian soldiers and police officers promised their support. Arrow Cross militiamen, arriving at the scene, fled after some of them had been pelted with rocks and two had been beaten up by local women. Feelings against the evacuation were running so high that those who tried to obey were attacked by the demonstrators and had their possessions scattered all over the area.

On 5 December the chief public notary and his assistant joined the protesters, declaring: "They are right, we aren't moving an inch either." The Arrow Cross arrested them, and, when the demonstrators demanded their release, also arrested eight workers in the crowd. Four armed communists charged the Arrow Cross headquarters and liberated the captives: the communist László Kormos killed three Arrow Cross men before he was shot dead. The demonstrators then moved from the town hall to Piac Square, where a German soldier on a motorcycle opened fire on them, killing a woman, and further inflaming their fury. On 6 December soldiers began to distribute their arms to civilians, and the evacuation was halted.

In Pestszentlőrinc the evacuation also foundered on the opposition of the population. Here a deputation called on the authorities to rescind the order, which could not have been carried out in any case for lack of troops.

In Kőbánya, Károly Kiss and István P. Horváth created a 40-strong communist resistance group in November. They stole a wagonload of weapons, explosives, and uniforms from Ferencváros Station, with which they formed a KISKA unit. Disguised in Arrow Cross uniforms, some of them shot "Brother" János Csordás, the district's Arrow Cross chief, and two other party leaders. Most important among their many armed operations were blowing up Rákoskeresztúr Arrow Cross headquarters and, jointly with the Stollár Group, defending the Légrády print works.

Another outstanding communist resistance group was that in Újpest, led by László Földes. Its best-known actions were rescuing the Újpest water tower, which had been mined by the Arrow Cross on 31 December, and blowing up the Újpest Arrow Cross headquarters after the liberation of 48 political prisoners held there on

9 January. In the latter action 12 members of the group entered the headquarters in Arrow Cross secret police uniforms, demanded that the prisoners be handed over for "execution" and, on the way toward the Danube, released them. They then returned to the headquarters and delivered a time bomb made of 14 kilograms of picric acid, claiming that it was gold. By the time the ruse was discovered, 28 Arrow Cross militiamen had been buried under the ruins of the building. The total number of substantial operations carried out by the Újpest group was 53.

There were several more bomb attacks by communist partisans. On 6 October the Marót Group destroyed a statue of Gyula Gömbös, a former right-wing prime minister of Hungary, and on 22 November the Szír Group devastated the Metropol Hotel, where high-ranking German officers were billeted. On 2 December the Szír Group blew up the pillars at the entrance to the Municipal Theater, where the Arrow Cross Party Congress was due to be held. By 3 December the rubble had been cleared, but the same day members of the Marót Group threw two acetone bombs into the crowd that had gathered there. Through this most spectacular of their actions the communists prevented the first and only mass meeting planned by the regime.

Eventually several members of the Szír Group were arrested, and only Gábor Csillik managed to escape in late December. He promptly reorganized the group and carried out further operations. Ironically, he was rearrested on 13 January by the Soviets, as was Dezső Weinberger, known as Szír, who later disappeared in the Gulag. The "liberators" were suspicious of everybody, and after the passing of the first wave, Soviet officers with more time on their hands often took resistance fighters prisoner together with others.

The Ságvári Group, organized by Lajos Turcsányi, an activist of the Communist Youth Federation, suffered a similar fate. Its members, "borrowing" the necessary uniforms, documents, and office equipment, established themselves in the vacant premises of the German Volksbund organization as the "staff of the 101st Mechanized Chemical Warfare Battalion." In this disguise they carried out several armed operations. Eventually they were captured by the Soviets and released from the Gödöllő prison camp only thanks to the intervention of the Communist Party.

Fourteen members of the communist Red Brigade were denounced and arrested by the Arrow Cross on 2 January. At the secret police station in the Royal Palace they were subjected to brutal torture. The worst was probably suffered by Éva Braun, as one of her fellow prisoners remembers:

> While I was being interrogated, I could hear terrible screaming and panting from the next room. The gendarme interrogating me behaved relatively decently. When he noticed that I was listening to the screams from the next room, he told me that they were "doing" Éva Braun. He said that she was being raped with a piece of wood. After my interrogation I was led through that room, where I saw Éva Braun lying on the floor half naked and weeping.

Later in January many of the prisoners were executed by Hungarian gendarmes on a terrace of the Royal Palace.

The Jewish resistance was primarily engaged in saving lives. Ottó Komoly, leader of the Hungarian Zionists and the Budapest Jewish Rescue Committee, had made contact with the Hungarian Front in 1943, and before the German occupation the committee had helped persecution victims from neighboring countries find refuge in Hungary or Romania. In September 1944 Friedrich Born, the representative of the International Red Cross in Budapest, had put Komoly in charge of the Red Cross's "A" Office for International Affairs. In reality this office was a cover for the Zionists, and one of its sections was directly involved in the resistance. After the Arrow Cross coup Komoly issued several hundred letters of safe conduct, some genuine and others false, and had food delivered to the ghetto. On 1 January 1945 two Hungarian officers called at his office, which had extraterritorial status, and invited him to a meeting to "talk things over." Komoly accompanied them and was never seen again.

From the beginning of the German occupation, the Jewish resistance issued tens of thousands of forged identity cards, letters of safe conduct, passports, registration certificates, and exemptions for munitions workers. Members of the radical Zionist Hashomer Hatsair organization, founded in the 1930s by Ernő Szilágyi, also undertook armed operations. In half a dozen cases, wearing Arrow Cross uniforms, they carried out rescue missions or killed genuine Arrow Cross activists. On 24 and 26 December respectively, with false "open orders," they liberated 30 and 137 captives, respectively, from the prison in Margit Boulevard, including György Nonn, who later became a notorious communist public prosecutor.

The Jewish communist actor György Aczél, who had converted to Christianity, worked as a liaison officer in the Zionist resistance. His task was to receive money, arms, and food for the Communist Party from the Zionists. His superiors were Gábor Péter, later the head of the communist secret police, and György Donáth. After Horthy's ceasefire attempt he disguised himself by growing a moustache, and reports about his escapades vary: "Aczél was remembered wearing either a gendarmerie, Gestapo, or German army officer's uniform, or a dress uniform, or a camouflage coat. . . . He was seen in a large black car or, according to others, in a jeep. . . . He was repeatedly heard shouting orders in German, pretending not to speak Hungarian (although in fact he did not speak German)."

Many army, police, and gendarmerie officers helped to save fugitives, of whom tens of thousands were hiding in the capital. Colonel András Dienstl, for instance, received an Arrow Cross gang looking for Jews in his house in his dress uniform, covered with medals, and simply sent them away. Gendarmerie Chief Inspector István Parádi attended to Wallenberg's personal protection and prevented numerous operations against Jews. Even in the entourage of the head of the State Security Police, Péter Hain, there were some who sabotaged the "final solution."

However, shortage of time, anti-Semitic propaganda, and lack of unanimity in the Hungarian middle class precluded the development of a concerted movement against the implementation of the anti-Jewish legislation. Some individuals tried, with little success, to appeal to the public. The wife of Count István Bethlen, for example, was arrested when she tried to persuade Christian women to pin a yellow leaf to their garments as a sign of solidarity after the introduction of the yellow star. Pál Tetétleni, managing director of the Bauxit company, was executed, together with his pregnant wife and two small daughters, for sheltering fugitives. Everywhere posters announced that anybody hiding Jews would be punished by immediate execution, and Arrow Cross militia carried out this threat whenever possible.

Early in October 1944 the U.S. Army's Office of Strategic Services (OSS) sent the Hungarian-American First Lieutenant Pál Kovács to Hungary to organize resistance and obtain military intelligence. Using Béla Jánosi's Dallam Group with its 20 members as his base, he contacted the Hungarian Front and several resistance organizations but was arrested on 5 December. Forty-six others were also seized, and most of them murdered by the Arrow Cross secret police between 15 January and 11 February.

The British dropped paratroopers on secret missions into Hungary. Among others, 22 Hungarian-Canadians were trained for that purpose, but only one of them managed to escape after being captured by Hungarian police, and to make his way to Budapest, where he was hidden by the resistance group of the number 11 garrison hospital.

The resistance movement created several KISKA battalions, with those in the III–VIII, XIII, and XIV Districts in particular carrying out armed operations. Most important was the XIII/1 Battalion, led by First Lieutenant Lajos Gidófalvy. This was formed on 18 October, and at the time of its dissolution in early January it claimed 1,200 members, although many belonged only on paper. This group, liaising with others, issued forged certificates, attacked Arrow Cross militia, and prevented the destruction of Ferdinánd Bridge and several factories. It planned to open the front line to the Soviets, but on 8 January most of its members were arrested by Arrow Cross security forces. Gidófalvy and several of his companions, who had managed to hide, were killed a few days later, probably while trying to prevent Erzsébet Bridge being blown up.

In September 1944, Aurél Desewffy, János Brencsán, János Szécsy, Antal Viczián—four members of Emericana, the largest university students' union—had formed a National Guard battalion which subsequently became a KISKA battalion. Apart from producing false documents, the students participated in rescue missions and armed resistance. By the time the encirclement was completed, they had stolen five wagonloads of food and military matériel (10,000 uniforms, 20,000 hand grenades, three antiaircraft guns with ammunition, 5,000 pairs of boots, and other equipment), which they threw into the Danube before the arrival of the Soviets. When the first Soviet soldier appeared, practically all of them defected, but most ended up in prison camp.

The primary task of a group led by Imre Radó and Endre Magyari, with 457 members operating under the guise of the Hungarian Publishing Company, was to forge documents, which were supplied even to German soldiers. On 29 December, as a result of betrayal, 71 members were arrested and—in the largest mass execution of resistance fighters—shot, along with 30 others, in the courtyard of the school at 52 Wesselényi Street.

József Ferenczy, subsequently a press tycoon, had organized several antiwar missions since the German invasion. On 15 October he established the VII/2 KISKA Company in order to provide legal status for his 86 men, who carried out several armed operations and hid fugitives. Hussar Captain Ede Gobbi produced forged exemption forms, which were distributed by his daughter, the actress Hilda Gobbi.

As the KISKA units had proved unreliable, the Arrow Cross authorities ordered them to be disbanded on 6 January—although several could be broken up only by armed force. Some of their members were drafted into the Hungarist Legion, while the majority either defected or escaped.

The work of Soviet reconnaissance is least documented. Major Mariya Fortus, of the 3rd Ukrainian Front, wrote several books about her activities, mixing myth and reality, as demonstrated, for example, by her report on the "Balaton operation." In January 1945 she claimed to have obtained documentation guarded by a Hungarian unit in the casemates of the Castle District concerning a "new German supertank." In fact, no German supertank was being manufactured in 1945, and no such documentation would have been kept outside Germany—least of all in a fortress surrounded by the enemy and without any manufacturing capacity. Nor would the Germans have passed any documentation about a "wonder weapon" yet to be produced to others, particularly to a fickle ally: in summer 1944 they had even refused to grant production rights for any of their existing tanks. Finally, neither Frigyes Wáczek, chief of staff of the unit concerned, nor its quartermaster, Alajos Vajda, knew anything about their division holding such documents.

Hungarian Soldiers on the Soviet Side

After Horthy's ceasefire attempt growing numbers of Hungarian soldiers began to defect to the Soviets, although most were motivated not by antifascist feelings but by the belief that it was pointless to continue the struggle. Major-General Kornél Oszlányi's order of 23 November 1944 exemplifies the response of the leadership:

> Incitement or conspiracy to desert will be punished by hanging. Commanders must use their weapons against deserters. Field gendarmes are to comb the woods and shoot any soldiers hiding or deserting. Those captured alive are to be court-martialed and punished by confiscation of their property and reprisals against their families. Defectors to the enemy must also be shot. The difficult situation is no longer due to the enemy but to the fact that the troops are contaminated and enemy propaganda is falling on fertile ground among some. Commanders must take more forceful action.

The number of soldiers hiding in Budapest ran to tens of thousands. The most resourceful set up fictitious military formations to cover their activities. Apart from the KISKA units these included the "101 Recruitment Center," which served only to hide fugitive soldiers. Defections were encouraged by the frontline propaganda of the Soviets, who often sent prisoners of war back to persuade those still fighting to cross over. During the entire siege the Soviets dispatched 739 Hungarian and 53 German soldiers on such missions, and 580 Hungarians and 27 Germans returned with

6,208 and 219 of their respective comrades. Defections of whole units began in late January 1945, when, according to Soviet reports, the 74th Artillery Detachment, the 204th and 206/II Antiaircraft Artillery Battalions, the IV Motorized Army Corps Battalion, and the I Bem József Mounted Artillery Battalion changed sides.

As the siege progressed, defectors were often given the choice between prison camp in Siberia and deployment against their countrymen. With memories still rife of Russian captivity during the First World War, they generally preferred to cross over. For the first time ever, defecting Hungarians were allowed to fight in Buda alongside the Soviets.

Previously, on Stalin's orders, even units that surrendered as a whole had been sent to prison camps, where recruitment for the Hungarian Legion and similar organizations had been discontinued by the end of 1943 because the Soviets had no desire to share the approaching victory with noncommunists. The reason why Hungarian volunteer units could be formed in Buda, mainly from the end of January 1945, was that the exhausted Red Army needed reinforcements, which its own command was unable to supply. The success of agitation among Hungarian soldiers made it seem reasonable to arm the defectors. Moreover, the ceasefire agreement of 20 January 1945 between the Soviet Union and the Hungarian Provisional National Government, which had been inaugurated on 22 December 1944, had removed any legal obstacle to the creation of Hungarian combat units.

Hungarian volunteers were first deployed with the Soviet 18th and 37th Soviet Rifle Corps. The difficulty of securing volunteers is described by one researcher: "Initially many officers in particular were reluctant to fight alongside the Soviet troops. The vacillation of the officers prevented many soldiers volunteering, although conversely many officers were induced to volunteer by the example of their men." Hussar Lieutenant Aurél Salamon remembers the problems of volunteering:

> The next morning there was another roll call. The soldiers were reeling with hunger and thirst. One or two fell down as a result of starvation or possibly nervousness.

A Hungarian-speaking officer stood in front of the row and uttered the decisive words: "Hungarian soldiers, those willing to fight the fascist Germans jointly with the Red Army in the new Hungarian units, step forward. Everybody will keep his rank and receive the same treatment as the Soviet soldiers."

Initially very few responded. The men suspected a trap and were thinking hard. It may have occurred to them that they could find themselves confronting their own relatives or be caught between the Germans and the Soviets. . . .

We knew that before the German campaign the great Stalin had liquidated thousands of his trained officers (for which a heavy price had then to be paid), without sparing even his marshals, for fear that one of them might turn into a Soviet Napoleon. . . . Then the shadow of Katyn, the massacre of Polish officers, loomed. . . .

The Hungarian soldier, facing nothingness, had a choice. He could become a victim of Hitler's ideology like thousands of his comrades or end his pointless life in some murderous prison camp, if he ever got there.

The other way pointed to the fight against the Germans. Whose heart had not been rent by the sight of our proud bridges tumbling into the water and the mournful cloud of smoke swirling above the city? The vainglorious crimes of the Nazis . . .

They began to undress the better dressed and equipped among the hesitating Hungarians. An infantry ensign came up to me and tried to unbuckle my belt. "You won't need this, Lieutenant," he said with an insolent grin. "I'll smash your head if you touch it," I snapped at the hyena. "I'm joining the unit against the Germans." The "comrade" slunk away with his tail between his legs. This was what had finally made me change sides.

When the looter had retreated, more and more people gathered around me. Three of our hussars, including my orderly Miklós Króczkai, opted for prison camp. "Miklós," I said to him, "you'll regret it. . . ." But no, he didn't want to go back to the front. So be it. We embraced each other, and he was the only one I ever saw again, more than three years later. The other two, Dobos and Koska, ended up in the mass grave of the camp.

Our diagnosis proved to have been correct. The numbers of those lost in the camps and on the front line did not differ greatly.

It was probably Ferenc Krupiczer, the interpreter of the Soviet 37th Rifle Corps, who set up the first volunteer units, followed by 11 others during the siege. The volunteers were allocated, after one or two days' training, to separate Hungarian groups numbering up to 183, the prescribed company size. Reserve Artillery Captain Kázmér Várady's group, the first to join battle on 21 January in Farkasrét Cemetery, suffered the heaviest casualties: by the end of the siege all its members but two, who had been gravely wounded, were dead.

The Hungarian volunteers were deployed at the most danger-ous points, which resulted in extraordinary casualties: several com-panies lost 50 to 80 percent of their strength. In all other respects the Soviet commanders treated them as comrades. The 83rd Marine Infantry Brigade's chief of staff, for example, issued the following order when Hungarians were attached to his unit: "Give them full provisions, regard them as our equals and avoid any rudeness or incident." The commander of the 37th Rifle Corps, Major-General Fedor Semionovich Kolchuk, repeatedly invited officers of the Hun-garian companies to dinner. The battle positions of other Soviet commanders were guarded by Hungarian volunteers.

More than 2,500 Hungarians defected—most in the final week of the siege—and fought on the Soviet side around Déli Station, Németvölgyi Road, Béla király Road, Gellért-hegy Hill, and the Castle District. They wore Hungarian uniforms, with strips of red German parachute silk tied round their arms and hats. Some 600 were killed. On 15 February 1945 the volunteer companies were amalgamated with a volunteer battalion set up three days earlier under Lieutenant-Colonel Oszkár Variházy, to form the 1st Hungarian Volunteer Regiment (later called Buda Volunteer Regiment)

During the last two weeks of the siege, Hungarians were capitulating in large numbers. The 10th Infantry Division had been trying to evade the fighting ever since the closure of the encirclement. Suspecting that the Germans would defend the Castle District to the bitter end, it had moved south from nearby Rózsadomb Hill to Horthy Miklós Square, and on the eve of the break-out, Captain Győző Benyovszky, the division's chief of staff, falsely reported that the route back was blocked by Soviet tanks. As a result, on the morning of 11 February, between 6,000 and 7,000 Hungarian soldiers, including several unscathed units of the division—for example, the 10th Signal Battalion and the 6th Infantry Regiment—were captured with all their equipment. The Soviets lined up the Hungarians and called on them to join the common struggle. Benyovszky remembers: "A Russian captain climbed on a table and told those who wanted to fight the Germans to turn right. When the whole crowd turned right, he was somewhat taken aback, because he hadn't expected such a success. He said that he needed a combat-ready unit, and so the soldiers of the Signal Battalion, who hadn't taken part in any fighting, became a volunteer company." Benyovszky struck up a conversation with a Soviet lieutenant-colonel, who invited him to help with the organization of a new army in Debrecen. In the confusion he was arrested by a Soviet sergeant and forced to join a passing transport of prisoners. Variházy, with the majority of his subordinates, was initially taken to a cellar in Budafok, where, according to his adjutant, First Lieutenant Gyula Létay, he "completely went to pieces. . . . The Russians even took away his leather coat."

On the next day the Soviets asked again who wanted to fight. Everybody, except the officers in charge of mail and duplicating, volunteered, and Létay even dragged two protesting field chaplains with him. This produced the first exclusively Hungarian volunteer battalion: until then volunteers had been able to fight in company strength only alongside the Soviet units.

The Buda volunteers took a particularly active part in resisting the break-out, which the Soviets rewarded by allowing them to raise a Hungarian flag on the Royal Palace beside their own. The palace itself was surrendered by the Germans on 12 February to a volunteer group led by First Lieutenant László Cseresnyés.

As a result of the Soviet security forces' habit of indiscriminately consigning any "dangerous elements" to the camps, some volunteer units were also taken prisoner. Thus, on 15 February, 2,534 members of the Buda Volunteer Regiment were assembled in the suburb of Kelenvölgy, disarmed, and directed to Jászberény, 80 kilometers east of Budapest, to be incorporated in the emerging 1st Infantry Division.

The fact that Hungarian units could participate in the action on the Soviet side should not be underestimated. Their very presence had a powerful effect on the population. They prevented many acts of violence and persuaded many Hungarian soldiers to abandon the struggle. Despite huge losses, they helped to shorten the siege and thereby reduce the number of victims.

Zero Hour: It's All Over

On the morning of 12 February 1945 a strange silence descended on the city. Only sporadic shots or machine-gun salvos could be heard. While the battle continued in the Buda hills, the streets of Buda were completely deserted except for some stray animals and a few Hungarian or German soldiers, half-demented with hunger and fear, searching for a hiding place. As the Soviet troops had also left, there were no armed forces in the center for several hours.

Encouraged by the silence, the civil servant József Finta set out after six weeks in a cellar to see his former workplace in the Castle District:

> In Retek Street I saw some burned-out tanks, but they weren't smoking anymore. Walking along Ostrom Street, I reached Bécsi Gate. I didn't meet . . . a soul—only dead bodies. . . .
>
> I got to the Castle District, not a soul anywhere. I walked along Werbőczy Street. Nothing but bodies and ruins, supply carts, and drays. . . . I got to Szenthárom-

42

Central Budapest, January 1945: soldiers' graves with starving horse

ság Square and decided to look in at the Council in case
I found somebody there. Deserted. I went up to the
office. Everything turned upside down, and not a soul.
I went down the stairs and turned right. . . . A man was
dragging himself along in front of me with his head
drooping. When I was level with him I realized that he
was István Bárcziházy Bárczy, the prime minister's
undersecretary of state. . . . A broken man, turned gray.
When I got quite close he looked up. "Mr. Undersecretary, where have you been?" I asked. "Jóska," he said,
"leave me alone. . . . Go and see for yourself if you can
bear it. . . ."

I walked to the prime minister's palace. The corner
section of the beautiful Baroque building was in ruins. . . .
Opposite the gate in the courtyard was the coach house.
I stepped in, and there was the carriage the king of Italy
had used when he came on a state visit, smashed to

pieces. Next to it the stables. . . . Two dead horses were lying on the floor, and not far from them, perhaps one or two meters away, a dead man, face down. I was so shaken that I turned round and ran out without looking where I was going. . . .

When I was about twenty meters from the entrance to the temporary military hospital, I saw two German soldiers coming out. Without weapons or anything, just like that. When they saw me they started running . . . toward Vérmező Meadow. They disappeared at the bottom of the steps, and I walked back to Bécsi Gate. I saw some dead bodies here and there, but no Russians.

In the deathly silence on my way home I didn't meet any Russians either. . . . I was in such a state that I was only looking in front of my feet to make sure that I didn't stumble over a body.

The student Dénes Kövendi went out at about the same time:

In the morning I walked into the college shouting, "Hurrah, we've been liberated," but was met by silence and black looks. It transpired that during the night several women had been raped and 10 or 15 students hiding there had been taken away for "malenki robot" [light work] (although they were allowed back home three days later). . . .

I immediately set out to see what had happened to my father and sister, from whom I hadn't heard since Christmas. They had taken refuge in the Baár Madas boarding school, which had been regarded by people from the country as a particularly safe haven in Budapest. I understood that the Russians had gotten there about New Year.

However, I had no way of knowing what the situation was like now. There were vague rumors about the break-out and about some Germans being left in the Castle District. So I started . . . toward Városmajor Grange, but when I turned into Alma Street some shots were fired. I wasn't sure whether they were meant for me, but in any case I sought shelter in a nearby villa. . . . In the doorway I found three young men who also wanted to go down that street . . . and this time there was no shooting. . . .

When we reached the row of trees near the Cartographical Institute, about 20 dead soldiers were lying on the opposite pavement. I think they were Hungarians and Germans. We didn't look at them very closely, but we could see more dead soldiers on the ground floor of a burned-out building that looked like a big shop or office. . . .

I left my temporary companions as I had to walk up Trombitás Street and they were going somewhere else. In the autumn I had heard that a former classmate of mine was living at number 2, and it seemed natural to drop in and find out what had been happening there.

When I opened the front door, I got the first (and last) real fright during the whole siege. Ten to 15 apparently high-ranking German officers were standing on the stairs in a line stretching from the front door to the mezzanine. . . . I had been programmed to be afraid of the Germans and to expect the Russians to liberate us (albeit somewhat unpleasantly). Now in my first confusion I thought that I had been captured by Germans. I mumbled something about what I had come for but didn't dare to ask about my classmate. All I wanted was to get out as quickly as possible. Nevertheless, I suspected that they weren't in a world-conquering mood either and might even have been frightened a little by my appearance. As they were going to be captured anyway, they were nervously waiting to get it over as soon as possible. They asked if I had seen any Russians. I said, not in that neighborhood. I asked whether I could continue up the road (meaning: would they please let me go). "As a civilian, you can certainly go," one of them said, and I ran for my life.

From Trombitás Street I sneaked into the boarding school from the back, without seeing either a Russian or anyone else. There I found my loved ones. . . .

The next morning I walked back to the college, feeling completely safe. I had no idea that the Russians were rounding up thousands of young men in civilian clothes in the streets. In any case I got there without any mishap.

Within the ghetto in Pest there had been no significant encounters, but the inmates nevertheless experienced some of the last skirmishes as the front line passed by them:

On 17 January toward 10 P.M. some SS men appeared from 8 Klauzál Street, having broken through the emergency passage between the shelters. They told us that they would be followed by a whole company within the hour and left, breaking through the emergency passage to 12 Klauzál Street. An hour later, however, a platoon of Red soldiers arrived from the street through the normal entrance to the shelter. The block commander (who had probably learned Russian as a prisoner in the First World War) told them what the SS men had said. They sent us out of the room into which the emergency passage opened . . . and hid behind the concrete water tanks in the larger room to await the Germans.

It could have been midnight when they arrived. The Russians let five or six enter before opening fire with their submachine guns. Luckily they could see even in the semidarkness that one German was carrying a panzerfaust, and they shot him before he could use it. Another threw a hand grenade at the Germans, which made quite a mess. It smashed three water tanks and the water poured into our part of the cellar, half a meter below the large room. We climbed on the wooden boxes we had turned into beds, trying to think of a way to reach the emergency exit if the water rose higher. . . . Of course, we didn't feel like going out into the street, where we could still hear the battle going on. In any case it was so cold out there that when we did go out on the next day the dead bodies piled up to be burned didn't even smell.

It could have been about one o'clock when they herded us from the cellar to the ground-floor apartments, where we waited till morning. The wounded SS man was still breathing heavily when we walked past him. His panzerfaust was lying on the corner of one of the concrete water tanks. No Red soldiers committed the slightest atrocity against anybody in the building while this platoon was there.

In Buda the buildings on the front line had been evacuated immediately before the break-out. On the afternoon of 10 February one of the evacuees observed this incident:

Along Olasz Avenue, with civilians from the neighboring streets and German prisoners of war, our procession grew to several hundred. That is how we reached the wooded stretch of land between the edge of the city and Budakeszi. . . .

The peaceful silence of the picturesque landscape was broken by swearing and the stamping of hooves. As we were stomping through the creaking snow, a Russian soldier appeared on horseback, with a submachine gun and drum magazine hanging from his shoulder on a leather strap. At that time I didn't know any Russian and couldn't understand the abuse he was letting loose on one German soldier who was walking along with his comrades, painfully dragging his thickly bandaged foot. We automatically stopped when we saw the Russian force his horse to knock the wounded man down and stamp on him. . . .

The German tried to get up and hobble on. The previous scene was repeated three times—as we heard while we walked on horrified—and then we could only assume that he hadn't got up again and had been left behind in the snow, either wounded or dead.

The Russian's fury was humanly understandable. He might have seen or suffered many German cruelties in the war . . . and come to hate all Germans. But . . . why had this particular prisoner among hundreds aroused his unbridled fury? If he wanted to kill him in revenge why didn't he simply shoot him rather than torture him to death? Why did he alone want revenge and none of his comrades who were escorting us? Could his thirst for revenge have turned on us as well?

To this day I can't find a satisfactory answer to these questions.

When the Soviets allowed some evacuees back home the day after the break-out, one of them witnessed the following scene:

On 12 February in the morning it was still dark when a patrol of three came in, saying: "Go home—the siege is over." They called at every villa. . . . My son and I had great difficulty pulling the sledge because the snow had melted in the meantime. By then we could see fully equipped German soldiers lying dead everywhere. . . .

In Olasz Avenue three armed Russians were walking ahead of us. When we reached the Cartographical Institute, the Russians stopped us. We didn't know what was going on. We were in the third row behind the patrol, followed by the crowd, women, children, sick people. Suddenly I saw a ragged, down-at-heel, stooped man in German uniform, without weapons or anything, coming toward us from Retek Street. The poor devil had made one mistake. He hadn't buttoned up his coat, and his iron cross was showing. As the patrol deliberated, we stood and waited to see what was going to happen. After talking for a while one of them beckoned to the German soldier: "Come along." He escorted him to the tracks of the Hűvösvölgy streetcar line on the other side of the street. Of course by then the streetcar wasn't running and the tracks were full of snow. He made the German walk ahead of him, and when he had almost reached the track shot him in the base of the skull in front of our eyes. The German fell forward . . . and was left lying on the ground.

The Treatment of the Prisoners of War

I was trudging toward Olasz Avenue with a large Russian soldier. He had a purple surcingle tied round his waist (who knows which prelate he had gotten it from) and kept showing me a silver chain that looked like gold. . . . It occurred to me that the surcingle symbolizes the taming of physical desires. I wonder if it did this warrior any good.
—Aurél Salamon

They really took a lot. From me a pair of boots, my spare jodhpurs, my flashlight—into which I had scratched "Stolen from First Lieutenant Péchy"—and many other trifles.
—György Péchy

Victors generally commit more outrages than those facing defeat. German atrocities against Soviet soldiers during the siege were relatively rare, and not many are known today. Contrary to international practice, the Germans forced prisoners to carry ammunition but treated them relatively humanely, not least because they knew that if they were captured—as was becoming more and more likely—they would be called to account for any acts of brutality. Typically, when Germany became a battleground, Hitler issued a special order: "Prisoners taken during the capture of towns or villages . . . must not be killed near the front because later on the civilian population would have to pay for it." In Hungary only a few German atrocities caused a stir and were duly exploited by the Soviet propaganda machine. Nor were the claims entirely groundless. In isolated cases Germans had indeed executed wounded

Soviet soldiers: a German sergeant attached to Major Viharos's combat group, for instance, had assembled a number of wounded in a cellar and shot them.

On the Soviet side the execution of wounded prisoners, particularly SS and auxiliary servicemen wrongly named "vlasovists," was common. These auxiliary servicemen, allocated mainly to the Service Corps, represented 5 to 10 percent of the German forces. A member of the Morlin Group remembers: "The Russians started to chase the Russian/Ukrainian prisoners who had been serving in the German army . . . out of one of the houses with their rifle butts. As they reached the square after running the gauntlet between the Russians, they were shot into a heap in front of us." Another prisoner recalls:

> When we had lined up, a Russian officer asked which of us were Russians. I knew the Russian mentality and language well enough to guess what that meant. About 15 to 20 stepped forward. There were probably some Hiwis ["volunteer helpers": either men fleeing from the Red Army or Soviet prisoners of war who joined the German army] among them, but most were Germans from Russia who had served in the Waffen SS. Before our eyes the Soviets set about them with their swords, and when they were lying on the ground, battered and stabbed all over, they were finally killed with a submachine gun.

The executions were unpredictable: "They were herding us toward Rózsadomb Hill. We stopped in front of a large villa. Two rows ahead of me they shot a prisoner in the head after a short exchange. He was wearing a Hungarian uniform but also spoke Russian. Was he a vlasovist? As he was dying with blood pouring from his head we stepped over him."

In the German military hospital underneath today's Széchényi Library, Soviet soldiers addressed each patient individually, and those in German uniforms who did not answer in German were shot on the spot. They raped and stabbed several nurses and threw hand grenades into the wards. Similar atrocities against German wounded occurred in almost every hospital.

The Soviet soldiers often took no prisoners and slaughtered even those Germans who surrendered. According to survivors, "dead German soldiers with their hands above their heads were lying in serried ranks on the embankment of the Cogwheel Railway," and similar executions are reported by many other sources.

The Waffen SS and the wounded were most at risk. The former were killed for political reasons, the latter because their care would have required too much effort and they could not work. In the sports ground in Budakeszi, SS soldiers were forced to dig their own graves before being shot. In Pilisszentkereszt both the Soviets and the Germans used axes to dismember prisoners who had been wounded in street fighting. Some wounded prisoners who could not walk were dragged along the road behind trucks or crushed alive by tanks. The latter fate befell the patients of the military hospital near the Ministry of War, who were carried out into the street expressly for that purpose. Ensign Norbert Major witnessed the following incident: "Two human figures were lying in Tóth Árpád Promenade. Suddenly we saw one of them raising his hand and then feebly dropping it. Nobody dared to do anything, but several of us asked the Soviet lieutenant who was escorting us to help. He drew his pistol, walked up to them and . . . shot them in the back of the neck. That completed the first aid." Soldiers captured during the break-out, when the Soviets no longer feared reprisals, were most likely to be executed. This is confirmed by the mutilated bodies exhumed from the mass graves in the environment of Buda and by the reminiscences of the foresters and other villagers who buried them. German and Soviet dead were often interred in common graves with a red star placed above them. German graves were destroyed by the Soviets in Pilisszentlélek and elsewhere.

One particularly dark episode was the death march of prisoners to Baja, when those unable to walk any farther were shot through the base of the skull and thrown into the ditch on the roadside by Soviet soldiers bringing up the rear. Iván Hermándy had witnessed four such executions when he too faltered and lay down, resigned to his fate. When the Soviets discovered that he was a Hungarian, they bundled him on a passing peasant cart that took him to a prison camp, where he was refused admission because he had arrived on his own. Finally he was propped up against a tree and abandoned.

At that stage the prisoners received hardly any food. The first meal given to one group transferred from the Sóskút camp was corn with salami, cooked in a gasoline drum; they were unable to eat, although they soon wished they had. One survivor remembers: "Sometimes we were allowed to rest. Then all the prisoners threw themselves into the puddles and ditches to drink. If there was a field of corn along the road, we all rushed to grab some, ignoring

43
Artist Sándor Ék painting his poster "The fascist beast cannot escape"

44
"GPU: it would be the same here," contemporary anti-Soviet poster

the shots fired at us at random. Hundreds died of dysentery after drinking the dirty snow water."

The executions were not carried out according to any master plan. The Soviet army command, unlike the German, issued no unequivocal orders but instead engaged in constant propaganda, portraying the enemy as vile, satanic, and fit only to be executed.

In every war Stalin's official propagandists called the enemy troops "wild beasts," "murderers," "scum," "barbarians," and "animals." During the winter war of 1939 they had used such terms to describe the Finns, who behaved in a relatively civilized manner, and the daily reading of Soviet soldiers included articles about men having their eyes gouged out or being burned alive, and about the barbarities of Finnish Red Cross nurses. During the Second World War they labeled the Germans "cannibals," "filth," "monsters," and "brutes." Printed envelopes issued to soldiers for their letters home frequently showed the picture of a child begging: "Dad, kill a German." In some units, forms called "Personal Revenge Account" were distributed with blanks for the number of Germans killed, the type of weapon used, and the confirmation of the commander.

In his propaganda piece *The German,* the Soviet author Ilya Ehrenburg styled even ordinary German conscripts "murderers," "wild beasts," or "starving rats" and declared: "We do not regard them as human beings. . . . Europe has long known that the best German is the dead German." Similar phrases are found in the writings of Aleksandr Aleksandrovich Fadeev, Aleksei Tolstoy, and the historian Evgeni Tarle, or in the novel *The Science of Hatred* by the Nobel Prize winner Mikhail Sholokhov.

Articles by Ehrenburg and his colleagues, which had been appearing in the frontline newspapers since July 1941, were compulsory reading for the Red Army. The mood they created was responsible for the death of many German prisoners. However, the experiences of Soviet soldiers who had personally witnessed the Germans' treatment of Jews and other civilians also played an important part in triggering atrocities.

The Soviet leadership must have been aware of the soldiers' conduct. The command of the political section of the 2nd Ukrainian Front stressed in a report that the German soldiers preferred death to captivity. The Red Army contained many officers who had served in the political police (Cheka, OGPU, NKVD) or the notorious OSNAS sabotage units. Lieutenant-Colonel G. S. Chebotarev in his memoir recalls commanding an "extermination unit" of the NKVD in the fight against Caucasian tribes in the 1930s. Others acquired ample experience in such operations as the suppression of the Tambov peasants' uprising, when projectiles filled with poison gas were used against civilians for the first time in history; the campaign against the kulaks; or the Katyn massacre. Regiments, battalions or NKVD units of this kind—professional murderers, trained to kill even innocent people—were attached to every Soviet army. Eyewitnesses report that they often took away the identification tags of those about to be executed in order to prevent them being recognized in the future.

The opposite sometimes also happened. First Lieutenant Wolfgang Betzler was congratulated by a Soviet soldier on his medals and given a hat by another when he had lost his own, while SS Hauptsturmführer Kurt Portugall recalls:

> After asking for my name, rank, and unit, they offered me a piece of bread and some vodka, remarking that I had probably not had anything to eat or drink for days and must be hungry. . . . The heat of the room made me break out in a sweat. The Russian major told me to open my camouflage suit. When I did so, he studied my stripes, SS runes, and medals with interest. Then he said: "I have great respect for the soldiers of the Waffen SS. You will now be transported to our hinterland. In our base there are as many bastards as in yours. I advise you to take off the SS runes and medals; it would be better for your health. I don't want your medals, none of us here wants them, because we are members of the guard units, who are the Russian Waffen SS."

Minutes earlier, Portugall recalled,

> two men who turned out to speak Russian were given a terrible beating. The Russians made them kneel down and swear by the Mother of God that they would never again take up weapons against their fatherland. These two comrades were Germans from the Volga who had emigrated in 1939 as a result of the pact between Hitler and Stalin. They were allowed to rejoin our line after being treated by Russian nurses, and each had a loaf of bread tucked under his arm.

An incident involving a number of Germans and Hungarians captured on Rózsadomb Hill was typical of the unpredictability of the Soviets. The prisoners were lined up and were being shot one after another by their vengeful captors. When the executioners came to Staff Captain Béla Barabás, a Soviet officer dashed out of a nearby villa and roared at the Soviet soldiers to stop. In another incident some postmen and conductors captured near Wolff Károly Street were saved by a Russian-speaking Hungarian officer who explained to the Soviets that their uniforms were not those of the Arrow Cross militia.

Sometimes well-meaning Soviet soldiers practically invited Hungarian prisoners to escape. Thus First Lieutenant István Kaszás, asking for water, was told by a Soviet guard to go wherever he liked, although after drinking a few mouthfuls, he rejoined the column because he was afraid of being unable to prove his identity if he were left behind. Elsewhere, at the end of a march, the officers were ordered to step out of line: instead of being shot as they expected, they were allowed to sleep in the farmhouses, together with their guards, while the lower ranks slept in the barns.

Sometimes people were captured by pure coincidence. The wounded Hussar Lieutenant István Tabódy was asked by a Soviet soldier if he spoke German. As soon as Tabódy had uttered an eager "ja," the soldier, with an enormous kick, propelled him into a batch of prisoners; he never had a chance to explain that he was a Hungarian.

As a result of the unbridled propaganda, "lawless behavior, unworthy of human beings" had spread among the Soviet soldiers, and "some units had become uncontrollable." Beginning in 1945, therefore, firm orders prohibiting the ill-treatment of innocent prisoners of war and civilians were given to almost every unit. A copy of such an order issued by Marshal Malinovsky fell into the hands of German and Hungarian troops early that year.

The Soviet atrocities in Budapest were not the only ones committed during the war and bear no comparison to the crimes of the German *Einsatzgruppen* in the Soviet Union or of Soviet soldiers in East Prussia. The fact that they occurred does not mitigate the culpability of the German National Socialist system.

The Soviet Crimes
Institutional Offenses

To some extent every army fighting a war violates human rights. The Red Army was no exception. There were significant differences between the two sides, however, as to the manner and extent of these violations. Before the siege Hungary had been a theoretically independent ally of the Germans, who therefore committed fewer atrocities there than, for example, in the Soviet Union. Although Germans participated in the persecution of the Jews, their role was largely restricted to "paperwork," and those most directly responsible were the Arrow Cross government and its executive organs.

German crimes in Budapest occurred primarily during the last phase of the siege and generally remained confined to looting and destroying property, as for instance in Pestszentlőrinc, where a number of workers' homes were blown up to provide a clear field of fire for the artillery. One of the most serious acts of violence against civilians took place in Dunaharaszti, where a group of Germans shot villagers protesting against the confiscation of their cattle. On Sashegy Hill another group drove a family with whom they had been billeted out of their own home, killing their young daughter in the process. However, such cases did not exceed a few dozen.

The Red Army had reached the Carpathian Basin in very different circumstances. The Soviets rightly regarded Hungary as an enemy state, and they also found communications with the population more difficult, because few Hungarians spoke Russian. Soviet soldiers were rarely granted leave, and there were no field brothels, which accounted for many of the rapes. They were allowed to send home parcels weighing up to ten kilograms, which was a hidden incentive to loot, as there was nothing else to send. Most, including the highest officers, had directly or indirectly experienced the behavior of the German and Hungarian occupiers of their country and were therefore frequently bent on revenge.

Although the near-genocidal activities of the Germans and Hungarians in the Soviet Union received a great deal of publicity from Soviet propagandists, they bore no immediate relation to those of the Soviet soldiers, who also perpetrated atrocities in Czechoslovakia or allied Yugoslavia. The causes of war crimes are mainly found in the system that tolerates, supports, or instigates them, determining the extent to which the rule of law and justice may be ignored and where institutional (and, to a degree, personal) limits to criminal behavior should be set. Armies commit crimes because the military command has an interest in deterrence. In the totalitarian Soviet state, with its partly Asiatic structures, the destructive impulses awakened by this approach surfaced with particular violence.

Many Soviet crimes, in addition to those committed by individuals on their own initiative, were ordered from above. In Budapest, as in other large cities, special units of the Red Army promptly began to collect valuables for the Soviet Union. According to the Swiss embassy, a small but meticulous group of officers "plundered the strongboxes—particularly American and British— in every bank and took away all the cash" shortly after the end of the siege. The Jews paid dearly for their "liberation": 95 percent of the works of art that were stolen are estimated to have belonged to famous Jewish collectors, including Móricz Kornfeld, Bertalan Demény, and Sándor Harsányi.

The country's public collections were systematically robbed by officers trained in art history, which is how the collection of Ferenc Hatvany disappeared from the safe of the Bank for Commerce. The only well still working in the neighborhood was in the cellar of the bank, and people who came to fetch water were able to observe Soviet soldiers carrying valuables away for days. It may have been no coincidence that the art dealer Márton Porkai, who lived next door, was seized by the NKVD at the same time. Events in the Hungarian General Credit Bank were reported by the manager:

> On 20 January 1945 a group of Russian officers came to the bank. They opened every safe and strongbox, at times by force. They took away 113 million pengős in cash, as well as about 800 suitcases and other containers deposited by clients, and emptied 1,400 safe-deposit boxes.
>
> It is impossible to estimate the value of the objects taken, but it is certain that it was a very large amount.

They also took securities worth several hundred million pengős, which belonged partly to clients and partly to the bank.

The Weiss Manfred Works in Csepel was dismantled and carried away by the Soviets on the grounds that it was German property (the Weiss family had handed its shares over to the SS in exchange for being allowed to escape to Switzerland). Jewish possessions stored in the vaults of the National Bank also fell into the hands of the Soviets, who continued loading crates of them onto trucks for days.

Along with the occupation of the city, the "cleansing" of the Communist Party began. The resistance activist Pál Demény, whose followers made up the majority of the Budapest Communist Party, was arrested on 13 February, allegedly because his faction had opposed the Moscow party line. No notice was taken of the fact that on 16 February, shortly after being released from Arrow Cross detention, he had written to the Communist leader Mátyás Rákosi asking for clarification of his position. The first step in "uniting the workers" in order to secure a Communist takeover was always the removal of dissidents.

A particularly murky case was that of Raoul Wallenberg, perhaps the most famous victim of the pathologically suspicious Soviet counterintelligence service. His fate has repeatedly been attributed to the fact that he had seen documents concerning the Katyn massacre. In 1943 the Hungarian forensic pathologist Ferenc Orsós had reported on his inspection of the scene of the massacre, and the Polish resistance had also sent details to Hungary. These documents were stored in the Hungarian General Credit Bank. Like Wallenberg, Béla Varga, the president of the Hungarian National Assembly in 1945, and Zoltán Mikó, the prominent resistance fighter, were familiar with the results of the investigation. It was therefore no coincidence that all three were seized by Soviet counterintelligence. The two Hungarians were initially sentenced to death. Béla Varga was saved by his interpreter, a Soviet colonel of Hungarian origin, who told him what to say: "Most important, if they ask you about Katyn, you know nothing." Mikó was executed on 15 August 1945. Mikó's assistant, Vilmos Bondor, who was sentenced to 25 years' imprisonment, was repeatedly asked during interrogations what he knew about Wallenberg and the "documents." Wallenberg himself was arrested on 19 January 1945 in Rákosszentmihály and died in the Soviet Union in unknown circumstances.

In addition, Wallenberg, Mikó, and Bondor had committed capital offenses, according to Soviet logic, simply by having contacts with espionage organizations. Wallenberg, whose position at the Swedish embassy was merely a blind, was financed by the U.S. World Refugee Board, which Soviet counterintelligence believed— not entirely without reason—to have links with the U.S. secret service. Mikó and Bondor for their part had commanded an Arrow Cross sabotage and intelligence unit. These facts alone would have been sufficient for the Soviets to treat the three men with utmost severity.

The paranoia of the Soviets was so great that they even arrested Communist members of the armed resistance and accused Zionist activists of spying for the Germans. Hardest hit were people who had been engaged in intelligence or counterintelligence, held the post of public prosecutor, or done business with foreign firms:

> Everybody was suspect, and when somebody was caught all his acquaintances, friends, relatives, debtors, and business partners, whose names were found in his notebook, were arrested. Every exporter was suspected of being a spy, and his documents were searched with the greatest enthusiasm; and if for some reason an unfortunate citizen was named in the files of an export company— whether as an employee, an expert, an inquirer, a lawyer, or a tenderer—he was locked up in a frontline prison.

The fact that such occupations and connections were associated by the Soviets with the worst crimes right from the outset reflects on their own totalitarian system. As an inevitable consequence of Stalinism, Soviet soldiers distrusted even their fellow soldiers and kept constant watch over each other.

The Wallenberg affair continued to claim victims long after the war. In 1952, in parallel with the "Jewish doctors' trial" in

Moscow, a show trial of Zionists was mounted in Budapest. The leaders of the Pest ghetto and the organizers of rescue operations were to be convicted of the "murder" of Wallenberg. Several hundred people were arrested, and in the course of interrogations many suffered injuries from which they never recovered. Miksa Domonkos, one of the celebrated rescuers, died as a result of torture on 25 February 1954. It was only thanks to the death of Stalin that the trials were broken off.

Even diplomats were not always spared, as Carl Lutz, the Swiss chargé d'affaires, experienced:

> Shortly after the capture of Budapest the Russian military also descended on us in the ruins of the British embassy. An officer demanded our embassy cars, some of which were no longer working, and gave me five minutes to get the missing "spare part." Then he drew his pistol, ran after me into the bunker, and shot at me several times. I barely managed to escape through the emergency exit of the air-raid shelter. Subsequently we were harassed and looted for ten days and nights by drunken soldiers.

A report of the Swiss embassy about the treatment of its staff and the loss of Jewish property reads:

> Soon after the arrival of the Russians the head of the Swiss embassy, Herr [Harald] Feller, and his chief clerk, Herr [Hans] Mayer, were arrested by the GPU [actually the NKVD, which had absorbed the GPU in 1934]. They have not been heard of since. . . . The premises of the embassy were looted four times. During one of the raids a Russian even put a noose around the neck of an embassy employee, Herr Ember, in an attempt to force him to hand over the safe key. When he still refused, the noose was drawn so tight that he lost consciousness. The Russians took the key from his pocket and cleared out the safe, taking deposits worth several million with them. . . . One of the large safes of the Swedish embassy that

the Germans had not managed to remove was removed
by the Russians with all its contents.

In several cases during the fighting, Soviet soldiers had forced
unarmed civilians to walk ahead of them as living shields. After the
fall of Budapest, Malinovsky granted his troops three days of "free
looting"—which included forcing women to act as prostitutes and
being held captive for a fortnight if they were considered attractive—to celebrate their victory. There were some well-meaning
Soviet officers who warned their Hungarian acquaintances of the
imminent danger.

The depredation of the capital became more and more systematic as the occupation progressed. In concerted actions all the
equipment of the hotels on Margit Island was stolen, as were many
sculptures in public places. In Budafok, a suburb famous for its
wine cellars, the Soviet district commanders and their political officers were replaced twice in quick succession because their exploits
under the influence of free alcohol had come to the attention of the
supreme command. In many cellars, the local residents, fearing the
unpredictability of drunken soldiers, had let the wine run out of
the barrels. In some places the wine was up to 40 centimeters high.
The occupiers not only drank, but actually waded, sat, and rolled
in it. According to Deseő's recollections, in a Budafok cellar nearly
20 Soviet soldiers were found drowned in wine.

In March 1945 the Swiss embassy reported on the methods of
the "liberators":

> Looting was ubiquitous and thorough, albeit not always
> systematic. One man had all his trousers stolen but not
> his jackets. Some small groups specialized in valuables,
> looking for gold, silver, and other metals with detectors.
> Trained dogs were also used. . . . Immovable furniture
> and large works of art were often simply destroyed.
> Often the looted homes were finally set on fire. . . .
>
> Today order is being kept by Hungarian police. How-
> ever, Russian soldiers frequently stop passers-by to relieve
> them of the contents of their pockets, particularly watches,
> cash, and sometimes even personal documents. . . .

The insecurity is made worse by the Russian practice of abducting people from the streets or flats to
secure laborers for public works. . . . In this way thousands of people are forced to work in the countryside
and in Budapest itself. After a while they are generally
allowed to return home, but are never given the opportunity to inform their relations of their whereabouts.
The current minister of public works, Count Géza Teleki, and a mayor of Budapest were led away without
prior warning and found only two days later, when a
Russian officer to whom they were able to talk finally
released them. Prince Pál Esterházy was discovered in a
cemetery burying dead horses. Near Gödöllő a large
concentration camp has been set up with about 40,000
internees, who are being deported to an unknown destination in the east. It is common knowledge that these
internees are given very little food unless they sign a
statement that they wish to join the Red Army or to
work in Russia of their own free will.

The concept of public work was rather loosely interpreted by the
Soviets:

If some work had to be done for the military, such as
moving a gun into position, pulling a broken-down car
from the road, or loading goods from a store onto a
truck, the Russians simply stopped pedestrians and set
them to work. . . . Sometimes the forced laborers worked
for half an hour, at other times for half a day. They were
either given food or not, just as the Russians pleased.

The Soviets' favorite spots for seizing laborers were those
with the heaviest pedestrian traffic. The Anker Palace corner, the
intersection of Kossuth Lajos Street and Múzeum Boulevard, and
the junction of the Great Boulevard and Rákóczy Road were particularly hazardous, and so were the bridges, where they used the
trick of announcing that people would only be allowed to cross in
groups of a hundred, whereupon all those rushing to be in the

45
Noncombatant Hungarian police officers on their way to a Soviet
prisoner-of-war camp

first group were forced to carry rubble instead of continuing their journey.

In February 1945 Malinovsky had some 50,000 men rounded up in order to deliver the 110,000 prisoners he had reported to the Soviet supreme command. Police officers, postmen, and firefighters in uniform were classified as prisoners of war from the outset, and many members of the Buda Volunteer Regiment suffered the same fate. As this was still not enough, people with German names listed in the municipal records were seized in their homes, as were many passers-by in the streets, including former victims of the fascists. To fill the gaps left by captives escaping from marches, residents were dragged out of their houses. The most notorious camps were those in Gödöllő, Cegléd, Jászberény, and Baja. Imre Kovács remembers Gödöllő:

> We stumbled across the railway lines and the three- or four-story buildings of the magnificent high school appeared in front of our eyes, surrounded by a double

barbed-wire fence. Both inside and outside the fence guards were doing the rounds, constantly yelling and shooting. In front of the fence huge groups of women, children, and old people stood calling out, and from behind it frightening shadows waved and answered. The guards did all they could to keep the visitors at a distance, firing warning shots at the more daring who advanced closer. . . . We really had the impression that the whole of Budapest was crammed together before us. Fur-coated gentlemen, distinguished in their bearing but shabby and worn out, were marking time in the courtyard next to streetcar conductors, street sweepers, postmen, and policemen. . . . For some reason the camp command was continually taking stock of the people. Names were flying through the air and there was swearing and cursing.

Only a small percentage of the Hungarians captured in Budapest and its environs could really be regarded as prisoners of war. The deportations of civilians assumed such proportions that János Gyöngyösi, the foreign minister in the Hungarian Provisional National Government, personally requested the head of the Allied Control Commission for Hungary, Marshal Kliment Yefremovich Voroshilov, to end them.

An overeager, one-eyed Soviet sergeant even detained a British and a U.S. member of the Allied Control Commission in the street, forcing them to load metal parts at a railway station for hours. They were not released until Major-General Chernishev, the city commander, with whom they had an appointment, personally found them. An eyewitness reports: "I didn't hear what they said to each other. Then the general yelled for the one-eyed soldier. . . . He beat him with a whip, and when he collapsed he kept kicking him. The sergeant was taken away on a stretcher."

Many houses that were still habitable remained occupied by Soviet soldiers for months. The owners were at best allowed into the gardens to rummage among the objects smashed and thrown out by the victors. One of them remembers what she found when she could finally return home:

The Russians stayed in the villa for more than six months. All that time they had not even carried the rubble out of the wrecked rooms. When they suddenly left at the end of the summer, a shocking sight awaited us. They had taken away practically everything they had not burned as firewood or thrown into the bomb craters. The piano, the paintings, the furniture, the carpets—at least those they had not cut up to make horse blankets or "curtain fringes" for their trucks—they had taken them all. And they had also taken 13 doors and a total of 72 window frames. . . .

In every room the remnants of my grandfather's library were stacked high: a pile of human excrement, an open book placed on top of it, another pile, another book, and so on. . . . The paper required for this "activity" had of course been torn out of the books in handfuls. . . . These towers stood in rows like proud skyscrapers, giving off an unbearable stench.

The Soviets brutally retaliated for any action taken against them. When an Arrow Cross sniper shot a Russian officer from an upper floor in Halmi Road, all the men found in the vicinity were herded to a park nearby and executed in front of the assembled residents of the district as "a warning." After the capture of Buda, mass executions took place in the courtyard of Margit Boulevard prison, Széna Square, and Torockó Square.

Looting and Rapes

What he told us was nothing short of hell on earth. Seventy percent of the women, from girls of 12 to mothers in the ninth month of pregnancy, raped; most men deported; every home looted; the city and its churches in ruins; in the restaurants and stores horses; in the streets, cemeteries, and ransacked shops thousands of unburied bodies; in the cellars people half-demented with hunger,

cutting pieces of flesh from horses dead for days; and so
on. This is how things may have been in Jerusalem when
the prophet Jeremiah uttered his laments.
—Bishop József Grősz

To some inhabitants of Budapest, the Soviet occupation meant life
and freedom, or at least deliverance from the Arrow Cross; to others—who often bore no direct responsibility for the fascist crimes—
it meant mass graves, rapes, or deportation to Siberia.

Worst of all was the sense of absolute defenselessness. Although the danger of being killed had been greater during the
siege, it had in some ways been easier to bear than the precarious
existence that followed. Since the air raids in summer 1944 everybody had known that the war would also claim civilian victims, but
few had expected the utter lawlessness and insecurity that came
with the "liberation."

The atrocities varied from one area of the city to another.
Where fighting had been most prolonged, the suffering of the population was greatest. In Buda, particularly around Gellért-hegy Hill,
the Castle District, and Rózsadomb Hill, law and order had not
returned even by the beginning of March 1945. Here almost all the
houses were looted several times by marauding Soviet soldiers or
deserters, Soviet patrols summoned to help, or Hungarian criminals.

The looters' behavior was unpredictable. Sometimes they
killed whole families, at other times they started to play with a
child's toys and left peacefully. Even the Soviet city command was
not spared: Lieutenant-General Zamertsev's car was stolen while he
was in the theater. Ferenc Kishont (aka Ephraim Kishon), the
Israeli humorist, who lived in Budapest at the time, recalls: "We
thought that the men who had defeated the gigantic National
Socialist war machine were superior in military terms. But all the
Soviets we met were just gifted black marketeers and passionate
rag-and-bone men. They were wearing a colorful medley of clothes
from the occupied territories. Some were pulling baby carriages
filled with plunder from their looting campaigns."

Both during and after the siege it was primarily the women
who looked after their families and often risked their lives, carrying

water, standing in line for food, nursing the sick, and trying to protect their loved ones. Most men did not venture out of the cellars, either because they had reason to fear capture—first by the Arrow Cross, then by the Soviets—or because they were less brave. Intruders were more often resisted by women, who often paid for their courage with their lives. A Swiss embassy report reads:

> The worst suffering of the Hungarian population is due to the rape of women. Rapes—affecting all age groups from ten to seventy—are so common that very few women in Hungary have been spared. They are sometimes accompanied by incredible brutalities. Many women prefer suicide to these horrors. . . . The misery is made worse by the sad fact that many Russian soldiers are diseased and there are absolutely no medicines in Hungary.

Mrs. Ödön Faragó kept a diary throughout the siege and stopped temporarily when the second wave of Soviet soldiers replaced those on the front line and the rapes began:

> I haven't been able to write for a week. This week has been hell. What we have been through is indescribable. We tremble whenever we hear a Russian. We fold our hands and pray to God to let him walk on. We have nothing left. They have taken our clothes, household linen, food, drink, everything. We have been up day and night, trembling. The seven weeks of the siege were child's play compared with the three weeks of torture we have endured since.

In February 1945 the communists of Kőbánya submitted the following appeal to the Soviets:

> For decades the workers of the world have been looking to Moscow like the ignorant laborer to Christ. It was from there that they expected . . . liberation from the barbaric vandalism of fascism. After long and painful persecution the glorious, longed-for Red Army has come, but what a Red Army! . . .

Kőbánya was the place where the liberating Red Army arrived on 2 January after heavy house-to-house fighting, leaving destruction, devastation and desolation in its wake. This was not because there were fascists among the rags and bits of furniture in the homes of the people who had been wage slaves for decades: among the working people of Kőbánya very few were pro-German and the rest hated the Nazis. Rather, it was an outbreak of rampant, demented hatred. Mothers were raped by drunken soldiers in front of their children and husbands. Girls as young as 12 were dragged from their fathers and mothers to be violated by 10 to 15 soldiers and often infected with venereal diseases. After the first group came others, who followed their example. . . . Several comrades lost their lives trying to protect their wives and daughters. . . .

The situation in the factories is terrible. Russian officers have created impossible conditions by ignoring the workers' committees, which contain many Communist Party members. The workers toil for three pengős an hour on an empty stomach with no more than a lunch of peas or beans all day. . . . The former fascist managers are treated with more respect than the workers' committees, because they supply the Russian officers with women. . . . Lootings by Russian soldiers are still the order of the day. . . . We know that the intelligent members of the army are communists, but if we turn to them for help, they have fits of rage and threaten to shoot us, saying: "And what did you do in the Soviet Union? You not only raped our wives before our eyes, but for good measure you killed them together with their children, set fire to our villages, and razed our cities to the ground." We know that Hungarian capitalism bred its own sadist brutes. . . . But we do not understand why a Siberian soldier talks like that . . . when the fascist attacks . . . never even reached the Urals, the dream of German fascism, let alone Siberia. . . .

It is no good praising the Red Army on posters, in the Party, in the factories, and everywhere, if men who have survived the tyranny of Szálasi are now herded along the roads like cattle by Russian soldiers, constantly leaving dead bodies behind. . . .

Comrades sent to the countryside to promote land distribution are being asked by the peasants what use the land is to them if their horses have been taken away from the meadows by the Russians—they cannot plow with their noses. If these things were stopped it would outshine all the frantic propaganda, and the Hungarian workers would regard the Red soldiers as gods.

In spring 1945 the leadership of the Hungarian Communist Party received this complaint from the branch in the village of Bicske:

Although the front line is now a long way from here, Bicske is in an even worse position than when we were evicted from our village for nine weeks [during the relief attempts from December 1944 to February 1945]. We have been robbed of everything, but marauding soldiers are still constantly stealing and looting. In peacetime we had more than 1,000 horses, now only 30, and the soldiers are still stealing them daily. . . . The people live in fear; . . . the women are treated most shamelessly. . . . Every day that passes the people have less confidence in the Party.

In the village of Pilisszentkereszt, which changed hands twice during the relief attempts, the local priest writes in his diary:

Till 6 January 1945 things were relatively quiet, although the soldiers, and even the officers, did a lot of looting and pillaging. Led by an officer, they robbed me three times. . . . From 6 to 11 January the GPU constantly interrogated me, twice opening fire with a submachine gun behind me (as a threat). . . . Antitank mines have so far claimed 13 dead and 87 more or less seriously wounded [of a total population of about 950]. . . . We have been ordered to destroy the mines that are being found. By now we have disarmed many hundred. Four men have been shot by the Russians. . . . The Russians camped in the church for two weeks. They broke the tabernacle open and scattered the host on the floor. They spread mattresses taken from my house and elsewhere in front of the altar, and raped girls and women on them. They used the side altars as tables and the tabernacle as a store cupboard for jam, lard, bacon, etc. They ruined the organ by playing dance music on it during their parties. They cut the vestments into thin ribbons . . . to make military insignia, decorations for their hats, and stripes for their trousers. They unscrewed the chalices after copiously drinking from them. . . .

They were going to execute me because—as a "bourgeois" who has a phone and a radio and can speak German—I must be spying for the Germans. . . .

46
Hungarian woman among male prisoners of war

My home has been completely plundered by the Russians. . . . Eighty percent of my furniture is a thing of the past. It was used as firewood. I have nothing left.

In various places specially hired prostitutes entertained the Soviets, while elsewhere housemaids sacrificed themselves for their employers, or mothers for their daughters. Generally women tried to look older than they were. Many wore shapeless clothes and smudged their faces or pretended to be suffering from diseases.

There are no precise records of the number of women raped in Hungary. Zamertsev spoke to Sándor Tóth of 1,800, but this was clearly only a fraction of all cases. The picture is also distorted by the fact that the existing figures do not show how many women died due to rapes, or were raped several times. In any case the situation was so grave that even Mátyás Rákosi, secretary general of the Communist Party, appealed to the Soviet authorities.

Statistics show 2 million women in Germany were raped, and some 60,000 children born as a result. Of the 1.4 million female inhabitants of Berlin at least 110,000 were raped and 1,156 subsequently gave birth. In Hungary similar statistics could be prepared only in towns temporarily recaptured by German and Hungarian troops. In Lajoskomárom 140 of 1,000 women residents sought medical treatment, and in Székesfehérvár 1,500 women were reported raped, but the estimated number was between 5,000 and 7,000, or 10 to 15 percent of the entire population—all this after a Soviet occupation lasting 30 days. In Budapest, according to information available to date, about 10 percent of the population were raped. In addition, about 1,000 German women in the Wehrmacht were captured, probably suffering most at the hands of the Soviets.

Significantly, in territories occupied by the Red Army—for example, in Germany—the number of people suffering from venereal diseases had grown by a factor of 20. In Hungary a compulsory treatment center was set up in every town with more than 10,000 inhabitants and elsewhere as necessary. In Budapest after the war 35,000 to 40,000 clandestine prostitutes were known to the police, apart from those listed in official records. This number is also more than 20 times the number before 1945. Nor was the increase caused by loose morals: when the fighting was over, the sense of helplessness, hunger, and sheer need to survive often drove women to prostitution.

The rapes are only partly explained by the fact that the soldiers wanted to satisfy their sexual urges. Rapes usually occurred in appallingly unhygienic conditions (with the victims unable to clean up for weeks in some cases) and often within a few meters of indifferent onlookers awaiting their turn. The soldiers could hardly have derived much pleasure from these violations, while running a considerable risk of contracting diseases which were incurable, as penicillin was not available in the Soviet Union at the time.

Mass rape as an archaic army rite was much more common among the Soviets than in any other European army. The defilement of women, providing the victors with a kind of collective recompense and gratification, has existed as a psychological phenomenon ever since the wars of ancient times. The better-organized an army, the less likely are its soldiers to obey such archaic urges. This is not to say that even the most civilized soldier may not commit sexual violence on some occasion, but he would be seeking his pleasure as an individual rather than as a conqueror. That is why the German or Hungarian soldiers' way of indulging in such excesses was completely different from that of the Soviets.

A horrifying picture is painted by a variety of reminiscences and reports. The youngest rape victims were less than 10, the oldest over 90. Some women were raped up to 22 times. Four cases are also known of men being raped by female soldiers. All this seems to confirm that these crimes were not simply sexually motivated but arose from more complex psychological impulses. One of several letters written by Soviet soldiers which fell into German hands illustrates how they felt about the women concerned: "There are enough women and they don't speak a word of Russian. So much the better: we don't have to try and persuade them—we just point the pistol at them, the order 'lie down' settles the matter, and we can move on."

Apart from the human aspect, the rapes probably did more harm to socialism as represented by the political system of the

USSR (and, tragically, to Russian culture) than the most savage
National Socialist propaganda. Even those who sympathized with
the Soviet Union, or belonged to the Communist Party, were
unable to understand these crimes. All they could do was remain
silent or resort to euphemisms, as did Lajos Fehér when writing
about his efforts to bring his fiancée to safety: "Because of the
situation that has arisen I have decided to rescue aunt Diera's
daughter Éva urgently from the Filatori fields." Iván Boldizsár
characterizes the same "situation" through a cynical joke:

> Grisha pulls out his wallet and hands his wife's photo
> round. She is a typical Caucasian, large and dark-eyed,
> beautiful rather than pretty. He is about to put the wal-
> let away, but the others in a chorus demand to see the
> rest of the photos. For a while Grisha plays hard to get,
> but finally produces them.
>
> "This is Ilonka, this is Marianna, this is Sári, this is
> Amália, this is again Ilonka, this is Magda, this is Márta,
> this is again Ilonka . . ." We all laugh. The pictures
> represent every age and social class.
>
> Through a gesture I ask him whether he had gotten
> them with his pistol.
>
> A new wave of laughter. Before Grisha can answer,
> Vassily explains:
>
> "A little bread, a little flour, a little lard, a tiny little
> bit of sugar."

The Soviet supreme command did not really appreciate the
problem, although in some cases it handed out punishments even
harsher than they would have been in western Europe. A case in
point was Yugoslavia. The leadership of the Yugoslav Communist
Party protested to Stalin against the rapes, which it regarded as
particularly grave, given that the country was an ally of the Soviet
Union. As Milovan Djilas recalls, Stalin rejected the protest:
"Doesn't Djilas . . . understand that a soldier who has marched
thousands of kilometers through pools of blood and through fire
and water will want to have a little fun with a wench or steal a
trifle?"

The saddest psychological consequence of the mass rapes, however, was not so much the discrediting of the Soviet system as the fact that for half a century these unspeakable and unforgettable experiences remained in the foreground, preventing the Hungarian people from personally confronting what had happened in their history before and during the Second World War. Whenever the question of direct or indirect individual responsibility for the fate of the Hungarian Jews or of Hungary's involvement in the war arose, the Soviet soldiers' behavior was immediately cited as a supposedly logical answer. "We also suffered a lot" was the common response.

While these experiences prevented Hungarians from coming to terms with their responsibility at a personal level, the Soviet political system imposed on Hungary did so at a social level. Márai, in his diary, describes what should have started in 1945: "The Jewish part of the problems has been resolved for a long time to come thanks to the arrival of the Russians: the liberation of the Jews has happened. Now the harder part of the problem is beginning: the liberation of the Gentiles." Before long he had to recognize that nobody had really been liberated. The outbreaks of anti-Semitism in Kunmadaras, Ózd, Makó, and Miskolc—often instigated by Communist Party members—provided somber proof that nothing had been resolved and no social or political liberation had taken place.

The Soviet Soldiers' Mentality as Reflected in Contemporary Recollections

"Were you looking forward to the arrival of the Russians?"

"Yes, as if they had been our own family. Rafi, for example, ran to meet them like a madman and embraced the first Russian in tears. The Russian said: Here, Jew, give me your leather coat."

—István Benedek and György Vámos

There have been many attempts to analyze the distinctive features of the Soviet troops' behavior. The reminiscences of contemporaries suggest that Soviet soldiers were more likely to act on extreme impulses than were their western or central European counterparts. In Hungary, as a result of the war and the subsequent Stalinist dictatorship, the negative aspects were more vividly remembered than the humane gestures shown toward the population by many of the occupiers, whose spontaneity manifested itself not only in violence but also in kindness at both the personal and institutional levels. Soviet soldiers frequently took children or whole families under their protection, and the same Soviet army that deported tens of thousands of innocent civilians to Siberia set up mobile kitchens for those left behind without asking for anything in return.

Budapest was the first Western-style metropolis in which Soviet soldiers were confronted with the material amenities of "bourgeois" culture after heavy fighting. In Bucharest and Belgrade they had been welcomed as allies, while Warsaw had been totally destroyed before their arrival. To many of them, flush toilets, large book collections, and eyeglasses were among the many

47
Soviet soldier feeding Hungarian children

novelties. Swiss consul Carl Lutz, who set out to look for the Soviet high command after the break-out, recalls: "We climbed over burned-out flamethrowers and tanks in the long tunnel under the Castle District, and when we finally reached the Soviet headquarters, we were met by an infernal racket. The officers were celebrating their victory, dancing on the tables blind drunk. I was allocated a Ukrainian as guard, but he ran away on the second evening." Occupation by the Red Army brought with it a clash of two fundamentally different cultures. The Hungarians regarded the Germans as civilized but capable of great cruelty, and the Soviets as basically well-meaning but savage, with ideas very unlike their own about the meaning of private property, duty, and responsibility.

The only thing many Soviet soldiers knew about the West was that at every step they would be meeting "bourgeoisie," which included anybody who possessed a watch, a bed, or a stove. They often had no idea of how to use modern toilets, which they called "stealing machines" because they swallowed everything—including objects left in them for cooling or cleaning—when they were flushed.

Watches and clocks seemed to have a mythical significance. The writer Endre Illés tells the story of a professor who had made friends with a group of Soviet privates and whose watch was stolen by some others. The professor's friends immediately set out to put matters right, and soon he was wearing a watch again—but not his own. An eyewitness of the "liberation" of an emergency hospital remembers:

> Suddenly two Soviet soldiers appeared at the entrance. One . . . told us in a loud voice to hand over our watches and jewelry, while his companion was pointing his submachine gun at us, with the safety catch released. Not a word was heard, until a woman . . . began to sob violently. The warrior, who had scarcely outgrown his childhood, was moved. "Don't cry," he kept saying as he stroked her and, reaching in his pocket, pressed two wristwatches into her hand. Then he went on looting.

Months after the siege a newsreel of the Yalta conference was being shown in the Budapest cinemas. When U.S. President Franklin

D. Roosevelt raised his arm to point something out to Stalin and his wristwatch became visible, several jokers in the audience shouted: "Mind your watch!"

Despite their propensity for savage acts, the Soviet soldiers had many taboos. One was hurting children. The following recollection is representative. The speaker, then aged 3, was discovered with his grandparents in a shelter by a Russian captain:

> "Daddy," I said, because his stubble made me think that he was my father, home from the front. The captain asked the others what I had said. Somebody answered in Serbo-Croat and he burst into tears. He hugged me, saying that he was a teacher with a child of the same age, and showed us a picture. Later he kept bringing us food. After the break-out he posted a guard in front of our house to protect us, and at times of free looting wouldn't allow any of us out into the streets.

An incident reported by Kishon is equally instructive:

> My sister Ági decided to thank our liberators personally. One evening, soon after the retreat of the Germans from our suburb, she dolled herself up in a dress with a low neckline and set out for the nearby Soviet command post. We waited for her half the night, worried out of our minds. She came home in the small hours in high spirits, telling us how politely the Russians had treated her. They had hugged and fed her and given her a food parcel to take home.
>
> In the afternoon we . . . discovered that in the whole district my sister was the only woman not to have been raped. . . .
>
> My sister was very young and naive at the time, which was probably what had saved her from the worst on that terrible night. But it is also possible that the Russians, like Muslims, respected a madwoman. . . .
>
> They were simple and cruel like children. With millions of people destroyed by Lenin, Trotsky, and Stalin,

or in the war, death, to them, had become an everyday affair. They killed without hatred and let themselves be killed without resisting.

The soldiers had tremendous respect for doctors and—because of their supposed political influence—writers. Márai recalls a fierce cossack who forced him to carry a sack full of loot several kilometers before asking him about his profession: "When he heard the magic word 'writer' he took the sack from me. With a frown, he pulled out his knife, cut a loaf of bread in two halves, handed one half to me, tucked the sack under his arm, and plodded on by himself."

Contrary to expectations, people were pressed into labor, plundered, or raped by the Red Army regardless of their religion. This caused great disillusionment among the Jews. Márai writes about the first meeting between the rabbi of Leányfalu and a Russian soldier. When the "patriarchal figure . . . revealed that he was a Jew" the soldier kissed him on both cheeks and said that he was also a Jew. Then he stood the whole family up against the wall and, searching the house with the thoroughness of a Moscow burglar, stole every valuable object.

A good impression of how the Soviets ran public affairs in Budapest is given by one observer:

> In the West the populations of territories about to be occupied received early radio broadcasts from [British] General [Bernard Law] Montgomery instructing them what to do when the British and American troops arrived. After the capture of Budapest weeks went by without either individuals or the authorities knowing which Russian commands to approach when the need arose. In fact, the Russians themselves did not know. Typically, the first Russian order appeared on 5 February, and the second, marked number 1, on 6 February. They were not signed by the commander in chief or the city commander, but by a certain Major Nefedov.

The end of the siege brought no relief to Budapest. People spoke about another city as a land of milk and honey: "Szeged is enjoying perfect law and order. There is no looting, in the streets the lights are burning and the streetcars running, in the theater plays are being performed, in the cinemas American and English films are being shown, and in the market everything is available." Of Budapest, however, the opposite was true. Apart from regular soldiers there were thousands of Soviet deserters in the city, living on pillage and fighting pitched battles with the NKVD and the police. As late as February 1946 eight robberies with murder occurred on a single day. Most of the culprits were Soviet soldiers, although many Hungarian criminals also took advantage of the power vacuum after the defeat.

On a happier occasion a group of Russian soldiers commandeered a bus and forced the driver at gunpoint to take them on a sightseeing tour, and some of the occupiers tried to become regular residents:

> If a Russian took a fancy to the bourgeois way of life or to a Hungarian woman, he decided to stay. He simply changed into civilian clothes and nobody cared. In our neighborhood a Russian who had been a cobbler at home, attracted by the good income and freedom, became a shoemaker's apprentice. . . . A Russian female soldier turned up on our caretaker's doorstep asking him for accommodation in the block as she wanted to leave the army; she had already found a proper job and promised to be a good tenant who would not disturb the others.

Hungarians soon started to defend themselves. As a first sign many tied ribbons around their arms in the British, U.S., French, Yugoslav, Swedish, Romanian, Portuguese, or Czechoslovak colors, while others wore the insignia of the Red Cross or public services such as Budapest Transport, the Hungarian State Railways, or the police. The last two were particularly popular because they were usually respected by the Soviets. Civilian guards were positioned in many apartment blocks. At the time of the air raids various metal objects had been fixed in front of every building and struck to announce the approach of the bombers. Now they were used to alert the security patrols when looters were coming.

During the interregnum after the siege, janitors became virtually absolute rulers. They negotiated with the Soviets, traded possessions found in their blocks, and laid down the duties of the tenants. As a leftover from the multinational Austro-Hungarian monarchy, many were of Slav descent, spoke a Slav language, and sympathized with their fellow Slavs. When a Mrs. K. B. resisted a Russian officer's attempt to rape her in a cellar, the janitor offhandedly remarked: "Why are you making such a fuss? You're a grown-up woman."

Many complaints about the excesses of soldiers were submitted to the Soviet authorities, who often took a strict line, executing the perpetrators on the spot. Malinovsky was said to have personally shot a Soviet major for rape. Naturally, the opposite also happened. The commander in Csepel, arguing that "the command wishes to spend its time in more useful ways," requested permission to call to account anybody who slandered the Red Army within his jurisdiction. Permission was granted, and the complaints miraculously ceased.

Life Goes On

Sheltering in the window of a ruined shop . . . a woman was selling potato fritters at ten pengős each. The fritters were cold, unappetizing, and of doubtful cleanliness. . . . But the starving people were no longer fussy; they stopped to buy and eat them.

Near the National Theater a young man was touting his merchandise: "Soviet stars to wear! . . . Only two pengős each! . . . Buy Soviet stars!"

The fritters were more popular.

—Sándor Tonelli

When the din of battle had subsided, the civilians began to return home from the cellars, the areas behind the front line, and the ghetto. As they entered their homes—particularly the villas on

Sashegy, Gellért-hegy, and Rózsadomb Hills—they stumbled over dead German, Russian, or Hungarian soldiers. Covered in plaster dust, between collapsed walls, fallen ceilings, and shattered glass, the bodies lay frozen stiff in unlikely postures, with their weapons, ammunition, and other possessions scattered around them. Their boots were usually missing, their clothes torn and black with dried blood, their documents strewn all over the floors by Russians searching their pockets. It was often necessary to sand down the furniture or window frames to remove the blood and brain matter that had soaked into them, or to dispose of the stained fabric of sofas and armchairs on which somebody had died. One of the first

48
Margit Boulevard after the siege

tasks was burying the decomposing bodies—both human and animal—that were found everywhere. The Soviet army drove all available civilians, including children as young as 12, out of their homes to do this.

Before Christmas 1944 and during January 1945, state employees were paid three months' salary in advance as the military situation was expected to make further payments impossible. For the average civil servant this amounted to between 1,200 and 2,000 pengős. When the fighting ended everybody wanted to make up for being unable to shop for weeks. By February people were paying 100 pengős for one kilogram of flour, 400 for sugar, 6,000 to 7,000 for a suit, and 3,000 for a pair of shoes—although this was nothing compared to the hyperinflation that followed later.

Conditions began to cause concern even in the Soviet high command. The first city commander, Major-General Chernishev, who had been motivated entirely by self-interest, was replaced in late February by Major-General Ivan Terentevich Zamertsev, who was to remain in charge until 1948. Colonel Kálmán Gál, head of the Budapest Security Battalion until 17 October 1944, became the first Hungarian city commander on 13 April 1945, but Zamertsev continued to make all the important decisions.

Four resistance fighters—Marquis Pál Odescalchi, the landowner Imre Biedermann, and First Lieutenants Guidó Görgey and Jenő Thassy—had arranged to meet their comrade László Sólyom, who had supplied them with explosives during the fighting, at the National Museum the day after the fall of Pest. Thassy recalls what happened when they arrived there on 19 January:

> The sun was shining. The broken pavement was covered in snow, blood, and mud. The place was swarming with Soviet soldiers arguing. The only civilians we could see were groups herded along by the Russians. The National Museum was still standing, although it had been damaged, and we could hardly believe our eyes when we saw László Sólyom standing at the iron railing near the entrance. . . . At one point a Soviet patrol stopped us,

but their commander seemed to be satisfied by the piece of rubber-stamped paper Sólyom shoved under his nose, and we were able to continue . . . to a yellow building with several stories opposite the Municipal Theater. Its façade still carried the inscription "Volksbund," but above it there was a freshly painted wooden board announcing "Budapest Central Office of the Hungarian Communist Party" . . . and next to it was a red flag with the hammer and sickle. . . . Sólyom led us to the far end of the corridor and told us to wait. He disappeared in one of the offices and soon came back with a lanky individual, who planted himself in front of us and said: "My name is János Kádár. I am the secretary of the Budapest section of the Communist Party. Comrade Sólyom has told me that you took part in the armed struggle for liberation. In recognition of your merit we offer you the opportunity to join our party. This is a particular honor. . . . I would like to have your answer immediately, you must make up your minds now.

The four men refused the offer and left. At the next street corner three of them (having parted from Biedermann) were arrested by Soviet soldiers. Thassy continues: "We confidently protested and presented the bilingual [Hungarian and Russian] documents we had received at the party office. The Russian NCO spat, tore up all three documents, and shoved us into the row of prisoners."

Kádár and the Budapest Communist Party leadership had met the first Soviet soldiers on 13 January 1945 in Kőbánya: as none of them spoke Russian, it took them a long time to explain who they were. Ten days later Kádár was appointed deputy police commissioner for Budapest. He was fully aware of the Soviet transgressions, on which he submitted a strictly confidential report on 9 February:

Despite all difficulties the organization of the National Guard began immediately after the arrival of the Soviet troops. . . . This was extremely difficult as the Soviet authorities were arresting the police officers at the police stations and barracks. Every day only 50 percent

of the police officers who set out on their rounds reached
their destination. The arrests assumed such proportions
that by now there are 2,000 to 3,000 police officers of all
ranks in the Gödöllő prison camp. The Soviet commands
made our work very difficult, particularly in the early
phases, and are still doing so. The newly established police
stations and headquarters were overrun by NKVD units,
whose continuous presence and unreasonable demands
are still wasting a large amount of our time and crippling
our work. . . . The confusion was exacerbated by the fact
that in a number of places several police forces were
formed at the same time. In some cases two individuals
were acting as police chiefs at the same station as a result
of orders given, without thinking of the consequences,
both by political parties and by ill-informed Soviet commands. . . . Another characteristic phenomenon is the
Jewish infiltration. . . . I must also mention the activities

49
Remains of a villa on Rózsadomb Hill

of illegal police forces such as the "Hungarian GPU," the "Miklós Guard," and the "Social-Democratic Organization for Internal Security." These have been, or are being, liquidated.

In view of the catastrophic situation, security forces from Debrecen and other provincial towns were brought to Budapest and armed by the Soviets (initially police patrols had only been equipped with batons). As Kádár notes, the civilians at first received these forces with joy but were soon bitterly disappointed by their abuses.

Arbitrary "people's judgments" and arrests by the Communist Party and its nascent police had begun even before the end of the siege. Labor-Service supervisors József Rotyis and Sándor Szivós were charged with 124 fascist murders and publicly hanged on 4 February 1945. Public executions, which were sometimes turned into popular festivals for political reasons, went on for several years. One eyewitness remembers: "The new communist audience continuously shouted in chorus at the hangman: 'Slowly, Bogár. Slowly, Bogár.' Many of us asked the Ministry of Justice to put an end to this barbarity. . . . When I visited Justice Minister István Ries, he refused my appeal. He said: 'The Jews need some satisfaction after suffering so much.'" By 12 April 1945 the number of "fascist and other reactionary elements" arrested in Budapest had reached 8,260, of whom only 1,608 were eventually released.

On 20 January the Provisional National Government had agreed to a ceasefire with the Soviet Union. One condition was that the Hungarian government take full responsibility for feeding the entire Red Army in Hungary—which had in any case confiscated most of the available food stocks and paid for them solely with unfunded military currency. This irresponsible issue of currency was one of the causes of the subsequent hyperinflation.

Despite the pleas of the Communist leaders, Malinovsky refused to supply any food to the Hungarian authorities. In view of the crucial importance of feeding the capital, the coalition parties vested extraordinary powers in Zoltán Vas, who was appointed government commissioner for public supplies on 13 February 1945. Vas confiscated all the food that had not been appropriated by the

Soviets and ordered the arrest of anyone who obstructed his work. He changed his mind only once: when János Gundel, owner of the famous Gundel Restaurant, was interned for allegedly overcharging, the intellectuals of Budapest raised such an outcry that he had to be released. Vas's first directives included the evacuation of Budapest's children and the creation of emergency kitchens in the city. The first food delivery arrived on 17 February. The minimum requirement was ten wagonloads a day, but initially this could not be achieved. In the interim many factories fed their own workers, bartering their products for food in the provinces. By spring 1945 the communal kitchens were feeding 50,000 people. Three hundred selected artists and scholars received special rations, nicknamed "Vas parcels."

Distributing food in the ruins was a major task: at first everything was transported by steam trains on streetcar lines repaired in a makeshift fashion. On 25 February, Vas ordered the introduction of food coupons in the city center, although it took until 1 June for the system to be up and running in all the suburbs. The rations amounted to 500 calories a day until the end of March and 1,000 calories afterward—compared with the minimum requirement of 2,000. Matters began to improve rapidly when the Soviet command agreed to lend the Hungarian government some of the supplies it had confiscated and to hand back many of the impounded public works: first to resume production, on 27 March, was the Gizella mill, although the "communal bread factory" with the largest capacity did not return to civilian use until the end of June.

Commerce centered on the Stock Exchange building and the square in front of it, as well as Teleki Square. Apart from currency and securities, people bought and sold fat, plum jam, copper vitriol, and everything else under the sun. Most dealers kept no merchandise but knew where goods could be purchased. Rucksacks were among the most common fashion accessories, carried by all who traveled to the countryside to do business, or who simply hoped that something would turn up. Equally popular were red silk shirts made from German parachutes hidden by civilians, either with some further use in mind or because of the Soviets' habit of opening ferocious artillery and mortar fire on whole residential areas where they saw signs of ammunition canisters having been dropped from the air; in the countryside such a shirt could even buy a goose. Horse blankets were turned into autumn and winter coats, tent canvas into jackets. Mechanically minded people would restore wrecked cars and motorcycles, or convert their engines into motors for chainsaws, grain mills, and flour grinders. Various surprising objects have been hoarded to this day: I myself have come across tank seats doubling up as footstools, food canisters dropped by parachute serving as moving crates, engine grease from a German panzer applied to garden tools, and a drum with the inscription "Reichsmarine" used for collecting rainwater.

In addition to watches, the Soviets were particularly eager to obtain lighters and fountain pens, both of which ranked almost as a currency. Watches with "red stones" were most popular, and some smart operators dotted the mechanisms inside with red enamel paint to fake the nonexistent jewels. A peculiar aspect of these commercial activities is highlighted by "Mayor Vas's ban, announced in the newspapers, on dealers placing in their shop windows notices in Russian about wanting to buy gold, silver, leather, and textile goods. Such notices would show the heroic Russian army of liberation in an untruthful light by fostering the belief that its members are marketing unlawfully acquired wares." The owner of a shop in the city center placed the following warning in Hungarian and Russian in his window: "I keep no merchandise in my shop. Please refrain from breaking in."

Most cars had been destroyed during the siege, and the remaining few had been confiscated by the Soviets. The first streetcar line began to operate on 8 February. Others did not follow suit until April and May, but by November most were running. Bus traffic resumed on 20 February with a single vehicle produced by a bus company on the Soviet command's order to do so within three days. The first horse-drawn cab appeared on 19 March. Telephone communications and radio broadcasts were restored on 1 May, as were mail deliveries. Industrial production restarted with the match factory in Budafok: the Soviets had undertaken to provide the factory with armed protection against looting by their own soldiers, and the workers initially received their wages in the form of

50
Procession of the Social Democratic Party's XII District section; above,
a crashed German glider whose pilot was decapitated

matches. The gasworks were back in action beginning 7 February,
although as late as November, because of the damage to the pipes,
only about 50 percent of the reconnected households received supplies. Last to recover were the drains and sewers, which had scarcely
reached 2 percent of their prewar performance by November. Collection of 45,000 cubic meters of rubbish in public squares began
in April and took several months to complete. The Soviets had
demanded only the immediate removal of dead bodies, which was

necessary to prevent epidemics—a task carried out mainly by the local population.

As water supplies remained erratic, laundry was often washed at public fountains and springs. The hot springs in Városliget Park were particularly popular, and the bronze statues in nearby Hősök Square served as clotheslines. Many people dug up their gardens to cover at least part of their food requirements—in summer 1945 in the XIV District alone 35,000 people were growing their own vegetables.

The first cinema reopened on 6 February 1945 in Pest, with the Soviet film *The Battle of Orel*. Soviet heroes were further celebrated with statues erected, on the orders of the 2nd Ukrainian Front's War Council, opposite the Gellért Hotel in Buda and on the Danube Promenade in Pest—after the areas concerned had been forcibly cleaned by civilians living nearby. Cabaret in Pest also came to life soon. The comedian Kálmán Latabár received a standing ovation when he appeared on stage and, pulling up his sleeves and trouser legs, revealed about 30 watches. His puns and jokes about the looting Russians reduced audiences to helpless laughter.

The villages near Buda had suffered greatly from the siege: many had changed hands several times, and Pilismarót, for example, had remained on the front line for three months. Between 10 and 20 percent of the inhabitants had been abducted, and all were robbed by the victors. Their destitution reached such proportions that by early March they were disinterring dead bodies in order to barter their clothes for seed corn in the more prosperous villages of Transdanubia. In Csolnok some villagers dug up a Soviet soldier, whom they had earlier been ordered to bury, and found on him five pairs of trousers stolen from a local Swabian, two of which proved perfectly usable. Boots were also recovered in this way and bartered weeks after the burial of their owners.

By April 1945 the population of Budapest had been reduced from 1,200,000 to 830,000, with 166,000 more women surviving than men. Some 38,000 Hungarian civilians, including Jews, were killed as a direct result of the siege, while 38,000 more failed to return from forced labor or prison camps. Hungarian soldiers

numbering 28,500 also died, making a total of approximately
104,500. Forty-four percent and 33 percent of the deaths, respectively, occurred in the I and II Districts in Buda. British and U.S.
air raids before the siege had damaged almost 40 percent of all
buildings, hitting hardest the IX District in Pest and the XII District in Buda (Tables 15, 16).

7

Epilogue

The battle for Budapest is remembered in history as one of the bloodiest city sieges of the Second World War in Europe. According to Soviet statistics, the Red Army's casualties in the struggle for the capital and in associated actions—including those against the German relief attempts—amounted to 240,056 wounded and 80,026 dead. The latter figure represents half of all the Soviets who died within the current—post-1946—Hungarian borders, meaning that every other Soviet soldier killed in Hungary gave his life for Budapest. The losses of matériel were of a similar order. In the 108 days of the Budapest operations—dating the siege, as the Soviets did, from 29 October 1944—Malinovsky's 2nd Ukrainian Front and Tolbukhin's 3rd Ukrainian Front lost a total of 135,100 small arms, 1,766 tanks and assault guns, 4,127 pieces of heavy artillery, and 293 aircraft. In Soviet statistics the total losses of the 2nd Ukrainian Front (29 October 1944 to 13 February 1945) and the 3rd Ukrainian Front (12 December 1944 to 13 February 1945) are attributed to the Budapest operation, even if they occurred in the Ercsi, Hatvan, or Nagybajom region. Thus it is extremely difficult to compare the losses of the two sides, particularly as figures given for those of the Germans and Hungarians during the operations in question are only approximate.

According to my own calculations, 25 percent of all Soviet casualties connected with Budapest stemmed from the relief attempts, 55 percent from the battle for the city itself, and 20 percent from actions that, in German and Hungarian records, are not directly associated with the capital. For operations within the territory of Hungary (as defined by the Trianon Treaty) the Hero of the Soviet Union medal was awarded to 382 individuals. Among the 276 awards referring to specific locations, operations in and around Budapest—particularly the Danube crossing at Ercsi, with 115 awards—account for a surprisingly large proportion (Table 17).

The number of German and Hungarian military casualties can only be estimated, because we do not know whether any Hungarians are included in the figures given for the relief attempts (making a possible difference of up to 10 percent). The total cannot have exceeded 60 percent of the Soviet casualties, even though practically the whole garrison was killed or wounded. The picture is further complicated by the fact that between November 1944 and the closure of the encirclement, numerous units were withdrawn from, and others moved to, the capital. Based on the available incomplete war reports and my own calculations, a total of some 137,000 Hungarian and German casualties (approximately 26,000 wounded, 48,000 dead, and 63,000 taken prisoner) compares with some 280,000 Soviet and Roman casualties (approximately 202,000 wounded, 70,000 dead, and 8,000 taken prisoner) (Table 18).

The diversion of Soviet troops to Budapest enabled the Germans to maintain their crumbling positions elsewhere in Hungary for some time. Even after Christmas 1944 they held the front line in Transdanubia only because the capital tied down substantial Soviet forces which they could not have matched. As the arrival of reinforcements enhanced the strength of the German front lines, the importance of Budapest as a fortress to be defended at all costs rapidly declined. In any case, the defenders, because of supply problems, even lacked the potential combat strength commensurate to their numbers; by the end of the first few weeks, for example, they had no heavy arms left. After the failure of the relief attempts it became clear that the stabilization of the front until the end of December would be paid for by the entire equipment of four German divisions and nearly 100,000 German and Hungarian soldiers, who could never be replaced.

The German command therefore could expect to profit from the siege only for a brief period. Nevertheless, it adhered to the same strategy to the very end. Three times enormous German reserves were concentrated for a counterattack but were preempted by the Soviets. The actions of these huge forces either remained largely defensive or miscarried because of lack of fuel, as in the last German offensive, when tanks had to be blown up to prevent them from falling into Soviet hands.

On 25 September 1944 the number of divisions thrown by the German Army Group South into the Hungarian theater of war was 14 (including 4 panzer divisions), with 277 tanks and assault guns (of which 192 were deployable and 85 under repair). By 10 January 1945 these numbers had increased to 28 divisions (including 9 panzer divisions), with 1,102 tanks and assault guns (499 deployable, 603 under repair), and by 15 March 1945 to 29 divisions (including 12 panzer divisions), with 1,796 tanks and assault guns (772 deployable, 1024 under repair). These increases reflect the growing importance the Germans attached to Hungary, and appear even more significant if one remembers that during the period in question four German divisions were completely annihilated and vanished from the battle order. In March 1945 half the German panzer divisions on the eastern front (about 30 percent of the total) were operating in Hungary, even though the Soviet troops were already within 60 kilometers of Berlin.

Although the Red Army finally succeeded in its objective, the siege, from the Soviet point of view, amounted to a series of defeats. Malinovsky's attempt to take the city failed four times: each time—on 7 November, in the third week of November, and in the first and last weeks of December 1944—the date had to be changed because the supreme command's orders were impracticable. Malinovsky himself was furious about the protracted fighting: "If I weren't obliged to account for your head in Moscow, I'd have you hanged in the main square of Buda," he roared at Pfeffer-Wildenbruch when he was at last able to interrogate him. The delay in the capture of the capital made it impossible to release sufficient Soviet forces for an effective stand against the Germans; typically, in early February 1945, when the Germans had only begun to move their 6th Panzer Army to Hungary, most Soviet units were still depleted as a result of the Konrad operations. Major-General Sergei

Shtemenko, chief of the Red Army's general staff in 1945, admits in his memoirs that the Soviet "plans to reach Vienna by the end of December and southern Germany in March were upset mainly by the lengthy siege of the Hungarian capital."

Battles for towns and cities differ in various respects from other types. In open-field battles one side generally collapses relatively early, while street battles may last weeks or months. One factor making the defenders' task in a city relatively easy is that utilities break down only gradually, enabling both soldiers and civilians to persevere despite the agony. Another factor is that the attackers have much greater difficulty finding their way in the confusing mass of buildings. Central control often ceases, and the operations disintegrate into dozens of small-scale actions, led by the commanders of units of between 50 and 250 soldiers. The effectiveness of heavy weapons is greatly reduced, and the defense must usually be overcome in hand-to-hand fighting. In Leningrad, for example, the garrison did not capitulate even after hundreds of thousands had starved or frozen to death. The rebels in the Warsaw ghetto were able to resist the German flamethrowers, bomber aircraft, and tanks for more than 30 days, although they had only small arms. And even American-style carpet bombing failed to obliterate the entire population of Germany's big cities.

As the attackers advance in a city, the fighting intensifies. The defenders' strength temporarily increases because their retreat, usually in concentric form, reduces the extent of the territory to be defended, with a larger proportion of heavy weapons available to defend each of the remaining sectors. During the encirclement of Budapest the length of the front line decreased by 90 percent and the territory held by the defense shrank to 3 percent of its original size within seven weeks. At the same time the rate of the decrease slowed: on 24 December the front line measured 87 kilometers in length, on 15 January, 21 kilometers, and on 11 February, 5 kilometers. The number of defenders declined even more slowly. On 24 December 1944 their ration strength (excluding the wounded) was 79,000 and their combat strength approximately 35,000; on 24 January 1945 about 40,000 and 15,000, respectively; and on 11 February 1945 about 32,000 and 11,000.

Nearly 30 percent of the military operations of the Second World War were battles for built-up areas. A sizable proportion of these took the form of city sieges, which proved the bloodiest of all. On the Italian front the average number of German casualties between 1943 and 1945 was 400 per week, and even on the western front it did not exceed 1,000. On the other hand, the suppression of the Warsaw uprising alone cost the German command 1,250 troops a week. In Budapest the number of German defenders fell from 45,000 to 24,000 in seven weeks: in other words, every week almost 3,000 German troops were lost, three times as many as on the western front, and that in addition to the Hungarian casualties. For the Soviets the siege of Budapest also proved to be one of the most costly operations of the Second World War. In 108 days of fighting for the Hungarian capital they suffered 320,082 casualties, as compared with 167,940 in Vienna (31 days), 352,475 in Berlin (23 days), 485,777 in Stalingrad (76 days), and 379,955 in Moscow (34 days). In these five offensives alone (out of a total of 51 significant defensive or offensive actions recorded by Soviet historians), more than 1,690,000 soldiers of the Red Army were killed or wounded, and 24,100 guns and mortars, 7,700 tanks, and 2,670 aircraft were lost—that is, the sieges cost the Soviets almost as many men and more matériel than the British or U.S. armies lost in the whole of the Second World War (Table 19). The only operations that took the Soviets longer to complete than the battle of Budapest were the defenses of Stalingrad and the Caucasus and the liberation of the Ukraine (125, 160, and 116 days, respectively), although even at Stalingrad the actual siege ended sooner and with considerably fewer civilian casualties than in Budapest. The staggering casualty figures throughout demonstrate that the Soviet supreme command considered no sacrifice too dear in the pursuit of its objectives.

To the German defenders in their hopeless situation, the battle of Budapest appeared as a "second Stalingrad." In Stalingrad, too, the fighting had continued to the last bullet, and when those still alive surrendered, they were no longer fit for action. It is symptomatic that a much smaller number than was usual of those captured at Stalingrad survived the ordeal of the camps: of 96,000 prisoners only 4,000 ever returned home. While no similar details about prisoners captured at Budapest are available, the overall military losses can be estimated, on the basis of the incomplete reports and the author's own calculations, as amounting to approximately 55,000 Hungarians and 47,000 Germans, a total of about 102,000 (Table 20).

Budapest withstood the siege longer than any other city defended by the Germans, although such pointless delaying tactics could also be observed elsewhere during the war. In his order of May 1944, Hitler had declared numerous cities "fortresses" and ordered them to resist the enemy until relief arrived. This order was generated by his pathological distrust of the Wehrmacht generals, who in his view did not take the National Socialist idea of total war seriously enough. He clung to the "fortress" theory even when it had clearly proved to have been at least partly responsible for the destruction of the German Army Group Center in Byelorussia in the summer of 1944. On that occasion the attacking Soviet spearheads simply bypassed the cauldrons, and after a few days there was already a distance of several hundred kilometers between the defenders and their own retreating units. Relief was therefore impossible, and the troops, left to their own devices, chose to break out rather than surrender. Some soldiers trekked 700 kilometers, hiding or fighting when necessary, to reach their comrades.

The German troops' morale remained unparalleled, even during the last weeks of the war: they literally fought to the last house and the last room before laying down their arms. Although their remarkable endurance prolonged the existence of the National Socialist dictatorship, it was not rooted in any loyalty to the regime. As suggested earlier, an important factor, apart from the traditional German military virtues, was the ordinary German privates' perception of the war as a total one, which left them no personal choice. Even those who had reservations about the totalitarian system had been influenced by the constant terror bombing, fear of the enemy, and the anti-German invectives of U.S. Secretary of the Treasury Henry Morgenthau and the Soviet author Ilya Ehrenburg quoted in Nazi propaganda.

The situation of the Hungarian soldiers was different. For them the war was not an existential issue. In 500 years of history Hungary had lost every war, so the Hungarians were more familiar than the Germans with defeat and its consequences. The fact that most Hungarian soldiers, being poor country folk, had little or nothing to lose did not improve their morale, and they were further handicapped by being obliged to fight—with vastly inferior weapons and therefore much less hope of success—alongside the Germans, who, to make matters worse, treated them as inferior beings.

In numerical terms, as we have seen, the casualties of the Hungarians did not exceed those of the Germans and remained far below those of the Soviets. Nevertheless, their sacrifice was the most senseless of the three. The Hungarian soldiers—whichever side they joined—could only play the part of extras in the destruction of their country. Many felt that way but considered themselves bound by their military oath to fight, even when they could clearly see the outcome of the war; others capitulated after Horthy's cease-fire bid. Ultimately they only had the choice between a greater and a lesser evil: perseverance prolonged a lost war for a bad cause, and surrender brought no true liberation.

Notes

1. Prelude

p. 2, "400,000 and 698,200": Ölvedi, pp. 114, 121. For the ration strength of the 2nd Ukrainian Front, see Krivosheev, p. 227.

p. 2, "their strength": The Soviet losses were calculated from the following sources: Ölvedi, p. 196; HL KTB Hgr. Süd 876/b, daily reports, 6–10 October 1944.

p. 3, "thereby be defended": Teleki, p. 173.

p. 4, "here as well": Kovalovszky, pp. 83, 79.

p. 5, "you keep it": Churchill, pp. 194–195.

p. 6, "Black Seas": For the text of Molotov's Berlin negotiations see Seidl, pp. 278–284.

p. 6, "parties and groupings": Zaharov, p. 216.

p. 7, "in civilian clothes": Styemenko 1972, quoted in Tóth 1975a, p. 22.

p. 7, "here than elsewhere": ibid.

p. 7, "as a whole": Although the Hungarian 1st Army had suffered significant losses after 15 October 1944 and some 15,000 soldiers had left their units, not only did it survive, but it was even able to delay the advance of Petrov's 4th Ukrainian Front through its counterattacks. As late as December 1944 Petrov's troops were still marking time in the northeastern Carpathians.

p. 7, "as quickly as possible": Major-General Matvey Vasilevich Zakharov's misleading comment on this conversation is characteristic: "At this time the [Hungarian] democratic government was being formed. The liberation of the city from the yoke of the German fascists would have accelerated its formation and would have been advantageous for the few wavering elements in the bourgeois parties and groups" (Zaharov, p. 216). In reality Zakharov knew that Stalin's "political question" pertained not to the propagandistic importance of the capture of the capital but to the later division of east and southeast Europe between the victors.

p. 8, "saying another word": Zaharov, p. 217.

p. 8, "on 26 October": Dombrády and Tóth, pp. 378–380.

p. 10, "Germans could regroup": ibid., p. 30.

p. 11, "21 September 1944": ibid., p. 382.

p. 12, "Slovak Technical Division": BA-MA KTB Hgr. Süd 19 V/51, document no. 7097.

p. 12, "on the earthworks": HL KTB Hgr. Süd 897/a, 14 November 1944.

p. 12, "will be open": BA-MA KTB Hgr. Süd 19 V/51, document no. 6660.

p. 12, "with the utmost urgency": HL VKF 304/a, orders of 12 October 1944.

p. 13, "diverted to the capital": The order for the Hussar Division to come to Pest and the prohibition on blowing up the bridges of Budapest were without doubt part of the planned ceasefire.

p. 13, "7th Assault Artillery Battalion": According to Billnitzer's manuscript (private collections), the Hungarian supreme command had already given the orders in question on 17 October 1944.

p. 13, "Kispest as reserves": HL VKF 306/b, 1 November 1944. Pfeffer-Wildenbruch's order to the Budapest Corps Group.

p. 14, "without success": Friessner, pp. 159–160.

p. 14, "going to survive": Kovalovszky, p. 82.

p. 14, "by the Russian tanks": Huszár, p. 125.

p. 15, "all five tanks": HL TGY, Marosújvári, pp. 9–10.

p. 15, "tanks were damaged": Huszár, p. 126.

p. 15, "southeast of Budapest": HL KTB Hgr. Süd 896/b, attachments 3 November 1944; Kovalovszky, pp. 180–211.

p. 15, "immediately destroyed": *Hadtudományi tájékoztató* 1944/10, p. 43.

p. 16, "ammunition and fuel": This is confirmed not only by Soviet sources but also by Soviet radio messages decoded by the German Army Group South. HL KTB Hrg. Süd 896/b, 5 November 1944.

p. 16, "stalled offensive": Tóth, 1975a, p. 41.

p. 18, "per 18 men": HL KTB Hgr. Süd 896/b, report of 11 November.

p. 18, "in the ground": The brutally mutilated bodies of surrendering SS soldiers were found after the successful counterattack. Records of the event are found among the November attachments of the war diary of the German Army Group South.

p. 18, "total failure": KTB Hgr. Süd RH 19 V/54, pp. 59, 116.

p. 18, "process of restructuring": BA-MA RH 24–72/44, strength report 12th Infantry Division, 25 October 1944.

p. 19, "escaped unscathed": HL TGY; Tassonyi, p. 19.

p. 19, "40 percent casualties": Martin and Ugron, p. 98.

p. 20, "four or five": Friessner, p. 176.

p. 20, "in the Carpathians": Tóth 1975a, p. 62.

p. 21, "to hold prisoners": Thuróczy, p. 69.

p. 21, "Tököl completely": Tibor Gencsy's memoirs, p. 18 (in the collection of the author).

p. 22, "they were silent": HL TGY, TGY Aurél Salamon 3179, p. 54.

p. 23, "all Soviet fronts": Tóth 1975a, p. 62.

p. 23, "Balkans undesirable": In October 1944 Stalin and Churchill had come to an agreement about the division of the Balkans. For details, see Kogelfranz, pp. 12–13.

p. 24, "the secondary section": Tóth, 1975a, pp. 62–63.

p. 26, "in midriver": ibid., p. 73.

p. 26, "his dead body": Tóth, 1975b, p. 280.

p. 26, "partly frozen river": Veress, p. 76.

p. 28, "to their enemies": Tomka (manuscript in the collection of the author).

p. 28, "crossing at Ercsi": For a list of those who received the Hero of the Soviet Union medal, see Tóth, *Hősök*, pp. 203–310. The total number of awards for fighting on Hungarian soil was 382, which includes 26 generals and 80 air force officers decorated for locally unspecified actions. The 115 soldiers honored for the crossing at Ercsi represent 42.7 percent of the remaining 276.

p. 29, "superior strength": Some 8,000 Hungarian and German troops were facing about 40,000 Soviet troops. At the breakthrough points, the disproportion between the attackers and the defenders was even greater.

p. 29, "Soviet soldiers killed": Hanák's battle report of 9 December (in the collection of the author); interview with Városi.

p. 30, "deserted to the enemy": Friessner, pp. 204–205.

p. 30, "1/II Parachute Battalion": HL KTB Hgr. Süd 897/a, 14 December 1944.

p. 31, "within 24 hours": *Népbírósági Közlöny* 1, 1945; *Hadtudományi Tájékoztató*, p. 191.

p. 31, "KISKA auxiliary security companies": For the KISKA auxiliary units, see Chapter 2.

p. 31, "within a few hours": note by Gödry (in the collection of the author).

p. 31, "10th Infantry Division": Martin and Ugron, p. 102.

p. 31, "fierce resistance": ibid., p. 104.

p. 33, "dig ourselves in": Thuróczy, pp. 72–74.

p. 33, "two Hungarian battalions": Csima, pp. 47–48.

p. 33, "joined the attackers": HL, documents of the 10th Infantry Division, telephone diary, 6 December 1944.

p. 34, "ceased to exist": ibid., 15 December 1944.

p. 34, "to the north": HL TGY, György Péchy, pp. 149–151.

p. 34, "on 15 December": HL TGY, Vajda, TGY 2772, p. 101; Csima, p. 48.

p. 35, "sizable Soviet thrust": HL KTB Hgr. Süd 897/b, 14 December 1944.

p. 37, "outnumbered the defenders": The figures given by Tóth (1975a, p. 131) are inaccurate, as he could not have known the actual strength of the German and Hungarian divisions. In the period concerned, the maximum numbers were 3,000 in the 1st Hussar Division, 6,000 in the 271st Volksgrenadier Division, 2,000 in the Kesseő Group, 4,000 in the 20th Infantry division, 12,000 in the armored groups of the 1st, 3rd, 6th, and 23rd German Panzer Divisions, and

7,000 in the German 153rd Field Training Division and other units. These forces, totaling 34,000 men, were attacked by some 150,000 soldiers in 16 infantry divisions and 4 mechanized or tank corps.

p. 38, "burying those inside": Tomka, p. 99.

p. 38, "30 kilometers deep": Veress, p. 86.

p. 38, "brief periods": BA-MA RW 49/145, report of 30 December 1944.

p. 40, "and fire": Thuróczy, p. 103.

p. 41, "Transdanubian hills": Teleki, p. 173.

p. 41, "defending Budapest": Fiala, p. 88.

p. 41, "provided by the Germans": HL KTB Hgr. Süd 897/a. 3 November 1944.

p. 42, "as in Warsaw": HL KTB Hgr. Süd 897/a, 26 November 1944.

p. 42, "an open city": interview with Wáczek, who was chief of staff of the 1st Armored Division when he carried out this order.

p. 42, "VI Army Corps": However, the Hungarian VI Army Corps remained in the Carpathians and, with the exception of the 10th Infantry Division, never reached Budapest.

p. 42, "in charge": BA-MA N 370/1. In many works of reference and historical studies Pfeffer-Wildenbruch is erroneously named Pfeffer von Wildenbruch. In reality he was not a member of the German aristocracy. For his personal details see Chapter 2.

p. 43, "previous agreements": HL VKF 306/a; Zákó, p. 101.

p. 43, "material damage": HL KTB Hgr. Süd 897/b, 23 November 1944.

p. 43, "special units": HL KTB Hgr. Süd 897/a attachments, 1 December 1944.

p. 44, "the last brick": Teleki, p. 173.

p. 44, "to Hitler's liking": See HL microfilm, reel no. 1071, Winkelmann's notes.

p. 45, "and the Wehrmacht": Maier, p. 493; HL Hgr. Süd 897/a attachments, 12 December 1944.

p. 45, "in German hands": HL KTB Hgr. Süd 897/a, 12 December 1944.

p. 45, "of this kind": BA-MA RW 49/145, 12 December 1944.

p. 46, "such a shower": HL TGY, Bíró 3053, p. 17.

p. 47, "a few days": Ferenc X. Kovács, p. 21 (in the collection of the author).

p. 47, "to that position": interview with Wáczek.

2. The Encirclement

p. 48, epigraph: Blanka Péchy, p. 34.

p. 49, "stop the enemy": Száva, 1975b, p. 212.

p. 50, "nothing to fear": Faragó, p. 1 (manuscript in the collection of the author).

p. 50, "also continued": Magyar Játékszín, 18/22, 21–27 December 1944.

p. 50, "in the Bia sector": MA KTB Hgr. Süd, 897/b, daily reports, 23 December 1944.

p. 51, "to the Buda side": Száva, 1975b, p. 248.

p. 51, "this nonsense?": Guderian, p. 347.

p. 52, "most appropriate step": For the procrastination over the relocation see War Diary of the German Army Group South. Extracts from the text are reproduced in Bayer. Balck actually regarded the defense of the capital as superfluous, since the relocated forces alone would have been enough to stabilize the situation in Transdanubia. The deployment of the IVth SS Panzer Corps would then have become unnecessary. For Guderian's comments on Hitler's decisions, see Maier, p. 330.

p. 52, "troops had advanced": interview with Kovács. The German and Hungarian commands received all the reports of the German Army Group South that concerned them.

p. 52: "patently wrong": This was claimed primarily by Gosztonyi, but the reports of the German Army Group South dated 22 and 23 December, which were based exactly on Pfeffer-Wildenbruch's reports, clearly demonstrate the opposite.

p. 52, "German divisional staffs": Schweitzer, BA-MA MSg2/4631, p. 1; Bondor, p. 63. Schweitzer kept the war diary of the 13th Panzer Division and received repeated reports on the encirclement as early as 23 December.

p. 52, "Pfeffer-Wildenbruch's personnel": MA KTB Hrg. Süd 898/b, 8 February 1945.

p. 53, "delivery of supplies": MA KTB Hrg. Süd 898/b, 8 February 1945.

p. 53, "road to Budakeszi": Pálfalvi, p. 73.

p. 53, "north of Páty": HL, documents of the 10th Infantry Division, war diary, p. 74.

p. 53, "reconnaissance activities": HL TGY, Bíró, 3053, p. 48.

p. 53, "alert all units": HL, documents of the 10th Infantry Division, war diary, 23 December.

p. 53, "Bicske and Budaörs": HL, documents of the 10th Infantry Division, telephone diary, 23 December.

p. 53, "toward Széna Square": HL TGY, Vajda, 2772.

p. 53, "the Hungarian command": interview with Kamocsay, who served with a training unit of the army.

p. 53, "already in Vienna": HL KTB Hrg. Süd 897/b, 24 December 1944.

p. 53, "mutual distrust": For Lieutenant-Colonel Usdau Lindenau's comments on the relations between the two general staffs, see Gosztonyi, 1984.

p. 54, "watched events passively": Hindy's reports and the reminiscences of his staff members (Paulics, Borbás, Kovács) support this impression. In an interview Kovács said: "We were also told that the villages in the neighborhood of Budapest had been overrun. We did nothing, and we couldn't have given the Germans a lot of advice, as they would in any case have simply told us to send Hungarian troops. On the other hand they were too brusque to accept any advice from us. They 'didn't need' it."

p. 54, "sighted nearby": HL TGY; letter from Pál Darnói.

p. 54, "have a pistol": interview with Pintér.

p. 55, "the phone link": BA-MA MSg, Hübner, p. 2.

p. 55, "I can do": interview with Kovács.

p. 55, "to the Germans": ibid.

p. 56, "gun at him": Gosztonyi, 1992, p. 230.

p. 56, "Christmas shopping": Portugall, p. 2 (in the collection of the author).

p. 57, "like wildfire": interview with Dalmy, passenger on the train.

p. 58, "a goulash": interview with Czeczidlowszky.

p. 58, "Mártonhegyi Road": Hingyi manuscript, p. 2 (manuscript in the collection of the author).

p. 59, "by a grenade": interview with Kamocsay.

p. 59, "speaking Russian": HL TGY, Elischer, p. 13.

p. 59, "János Hospital": This was called Új [new] Szent János Kórház at the time. The old János Kórház, on the south side of Széna Square, was destroyed during the siege.

p. 60, "the other side": Zolnay 1986, pp. 411–412.

p. 60, "had reached Buda": BA-MA RH 2/1950.

p. 60, "different reason": For example, interview with Michael Klein: "At Szépilona on Christmas Day the Soviets were collecting the engagement and wedding rings and watches of the civilians they came across in the streets, instead of attending to their military duties."

p. 61, "the late morning": interview with Neuburg.

p. 61, "the VII District": letter from György Válas (in the collection of the author).

p. 61, "Esztergom to Budapest": Flekács, p. 1 (in the collection of the author).

p. 62, "signal rockets": interview with Kamocsay.

p. 62, "the Danube Bend": For further details of the capture of the villages in the county of Pest, see Krizsán.

p. 62, "four T-34s": Csiffáry, p. 18.

p. 62, "German brothers-in-arms": The commander's behavior illustrates the mood among the Hungarian regular officers and also explains the attitude of the Hungarian troops during the siege. Although by now the majority of regular officers could see the futility of continuing the war and tried to keep their troops out of the fighting, they were unable to make up their minds either to turn against their allies or to lay down their arms.

p. 62, "at the last moment": interview with Safáry.

p. 63, "at Süttő station": Nagy, Gábor 1983, p. 431.

p. 64, "and the city fall": OSZK, Csécsy, 24 December 1944.

p. 64, "the Christmas tree": Varga, p. 1 (in the collection of the author).

p. 65, "had been killed": Hingyi manuscript, p. 3 (in the collection of the author).

p. 65, "north of Érd": Csebotarev, 1975, pp. 121–123.

p. 66, "part of the crew": HL TGY, Dénes Horváth, pp. 1–2.

p. 66, "at every point": Pálfalvi, p. 69.

p. 67: "shooting suddenly started": interview with Sasvári.

p. 67, "were quite surprised": Vass, *Egyetemisták* (private collections), p. 18.

p. 68, "youth organizations": HL TGY, Elischer, p. 13. István Zsakó, the Arrow Cross youth leader, also offered to evacuate the University Battalion, but Elischer did not wish to share a joint enterprise with the Arrow Cross and therefore remained in Budapest with his unit.

p. 68, "divisional staff": HL, documents of the 10th Infantry Division, war diary, p. 77.

p. 68, "left for Szentendre": letter to the author from József Varga, 23 January 1944.

p. 68, "and Budakalász": *Okmányok;* interview with Dobai.

p. 69, "their uniforms": Sólyom and Szabó, p. 54.

p. 69, "Szentendre presbytery": Katona, p. 47.

p. 69, "white armbands": Márai, 1990b, p. 285.

p. 69, "cut the fuses": *Pest Megyei Hírlap*, 24 June 1973.

p. 69, "were taken prisoner": Zaharov, p. 229. This number seems to be exaggerated. The forces trapped in the Danube Bend were insignificant, consisting mainly of battalions defending the river bank with only 1,000–2,000 troops.

p. 70, "70,000 prisoners": This number is obtained by adding up the figures published in *Szabadság* between 24 December 1944 and 16 February 1945.

p. 70, "138,000 prisoners": Zaharov, p. 262.

p. 70, "in the encirclement": HL KTB Hgr. Süd 897/b, report of 31 December 1944.

p. 70, "around 40,000": letter from Horváth to Gosztonyi, 8 November 1961, HL TGY 3070, Darnói.

p. 70, "corps as 300": HL, documents of the IX SS Mountain Army Corps, report of 14 January.

p. 70, "within the cauldron": HL TGY, Bíró 3251; HL, documents of the 10th Infantry Division show that between 28 January and 1 February some 1,000 men were captured on Rózsadomb Hill. On 11 February several thousand more were captured.

p. 71, "artillery observers": interview with Czeczidlowszky.

p. 72, "or badly wounded": Ravasz, p. 383.

p. 72, "police raids": Városy, p. 21 (in the collection of the author); interviews with Lénárt and Csány.

p. 73, "were underemployed": interview with Városy.

p. 73, "strength of 14,000": interview with Wáczek.

p. 73, "infantry to the Germans": BA-MA KTB Hgr. Süd 897/b, report of 16 December 1944.

p. 73, "no investigations followed": interview with Wáczek.

p. 73, "of the siege": interview with Létay.

p. 73, "never informed": interview with Benyovszky.

p. 73, "weaponry accounts": interview with Czeczidlowszky; recollections of Bíró (HL TGY).

p. 73, "numbered only 30 to 40": HL VKF, box 306/b, 2 November 1944.

p. 73, "informed on him": HL TGY, Bíró 3251.

p. 74, "own free will": e.g., Lieutenant László Szentendrei of the Hungarian 10th Infantry Division, who joined the German Feldherrnhalle Division (interview with Szentendrei). Civilian volunteers are mentioned in Kern.

p. 74, "222 armored trucks": Soviet archival sources, for example Zaharov, p. 259.

p. 75, "German insignia": interview with Sasvári. The unit in question was probably the 201st Heavy Artillery Battalion.

p. 75, "against their officers": Balck, p. 611; Balck: unpublished papers, BA-MA N 647/v. 13, p. 5.

p. 76, "for that purpose": HL TGY, Salamon, Aurél, 3116, p. 95. Most reports about soldiers committing suicide come from survivors of the break-out (see Chapter 4).

p. 76, "300,000 rations": HL KTB Hgr. Süd 897/5, 8 February 1945, report from Colonal-General Balck.

p. 77, "youthful bravado": Kovács, pp. 12, 36 (manuscript in the collection of the author).

p. 77, "my lads": interview with Gerő Ungváry.

p. 79, "recaptured territories": BA-MA RH 2/2468, report of November 1944.

p. 79, "400 twice": interview with Wáczek.

p. 79, "outnumbered them": for example, Klein, p. 44 (manuscript in the collection of the author).

p. 79, "wanted to live": BA-MA RH 2/2458. As a characteristic example of the Soviet command's ruthlessness, the 214th Guard Cavalry Regiment in its entirety was reclassified as a penal unit and its commander degraded merely because the unit had lost its flag in the tank battle of Debrecen (BA-MA RH 2/1996, report of 18 January 1945). A Russian captain in action on Sashegy Hill told civilians that even those with bone injuries were sent back to the front two days later because their commanders "wanted to be rid of them" (interview with Benefi).

p. 79, "back than forward": HL TGY, Bíró 3053, p. 28.

p. 80, "Soviet division 7,509": BA-MA RH 2/1330.

p. 81, "requisitioned locally": BA-MA RH 2/2458.

p. 81, "under Castle Hill": Gosztonyi wrongly describes this as the "Horthy shelter": the regent's shelter was underneath the Royal Palace.

p. 82, "office hours": Lieutenant-Colonel Wolff's report, BA-MA N 647/13.

p. 82, "division's combat strength": BA-MA, Schweitzer, p. 5.

p. 83, "ignorance of the situation": BA-MA N 647/13.

p. 85, "such things": BA-MA N 647/13.

p. 85, "not be replaced": Balck, pp. 611, 661.

p. 86, "a poor man": interview with Benyovszky.

p. 90, "obedient and disciplined": MA Hindy's record sheet.

p. 90, "fair judgments": ibid.

p. 91, "from the hook": Bokor, 1982, p. 344.

p. 91, "to support me": ibid., p. 345.

p. 92, "with my life": ibid., pp. 221–222.

p. 92, "were to capitulate": Tomka, p. 49 (manuscript in the collection of the author).

p. 92, "moral slough": HL, Trial of Hindy.

p. 93, "whenever I could": In reality he could have done much more if he had taken more positive action to oppose the Germans.

p. 93, "and executed": Varga, p. 221.

p. 93, "were deserters": ibid., p. 218.

p. 94, "he walked": HL TGY Paulits, p. 40.

p. 95, "of the service": Assault guns were first deployed in the field in 1940. As they were produced in limited quantities, assault artillery units were used in Budapest mainly as infantry.

p. 97, "hail of bullets": interview with Bődy.

p. 97, "time he came": interview with Lám.

p. 97, "17 February 1945": interview with Hingyi.

p. 99, "all Soviet armies": According to Soviet figures the seven corps had 3,341 tanks—almost as many as the total number of tanks on the German side (Suworow, p. 176).

p. 101, "Military District": *Sovetskaya Voyennaya Entsiklopediya*: Malinovsky, vol. 5, pp. 100–101; Tolbukhin, vol. 8, p. 63.

p. 102, "constantly interfering": Bondor, p. 38.

p. 102, "riding crop": interview with Galántay.

p. 102, "not even armed": HL, Trial of Hindy.

p. 103, "7 January 1945": *Budai Összetartás,* 7 January 1945.

p. 104, "in pouring rain": letter to the author from Galántay, 21 September 1994.

p. 105, "of Vannay's men": Így élt.

p. 105, "east of Pest": letter to the author from Galántay, 17 August 1997.

p. 106, "take no prisoners": interview with Galántay.

p. 106, "Kútvölgy Valley": ibid.

p. 107, "escape once more": *Népbírósági Közlöny* 5, no. 2, February 1946. Deutsch was subsequently cleared of collaboration with the Arrow Cross by the People's Court.

p. 107, "of the embankment": HL TGY, Szalai, pp. 57–58.

p. 108, "any particular faction": HL TGY, Elischer, p. 3.

p. 108, "Assault Battalion began": HL TGY, Vass, *Egyetemisták,* pp. 9–11.

p. 108, "Anglo-Saxon lines": HL TGY, Elischer, pp. 3–4.

p. 109, "pointless slaughter": Sipeki, p. 1 (manuscript in the collection of the author).

p. 110, "and Europe": HL TGY, Elischer, p. 13.

3. The Siege

p. 111, "southeast of the city": interview with Baló.

p. 112, "were captured": HL, documents of the 10th Infantry Division, telephone diary, 25 December.

p. 112, "an acute problem": report from Ernst Schweitzer, 26 February 1945 (manuscript in the collection of the author).

p. 113, "attacking the building": HLK TGY, Aurél Salamon, 3179, p. 65.

p. 113, "two enemy assaults": Tóth, 1975b, p. 336.

p. 113, "commander wounded": There are conflicting accounts of the attack. According to the war diary of the 10th Infantry Division, the battalion panicked after retaking the original positions, while according to surviving members (e.g., Galántay), the withdrawal was due to the approach of Soviet troops from the rear.

p. 114, "to break out": Bayer, p. 332.

p. 114, "forbidding the break-out": Gosztonyi, 1992, p. 230.

p. 115, "the time being": HL VKF, box 306/b, situation report of 30 December 1944.

p. 115, "Soviet Union medal": Tóth, 1975b, p. 336.

p. 115, "at once": Csima, p. 50.

p. 116, "Nazi fascist atrocities": for example, Chebotarev, Necheporuk, Tóth, Máté, Balázs Szabó.

p. 117, "left-hand front wheel": Gosztonyi, 1989a, p. 137.

p. 118, "and other inaccuracies": The distance to the Hofherr-Schrantz machine factory was 2 kilometers; according to the map the death of the delegates would have occurred not 150–200 meters but 400 meters from where he stood; and there were no cobbled streets anywhere in the neighborhood. I am indebted to József Baki for drawing my attention to these contradictions, which I subsequently verified personally.

p. 119, "we set off": Csebotarev, 1967/4, p. 724.

p. 120, "motionless in the road": Gosztonyi, 1989a, p. 145.

p. 120, "fell on the road": Csebotarev, p. 725, suggests that the delegates were attacked with both shells and light weapons.

p. 120, "also wounded": Klein, 1994 (private collections, manuscript in archive of Pongrácz); Gosztonyi, 1989a, p. 145.

p. 121, "in the area": Gosztonyi, 1989a, p. 142.

p. 121, "taken prisoner": BA-MA MSg, Schweitzer, p. 3, reiterated in a letter to the author in 1996.

p. 121, "launched an investigation": Violations of international law were dealt with by a special section of the supreme command, whose task during the war was to start proceedings against both the enemy armies and Germans accused of war crimes.

p. 122, "the environment": BA-MA RW 4/900.

p. 122, "Soviet war propaganda": ibid.

p. 122, "international obligations": ibid., Pfeffer-Wildenbruch also received this order, but had it rescinded. Tóth (1974, p. 256) mistakenly dates it before the death of the delegates.

p. 122, "reports whatsoever": Zayas, passim.

p. 123, "explain it": HL, Trial of Hindy.

p. 123, "released in 1953": Klein, 1994, and undated letter (private collections, archive of Pongrácz).

p. 125, "brigades and regiments": 5th Guard Artillery Division (17th Gun, 18th Howitzer, 95th Heavy Artillery, 27th Mortar Brigades), 16th Artillery Division (52nd and 109th Howitzer, 61st Gun, 90th Heavy Howitzer, 114th Mortar Brigades), 22nd Special Antitank Artillery Brigade, 41st Gun Guard Brigade, 152nd Army Gun Artillery Brigade, 48th, 66th, 80th Mortar Regiments, 5th Antiaircraft Artillery Division (Zaharov, pp. 472–473).

p. 125, "assault gun regiments": According to Zaharov, pp. 472–474, the 3rd and 39th Tank Brigades, and the 30th Independent Heavy Tank Regiment.

p. 125, "one tank brigade": interview with Hingyi.

p. 126, "organizing this action": Tóth, 1975b, p. 341.

p. 126, "armored trucks": Schweitzer, Report (in the collection of the author).

p. 126, "taken prisoner": HL VKF, box 306, Budapest situation report of 31 December.

p. 126, "north of Sashalom": Czoma, p. 337.

p. 127, "Tiger tank": There were no Tiger tanks in Budapest. Péchy probably confused them with Panther tanks.

p. 127, "men withdrew": HL TGY, György Péchy, p. 161.

p. 128, "the Romanians": Csima, p. 54.

p. 128, "two days earlier": ibid.

p. 128, "stranded barge": Maier, p. 56; HL KTB Hgr. Süd 897/b, 2–4 January 1945.

p. 129, "direct-fire guns": Tóth, 1975a, pp. 227–228.

p. 129, "of projectiles": Zaharov, pp. 264–265; Tóth, 1975a, pp. 227–228.

p. 131, "Soviet-held areas": interview with Entzmann.

p. 132, "was 865": HL, documents of the 13th Panzer Division, strength reports of 7 and 14 January 1945.

p. 132, "about 10 January": BA-MA MSg, Schweitzer, p. 5.

p. 133, "used up": KTB Hgr. Süd, report of 5 January 1945.

p. 133, "unsuccessful counterattacks": letter to the author from Vályi, p. 5; interview with Mányoki.

p. 134, "of them dead": interview with Hanák.

p. 135, "stands and stables": Schöning (documents in the collection of the author).

p. 135, "6 January 5, 621": Maier, p. 44.

p. 135, "MÁV housing estate": Városy, p. 22 (manuscript in the collection of the author).

p. 136, "during the afternoon": HL, documents of the 10th Infantry Division, war diary, p. 93.

p. 137, "an early solution": HL KTB Hgr. Süd 897/b, 9 January 1945.

p. 137, "the men killed": *Hadtudományi,* p. 192.

p. 137, "of the park": ibid.

p. 140, "its assault guns": *Hadtudományi,* p. 76.

p. 140, "of Orczy Square": Városy, p. 24 (manuscript in the collection of the author).

p. 140, "previous day": HL, documents of the 10th Infantry Division, order book, 11 January 1945.

p. 140, "Pilis Hills": HL KTB Hgr. Süd 897/b attachments, report of 11 January 1945.

p. 140, "Tisztviselőtelep estate": HL TGY, Vajda, 2772, p. 112.

p. 140, "southeastern section": interview with Baló.

p. 141, "NCOs were killed": Csima, pp. 59–60.

p. 141, "soon after 15 January": HL, documents of the 13th Panzer Division, report of 13 January 1945.

p. 142, "by saboteurs": HL TGY, Mucsy, p. 18.

p. 142, "to defect": Maier, p. 61; KTB Hgr. Süd, report of 13 January 1945.

p. 142, "as many as five times": interview with Kutscher.

p. 142, "patients and staff": interview with Kamocsay and HL TGY, Vass, *Egyetemisták* (private collections), p. 38.

p. 142, "and conflagrations": HL VKF, box 306/b, report of 14 January 1945.

p. 142, "is disastrous": HL KTB Hgr. Süd 897/b, 14 January 1945.

p. 143, "from it barricaded": Billnitzer, VII, p. 22 (private collection; I would like to thank Sándor Tóth for allowing me to use this manuscript).

p. 144, "defenders to surrender": HL VKF, box 306/b, report of 15 January 1945.

p. 144, "for Germans": HL TGY, Mucsy, p. 19.

p. 144, "Zrínyi assault gun": interview with Bődy.

p. 144, "Kálvin Square": HL, documents of the 13th Panzer Division, report of 15 January 1945.

p. 145, "with his secret": HL TGY, Bíró 3251, p. 28.

p. 145, "in my pocket": Gosztonyi, *Politikusok,* p. 30.

p. 147, "a Soviet assault": HL TGY, Mucsy, p. 19.

p. 147, "(northern section)": HL, documents of the 13th Panzer Division, report of 16 January 1945.

p. 147, "hit by a bomb": ibid.

p. 147, "blown up": HL VKF, box 306/b, report of 16 January 1945.

p. 148, "in Siberia": Gosztonyi, 1990, p. 189.

p. 148, "to evacuate": Maier, p. 63.

p. 148, "the relocation": interview with Kamocsay.

p. 148, "do about him": interview with Ferenc X. Kovács.

p. 151, "many times": HL TGY, Vajda, 2772, p. 118.

p. 151, "hardly walk": Benyovszky's diary (in the collection of the author).

p. 151, "hurrying toward Buda": Bayer, p. 347.

p. 152, "preceding it": interview with Wohltmann.

p. 152, "lived there": HLK TGY, Vass, *Egyetemisták* (private collections), p. 39.

p. 152, "Nyugati Station": HL TGY, Gödry.

p. 153, "Hungarist group": Hingyi, Nyilas (private collections).

p. 153, "Kelenföld Station": HL, telephone diary of the 10th Infantry Division, 26 December 1944.

p. 154, "caved-in cellars": *Tétény–Promontor,* pp. 361–362.

p. 154, "baptism of fire": *Hadtudományi,* p. 189.

p. 156, "very likable": HL TGY, Elischer, p. 16.

p. 156, "Russians retreated": HL TGY, Vass, Egyetemisták (private collections), p. 20.

p. 158, "to the front line": Asik, p. 261.

p. 158, "white flag": interview with Vasváry.

p. 159, "radio transmitter": interview with Major.

p. 159, "behind the cemetery": HL TGY, Horváth, p. 2.

p. 159, "flag seized": HL, documents of the 13th Panzer Division, report of 15 January 1945.

p. 159, "most of the cemetery": interview with Sasvári.

p. 160, "to the field": Galántay, *Boy* (private collections); lectures at the Sandhurst and Budapest military academies (in the collection of the author).

p. 160, "some German units": Galántay, *Defense;* interviews with Galántay, Vass, and Sasvári.

p. 160, "heavy fighting": HL TGY, Vass, *Egyetemisták* (private collections), p. 30.

p. 161, "civilian clothes": interviews with Hingyi and Kokovai.

p. 161, "Ördög-árok culvert": interviews with Hingyi and Galántay.

p. 161, "by day impossible": HL, documents of the 13th Panzer Division, report of 16 January.

p. 164, "reed blinds": Sulyánszky, p. 17 (in the collection of the author).

p. 164, "machine guns": interview with Galántay.

p. 164, "medieval ruins": letter from Litteráti-Loótz to Gosztonyi, 1973.

p. 164, "bank of the island": HL, war diary of the 10th Infantry Division, 21 January 1945.

p. 165, "no casualties": letter from Litteráti-Loótz to Gosztonyi, 1973.

p. 166, "without any losses": ibid.

p. 166, "icy river": ibid.

p. 166, "Dörner group": HL, documents of the 13th Panzer Division, report of 21 January 1945; diary of Városy, p. 25 (in the collection of the author).

p. 167, "12 guns": HL, documents of the 13th Panzer Division, report of 21 January 1945.

p. 167, "soldiers were killed": letter from Galántay to the author, 17 August 1997.

p. 167, "transferred from Pest": The 30th Rifle Corps and 68th Guard Rifle Division had been deployed against the relief attempts, and all the other units in action in Pest before 18 January regrouped to Buda.

p. 168, "722 blocks": Zaharov, p. 260.

p. 168, "multistory building": Tóth, 1975b, p. 355.

p. 168, "enemy losses high": HL, Documents of the 13th Panzer Division, report of 22 January 1945.

p. 169, "Buda bank": notes by Dema, p. 2 (in the collection of the author).

p. 170, "in our hands": HL, Documents of the 13th Panzer Division, report of 23 January 1945.

p. 170, "hold the front": ibid., report of 24 January 1945.

p. 170, "upper floor": interviews with Hanák and Városy.

p. 170, "from the west": interview with Benefi.

p. 171, "were missing": Vass, *Egyetemisták,* p. 39.

p. 171, "supply units": HL, documents of the 10th Infantry Division, war diary, 21 January 1945.

p. 171, "seen battle": interview with Bíró.

p. 172, "from behind": interview with Hanák.

p. 172, "defenders' fire": HL VKF, box 306/b, report of 26 January 1945.

p. 172, "slaughter in Budapest": Friedrich, pp. 96–97 (private collections).

p. 173, "until relieved": report by Schweitzer, p. 4 (copy in the collection of the author).

p. 173, "by this time": Maier, p. 90.

p. 174, "is shocking: ibid., p. 89.

p. 174, "out of ammunition": letter to the author from Galántay, 20 March 1995.

p. 175, "same fate": Billnitzer's diary, VII/p. 22 (manuscript in the collection of the author).

p. 175, "the end": Maier, pp. 90–100.

p. 175, "to the north": BA-MA MSg, Schweitzer, p. 8.

p. 176, "before Castle Hill": interview with Galántay.

p. 176, "risk of diseases": Maier, p. 100.

p. 177, "of Sashegy Hill": HL TGY, Horváth, p. 3.

p. 177, "29 automatic guns": HL VKF, box 306/b, report of 31 December 1944.

p. 178, "cases of typhus": Maier, p. 102.

p. 178, "old battle line": HL VKF, box 306/b, report of 2 February 1945.

p. 178, "Városmajor Street": Major, p. 2 (manuscript in the collection of the author).

p. 179, "relief of Budapest": BA-MA KTB Hgr. Süd, report of 4 February 1945.

p. 179, "bitter end": ibid.

p. 179, "unilateral surrender": interview with Wáczek.

p. 179, "their destinations": Hingyi, 1994b, p. 56.

p. 180, "more casualties": Major, p. 3 (manuscript in the collection of the author).

p. 181, "hospital treatment": Maier, p. 107.

p. 181, "near Németvölgy Cemetery": Lukács, p. 175 (manuscript in the collection of the author).

p. 181, "of development": HL VKF, box 306/b, report of 6 February 1945.

p. 181, "the detachment surrendered": letter to the author from Joó.

p. 182, "German fire": Sárközi, 1995, p. 112.

p. 182, "wiped out": interview with Sasvári.

p. 182, "Castle District": interview with Keller.

p. 183, "cessation of hostilities": HL, war diary of the 10th Infantry Division, 8 February 1945.

p. 184, "antitank gun": HL TGY, Kokovay, p. 10.

p. 185, "and perished": Tóth, 1980, pp. 40–41.

p. 186, "violent gun battle": Vass, Dénes, p. 47.

p. 186, "any casualties": Noel, p. 3 .

p. 186, "with shells": Tóth, 1980, pp. 43–44.

p. 186, "entirely charred": Sulyánszky, p. 29 (manuscript in the collection of the author).

p. 187, "break-out attempt": Dombrády and Nagy, p. 124.

p. 187, "Sziklakápolna chapel": Bolyos, p. 67 (private collection; I would like to take this opportunity to thank Pál Dobay for giving me access to his collection); Tóth, 1980, p. 23.

4. Relief Attempts

p. 188, "forces to Hungary": letter from Ernst Philipp to Gosztonyi, 23 July 1985.

p. 189, "Hungary bottom": Boldt, p. 28.

p. 189, "eastern front": Száva, 1975a, p. 224.

p. 190, "(later Brigade)": The Hungarian First Lieutenant and SS Obersturmbannnführer Károly Ney—degraded and dismissed from the Honvéd army for disobeying orders—had recruited this group, which by the end of the war numbered 5,000 members, from right-wing veterans of the eastern front. After the war he worked as a CIA agent, organizing clandestine arsenals and sabotage groups in Austria.

p. 191, "German relief attempts": 1st, 2nd, 4th, 9th Guard Corps; 7th Mechanized Corps; 5th, 18th, 23rd Tank Corps; 4th, 6th Guard Corps; 5th Cavalry Corps.

p. 191, "fast-moving units": 7th Mechanized Corps, 5th Cavalry Guard Corps, 2nd Mechanized Guard Corps.

p. 191, "Germans' strength": Tóth, 1975a, p. 157.

p. 192, "further forces": ibid., p. 156. The units concerned were the 49th and 109th Guard Rifle Divisions and parts of the 2nd Mechanized Guard Corps.

p. 193, "the relief units": Maier, p. 45.

p. 194, "out of action": HL KTB Hgr. Süd 898/b, report of 9 January 1945.

p. 194, "for jaunts": Maier, p. 53.

p. 195, "good progress": ibid.

p. 196, "encirclement opened": information from Tóth (based on a report by Ferenc Krupiczer, interpreter of the 37th Rifle Corps).

p. 196, "Obergruppenführer Pfeffer-Wildenbruch": Maier, p. 55.

p. 198, "500 Soviet ones": Soviet figures from Veress, pp. 169–173; German from BA-MA KTG Hgr. Süd RH 19 V/59, strength reports.

p. 198, "under control": Zaharov, p. 245.

p. 199, "by the Luftwaffe": Száva, 1975b, p. 242.

p. 199, "around the capital": Earlier studies wrongly report a distance of 18 kilometers. The bridgehead at the easternmost occupied village was about 25 kilometers from the nearest point of the encirclement on Sashegy Hill.

p. 199, "still in action": Gosztonyi, 1989b, p. 55.

p. 199, "prevent a break-out": Veress, p. 169.

5. The Break-Out

p. 201, epigraph: Wolff's report, BA-MA N 647/13, p. 5.

p. 203, "of breaking out": This happened, for example, in late April 1945, when the 12th Army under Colonel-General Wenck broke through the Soviet encirclement of Berlin and was captured by the British and Americans. Even in May 1945 Germans continued to fight rather than surrender to the Soviets.

p. 204, "no other solution": Garád, p. 5 (manuscript in the collection of the author).

p. 204, "80,000–100,000": BA-MA RH 10 V/60, in: Maier, p. 518.

p. 204, "before the break-out": Cf. letter from Wolff (copy in the collection of the author).

p. 206, "would start": Cf. Garád (private collections), Hübner (BA-MA), and Mückl (BA-MA).

p. 207, "in the country": Nagy, László.

p. 207, "over a drink": BA-MA MSg, Schweitzer, p. 8.

p. 207, "civilian clothes": interview with Kokovay.

p. 207, "Déli Station": interview with Hingyi.

p. 207, "Széll Kálmán Square": Csebotarev, 1967/4, p. 128.

p. 207, "and memoirs": HL TGY, Kokovay; interviews with Galántay and Rácz.

p. 208, "Kis-Sváb-hegy Hill": Although Soviet sources contain no indication of any plan in preparation for a German break-out, this can be traced accurately through Boldizsár's and Zolnay's memoirs and local residents' statements.

p. 208, "were evacuated": letter to the author from Antalóczi, 9 February 1995.

p. 208, "were betrayed": Gosztonyi, based on an eyewitness account, claims that a woman living in a shelter next to the radio-communication center of the IX SS Mountain Army Corps was a Soviet spy; the attractive blonde, who described herself as a Transylvanian refugee, had intimate relations with

Germans but was suddenly speaking Russian when she was taken away in a jeep occupied by NKVD officers after the break-out. These events are confirmed by the accounts of Wáczek and Hingyi, but they do not prove that the Soviets knew anything directly related to the break-out. Tóth (1980) suggests that the captain of the German radio-communication center, seen after the siege in Soviet uniform, had betrayed the break-out, and that Pfeffer-Wildenbruch's radio messages had been intercepted by a Hungarian officer who had defected to the Soviets. The betrayal hypothesis is not confirmed by any contemporary Soviet or Hungarian writers, who merely claim that the break-out did not surprise the Soviets. If the Soviet command had known about any betrayal, there would be some archival sources to prove it. Nor would there have been any reason to keep such an event secret after the war.

p. 208, "Grange area": Sárközi, 1995, p. 71.

p. 208, "out of the Castle District": Hübner, BA-MA MSg 2/238.

p. 209, " leader Veresváry": OSZK, Faragó, p. 66.

p. 209, "10 and 11 P.M.": Cf. Friedrich (private collections), Schweitzer (BA-MA MSg and private collections), et al.

p. 209, "previous evening": At 11 A.M. Győző Benyovszky, the Hungarian 10th Infantry Division's chief of staff since the defection of Béla Botond, had surreptitiously sent a patrol to Döbrentei Square with orders to return with the news that the Soviet tanks had arrived there. This was intended to discourage the soldiers near the Gellért Hotel from setting out toward the Castle District.

p. 210, "with the palace": letter from Galántay (in the collection of the author).

p. 210, "carry them out": reports of Helmuth Wolff, BA-MA N 643/vl3; Balck unpublished documents, BA-MA N 647/14.

p. 211, "like animals": Friedrich, p. 102 (private collections).

p. 211, "into disaster": Bayer, p. 371.

p. 212, "Szentjános hospital": Noel, p. 3.

p. 212, "bodies everywhere": HL TGY, Vajda, 2772, p. 139.

p. 213, "post office building": letter to the author from Galántay. The same event is reported in Blanka Péchy, p. 87.

p. 213, "with sugar": interview with Keller.

p. 216, "northwest from there": interview with Wáczek.

p. 216, "the 1a's": A 1a was an officer in a division's operative section.

p. 216, "an enemy": Cf. Schweitzer's diary and letters, partly in the collection of the author and partly at BA-MA MSg.

p. 217, "are gone": BA-MA RH, Nachtmann, p. 3.

p. 217, "Ostrom Street": The mass grave in Ostrom Street was exhumed in the 1950s.

p. 217, "resigned wounded": Garád, p. 7 (manuscript in the collection of the author).

p. 218, "woods beyond": notes by Dávid (manuscript in the collection of the author).

p. 219, "shoots himself": BA-MA MSg, Schweitzer.

p. 219, "pitch dark": Garád, p. 11 (manuscript in the collection of the author).

p. 219, "once more": Billnitzer, p. 8 (in the collection of the author).

p. 220, "nearly 3,200": letters from Wolff (Gosztonyi collection, 1961, Hingyi collection, 1988).

p. 221, "beaten army": OSZK, Lichtenberg.

p. 222, "in good time": HL, Trial of Hindy.

p. 223, "any comments)": Ferenc X. Kovács, p. 40 (manuscript in the collection of the author).

p. 223, "German seaside": HL TGY, Paulics, p. 50.

p. 223, "to everybody": letter from Borbás, August 1979, in: Gosztonyi, 1992, p. 239.

p. 223, "about 11 P.M.": The exact time is not known. Ferenc X. Kovács claims that the action started at midnight, while one of his officers recalls 6 o'clock. Both versions are probably wrong.

p. 223, "heavy weapons": interview with Kovács.

p. 224, "above ground": HL TGY, Paulics, p. 53.

p. 224, "them again": BA-MA MSg, Hübner, p. 11.

p. 224, "right and left": Noll, p. 4.

p. 225, "grim death": HL TGY, Paulics, p. 54.

p. 225, "before surrendering": letter to the author from Betzler, 30 November 1996.

p. 225, "join Pfeffer-Wildenbruch": Ferenc X. Kovács, p. 5 (manuscript in the collection of the author).

p. 226, "receive them": Máté, p. 180.

p. 226, "similar fashion": Gosztonyi erroneously claims that Dörner was killed in a gun battle at the exit. Ferenc X. Kovács met Dörner on 13 February as he was being taken, gravely wounded, to a collecting point in Béla király Road. "They will shoot us all," Dörner said lethargically; he was never seen again.

p. 227, "was breaking": Noll, p. 4.

p. 227, "streetcar depot": BA-MA MSg, Mückl, p. 31.

p. 228, "the latter": Noll, p. 4.

p. 229, "was able": HL TGY, Paulics, p. 60.

p. 229, "way for her": Ferenc X. Kovács, p. 6 (manuscript in the collection of the author), and interview.

p. 230, "from her": HL TGY, Paulics, p. 60.

p. 230, "starting point": interview with Kovács.

p. 231, "their weapons": HL TGY, Paulics, p. 61.

p. 232, "bundles behind them": Garád, pp. 8–9 (manuscript in the collection of the author).

p. 233, "moved on": HL TGY, Kokovay, pp. 2–3.

p. 234, "More casualties": BA-MA MSg, Schweitzer, p. 15.

p. 234, "ambush in Nagykovácsi": interview with Hingyi. Apparently a Soviet soldier in German uniform had told them that Nagykovácsi was deserted.

p. 234, "to tree": HL TGY, Bíró, p. iv.

p. 234, "and raids": recollection of Corporal Dániel Váli, in letter to the author from Galántai.

p. 235, "wounded Germans": BA-MA RH, Nachtmann, p. 4.

p. 236, "the carts": Garád, p. 12 (manuscript in the collection of the author).

p. 236, "comes again": BA-MA RH, Nachtmann, p. 4.

p. 236, "shot immediately": ibid., p. 7.

p. 236, "stood there": HL TGY, Kokovay, p. 4. Eventually Flügel was helped to get away.

p. 237, "cube of bread": BA-MA MSg, Schweitzer, p. 28.

p. 237, "of madness": BA-MA RH, Nachtmann; BA-MA MSg, Schweitzer.

p. 237, "Szilasi Szabó": Hingyi manuscript, p. 3 (in the collection of the author).

p. 238, "after the other": interview with Boosfeld, by courtesy of Peter Zwack Jr.

p. 238, "3rd Cavalry Brigade": Cf. letters from Wolff, 1961 and 1980 (in Gosztonyi collection). However, Wolff remembered the geographical details incorrectly.

p. 238, "own lines": interview with Kutscher.

p. 239, "German position": Schöning's unpublished documents (in the collection of the author).

p. 240, "on stretchers": HL TGY, Kokovay, pp. 5–6.

p. 240, "German lines": Gosztonyi, without naming his sources, cites 785 men, possibly based on Wolff's reports. This incorrect figure first appeared in 1957 in an article entitled "Als Budapest zum erstenmal starb" [When Budapest died for the first time] in the *Wiking Ruf* journal, from where it was probably adopted by all other writers. Wolff's memory seems far from perfect, particularly comparing his later letters with his report of 15 February 1945. According to the German Army Group South's documents, 624 had gotten through by 16 February (Mayer, p. 120). Most were Germans belonging to the SS and the Wehrmacht.

p. 241, "fresh again": BA-MA MSg, Schweitzer.

p. 242, "made it": ibid. Schweitzer's toes were subsequently amputated.

p. 244, "over the place": BA-MA MSg, Hübner, pp. 12–13.

p. 245, "as a farewell": HL TGY, Konkoly-Thege, pp. 152–153.

p. 245, "Military History": Cf. M. v. K. (private collections); interview with Hingyi; OSZK, Faragó, p. 67.

p. 245, "as they were": BA-MA MSg, Hübner, p. 14.

p. 246, "help them": HL TGY, Konkoly-Thege, p. 155.

p. 246, "urine drum": BA-MA MSg, Hübner, p. 14.

p. 246, "10:30 P.M.": Bayer, p. 112.

p. 247, "the cavalry corps": The cavalry corps in question, led by Lieutenant-General Gustav Harteneck, was stationed between Csákvár and Esztergom and included the 711th and 96th Infantry Divisions, the 3rd Cavalry Brigade, and the 6th Panzer Division, as well as the Hungarian 1st Hussar Division, but had no significant armored units of its own.

p. 247, "our disposal": Maier, pp. 113–115.

p. 247, "from the air": ibid., p. 519.

p. 249, "to penetrate": ibid., pp. 115–116.

p. 249, "assist the escapees": interview with Kokovay, who escaped through Mány.

p. 250, "[South Wind] enterprise": The objective of the Südwind operation was to destroy the Soviet forces that had broken through north of the Danube.

p. 251, "is 624": BA-MA RH 19V/61, Maier, p. 520.

p. 251, "16 February 1945": Maier, pp. 520–521.

p. 252, "terrible sight": Komiszarov, pp. 139–140.

p. 253, "or rifles": Tóth, 1980, p. 52.

p. 254, "two generals": Andrjusenko, pp. 141–142.

p. 254, "mentioning it": ibid., p. 142.

p. 255, "of flesh": interviews with Finta, Aurél Salamon, Dobay, and Wáczek.

p. 255, "meters high": Wáczek saw between 400 and 500 bodies in Vérhalom Square.

p. 256, "same fiction": BA-MA. Pfeffer-Wildenbruch's unpublished documents contain many contemporary newspaper cuttings of this kind.

6. The Siege and the Population

p. 257: epigraph: *Magyarság* (journal), 9 November 1944.

p. 258, "slow progress": *13. Panzerdivision*, p. 7.

p. 258, "leaders departed": Ránki, 1968, p. 910.

p. 258, "the explosion": Kovalovszky, p. 88.

p. 259, "fitting the charge": HL TGY, Almay, 3091.

p. 260, "Bolshevik horde": Glatz, p. 144.

p. 260, "during the siege": Kutuzov-Tolstoy, pp. 330–331.

p. 260, "favorite dog": Zamercev, p. 54.

p. 260, "started work": Glatz, p. 142.

p. 260, "been rescinded": Teleki, p. 166.

p. 260, "voluntary labor": OSZK, Tonelli, *Budapest,* p. 79.

p. 261, "German army": HL, Documents of the Hungarian 10th Infantry Division, attachments.

p. 261, "carrying canisters": interview with Hingyi.

p. 261, "Heroes of Budapest": Teleki, p. 335.

p. 261, "roast chicken": Kovalovszky, pp. 207–208.

p. 261, "be expected": HL KTB Hgr. Süd 897/b, 23 December 1944.

p. 262, "the ghetto": Teleki, p. 213.

p. 263, "Margit Bridge": OSZK, Tonelli, *Budapest,* p. 79.

p. 263, "we can talk": Seidl, Marietta, p. 2 (manuscript in the collection of the author).

p. 263, "expecting defeat": HL TGY, Szalay.

p. 263, "we are having": interview with Nádasdy.

p. 263, "for scaremongering": interview with Galántay.

p. 263, "artillery units": According to a report by Hindy, the Hungarians had 22,000 horses. Gosztonyi, 1990, p. 46.

p. 263, "as stables": interview with Bődy.

p. 264, "nervous strain": Noll, p. 2.

p. 264, "people then": interview with Major.

p. 265, "for a break-out": Gosztonyi, 1990, pp. 46–49.

p. 266, "concrete facts": HL VKF, box 306/b, 31 December 1944.

p. 266, "liberation of Budapest": HL 21, I. 107, Documents of national Chief Inspector, Henkei Group, situation report of 31 January 1945.

p. 266, "their opinion": BA-MA RH 2/1950.

p. 266, "from above": Maier, p. 49; KTB Hgr. Süd, daily report of 8 January 1945.

p. 267, "the ice": Bokor, 1995.

p. 267, "tactical command": Gosztonyi, 1990, pp. 48–50.

p. 268, "destruction of Budapest": HK VKF, box 306/b, report of 15 January 1945.

p. 268, "burning ruins": ibid., report of 16 January 1945.

p. 268, "German troops": ibid., report of 17 January 1945.

p. 269, "in consequence": HL VKF, box 306/b, letter from Beregfy to General Hans Greiffenberg.

p. 269, "to beg": HL VKF, box 306/b, report of 3 February 1945.

p. 270, "the front line": ibid., report of 5 February 1945.

p. 270, "fairy tale": ibid., report of 6 February 1945.

p. 270, "cellars in Buda": Cs. Lengyel, p. 193.

p. 271, "to the Soviet": Bárdos.

p. 271, "constantly dripping": OSZK, Tonelli, p. 97.

p. 271, "the water works": Oldner, p. 12 .

p. 272, "her diary": Blanka Péchy, p. 68.

p. 272, "the action": Gosztonyi, 1994, p. 53.

p. 273, "during the night": HL TGY, Almay, 3091, p. 31.

p. 273, "the former": Teleki, p. 132.

p. 274, "Wehrmacht unit": Sólyom and Szabó on Kröszl.

p. 274, "vigorous protests": Teleki, p. 123.

p. 275, "following morning": interview with Lám.

p. 275, "own submachine gun": Ferenc X. Kovács, p. 9 (manuscript in the collection of the author); interview with Kovács.

p. 275, "persecution victims": *Képes figyelő*, 1945, no. 13.

p. 275, "*Budapester Kesselnachrichten*": Although no copy of the latter has been preserved, Galántay confirmed its existence in an interview. The Soviets published a propaganda paper with the same title, a copy of which is held in the Museum of Military History.

p. 277, "beyond imagination": Gosztonyi, 1990, p. 56.

p. 278, "millions of lice": Ney, *Budapest,* pp. 41–45 (manuscript in the collection of the author).

p. 278, "starving to death": reported by Dr Katalin Sárlai of the Fővárosi Szent István Hospital, who had heard the story from a former nurse. The phenomenon, known as induced lactation, is frequently mentioned in medical literature.

p. 278, "on 22 January": OSZK, Tonelli, p. 91.

p. 278, "marble façade": reported to the author by Pintér.

p. 279, "everything they had": interview with Kézdi-Beck.

p. 282, "hidden everywhere": diary of Deseő (in the collection of the author).

p. 283, "and the Castle": Márai, 1945.

p. 283, "caught him": Zamercev, p. 123.

p. 284, "the difference": Eszenyi, pp. 411–412.

p. 284, epigraph: Teleki, p. 145.

p. 285, "the SD": In addition to the organization of Jewish transports to the concentration camps, the SD (*Sicherheitsdienst*) carried out intelligence and counterintelligence duties in parallel with the Gestapo.

p. 285, "the Gestapo": The Gestapo had also taken on the duties of the Abwehr (military intelligence) beginning 19 February 1944.

p. 286, "hours a day": Szirmai, p. 270.

p. 286, "of the capital": Ránki, 1968, p. 912.

p. 286, "in the street": interview with Aczél.

p. 287, "of 81": Lévai, 1947, p. 24.

p. 287, "in the canal": Lévai, 1946b, p. 128.

p. 287, "into the Danube": Gosztonyi, 1990, p. 50.

p. 288, "German occupation": Some German units publicly executed Jews, and pogroms took place, for example, in Lemberg and Riga.

p. 288, "the population": Cf. especially Bibó.

p. 288, "vindictive swine": Blanka Péchy, p. 67.

p. 289, "take revenge": Fenyő, 3 January 1945.

p. 289, "keep it?": Márai, 1990a, p. 285.

p. 289, "death register": Teleki, p. 150.

p. 289, "in the streets": Lévai, 1946b, p. 120.

p. 289, "last journey": memoir of Dema (in the collection of the author).

p. 290, "he said": interview with Rácz.

p. 290, "a price": Lévai, 1946a, p. 226.

p. 291, "divorced her": *Népbírági Közlöny*, 25 May 1946.

p. 291, "possible manner": Teleki, p. 135.

p. 292, "been persecuted": Stark, pp. 33–40.

p. 292, "the population": Sólyom and Szabó, p. 123.

p. 293, "or anywhere": *Soproni Hírlap*, 18 October 1944.

p. 293, "recognized 34,800": Teleki, p. 139.

p. 293, "to the Germans": Lévai, 1947, p. 59.

p. 295, "his ring": Elek, p. 92.

p. 295, "they wanted": Lévai, 1947, p. 76.

p. 295, "himself Jewish": ibid., p. 16.

p. 296, "the persecutions": Lévai, 1946b, p. 88.

p. 297, "as Jews": Jerezian, p. 61.

p. 299, "mutilated body": Kis, pp. 24–26.

p. 300, "Swiss Embassy": Lévai, 1947, p. 104.

p. 300, "ghetto alive": ibid., p. 107.

p. 300, "been 8": Lévai, 1946a, p. 262.

p. 300, "gas taps": Lévai, 1947, p. 113.

p. 301, "machine-gunned them down": Határ, p. 918.

p. 302, "the 50 people": Szekeres, p. 571.

p. 302, "and officers": interview with Hermándy.

p. 302, "another Katyn": Lévai, 1947, p. 135.

p. 302, "forbade the pogrom": Lévai, 1947, p. 135. Gosztonyi in his writings erroneously attributes the rescue of the ghetto to Pfeffer-Wildenbruch and his SS soldiers. Schmidhuber never belonged to the SS.

p. 303, "two hours": Szekeres, p. 578.

p. 303, "in the street": OSZK, Csécsy.

p. 305, "come from": HL TGY, Lám, pp. 147–148.

p. 306, "the capital": Ferenc X. Kovács, p. 19 (manuscript in the collection of the author).

p. 307, "soldiers' coats": Imre Kovács, p. 112.

p. 309, "forces pass": Sipeki Balás, p. 3 (manuscript in the collection of the author).

p. 309, "1.b section": Possibly Colonel Béla Tatay. The 1.b section was the anti-espionage and intelligence section.

p. 309, "awkward position": Sipeki Balás, p. 3.

p. 309, "issued by Mikó": Vass, *Egyetemisták* (private collections), p. 17.

p. 309, "15 August 1945": Bondor, p. 187. Works of reference usually give wrong dates for Mikó's execution.

p. 310, "prisoners of war": ibid.; interview with Ferenc X. Kovács.

p. 310, "10th Infantry Division": In 1946 András was arrested by the ÁVO (State Security Police) on trumped-up charges and received a death sentence, commuted to ten years' hard labor.

p. 310, "his unit": interviews with Benyovszky and Bíró. Major Aladár Zvolenszky, commander of the 1.b section, had already contacted the Soviets in the Carpathians and eventually defected with his entire unit.

p. 310, "the occupants": Ferenc X. Kovács (manuscript in the collection of the author); Blanka Péchy, p. 43.

p. 312, "liaison officer": Kádár spent much of the siege as an administrator employed by a baroness. His younger brother, Jenő Csermanek, also participated in the resistance and was killed three years later, when he fell from a balcony while trying to raise a red flag at his place of work.

p. 312, "committee of 13": According to party-line historians, the members of the Moscow faction "prevailed in the committee leadership, not because of their number but because of their experience of illegal struggle, their sensible program, and their personal courage" (Gazsi and Pintér, p. 174). In reality the Demény faction was stronger in every respect.

p. 312, "in Csepel": Gazsi and Pintér, pp. 179–185.

p. 313, "inch either": ibid., p. 182.

p. 313, "a woman": Csepel, p. 392.

p. 314, "the building": *Újpest,* p. 208.

p. 314, "the Gulag": Benedek and Vámos, p. 39.

p. 315, "Communist Party": *A magyar antfasiszta,* pp. 283–284.

p. 315, "and weeping": Gazsi and Harsányi, p. 682.

p. 315, "seen again": Grossmann, pp. 271–272.

p. 316, "speak German)": Révész, p. 19.

p. 316, "final solution": Szita, pp. 86–88.

p. 317, "yellow star": ibid., p. 88.

p. 318, "prison camp": M. Kiss, p. 300.

p. 318, "Balaton operation": Fortusz, p. 48.

p. 319, "forceful action": HL TGY, Bíró, 3053, p. 21

p. 320, respective comrades": Száva, 1975a, p. 267

p. 320, "their men": Tóth, 1980, p. 25

p. 322, "differ greatly": HL TGY, Aurél Salamon, 3116, pp. 16–17.

p. 322, "company size": *Hadtudományi* 1994/10, p. 185

p. 322, "were dead": Száva, 1975a, p. 282.

p. 322, "their strength": HL TGY, Sárközi-Csécsy, p. 18.

p. 322, "or incident": Tóth, 1980, p. 27.

p. 323, "volunteer company": interview with Benyovszky.

p. 323, "leather coat": interview with Létay.

p. 323, "with him": ibid.

p. 324, "László Cseresnyés": Gosztonyi, 1992, p. 240.

p. 326, "over a body": interview with Finta.

p. 328, "any mishap": letter to the author from Kövendi.

p. 329, "was there": letter to the author from Válas.

p. 330, "these questions": reminiscence of Salfay (in the collection of the author).

p. 331, "on the ground": interview with Finta.

p. 331, 1st epigraph: HL TGY, Aurél Salamon, 3116, p. 28.

p. 331, 2nd epigraph: HL TGY, György Péchy, p. 165.

p. 331, "known today": Among Hungarian reminiscences known to the author, only those of Konkoly-Thege (HL TGY), Aurél Salamon (HL TGY), and Gyalog mention a few such cases.

p. 331, "pay for it": HL KTB Hgr. Süd, 898/b.

p. 331, "a stir": Zaharov, p. 250.

p. 332, "shot them": HL TGY, Konkoly-Thege, p. 116.

p. 332, "named 'vlasovists'": Lieutenant-General Andrei Vlasov was captured by the Germans in 1942 and commissioned in September 1944 to set up the anti-Soviet "Russian Liberation Army." Although none of his soldiers were sent to Budapest, Soviet propaganda described every Soviet national serving on the German side as a "vlasovist".

p. 332, "front of us": HL TGY, Rhédey, p. 8.

p. 332, "submachine gun: Bayer, p. 389.

p. 332, "over him": HL TGY, Konkoly-Thege, p. 156.

p. 332, "the spot": M. v. K. (in the collection of the author).

p. 332, "the wards": BA-MA, letter from Carl Lutz to Pfeffer-Wildenbruch, N 370/6.

p. 332, "every hospital": In addition to the sources above, interviews with Mrs. Ferenc X. Kovács, Baló, and Entzmann.

p. 333, "Cogwheel Railway": HL TGY, Salamon, Zsigmond, p. 3.

p. 333, "other sources": interviews with Hingy, Tomcsányi, and Aurél Salamon, and reminiscences of local residents. In the Buda hills and around Perbál and Tök many Germans were found executed. Payer (p. 209) reports the execution of 300 in Perbál, and an anonymous letter in Gosztonyi's collection relates similar atrocities near Tök. These examples can be multiplied.

p. 333, "at risk": In an apartment at 2 Trombitás Street, Soviet soldiers emptied a submachine gun into a gravely wounded German officer who was lying on a couch (interview with Tomcsányi). By 13 February wounded Germans were still being "accidentally" shot around Széll Kálmán Square (interview with Aurél Salamon).

p. 333, "being shot": Friedrich, p. 140 (private collections).

p. 333, "street fighting": interview with Dobay.

p. 333, "by tanks": reports by Ottó Fritzsch, István Janositz, and Ferenc Stofficz in the Dobay collection, and interview with Dobay.

p. 333, "that purpose": interview with Aurél Salamon.

p. 333, "first aid": interview with Major.

p. 333, "the rear": Bayer, pp. 388–389; Portugall, p. 7 (manuscript in the collection of the author); interviews with Bartha and Ferenc X. Kovács.

p. 334, "and abandoned": interview with Hermándy.

p. 334, "they had": interview with Bődy.

p. 335, "snow water": Bayer, p. 388.

p. 335, "be executed": The German command had given orders for two groups of prisoners to be executed: Jews and political officers. The "commissar order," relating to the latter group, was not carried out consistently and was finally rescinded in 1942: subsequently many former political officers played a leading role in the Vlassov army. Initially the position of prisoners in Soviet hands was unclear, because on the one hand the Soviet Union did not recognize the prisoner-of-war status, and on the other hand many commanders interpreted the slogan "death to the German intruders" as meaning that any prisoners were to be liquidated. This situation ended in 1942, when Stalin issued a special order to the effect that the Red Army would take German soldiers and officers prisoner if they surrendered. Boog, pp. 778–790.

p. 336, "Red Cross nurses": Hoffmann, pp. 85–86.

p. 336, "and 'brutes'": Marshall Buddonny's battle order no. 5, 16 July 1941, BA-MA RH 24-3/134.

p. 336, "kill a German": Sander and Johr, p. 124.

p. 336, "the commander": Walendy, I, p. 10.

p. 336, "dead German": Boog, p. 784; Hoffmann, pp. 85–86.

p. 336, "to captivity": Száva, 1975b, p. 266.

p. 336, "notorious OSNAS": Cheka: Extraordinary Commission for Combating Counterrevolution and Sabotage, 1917–1922; GPU: State Political Administration (political police), 1922–1923; NKGB: People's Commissariat for State Security, beginning in 1941; NKVD: People's Commissariat for Internal Affairs, beginning in 1922; OSNAS: units with special designations within the NKVD.

p. 336, "the 1930s": Csebotarev, 1967/4, p. 713.

p. 337, "Soviet army": According to an account given to the Hungarian press by Aleksandr Lebed, a former commander of the 14th Moldavian Army, on 16 July 1941 Stalin had ordered the creation of special units to execute fugitives and other suspects, and on 17 November he set up further units to destroy all settlements adjoining the front line. Some units operating behind the front were to wear German uniforms in order to increase hatred for the occupiers. Although their activities were not as thoroughly organized as those of the SS *Einsatzgruppen,* they also ignored the conventions governing war.

p. 337, "the future": interview with Tamás Katona, who witnessed such an incident at the age of 13.

p. 337, "Russian Waffen SS": Portugall, p. 7 (manuscript in the collection of the author).

p. 337, "his arm": ibid., p. 6.

p. 338, "Cross militia": Lukács, p. 176 (manuscript in the private collection of Mrs. Ernő Lakatos).

p. 338, "left behind": interview with Kaszás.

p. 338, "a Hungarian": interview with Tabódy.

p. 338, "become uncontrollable": BA-MA RH 19 XV/6, 22 February 1945; RH 2/2685, 26 March 1945.

p. 338, "every unit": Hoffmann, pp. 274–276.

p. 338, "East Prussia": For the latter see de Zayas.

p. 339, "their cattle": Szekeres, p. 565.

p. 339, "the process": interview with Benefi.

p. 340, "the siege": Gosztonyi, 1989a, p. 175.

p. 340, "Sándor Harsányi": *Szombat,* 1997, no. 2.

p. 340, "for days": Gazsi, 1995, p. 28.

p. 341, "the bank": Kogelfranz, p. 96.

p. 341, "trucks for days": letter to the author from Czagányi, 19 February 1995.

p. 341, "Katyn massacre": for example, Bondor; Gazsi, 1995.

p. 341, "know nothing": Gazsi, 1995, p. 29.

p. 342, "secret service": ibid., p. 22.

p. 342, "the Germans": Benedek and Vámos, p. 59.

p. 342, "frontline prison": Imre Kovács, p. 186.

p. 343, "broken off": Ember.

p. 343, "drunken soldiers": BA-MA letter from Lutz to Pfeffer-Wildenbruch, N 370/6.

p. 344, "its contents": Montgomery, p. 206.

p. 344, "living shields": HL TGY, György Péchy, p. 161; HL VKF, box 306/b, report of 15 January 1945.

p. 344, "considered attractive": interview with Sasváry.

p. 344, "their victory": Kogelfranz, p. 96.

p. 344, "supreme command": Zamercev, p. 67.

p. 344, "drowned in wine": diary of Deseő (in the collection of the author).

p. 345, "free will": Montgomery, pp. 203–209.

p. 345, "Russians pleased": OSZK, Tonelli, *1944–45*, p. 145.

p. 346, "rounded up": The records are incomplete. Existing documents refer to 94,788 and 18,977 deported from today's Hungary and Budapest, respectively, but the real figures were multiples of these: researchers are unanimous that 50,000 were taken away from Budapest alone. About 20 percent of all the deportees were women and children (Ravasz, p. 498).

p. 347, "and cursing": Imre Kovács, p. 191.

p. 347, "a stretcher": letter from to the author from Csongrádi.

p. 348, "unbearable stench": Marietta Seidl, p. 2 (manuscript in the collection of the author).

p. 348, "a warning": interview with Rádi.

p. 348, "Toroczkó Square": interviews with Finta and Wáczek.

p. 349, epigraph: quoted in Szakács and Zinner, p. 19.

p. 349, "looting campaigns": Kishon, p. 74.

p. 350, "in Hungary": Montgomery, p. 207.

p. 350, "endured since": OSZK, Faragó, p. 66.

p. 352, "as gods": Szakács and Zinner, pp. 10–12.

p. 352, "the Party": ibid., p. 9.

p. 354, "nothing left": *Ötven* (manuscript in the collection of the author).

p. 354, "from diseases": The sufferings of rape victims are described in shocking detail in Polcz.

p. 354, "as a result": Sander and Johr.

p. 354, "gave birth": ibid., p. 54.

p. 354, "the population": HL, Documents of national Chief Inspector, box 21, no. 667.

p. 354, "as necessary": *Képes Figyelő*, 1945, no. 13.

p. 354, "official records": *Ítélet*, no. 38, 3 October 1946.

p. 355, "female soldiers": interview with Szablya; communication by Vadász.

p. 355, "move on": BA-MA RH 2/3031.

p. 356, "Filatori fields": Fehér, 1979, p. 575.

p. 356, "of sugar": Boldizsár,1982, p. 178.

p. 356, "Soviet Union": "In autumn 1944 . . . soldiers of the Soviet Union often committed such grave atrocities against the population and the officers of the Yugoslav army that this became a political problem for the new order and the Communist Party." Djilas, p. 81.

p. 356, "a trifle": ibid., p. 86.

p. 357, "the Gentiles": Márai, 1990a, p. 287.

p. 357, epigraph: Benedek and Vámos, p. 67.

pp. 358–359, "many novelties": For information on rapes see also the diary of Lieutenant Khoroshich in HL TGY, Lisszay.

p. 359, "second evening": BA-MA N 370/6, letter from Lutz to Pfeffer-Wildenbruch, 14 February 1956.

p. 359, "stealing machines": interview with Mrs. Kovács.

p. 359, "his own": ibid.

p. 359, "on looting": Steinert, p. 388.

p. 360, "the streets": interview with Benefi.

p. 361, "without resisting": Kishon, p. 75.

p. 361, "by himself": Márai, 1990b, p. 10.

p. 361, "valuable object": Károly Kiss, 1 April 1995.

p. 361, "Major Nefedov": OSZK, Tonelli, *1944–45,* pp. 144–146.

p. 362, "is available": ibid., p. 139.

p. 362, "the others": ibid., p. 150.

p. 363, "grown-up woman": interview with Mrs. K. B.

p. 363, "miraculously ceased": Zamercev, p. 97.

p. 363, epigraph: OSZK, Tonelli, *1944–45,* p. 239.

p. 365, "do this": interview with Sasvári.

p. 366, "minds now": Thassy, pp. 458–459.

p. 366, "of prisoners": ibid., p. 461.

p. 368, "being, liquidated": Szakács and Zinner, pp. 83–84.

p. 368, "February 1945": The Hungarian Communist Party had asked in advance for the Soviet city command's permission, to ensure that "the demonstrators attending would not be rounded up for labor" (Szakács and Zinner, p. 94).

p. 368, "so much": Sulyok, p. 275.

p. 368, "eventually released": Szakács and Zinner, p. 94.

p. 370, "the air": interview with Gábor Seidl.

p. 370, "acquired wares": OSZK, Tonelli, *1944–45,* p. 244.

p. 370, "breaking in": ibid., p. 250.

p. 370, "8 February": *Szabadság,* 8 February 1945.

p. 370, "three days": Szirtes, p. 10 (manuscript in the collection of the author).

p. 370–371, "of matches": *Tétény-Promontor,* p. 365.

p. 371, "to complete": *Vas.*

p. 372, "own vegetables": *Kossuth Népe* 10 (June 1945).

p. 372, "helpless laughter": Bárdos.

p. 372, "their owners": interview with Dobay.

7. Epilogue

p. 374, "80,026 dead": Krivosheev, pp. 211–212. Gosztonyi (1994, p. 59) without source references, refers to 240,136 wounded and 79,946 dead.

p. 374, "293 aircraft": Krivosheev, p. 372.

p. 376, "of Berlin": BA-MA RH2 Ost Karten (Panzerlage), 4999–6257.

p. 376, "interrogate him": Gosztonyi, 1992, p. 239.

p. 377, "Hungarian capital": Gosztonyi, 1982, part 4, p. 160.

p. 377, "and 15,000": HL, Documents of 13th Panzer Division, report of 24 January 1945.

p. 377, "about 32,000": Pfeffer-Wildenbruch reported 43,900 before the breakout, including 11,600 wounded.

p. 378, "troops a week": Glatz, p. 99.

p. 378, "108 days": The battle for Budapest lasted 108 days according to Soviet records (which date it from the beginning of the entire operation on 29 October 1944), and 102 days according to German and Hungarian records (which date it from the arrival of Soviet forces at the administrative border of the capital on 4 November 1944).

Tables

Table 1. Hungarian and German forces between the Danube and Tisza Rivers on 31 October 1944

Hungarian 3rd Army

Unit	Combat strength[a]	Tanks and assault guns	Guns	Combat value/ Notes[b]
10th Infantry Division	2,000	0	9	IV (arriving from Carpathians)
7th Assault Artillery Battalion	0	9	0	II
23rd Reserve Division	3,600	0	26	Less than IV
1st Hussar Division	3,700	0	30	II
1st Armored Division	700	20	7	III
5th and 8th Reserve Divisions	3,300	0	26	Less than IV
20th Infantry Division	1,500	0	15	IV

Table I. Hungarian and German forces between the Danube and Tisza Rivers on 31 October 1944—cont'd

		Hungarian 3rd Army		
Unit	Combat strength[a]	Tanks and assault guns	Guns	Combat value/ Notes[b]
23rd Panzer Division (German)	1,000	50	30	II (arriving from east of the Tisza on 31 October– 1 November) with 503rd Heavy Armored (Tiger tank) Battalion
24th Panzer Division (German)	1,600	18	45	II (behind the front line)
Total	17,400	97	188	

Source: BA-MA KTB Hgr. Süd RH 19/V54, situation report of 25 October 1944.
[a]Combat strength, according to German military terminology, signifies the number of troops available in any one unit for deployment on the front line, not counting artillery men, army service corps, radio operators, pioneers, etc. The combat strength usually amounts to some 30–50 percent of the unit totals.
[b]The German combat value reports list four different categories: I—entirely fit for attack, II—partially fit for attack, III—entirely fit for defense, IV—partially fit for defense.

Table 2. Soviet forces between the Danube and Tisza Rivers on 31 October 1944

2nd Ukrainian Front—Soviet 46th Army

Unit	Combat strength	Armored vehicles	Guns	Notes
2nd Mechanized Guard Corps	c. 12,000	248	c. 60	entirely replenished, fresh unit
4th Mechanized Guard Corps	c. 6,000	73	c. 50	arriving from Belgrade on 1 November
10th Rifle Corps	c. 8,000	0	c. 90	
23rd Rifle Corps	c. 10,000	0	c. 90	entirely replenished, arriving from Mezőhegyes on 1 November
31st Guard Rifle Corps	c. 8,000	0	c. 90	
37th Rifle Corps	c. 8,000	0	c. 90	
Total	c. 52,000	321	c. 470	

Source: Tóth 1975, pp. 15–16. Figures qualified by "c." are my estimates.

Table 3. German units regrouped to the Great Hungarian Plain

Unit	Infantry combat strength	Tanks and assault guns	Guns	Time and place of arrival
1st Panzer Division	1,000	13	30	Pilis-Cegléd, 1 November
13th Panzer Division	1,100	9	14	Dunakeszi-Ócsa, 1 November

Table 3. German units regrouped to the Great Hungarian Plain—cont'd

Unit	Infantry combat strength	Tanks and assault guns	Guns	Time and place of arrival
Feldherrnhalle Panzergrenadier Division	900	21	15	Örkény
8th SS Cavalry Division	3,060	10	37	Üllő, 2 November
22nd SS Cavalry Division	7,000	9	57	Dunaharaszti-Soroksár, 1 November
503rd Heavy Armored Battalion	0	41	0	Örkény-Pilis-Üllő, 3 November
Total	13,060	103	153	

Source: BA-MA KTB Hgr. Süd RH 19/V 54, situation reports of 25 October and 3 November 1944. The figures for the 503rd Heavy Armored Battalion are my estimates.

Table 4. German and Hungarian combat forces in the Hatvan region

Unit	Infantry combat strength	Heavy antitank guns	Tanks and assault guns	Guns
76th Infantry Division	1,000	9	7	32
Parts of the Hungarian 2nd Armored Division	800	2	16	24
18th SS Panzergrenadier Division	1,000	8	5	42
4th SS Panzergrenadier Division	900	9	13	32

Continued

Table 4. German and Hungarian combat forces in the Hatvan region—cont'd

Unit	Infantry combat strength	Heavy antitank guns	Tanks and assault guns	Guns
Parts of the 13th Panzer Division	700	1	6	36
46th Infantry Division	900	15	5	62
357th Infantry Division	800	8	5	42
German and Hungarian Total	6,100	52	57	270
Soviet opposition	c. 50,000	?	510	2,074

Source: The situation reports of the German divisions are found in the attachments to the war diary of the German Army Group South (HL KTB Hrg. Süd 897/a,b).

Table 5. The 2nd Ukrainian Front and the opposing German and Hungarian forces

Men and matériel	Soviet	German and Hungarian	Ratio
Personnel	528,000	127,000	4.2:1
Guns	10,867	2,800	3.9:1
Mortars (not including katyushas and smoke-bomb throwers)	3,974	880	4.5:1
Tanks and assault guns	565	c. 140	4:1

Source: Hazánk, p. 70. Minasyan's figures needed amendment, with the help of the Army Group South's war diary, only in respect of the German tanks and assault guns.

Table 6. German and Hungarian units on the Margit Line

Unit	Defended front sector	Combat strength
Sections of German 271st Volksgrenadier Division and Hungarian 23rd Reserve Division	20 km	3,000
8th SS Police Regiment (non-Germans)	10 km	800
Kesseő Group and sections of Hungarian 1st Hussar Division	30 km	800
German 153rd Field Training Division	20 km	c. 1,500
German 1st Panzer Division	10 km	c. 900
Hungarian 20th Infantry Division	10 km	800
Total	100 km	c. 7,800

Source: HL KTB Hgr. Süd 897/a, attachments.

Table 7. Soviet and German/Hungarian forces west of Budapest between 24 and 25 December 1944

Unit	Tanks and assault guns	Infantry
Soviet 18th Tank Corps	c. 109 T-34 tanks and 24 assault guns[a]	c. 3,000
Soviet 31st Guard Rifle Corps	0	c. 16,000
Soviet totals	c. 133	c. 19,000
Hungarian 16th and 20th Assault Gun Divisions	29 Hetzer assault guns	0

Continued

Table 7. Soviet and German/Hungarian forces west of Budapest between 24 and 25 December 1944—cont'd

Unit	Tanks and assault guns	Infantry
Parts of German 271st Volksgrenadier Division	0	c. 1,500
Hungarian 20th and 23rd Infantry Divisions	0	c. 1,200
German Division Group Pape (on its way)	62 tanks IV and V	c. 1,000
German and Hungarian totals	91	c. 3,700

[a]Gábor Nagy, 1983, p. 429. Figures marked "c." are my estimates.

Table 8. Hungarian units in the Budapest cauldron on 25 December 1944

Unit	Ration strength	Combat strength (deployable infantry only)[a]	Guns	Tanks and assault guns	Heavy antitank guns
10th Infantry Division[b]	7,500	1,000	25	0	13
12th Reserve Division	4,000	500	26	0	12
12th Tank Division[c]	5,000	500	3	7	3
I, II University Assault Battalions	1,000	1,000	0	0	0
Vannay Flying Squad Battalion	1,000	800	0	0	1
Parts of I Hussar Division[d]	1,000	250	8	0	4

Table 8. Hungarian units in the Budapest cauldron on 25 December 1944—cont'd

Unit	Ration strength	Combat strength (deployable infantry only)[a]	Guns	Tanks and assault guns	Heavy antitank guns
Parts of 6 assault artillery battalions[e]	2,000	1,000	0	30–32	8
6 antiaircraft and searchlight battalions[f]	2,000	800	168	0	0
5 gendarmerie battalions[g]	1,500	1,000	0	0	0
Technical and pioneer groups[h]	7,000	2,000	0	0	0
Budapest Guard Battalion[i]	800	800	0	0	4
I, II Budapest Assault Companies[j]	1,000	1,000	0	0	0
Combat groups drafted in Budapest[k]	2,000	1,600	0	0	10
Budapest Security Battalion[l]	300	300	0	0	0
Army artillery[m]	500	0	20–30	0	0
Budapest police and its combat groups[n]	7000	2,000	0	0	0
Budapest military institutes and supply units[o]	3,000	0	0	0	0
Hungarist combat units[p]	1,500	500	0	0	0
KISKA units	7,000	0	0	0	0

Continued

Table 8. Hungarian units in the Budapest cauldron on 25 December 1944—cont'd

Unit	Ration strength	Combat strength (deployable infantry only)[a]	Guns	Tanks and assault guns	Heavy antitank guns
Total	55,100	15,050	250–260	37–39	55
Excluding KISKA and military institutes	45,100	15,050	250–260	37–39	55
Combat troops (excluding police)	38,100	13,050	250–260	37–39	55

[a]HL, Documents of the 10th Infantry Division. According to telephone diary, 16 December 1944, the ration strength of the division was 7,990.

[b]Most of the artillery remained outside the encirclement and operated within the Szent László Division.

[c]The sources for this item are the war diary of the 10th Division, the studies in the Archive of Military History in Budapest, and interviews with the commanders and members of the units. In earlier accounts numerous units are either omitted or listed incompletely or wrongly.

[d]4th Hussar Regiment, 2nd Antitank Company, I Bem József Cavalry-Artillery Detachment, I Special Hussar Battalion, 4th Motor Pioneer Company.

[e]1st, 7th, 10th, and fragments of 13th, 16th, 25th Assault Artillery Battalions.

[f]201st, 206th, 208th, 217th, I Antiaircraft Battalions, and 201st Antiaircraft Searchlight Battalion.

[g]Galántai, Zilahi, Székelyudvarhelyi, Besztercei, Pécsi Gendarmerie Battalions. Their ration strength oscillated between 150 and 700 and is therefore calculated as 300 on average.

[h]A total of 11 battalions and 25 companies.

[i]One battalion per district plus ELTE [Eötvös Loránd University] KISKA Battalion and Táncsics Battalion (at the time code-named I Hungarist University Reconnaissance Battalion), totaling 16 battalions.

[j]These had been set up in November 1944 under the command of Ferenc Kubinyi and Gusztáv Hellebronth (interviews with Hingyi and Hellebronth).

[k]Berend, Korányi, Déri, Morlin, Viharos Combat Groups. The first three had been made up largely from antiaircraft units which had lost their guns, and the fourth from students of the Nagyvárad cadet academy.

[l]Consisting of cadets.
[m]9th, 21st Field Artillery Detachments, 106th Heavy Artillery Detachment, 20/4 Mortar Battery, 4/2 Artillery Battery.
[n]1 security regiment, 1 bicycle battalion, 2 antiaircraft companies, 1 training battalion, 1 armored vehicle detachment, and other police contingents.
[o]IV Motor Supply Detachment (and probably some other units with unknown designations).
[p]Central Hungarist Combat Group (Pál Prónay), North Pest Hungarist Combat Group (István Evetni), Svábhegy Group (Antal Ostián), City Center Hungarist Combat Group (Béla Kollarits), Óbuda Group, Zugló-Kőbánya Combat Group, Csepel Hungarist Combat Group (commanders unknown).

Table 9. German troops and proportions of German and Hungarian troops in Budapest on 24 December 1944

Unit	Ration strength	Guns	Tanks and assault guns (deployable or under repair)	Heavy antitank guns
8th SS Cavalry Division[a]	c. 8,000	c. 30	29	17
22nd SS Cavalry Division[b]	11,345	37	17	14
Feldherrnhalle Panzergrenadier Division[c]	7,255	38	24	9
13th Panzer Division[d]	4,983	35	17	8
Parts of the 271st Volksgrenadier Division[e]	c. 1,000	c. 6	0	c. 4
1st SS Police Regiment	c. 700	0	0	?
I/40 Heavy Antiaircraft Battalion	c. 500	12	0	0

Continued

Table 9. German troops and proportions of German and Hungarian troops in Budapest on 24 December 1944—cont'd

Unit	Ration strength	Guns	Tanks and assault guns (deployable or under repair)	Heavy antitank guns
12th SS Police Armored Vehicle Company	c. 100	0	0	0
Various combat groups	c. 1,500	0	0	c. 10
12th Antiaircraft Artillery Assault Regiment[f]	c. 1,000	c. 48	0	0
573rd Heavy Antiaircraft Detachment	c. 200	12	0	0
Europa Battalion	c. 300	0	0	0
500th Battalion for Special Use (penal battalion)[g]	c. 200	0	0	0
Noncombatants and others trapped in Budapest[h]	2,500	0	0	0
Troops directly attached to the IX SS Mountain Army Corps[i]	c. 1,500	c. 9	0	0
Sick and wounded caught up in Budapest	c. 1,500	0	0	0
Total	c. 42,600	c. 234	87	c. 62
Total excluding sick and wounded	c. 41,000	0	0	0

Table 9. German troops and proportions of German and Hungarian troops in Budapest on 24 December 1944—cont'd

Unit	Ration strength	Guns	Tanks and assault guns (deployable or under repair)	Heavy antitank guns
Total including Hungarian forces[j] (armored infantry vehicles)	c. 79,000	c. 489	c. 125 (221)	117
Percentage of Hungarians	46	53	30	47
Percentage of Germans	54	47	70	53

Source: The only strength reports still in existence are those concerning the 8th and 22nd SS Cavalry Divisions, the Feldherrnhalle Panzergrenadier Division, and the 13th Panzer Division. Figures given there were reduced by the number of troops left outside the capital after 24 December (BA-MA RH 10/139). Of the heavy arms listed only 60–70 percent were usable. For the units, see the strength reports in KTB Hgr. Süd 897/b and the reports of the IX SS Mountain Army Corps in the Archive of Military History in Budapest. Contrary to Gosztonyi's statement, the 6th SS Police Regiment was never in Budapest.

[a]BA-MA RH 10/105.

[b]BA-MA RH 10/328, exluding about 800 soldiers of the pioneer battalion left outside the cauldron after 24 December.

[c]BA-MA RH 10/206, excluding 1 battalion, 2 panzer companies, and 3 artillery batteries left outside the encirclement.

[d]Only 60 percent of the 13th Panzer Division was in action in Budapest. One panzer battalion, 1 antitank battalion, 1 antiaircraft battalion, and the II Battalion of the 93rd Panzergrenadier Regiment were either left outside the encirclement or were not even in Hungary. BA-MA RH 10/151.

[e]Remnants of the 977th and 978th Grenadier Regiments, 2 artillery batteries, and 1 SS police company.

[f]Including 147th, 632nd, I/40, and II/241 Artillery Battalions (BA-MA RH 10/139).

Continued

gThe Bataillon zur besonderen Verwendung (Battalion for special use) served as a penal unit for Wehrmacht soldiers, who were eventually allowed to rejoin their original units if they committed no further offenses.
hParts of 26th Field Gendarmerie Detachment, 9th Antitank Gun Battalion, 3rd SS Artillery Regiment, 4th SS Police Regiment, parts of the 109th SS Signal Detachment.
i959/I Artillery Battery, 504th Nebelwerfer Battalion, I and II/127 Pioneer Brigades, I/771 Pioneer Company, parts of 59th Pontoon Battalion. BA-MA RH II III/40 K3 and HL KTB Hgr. Süd 897/b, strength report of 1 January 1945.
jThis figure is confirmed by the confession of General Staff Colonel Gyula Vörös, who had defected to the enemy: Luknitsky [Luknyickij], p. 100.

Table 10. Soviet units in action in Pest and Buda (excluding artillery and direct attachments)

At the Pest Bridgehead and on Csepel Island	
3–5 November 1944	2nd, 4th Mechanized Guard Corps
3 November–mid-December 1944	10th Guard Rifle Corps (49th, 86th, 109th Guard Rifle Divisions), 23rd Rifle Corps (99th, 316th Guard Rifle Division, 68th Guard Division merged with 18th Rifle Division on 20 December)
3 November–1 December 1944	37th Rifle Corps (320th Rifle Division, 59th, 108th Guard Rifle Divisions)
15 November 1944–16 January 1945	7th Romanian Army Corps (2nd, 19th Infantry Divisions, 9th Cavalry Division), 66th Guard Rifle Division
15 November 1944–18 January 1945	36th Guard Rifle Division
beginning 12 December 1944	30th Rifle Corps (25th, 36th Guard Rifle Divisions, 151st, 155th Rifle Divisions)
from mid-December 1944a	18th Special Rifle Corps (297th, 317th Rifle Divisions)
3–18 January 1945	337th Rifle Division

Table 10. Soviet units in action in Pest and Buda (excluding artillery and direct attachments)—cont'd

In Buda	
beginning 24 December 1944	75th Rifle Corps (59th Rifle Division, 108th Guard Division, 320th Rifle Division), 83rd Marine Infantry Brigade
24 December 1944– 3 January 1945	2nd Mechanized Guard Corps, 49th Guard Rifle Division, 10th Guard Rifle Division (180th, 109th Guard Rifle Divisions), 23rd Rifle Corps (99th, 316th Rifle Divisions)
3–21 January 1945	37th Rifle Corps (from troops of 10th Guard Rifle Corps), 99th, 316th Rifle Division without its staff
beginning 21 January 1945	18th Special Rifle Corps (66th Guard Rifle Division, 297th, 317th Rifle Divisions)

Sources: Tóth, 1975a, pp. 128, 247; BA-MA KTB Hgr. Süd RH V/58–62 and situation maps. The table is incomplete because of the inaccessibility of Soviet sources and contradictions in publications to date. In addition to the units named, the following took part in the siege to the end: 21st Airborne Regiment, 123rd Cannon Artillery Brigade, 202nd Special Light Artillery Brigade, 110th Independent Antitank Division, 28th Mortar Brigade, 9th and 60th Antiaircraft Artillery Divisions, 11th, 12th, and 14th Technical Brigades, 12th and 16th Special Signal Regiments, 336th Frontier Guard Regiment, 3 divisions and 13 regiments of 3rd Fighter Aircraft Army Corps, and several other special battalions and regiments, all of which were given the epithet Budapest.

[a]On the supreme command's order of 14 November, the 18th Special Rifle Corps and the 30th Rifle Corps were regrouped to the 2nd Ukrainian Front from the 4th Ukrainian Front in the Carpathians. The regrouping was not completed until mid-December, and the 30th Rifle Corps first moved to the northeastern defense ring of Budapest after the breakthrough at Hatvan.

Table II. Respective strengths of the defenders and attackers, 24 December 1944–11 February 1945

	Strength of German and Hungarian forces (excluding wounded)		Strength of Soviet and Romanian forces		Proportions	
	Ration strength	Combat strength	Ration strength	Combat strength	Ration strength	Combat strength
24 December 1944	79,000	35,000	177,000	100,000	1:2.2	1:2.9
3 January 1945	70,000	30,000	145,000	80,000	1:2.1	1:2.7
20 January 1945	45,000	16,000	80,000[a]	40,000	1:1.8	1:2.5
11 February 1945	32,000	11,000	75,000	36,000	1:2.3	1:3.3

Source: The figures are based on the sources cited, with the exception of my own estimates for Soviet combat strengths.
[a]The Romanian 7th Army Corps, the 30th Rifle Corps, and the 68th Rifle Division were withdrawn from the siege on 18th January.

Table 12. Tanks and assault guns of the German Army Group South and the Soviet forces in the Carpathian Basin on 1 January 1945

	Tanks and assault guns	Note
Army Group South	494	554 more under repair
2nd and 3rd Ukrainian Fronts[a]	1,066	numbers under repair unknown
1st Mechanized Guard Corps	246	arriving beginning 18 December (from 4th Ukrainian Front); by 31 January 162 tanks and assault guns ready for action
2nd Mechanized Guard Corps	54	
4th Mechanized Guard Corps	c. 60	from 8 January attached to 6th Tank Army
5th Cavalry Corps	c. 50	on 28 January 37 tanks and assault guns
7th Mechanized Corps	101	according to German reports, 57 tanks lost by 10 January and 40 left on 27 January[b]
6th Armored Guard Army (5th Armored Guard Corps, 9th Mechanized Guard Corps), 27th Special Tank Brigade	162	on 13th January 72 tanks and assault guns left[c]
18th Tank Corps	150	on 25 December 165 tanks and assault guns
23rd Tank Corps	193	corps was not deployed until the second half of January and reported 152 tanks on 24 January[d]

Continued

Table 12. Tanks and assault guns of the German Army Group South and the Soviet forces in the Carpathian Basin on 1 January 1945—cont'd

	Tanks and assault guns	Note
Tanks and assault guns directly responsible to the fronts	50	the two fronts probably had 7 assault gun regiments, whose exact combat strength is unknown[c]

[a]Svirin, p. 77 cites 1,016 tanks and assault guns, not including the special tank and assault-gun regiments.
[b]Veress, pp. 131, 170.
[c]Minasyan, p. 357.
[d]Ibid., p. 363.
[e]30th Special Heavy Armored Regiment, 78th Armored Breakthrough Guard Regiment, 1202nd Assault-Gun Regiment, 366th Heavy Assault Gun Guard Regiment, 373rd Special Assault-Gun Guard Regiment, 382nd Assault-Gun Guard Regiment, 1453rd Assault-Gun Regiment.

Table 13. German and Soviet strengths in the southern section at the time of operation Konrad II (7–11 January 1945)

Unit	Tanks and assault guns	Guns	Infantry (combat strength)
4th Cavalry Brigade	c. 43	28	1,800
1st Panzer Division	c. 19	36	1,100
3rd Panzer Division	5	28	900
23rd Panzer Division	c. 24	24	1,900
503rd Heavy Panzer (Tiger) Division	c. 25	0	0
German total	c. 116	116	5,700
20th Guard Rifle Corps + 6 artillery regiments	0	c. 140	c. 6,000

Table 13. German and Soviet strengths in the southern section at the time of operation Konrad II (7–11 January 1945)—cont'd

Unit	Tanks and assault guns	Guns	Infantry (combat strength)
7th Mechanized Corps	c. 70	80	c. 2,000
93rd Rifle Division	0	c. 20	c. 1,500
63rd Cavalry Division	0	c. 20	c. 1,000
Soviet total	c. 70	c. 260	c. 10,500

Source: BA-MA KTB Hgr. Süd 898/b, report of 9 January 1945. The Soviet figures are my estimates.

Table 14. Losses of the Budapest garrison during the siege and the break-out (approximate percentages)

	Number	Percentage
Garrison on 24 December 1944	c. 79,000	100
Captured or killed in Pest[a]	c. 22,000	28
Captured or killed in Buda up to 11 February	c. 13,000	16
Garrison at the start of the break-out[b]	c. 44,000 (incl. 11,600 wounded)	56
Captured during the break-out between 11 and 15 February[c]	c. 22,350	28
Captured after 15 February (estimate)	max. 1,000	1
Escaped	max. 700	1
Hidden in the hinterland[d]	max. 700	1
Total killed during the break-out[e]	c. 19,250	24

[a]Soviet sources cite 35,830 men and 291 tanks, but the date (possibly 3 November) is not clear. The Hungarians suffered the larger part of these losses because the majority of them, by chance or by design, had not transferred to Buda.
[b]By 11 February 35,000 men were killed, missing, or captured.
[c]As reported to the Soviet supreme command on 16 February 1945.

Continued

[d]Mainly Hungarians.

[e]The Soviet 23rd Army Corps reported 4,700 enemy soldiers dead and 1,300 captured (Andrjusenko, p. 52). The 5th Guard Cavalry Corps and the 10th Guard Rifle Corps, which also took part in the prevention of the break-out, reported similar numbers.

Table 15. Hungarian losses due to the siege

Civilians

a	Population in June 1944	1,200,000
b	Population in April 1945	830,000
c	Killed by military action	13,000[a]
d	Killed by starvation, disease, etc.	25,000
e	Subtotal of dead (c + d)	38,000[b]
f	Jewish dead (included in e)	15,000[c]
g	Dead by execution (included in e)	c. 7,000[d]
h	Deported for forced labor	c. 50,000
i	Failed to return from forced labor	c. 25,000[e]
j	Taken prisoner of war	c. 50,000
k	Failed to return from prisoner of war camps	c. 13,000[f]
l	Total of dead (e + i + k)	c. 76,000

Soldiers

m	Taken prisoner of war	c. 40,000
n	Failed to return from prisoner of war camps	c. 12,000
o	Killed, 3 November 1944–15 February 1945	c. 16,500
p	Total of dead (n + o)	28,500
r	Grand total of dead (l + p)	c. 104,500

[a]*Hadtudományi*, 1994/10, p. 161.

[b]Before 1944 and after 1945, 18,000 people a year on average died in the capital. In 1944 the figure rose to 25,855, and in 1945 to 49,364—an average of 37,600 in the two years comprising the siege. A significant proportion of the population had fled beforehand. Many had been killed by Allied air raids.

[c]This figure covers both the Arrow Cross terror and the Soviet occupation.

[d]Lévai reports 6,200 cases tried by the People's Court. The most notorious Arrow Cross group, in Zugló, alone killed 1,200 people.

[e]*Hadtudományi*, 1994/10, p. 163.

[f]According to Tamás Stark on average 70 percent of prisoners returned home from Soviet captivity. *Hadtudományi*, 1994/10, p. 163.

Table 16. Condition of homes after the siege

Homes	Number	Percentage
Habitable	215,653	73.0
Partly habitable	47,322	16.0
Uninhabitable but reparable	18,775	6.4
Destroyed	13,588	4.6

Source: Kővágó, p. 47.

Table 17. Hero of the Soviet Union medals awarded for operations in Hungary (within its 1938 borders)

	Number	Percentage
Total of localized awards	276	
Danube crossing at Ercsi	115	41.7
Actions on the outskirts of Budapest	15	5.4
Actions in Budapest	24	8.7
Defensive actions against the break-out	6	2.2
Defensive actions against the relief attempts	4	1.4
Total for operations related to Budapest	164	59.4
For other operations	112	40.6

Source: Tóth, 1975a.

Table 18. Comparison of the military casualties of the siege

Casualties 3 November 1944–11 February 1945	Wounded	Dead	Prisoners	Total
Casualties of the Soviet army[a]	c. 130,000	c. 44,000	max. 2,000	c. 176,000
Casualties of the Romanian 7th Army Corps[b]	c. 12,000	c. 11,000	max. 1,000	c. 24,000
Casualties of the Hungarian and German garrison	included among prisoners	c. 40,000	c. 62,000	c. 102,000
Soviet casualties of Konrad operations	c. 60,000	c. 15,000	c. 5,100[c]	c. 80,000
Hungarian and German casualties of Konrad operations[d]	c. 26,000	c. 8,000	max. 1,000	c. 35,000
Total Hungarian and German casualties	c. 26,000	c. 48,000	c. 63,000	c. 137,000
Total Soviet and Romanian casualties	c. 202,000	c. 70,000	c. 8,000	c. 280,000

[a]As noted above, 25 percent of the total Soviet losses were attributed to the Konrad operations and 55 percent to the siege of the capital.

[b]Estimates based on *Hadtudományi*, and incomplete details in Maniescu and Romanescu.

[c]According to the summary report of the Army Group South, between 24 December 1944 and 10 February 1945 a total of 5,138 people were taken prisoner. In Soviet sources prisoners appear under "dead and missing," as they were originally listed as missing.

[d]The Balck Army Group reported 34,108 casualties between 24 December 1944 and 10 February 1945, which did not include those missing—at least 1,000 according to my calculations (KTB Hgr. Süd, Maier, p. 521).

Table 19. Losses of the Soviet army in its major offensives

Operation (length)	Casualties		Tanks		Guns and mortars		Aircraft	
	Total	Daily	Total	Daily	Total	Daily	Total	Daily
Budapest (108 days)	320,082	2,964	1,766	16	4,127	38	293	2–3
Vienna (31 days)	167,940	5,417	603	19	1,005	32	614	20
Berlin (23 days)	352,475	15,325	1,997	87	2,108	92	917	40
Stalingrad (76 days)	485,777	6,392	2,915	38	3,591	47	706	9
Moscow (34 days)	379,955	11,175	429	13	13,350	393	140	4

Source: Krivosheev, pp. 174, 182, 212, 217, 219, 224–227, 368–373.

Table 20. Hungarian and German military losses during the siege

	Hungarian	German	Total
Strength of defense on the Attila Line at beginning of November 1944	c. 54,000	c. 48,000	c. 102,000
Losses (dead, missing, wounded, taken prisoner) in Pest between 3 November and 24 December 1944	c. 17,000	c. 6,000	c. 23,000
Prisoners of war (among the above)	c. 9,500	c. 500	c. 10,000
Strength of defense on 24 December 1944	c. 38,000	c. 41,000	c. 79,000
Losses in Pest between 24 December 1944 and 18 January 1945	c. 12,000	c. 10,000	c. 22,000
Prisoners of war (among the above)	c. 9,000	c. 1,000	c. 10,000
Casualties in Buda between 24 December 1944 and 13 February 1945, including break-out	c. 26,000	c. 31,000	c. 57,000
Prisoners of war (among the above)	c. 20,000	c. 10,000	c. 30,000
Total losses	c. 55,000	c. 47,000	c. 102,000

Bibliography

In the notes, references to books and articles are given by the surname of the author or editor, or an abbreviated title. The location of archival material (contemporary documents and collections of studies in Hungarian, Wehrmacht files and collections of manuscripts in German, manuscripts in Hungarian) is indicated through the abbreviated name of the archive and section concerned. Memoirs, reports, diaries, letters, etc., in private collections are identified as such, as are interviews conducted by the author with survivors. Many of the sources I have used are available only in Hungarian: in these cases an English working title is supplied in square brackets. Where I have used Hungarian translations of books published in other languages, the titles of the originals are also quoted, as are the titles of any published English versions. The names of Russian writers whose works I used in Hungarian translation are transliterated according to Hungarian conventions in the page references in the Notes, and according to both Hungarian and English conventions in the lists below. Quotations from the War Diary of the German Army Group South (KTB Hgr. Süd) taken from the holdings of either the Hungarian Archive of Military History in Budapest or the German Federal Archive's Military Archive in Freiburg are designated HL and BA-MA, respectively. In the section on books and articles the title of the journal *Hadtörténeti Közlemények (Contributions to Military History)*, in which many of the articles appeared, is abbreviated as *HK*.

Books and Articles

Adonyi-Naredy, Ferenc, and Kálmán Nagy. *Magyar huszárok a II. világháborúban* [Hungarian hussars in the Second World War]. Sárvár, 1990.

Aly, Götz, and Christian Gerlach. *Das letzte Kapitel: Die Vernichtung der ungarischen Juden* [The last chapter: The destruction of the Hungarian Jews]. Munich, 2002.

"Ami Budán a 'Kitartás' nyomában maradt . . . " [What was left of Buda after the "Endurance" . . .]. In *Feltámadás,* 19 February 1945.

Andrjusenko, Szergej Alekszandrovics. "A Duna hullámain II." [Sergei Aleksandrevich Andrushenko, On the waves of the Danube II.] In: *HK*, no. 1, 1966.

Anghi, Csaba (ed.). *A 100 éves állatkert* [The 100-year-old zoo]. Budapest, 1966.

Árokay, Lajos. *Emlékező tájak* [Landscapes that remember]. Budapest, 1970.

Asik, Mihail. "Emlékeim a Budai Önkéntes Ezred harcaiból." [Mikhail Ashik, My memories of the battles of the Buda Volunteer Battalion.] In *HK*, no. 2, 1981.

Asztalos, István. *Író a Hadakútján* [A writer on the road of the armies]. Budapest, 1978.

Bajtársi Levél [Letter to comrades (newspaper)].

Baktai, Ferenc. *A kőbányai előörs* [The Kőbánya outpost]. Budapest, 1956.

Balassa, Erik. "'Csia Testvér! Kérem ezt az ügyet rövid úton kivizsgálni . . .'" ["Brother Csia, please investigate this matter right away . . ."]. In *Képes Figyelő*, no. 13, 1945.

Balck, Hermann. *Ordnung im Chaos: Erinnerungen 1893–1948* [Order in chaos: Memories, 1893–1948]. Osnabrück, 1980.

Bangha, Ernő. *A magyar királyi testőrség 1920–1944* [The Royal Hungarian Bodyguard, 1920–1944]. Budapest, 1990.

Bárdos, Lajos. "Nincsen Isten—Istenünkön kívül: Ostromnapló" ["There is no god—apart from our god: A siege diary"]. In *Jel*, no. 3, 1997.

Bayer, Hanns. *Kavalleriedivisionen der Waffen-SS* [Cavalry divisions of the Waffen SS]. Heidelberg, 1980.

Béke és Szabadság [Peace and liberty (newspaper)].

Benedek, István, and György Vámos. *Tépd le a sárga csillagot* [Tear off the yellow star]. Budapest, 1990.

"Beszélnek a szemtanúk" [The eyewitnesses speak]. In *Ország-Világ*, nos. 14–16, 1968.

Bibó, István. "The Jewish Question in Hungary after 1944." In *Democracy, Revolution, Self-Determination*. Boulder, 1991.

Bokor, Péter. *Végjáték a Duna mentén: Interjúk a filmsorozathoz* [Endgame on the Danube: Interviews on the film series]. Budapest, 1982.

———. "Verolino Érsek, az ostrom tanúja" [Archbishop Verolino, witness to the siege]. In *Magyar Hírlap*, 11 February 1995.

Boldizsár, Iván. "Értem esett el" [He died for me]. In *Magyar Nemzet*, 13 February 1945.

———. "Buda 1945. február 13." [Buda, 13 February 1945]. In *Magyar Nemzet*, 13 February 1951.

———. *Don-Buda-Paris*. Budapest, 1982.

Boldt, Gerhard. *Hitler: die letzten zehn Tage in der Reichskanzlei*. Munich, 1976. [*Hitler: The Last Ten Days*. Trans. Sandra Bance. New York, 1973.]

Bondor, Vilmos. *A Mikó rejtély* [The Mikó mystery]. Budapest, 1995.

Boog, Horst, et al. (eds.). *Das Deutsche Reich und der Zweite Weltkrieg, Band 4: Der Angriff auf die Sowjetunion*. Stuttgart 1983. [*Germany and the Second World War*. Vol. 4, *Attack on the Soviet Union*. Trans. Dean S. McMurry et al. Oxford, 1998.]

Boros, Pál (ed.). *Pest megye felszabadulása és az új élet megindulása a korabeli sajtó tükrében* [The liberation of Pest County and the beginning of new life as reflected in the press of the time]. Budapest, 1970.

Braham, Randolph B. *The Politics of Genocide: The Holocaust in Hungary.* 2 vols. New York, 1981.

Budai Összetartás [Buda solidarity (newspaper)].

Budai Polgár [Buda citizen (newspaper)].

Budapest (newspaper).

Budapester Kesselnachrichten [News from the Budapest cauldron (newspaper)].

Buligin, V. A. "Visszaemlékezés a Magyarország felszabadításáért folyó harcra" [Recollections of the struggle for the liberation of Hungary]. In *HK*, 1961/1.

Churchill, Winston S. *The Second World War,* vol. 6. London, 1954.

Command (magazine).

Csapó, György. "Ahol Steinmetz utolsó éjszakáját töltötte" [Where Steinmetz spent his last night]. In *Magyar Nemzet* 304, 1954.

Csebotarev, G. Sz. *A béke katonái* [The soldiers of peace], Budapest, 1975. [G. S. Chebotarev, *Soldaty mira.* Moscow, 1950.]

———. "A parlamenter halála." [G. S. Chebotarev, The death of the parley delegate]. In *HK*, no. 4, 1967.

Csepel története [The history of Csepel]. Budapest, 1965.

Cseres, Tibor. *Bizonytalan század* [The insecure company]. Budapest, 1968.

Csiffáry, Nándor. "Dorog a II. világháborúban" ["Dorog in the Second World War"]. In *Dorogi Füzetek* 5, 1995.

Csima, János. "A 7. román hadtest a Budapest felszabadításáért folytatott harcokban" [The Romanian 7th Corps in the battles for the liberation of Budapest]. In *HK* 1965/1.

Cs. Lengyel, Beatrix. "Budapest ostroma: Széchenyi Viktor gróf feljegyzései 1944. december 24.–1945. február 12." [The siege of Budapest: Count Viktor Széchenyi's notes, 24 December 1944–12 February 1945]. In *Tanulmányok Budapest múltjáról* [Studies in Budapest's past] 24 (1991).

Czoma, László (ed.). *Tanulmányok Rákospalota-Pestújhely történetéből* [Studies in the history of Rákospalota and Pestújhely]. Budapest, 1974.

Darnóy, Pál. "A Budapestért vívott harc" ["The struggle for Budapest"]. Series of articles in *Hadak útján,* 1962–1970.

Darvas, József. *Város az ingóványon* [City in the mire]. Budapest, 1945.

Délmagyarország [Southern Hungary (newspaper)].

Dernői Kocsis, László. "Pest 1945. január 18.: Zuglótól a Belvárosig" [Pest 18 January 1945: From Zugló to the city center"]. In *Magyar Nemzet* 14, 1955.

Déry, Tibor. *Két Emlék* [Two memories]. Budapest, 1955.

———. "Alvilági játékok" ["Games in the underworld"]. In *Magyar írók tanúságtétele 1944–45* [Hungarian writers' testimonies, 1944–1945]. Budapest, 1975.

Dezsényi, Miklós. *A szovjetorosz hajóraj harcai Magyarország felszabadításáért* [The Soviet fleet's battles for the liberation of Hungary]. Budapest, 1946.

Djilas, Milovan. *Találkozások Sztálinnal.* Budapest, 1989. [*Razgovori sa Staljinom.* Belgrade, 1990. *Conversations with Stalin.* Trans. M. B. Petrovich, New York, 1962.]

Dombrády, Lóránd, and Gábor Nagy. *Fegyverrel a hazáért: Magyar ellenállási és partizánharcok a második világháború idején* [With arms for the homeland: Hungarian resistance and partisan actions in the Second World War]. Budapest, 1980.

Dombrády, Lóránd, and Sándor Tóth. *A Magyar Királyi Honvédség 1919–1945* [The Royal Hungarian Honvéd Army, 1919–1945]. Budapest, 1987.

Dorogi Füzetek [Dorog pamphlets].

13. Panzerdivision. Das waren wir, das erlebten wir. Der Schicksalsweg der 13. Panzerdivision [The 13th Panzer Division, what we were, what we lived through: The fateful journey of the 13th Panzer Division]. Hanover, 1971.

Duna Tudósító [Danube reporter (newspaper)].

"Egy farkasréti lakós naplója" "[Diary of a Farkasrét resident"]. In *Magyar Nemzet,* 30 January 1949.

Egyesületi Értesítő [Association bulletin].

Ehrenburg, Ilja. *A német.* [Ilya Ehrenburg, The German.] Budapest, 1945.

Elek, László. *Az olasz Wallenberg* [The Italian Wallenberg]. Budapest, 1989.

Életünk [Our lives (newspaper)].

Ember, Mária. *Ránk akarták kenni* [They tried to pin it on us]. Budapest, 1992.

Eszenyi, László. *Trianoni nemzedék* [The Trianon generation]. Dabas, 1990.

Fáklya [Torch (newspaper)].

Fancsali, Petronella (ed.). *Budapest felszabadulásának kronológiája: A hadműveletek előrehaladása szerint, bibliográfiai utalásokkal* [Chronology of the liberation of Budapest: Following the progress of the military operations, with bibliographical notes]. Budapest, 1954.

Fehér, Lajos. *Harcunk Budapestért* [Our struggle for Budapest]. Budapest, 1955.

———. *Így történt* [This is how it happened]. Budapest, 1979.

Feltámadás [Resurrection (newspaper)].

Fenyő, Miksa. *Az elsodort ország (visszaemlékezések)* [The country that was swept away (memoirs)]. Budapest, 2d ed., 1986.

Fiala, Ferenc. *Így történt* [This is how it happened]. London, 1968.

Fogarassy-Feller, Michael. *Die Geschichte und Volkskunde der Gemeinde Werischwar/Pilisvörösvár* [The history and ethnology of Pilisvörösvár]. Budapest, 1994.

Fortusz, Marija. *Visszaemlékezéseim.* [Mariya Fortus, My memories.] Budapest, 1982. [*Balaton.* Simferopol, 1971].

Friessner, Hans. *Verratene Schlachten* [Betrayed battles]. Hamburg, 1956.

Gács, Teri. *A mélységből kiáltunk hozzád* [Out of the depths we cry to thee]. Budapest, 1946.

Galántay, Ervin. "Budapest védelme 1944–1945" [The defense of Budapest, 1944–1945"]. In *Duna Tudósító* 36, no. 2, 1999.

———. *The Defense of Budapest: Rise and Fall of the Volunteer VANNAY Battalion*. Sandhurst, n.d.

Gazsi, József (ed.). *Magyar szabadságharcosok a fasizmus ellen, 1941–1945* [Hungarian freedom fighters against fascism, 1941–1945]. Budapest, 1966.

———. *Akit Mózesként tiszteltek: Wallenberg füzetek II* [The man they honored like Moses: Wallenberg pamphlets II]. Budapest, 1995.

Gazsi, József, and István Pintér (eds.). *Fegyverrel a fasizmus ellen: Tanulmányok a magyar ellenállás és partizánharcok történetéből* [With arms against fascism: Studies in the history of Hungarian resistance and partisan actions]. Budapest, 1968.

Gerevich, László (ed.). *Budapest története* [The history of Budapest]. Budapest, 1980.

Gibson, Hugh (ed.). *The Ciano Diaries, 1939–1943*. New York, 1946.

Glatz, Ferenc (ed.). *Az 1944. év Históriája: História évkönyv 1984* [The history of 1944: History yearbook, 1984]. Budapest 1984.

Gobbi, Hilda. *Megszállás, ostrom, felszabadulás* [Occupation, siege, liberation]. In *Béke és Szabadság* 13, 1955.

Gosztonyi, Péter. *Der Kampf um Budapest 1944–45* [The battle for Budapest, 1944–1945]. Munich, 1964a.

———. "Der Kampf um Budapest 1944–45" [The battle for Budapest, 1944–1945]. In *Studia Hungarica*, 1964b.

———. *Endkampf an der Donau* [The final battle on the Danube]. Munich, 1969.

———. "Die militärische Lage in und um Budapest im Jahre 1944" [The military situation in and around Budapest in 1944]. In *Ungarn Jahrbuch* [Hungary yearbook] 8, 1977.

———. "Ungarns militärische Lage im Zweiten Weltkrieg" [The military situation of Hungary in the Second World War]. In *Wehrwissenschaftliche Rundschau* [Review of military science] 2–5, 1982.

———. "Budapest ostroma" [The siege of Budapest]. In *Magyar Nemzet*, 6 December 1984.

———. *Háború van, háború* [It is war, war]. Budapest, 1989a.

———. *Légiveszély Budapest* [Enemy aircraft approaching Budapest]. Budapest, 1989b.

———. *Vihar Kelet-Európa felett* [Storm over Eastern Europe]. Budapest, 1990.

———. *A magyar Honvédség a második világháborúban* [The Hungarian Honvéd Army in the Second World War]. Budapest, 1992.

———. "Harc Budapestért" [Struggle for Budapest]. In *Magyarok Világlapja*, October 1994.

———. *Budapest lángokban* [Budapest aflame]. Budapest, 1998.

———. *Politikusok, katonák, események* [Politicians, soldiers, events]. Munich, n.d.

Grossman, Sándor. *Nur das Gewissen: Carl Lutz und seine Budapester Aktion: Geschichte und Porträt* [Nothing but conscience. Carl Lutz and his enterprise in Budapest: History and portrait]. Wald, 1986.

Guderian, Heinz. *Erinnerungen eines Soldaten* [Memories of a soldier]. Heidelberg, 1952. [*Panzer Leader*. Trans. Constantine Fitzgibbon. London, 1957.]

Gyalog, Ödön. *Horthy Miklós katonája vagyok: Egy tüzérszázados emlékei* [I am Miklós Horthy's soldier: Memories of an artillery captain]. Budapest, 1992.

Györffy-Spáczay, Hedvig. "A IX. SS-Hadtestparancsnokság titkos napi jelentései a Budapesten folyó harcokról" [The IX SS Corps Command's secret reports on the fighting in Budapest]. In *HK*, no. 1, 1975.

György, István. *Kétezerötszázan voltak* [There were two thousand five hundred of them]. Budapest, 1975.

Hadak Útján [On the road of the armies (newspaper)].

Hadtörténeti Közlemények [Contributions to military history].

Hadtudományi Tájékoztató: A Budapesti csata 1944–1945: Az 1994. 12. 15–16-án megtartott tudományos ülésszak anyaga [Guide to military science. The battle of Budapest, 1944–1945: Material from a conference held on 15–16 December 1994]. Budapest, no. 10, 1994.

Határ, Győző. "Életút. Minden hajó hazám" [Journey through life: Every ship is my home]. In *Életünk* 11–12, 1994.

Hazánk felszabadulása, 1944–1945 [The liberation of our homeland, 1944–1945]. Budapest, 1970.

Herczeg, Ferenc. *Hűvösvölgy: Herczeg Ferenc emlékezései* [Hűvösvölgy: Memories of Ferenc Herczeg]. Budapest, 1993.

Hidegkúti Hirek [Hidegkút news (newspaper)].

Hingyi, László. "Magyar önkéntes alakulatok Budapest védelmében" [Hungarian voluntary formations in the defense of Budapest]. In *Hadtudományi Tájékoztató*, 1994a.

———. "Budapest légi ellátása" [Airborne supplies to Budapest]. In Ravasz, 1994b.

Hoffmann, Joachim. *Stalins Vernichtungskrieg* [Stalin's war of annihilation]. Munich, 3d ed., 1996.

Honcsar, Olesz. *Zászlóvivők*. Budapest, 1979. [Oles Honchar, *Znamenostsy*. Moscow, 1990. *Standard-Bearers*. Trans. N. Jochel. Moscow, 1948].

Hungarista [Hungarist (newspaper)].

Huszár, János. *Honvéd ejtőernyősök Pápán 1939–1945: A Magyar Királyi "vitéz Bertalan Árpád" Honvéd Ejtőernyős Ezred története* [Honvéd paratroopers in Pápa: The history of the Royal Hungarian "vitéz Bertalan Árpád" paratroop regiment]. Pápa, 1993.

Igaz Szó [True word (newspaper)].

"Így élt és ölt a Vannay-zászlóalj" [How the Vannay Battalion lived and killed]. In *Kossuth Népe* 37, 1945.

"Így vitte vágóhídra a budapesti rendőröket Hitschler SS-tábornok" [How SS General Hitschler led Budapest's policemen to the slaughter]. In *Népbírósági Közlöny* 2, 1946.

Itélet [Judgment (newspaper)].

Izsáky, Margit. *Ország a keresztfán* [A country on the cross]. Budapest, 1945.

Jel [Sign (newspaper)].

Jerezian, Ara. *A védett ház* [The protected house]. Budapest, 1993.

Juhászi, Imre. *Az ostrom: Regényes korrajz Budapest ostromából* [The siege: A fictionalized period portrait of the siege of Budapest]. Budapest, 1947.

———. "Négy nap Budán 1945-ben" [Four days in Buda in 1945]. In *Népszava* 25–28, 1955.

Kabdebó, Lóránd. *A háborúnak vége lett* [The war is over]. Budapest, 1983.

Kadosa (Kiss), Árpád. *Viszontlátásra, hadnagy úr* [So long, lieutenant]. Budapest, 1989.

Kántor, Zsuzsa. *Feledhetetlen ifjúság* [Unforgettable youth]. Budapest, 1955.

Katona, Gyuláné Sz. Katalin. *A Szentendrei Római Katolikus Egyház és Plébánia története 1002–1992* [The history of the Roman Catholic Church and Parish of Szentendre, 1002–1992]. Szentendre, 1996.

Kemény, Simon. *Napló: 1942–1944* [Diary: 1942–1944]. Budapest, 1987.

Képes Figyelő [Illustrated observer (newspaper)].

Kern, Erich. *Die letzte Schlacht. Ungarn 1944–45* [The last battle: Hungary, 1944–45]. Preussisch-Oldendorf, 1960.

Kertész, Róbert. "Egy gyerek ostromnaplója" [A child's siege diary]. In *K. R., Ne felejts* [Do not forget]. Budapest, 1955.

Kis, Ervin. *Vallomás és körülmények* [Confession and circumstances]. Budapest, 1965.

Kishon, Ephraim. *Volt szerencsém. Kishont Ferenc önéletrajza.* [I was lucky: Autobiography of Ferenc Kishont]. Budapest, 1994.

Kiss, Károly. "Találkozások a Vörös Hadsereggel" [Encounters with the Red Army]. In *Magyar Nemzet,* 1 April 1995, 30 September 1995.

Kiss, Sándor M. (ed.). *Magyarország 1944. Fejezetek az ellenállás történetéből* [Hungary 1944: Chapters from the history of the resistance]. Budapest, 1994.

Klietmann, K.G. *Die Waffen-SS: Eine Dokumentation* [The Waffen SS: A documentation]. Osnabrück, 1965.

Kogelfranz, Siegfried. *Jalta öröksége—az áldozatok, és akik megúszták* [The heritage of Yalta: The victims and the survivors]. Budapest, 1990. [*Das Erbe von Jalta.* Paris, 1985.]

Komiszarov, N.V. "Harc Budapestért" [The struggle for Budapest]. In *HK* 1, 1980.

Kossuth Népe [Kossuth's people (newspaper)].

Kőszegi, Imre. *Budavár ostroma 1945-ben* [The siege of the Buda Castle district in 1945]. Budapest, 1945.

Kovács, Béla. "Tizenhat pilisi hős" [Sixteen Pilis heroes]. In *Új Világ* 2, 1955.

Kovács, Imre. *Magyarország megszállása* [The occupation of Hungary]. Budapest, 1990.

Kővágó, József (ed.). *Budapest közállapotai az 1945–46-os tél küszöbén* [The general situation of Budapest on the threshold of winter, 1945–1946]. Budapest, 1946.

Kovalovszky, Miklós. *Lidércnyomás: Napló 1944. október 8.–1945. január 8.* [Nightmare: A diary, 8 October 1944–8 January 1945]. Budapest, 1995.

Kövendy, Károly. *Magyar Királyi Csendőrség: A csendőrség békében, háborúban és emigrációban* [Royal Hungarian Gendarmerie: The gendarmerie in peace, war, and emigration]. Toronto, 1973.

Kraetschmer, E. G. *Die Ritterkreuzträger der Waffen-SS* [Waffen SS bearers of the Knight's Cross]. Preussisch Oldendorf, 1982.

Krivosheev, G. F. (ed.). *Grif sekretnosti snyat: Poteri Vooruzhennykh sil SSSR v voinakh, boevykh deystviyakh i voennykh konfliktakh.* Moscow, 1993. [*Soviet Casualties and Combat Losses in the Twentieth Century.* Trans. Christine Barnard. London, 1997.]

Krizsán, László (ed.). *Okmányok a felszabadulás történetéhez Pest megyében* [Documents on the history of liberation in Pest County]. Budapest, 1960.

Kutuzov-Tolstoy, Mikhail Pavlovich. *Mein Leben: Von Petersburg nach Irland,* Marburg/Lahn, 1988. [Michael Pavlovich Kutuzov-Tolstoy, *The Story of My Life.* Marburg/Lahn, 1986.]

Kuznetsov, P. G. *Marshal Tolbukhin.* Moscow, 1966.

Láng, Judit. "Negyvennégy (közreadja Frank Tibor)" [Forty-four (published by Tibor Frank)]. In *Történelmi Szemle* 2, 1982.

Lestyán, Sándor. "Az utolsó órák" [The last hours]. In *Magyar Nemzet,* 30 January 1949.

Lévai, Jenő. *Fekete könyv a magyar zsidóság szenvedéseiről.* Budapest, 1946a. [*Black Book on the Martyrdom of Hungarian Jewry.* Ed. Lawrence P. Davis. Zürich, 1948.]

———. *Szürke könyv magyar zsidók megmentéséről* [Gray Book on the rescue of Hungarian Jews]. Budapest, 1946b.

———. *A pesti gettó csodálatos megmenekülésének története* [The story of the miraculous escape of the Pest ghetto]. Budapest, 1947.

Luknyickij, Pavel. *Magyar napló* [Hungarian diary]. Budapest, 1980. [Pavel Luknitsky, *Vengerskii dnevnik: noiabr 1944–aprel 1945.* Moscow, 1973.]

A magyar antifasiszta ellenállás és partizánmozgalom 1939–1945 Válogatott bibliográfia [The Hungarian antifascist resistance and partisan movement, 1939–1945: A select bibliography]. Budapest, 1982.

Magyar Futár [Hungarian courier (newspaper)].

Magyar Hírlap [Hungarian news (newspaper)].

Magyar Játékszín [Hungarian stage (newspaper)].

Magyar Nemzet [Hungarian nation (newspaper)].

Magyarok Világlapja [Hungarian world journal (newspaper)].

Magyarság [Hungarians (newspaper)].

Maier, Georg. *Drama zwischen Budapest und Wien: Der Endkampf der 6. Panzer-armee 1945* [Drama between Budapest and Vienna: The final battle of the 6th Panzer Army, 1945]. Osnabrück, 1985.

Mándy, Iván. "Arcok és árnyak" [Faces and shadows]. In *Vendégek a palackban* [Guests in the bottle]. Budapest, 1949.

Maniescu, Antone, and Gheorghe Romanescu. *Armata Romana in razboiul anti-hitlerist* [The Romanian army in the war against Hitler]. Bucharest, 1980.

Márai, Sándor. "Budai séta" [A walk in Buda]. In *Budapest,* December 1945.

———. *Napló: 1943–1944* [Diary: 1943–1944]. Budapest, 1990a.

———. *Napló: 1945–1957* [Diary: 1945–1957]. Budapest, 1990b.

Markin, Ilya. *Na beregakh Dunaya* [On the banks of the Danube]. Moscow, 1953.

Markó, György. "'A jelszó mozijegy'" ["The password is cinema ticket"]. In *Új Tükör,* 30 October 1988.

Martin, Kornél, and István Ugron. "Fejezetek a Szent László hadosztály tör-ténetéből" [Chapters from the history of the Szent László Division]. In *HK* 3, 1995.

Máté, György. *Budapest szabad!* [Budapest is free!]. Budapest, 1980.

Matolcsy, Károly. "Az 'utolsó nap' a Várban" [The "last day" in the Castle dis-trict]. In *Magyar Nemzet,* 13 February 1955.

Mészáros, Sándor. "A Budapesten körülzárt német-magyar hadseregcsoport légi ellátása" [Airborne supplies to the German and Hungarian army group encir-cled in Budapest]. In *Aero Historia,* December 1988, June 1989, December 1989.

Minasyan, M. M. *Osvobozhdenie narodov Yugo-Vostochnoy Yevropy. Boyevye dey-stviya Krasnoy Armii na territorii Rumynii, Bolgarii, Vengrii i Yugoslavii v 1944–1945 gg* [The liberation of the people of southeast Europe: Operations of the Red Army in the territories of Romania, Bulgaria, Hungary, and Yugo-slavia, 1944–1945]. Moscow, 1967.

Montgomery, John Flournoy. *Magyarország, a vonakodó csatlós.* Budapest, 1993. [*Hungary: The Unwilling Satellite.* New York, 1947.]

Nagy, Gábor. "A 3. Ukrán Front felszabadító hadműveleteinek első szakasza" [The first phase of the 3rd Ukrainian Front's liberation operations]. In *HK* 2, 1972.

———. "Adalékok Komárom megye felszabadulásának történetéhez" [Contribu-tions to the history of the liberation of Komárom county]. In *HK* 3, 1983.

Nagy, Lajos. *Pincenapló* [Cellar diary]. Budapest, 1945.

Nagy, László. "Mi történt február 11-én" [What happened on 11 February]. In *Budai Polgár,* 22 July 1945.

Némethy, Károly. "Karácsony Budapest 1944" [Christmas, Budapest, 1944]. In *Budapest,* 1945.

Nemzetőr [National guard (newspaper)].

Népbírósági Közlöny [The people's court gazette (newspaper)].

Néphadsereg [The people's army (newspaper)].

Néplap: Debrecen [The people's journal: Debrecen (newspaper)].

Népszabadság [The people's liberty (newspaper)].

Népszava [The people's word (newspaper)].

Neulen, Hans Werner. *An deutscher Seite: Internationale Freiwillige von Wehrmacht und Waffen-SS* [On the German side: International volunteers of the Wehrmacht and Waffen SS]. Munich, 1985.

Noel, Péter. "Az Egyetemi Rohamzászlóalj kitörési kísérlete" [The break-out attempt of the University Assault Artillery]. In *Bajtársi Levél* 5, 1974.

Noll, Reinhard. "Im Kessel von Budapest" [In the Budapest cauldron]. In *Wiking Ruf* 3, 1953.

Nonn, György. *Így szabadultam* [How I escaped]. Budapest, 1975.

Nyecseporuk, N. A. "A magyar föld felszabadítása." [N. A. Necheporuk, The liberation of the Hungarian soil]. In *HK* 1, 1967.

Nyíri, János. *Die Judenschule* [The Jewish school]. Munich, 1989.

Oldner, Vladimir. "A budapesti harcok krónikája" [Chronicle of the fighting in Budapest]. In *Néphadsereg,* 12 February 1955.

Ölvedi, Ignác. *A budai Vár és a debreceni csata: Horthyék katasztrófapolitikája 1944. őszén* [The Buda Castle district and the battle of Debrecen: The Horthy Regime's catastrophic policy in autumn 1944]. Budapest, 1974.

Örkény, István. *Budai böjt* [Fasting in Buda]. Budapest, 1948.

———. *Hóviharban* [In the snowstorm]. Budapest, 1954.

Ország-Világ [Country-World (newspaper)].

"Összefoglaló kimutatás Magyarország háborús kárairól" [Summary report on war damage to Hungary]. In *Magyar Statisztikai Zsebkönyv* [Statistical pocket book of Hungary]. Budapest, 1947.

Összetartás [Solidarity (newspaper)].

Ot Volzhskikh stepey do avstriyskikh alp. Voyevoy put' 4-oy gvardeyskoy armii [From the Volga steppes to the Austrian Alps: The war route of the 4th Guard Army]. Moscow, 1971.

Pálfalvi, Nándor. *Esküszöm, hogy hű leszek* [I swear to be faithful]. Budapest, 1990.

Palich-Szántó, Olga. "A vérző város: A németek menekülése a Várból" [The bleeding city: The Germans' escape from the Castle district]. In *Magyar Nemzet,* 3 March 1949.

Pápai újság [Pápa news (newspaper)].

Papné Wighard, Edit (ed.). *Napló a pincében töltött napokról: Budapest ostroma egy diáklány élményeinek tükrében* [Diary of the days spent in the cellar: The siege of Budapest as reflected in the experiences of a schoolgirl]. Budapest, 1994.

Payer, András. *Armati Hungarorum.* Munich, 1985.

Péchy, Blanka. *Este a Dunánál* [Evening on the Danube]. Budapest, 1977.

Pesterzsébet. Soroksár: Budapest XX. kerületének múltja és jelene: Tanulmányok [Pesterzsébet, Soroksár. Past and present of the XX district of Budapest: Studies]. Budapest, 1972.

Pest Megyei Hírlap [Pest County news (newspaper)].

Petyke, Mihály. *A Gestapó foglya voltam* [I was a captive of the Gestapo]. Budapest, 1945.

Polcz, Alaine, *Asszony a fronton: Egy fejezet életemből.* Budapest, 1991. [*A Wartime Memoir: Hungary, 1944–1945.* Trans. Albert Tezla. Budapest, 1998.]

Pongrácz, György. "Mi van az Aszú utcában" [What is happening in Aszú Street]. In *Hidegkúti Hírek,* 6, 1993.

———. "Hol legyen Buda környékén az 1945-ös budai kitörésnél elesettek katonai temetője" [Where is the cemetery containing the soldiers killed during the Buda break-out in 1945?]. In *Hidegkúti Hírek,* 5, 1994.

Ránki, György. *A Wilhelmstrasse és Magyarország: Német diplomáciai iratok Magyarországról, 1933–45* [Wilhelmstrasse and Hungary: German diplomatic documents about Hungary, 1933–1945]. Budapest, 1968.

——— (ed.). *Hitler hatvannyolc tárgyalása* [Sixty-eight discussions of Hitler]. Budapest, 1983.

Ravasz, István (ed.). *Magyarország a Második Világháborúban: Lexikon* [Hungary in the Second World War: Encyclopedia]. Budapest, 1994.

Révész, Sándor. *Aczél és korunk* [Aczél and our era]. Budapest, 1997.

Ruffy, Péter. *A tábornok úr (Ferencvárosi szél)* [The general (Wind in Ferencváros)]. Budapest, 1970.

Sander, Helke, and Barbara Johr. *Befreier und Befreite: Krieg, Vergewaltigungen, Kinder* [Liberators and liberated: War, rapes, children]. Frankfurt, 1995.

Sárközi, Sándor. *Küzdelmes katonaévek* [Hard years in military service]. Budapest, 1979.

———. *Budán harcoltak* [They fought in Buda]. Budapest, 1995.

Das Schicksal der Deutschen in Ungarn, herausgegeben vom ehemaligen Bundesministerium für Vertriebene, Flüchtlinge und Kriegsgeschädigte [The fate of the Germans in Hungary, published by the former Federal Ministry of Displaced Persons, Refugees, and War Victims]. Augsburg, 1994.

Schmidt, Mária. *Kollaboráció vagy kooperáció: A budapesti Zsidó Tanács* [Collaboration or cooperation: The Budapest Jewish Council]. Budapest, 1990.

Seidl, Alfred (ed.). *Die Beziehungen zwischen Deutschland und der Sovjetunion: Dokumente des Auswärtigen Amtes* [The relations between Germany and the Soviet Union: Documents of the German Foreign Ministry]. Tübingen, 1949.

Simmler, Karl. *Die Belagerung von Budapest* [The siege of Budapest]. Zürich, 1989.

Soldaten-Jahrbuch 1994 [Soldiers' yearbook 1994]. Munich, 1994.

Sólyom, József, and László Szabó. *A zuglói nyilasper* [The Zugló Arrow Cross trial]. Budapest, 1967.

Soproni Hírlap [Sopron news (newspaper)].

Söptei, István (ed.). *Az I. Huszárhadosztály a II. Világháborúban: Harctéri naplók, visszaemlékezések* [The I Hussar Division in the Second World War: Battlefield diaries and reminiscences]. Sárvár, 1992.

Sovetskaya Voyennaya Entsiklopediya [Soviet war encyclopedia]. Moscow, vol. 5, 1978; vol. 8, 1980.

Srágli, Béla, and László Bogár. "Tíz évvel ezelőtt . . . A budapesti felszabadító harcok" [Ten years ago . . . The battles of liberation in Budapest]. In *Néphadsereg* 1, 8, 11, 14, 25, 31, 33, 35, 37, 1955.

Stark, Tamás. *Zsidóság a vészkorszakban és a felszabadulás után, 1939–1945*. Budapest, 1995. [*Hungarian Jews During the Holocaust and After the Second World War, 1939–1949*. Trans. Christina Rozsnyai. Boulder, 2000.]

Steiner, Felix. *Die Armee der Geächteten* [The army of the outlawed]. Oldendorf, 1971.

Steinert, Gyula. "Budapest ostroma egy orvos szemével" [The siege of Budapest through the eyes of a doctor]. In *Vigilia* 5, 1995.

Strassner, Peter. *Europäische Freiwillige: Die Geschichte der 5. SS-Panzer-Div. Wiking* [European volunteers: The history of the 5th SS Panzer Division Wiking]. Osnabrück, 1977.

Styemenko, Szergej M. *Ahol a győzelmet kovácsolták* [Where victory was forged]. Budapest, 1969. [Chapters from Sergei M. Shtemenko, *Generalnyy shtab v gody voyny*. Moscow, 1968. *The Soviet General Staff at War: 1941–1945*. Moscow, 1985–1986.]

———. "Európa szívében" [In the heart of Europe]. In *Fáklya* 10, 1972.

Sulyok, Dezső. *A magyar tragédia* [The Hungarian tragedy]. Newark, 1954.

Suworow, Viktor. *Der Eisbrecher: Hitler in Stalins Kalkül*, Stuttgart, 9th ed., 1996. [Victor Suvorov, *Ledokol. kto nachal vtoruyu mirovuyu voynu?* Moscow, 1992. *Ice-breaker: Who Started the Second World War?* Trans. Thomas B. Beattie. London, 1990.]

Svéd, László, and Ágnes Szabó (eds.). *Dokumentumok a magyar párttörténet tanulmányozásához 5, 1939. szeptemberétől 1945. áprilisáig* [Documents for the study of Hungarian party history 5, September 1939–April 1945]. Budapest, 1955.

Svirin M., et al. *Tankove Srazennya. Boj u Ozera Balaton: Yanvar-Mart 1945* [Tank battles at Lake Balaton, January–March 1945]. Moscow, 1999.

Szabadság [Freedom (newspaper)].

Szabó, Balázs. "A 2. Ukrán Front budapesti hadműveletének I. szakasza" [The first phase of the 2nd Ukrainian Front's Budapest operations]. In *HK* 4, 1964.

———. "A 2. Ukrán Front budapesti támadó hadmuveletének II. szakasza" [The second phase of the 2nd Ukrainian Front's Budapest assault operations]. In *HK* 1, 1970.

Szabó, Borbála. *Budapesti napló (1944. november–1945. január)* [Budapest diary (November 1944–January 1945)]. Budapest, 1983.

Szakács, Sándor, and Tibor Zinner. *A háború megváltozott természete—Adatok és adalékok, tények és összefüggések, 1944–1948* [The altered nature of war: Information and contributions, facts and connections, 1944–1948]. Budapest, 1997.

Szalai, György. *Kőbánya története* [The history of Kőbánya]. Budapest, 1970.

Szántó, Piroska. *Bálám szamara (Visszaemlékezések)* [Balaam's ass (memoirs)]. Budapest, 1989.

Száva, Péter (ed.). *Fejezetek hazánk felszabadulásának történetéből* [Chapters from the history of the liberation of our homeland]. Budapest, 1975a.

——. (ed.). *Magyarország felszabadítása* [The liberation of Hungary]. Budapest, 1975b.

Szekeres, József (ed.). *Források Budapest történetéhez, 1919–1945* [Sources for the history of Budapest, 1919–1945]. Budapest, n.d.

Szentgróti, Éva. "Egy szovjet hadijelentés nyomában" [On the track of a Soviet war report]. In *Magyar Nemzet* 37, 1955.

Szép, Ernő. *Emberszag: Visszaemlékezések.* Budapest, 1989. [*Smell of Humans: Memoir of the Holocaust in Hungary.* Trans. J. Bakti. Budapest, 1994.]

Szidnainé Csete, Ágnes. *A 125 éves budapesti állat- és növénykert története: 1866–1991* [The 125-year history of the Budapest Zoo and Botanical Gardens, 1866–1991]. Budapest, 1991.

Szilágyi, István. "A kör bezárul (Tanulmányrészlet)" [The circle closes (Part of a study)]. In *Három fekete évtized* [Three black decades]. Budapest, 1946.

Szirmai, Rezső. *Fasiszta lelkek: Pszichoanalítikus beszélgetések háborús főbűnösökkel a börtönben* [Fascist souls: Psychoanalytical conversations with major war criminals in prison]. Budapest, 1993.

Szita, Szabolcs (ed.). *Magyarország 1944: Üldöztetés—Embermentés* [Hungary 1944: Persecution—rescue]. Budapest, 1994.

Szmirnov, Szergej. "Harcban született barátság." [Sergei Smirnov, friendship born in battle.] In *Új Világ* 7, 1949.

——. *Harcban Budapestért* [In battle for Budapest]. Budapest, 1952. [Sergei Smirnov, *Na polyakh Vengrii.* Moscow, 1954.]

Szombat [Saturday (newspaper)].

Sztéhló, Gábor. *Isten kezében.* Budapest, 1984. [*In the Hands of God.* Budapest, 1994.]

Teleki, Éva. *Nyilas uralom Magyarországon* [The Arrow Cross rule in Hungary]. Budapest, 1974.

Tersánszky, Józsi J. *Egy kézikocsi története* [The story of a handcart]. Budapest, 1949.

——. *Nagy árnyakról bizalmasan (Visszaemlékezések)* [In confidence about large shadows (Memories)]. Budapest, 1962.

Tétény-Promontor: Budapest XXII. kerületének története [Tétény-Promontor: The history of the XXII district of Budapest]. Budapest, 2d ed., 1988.

Thassy, Jenő. *Veszélyes vidék: Visszamlékezések* [Dangerous region: Reminiscences]. Budapest, 1999.

Thuróczi, György. *Kropotov nem tréfál* [Kropotov is not joking]. Debrecen, 1993.

Tiszay, Andor. *Budapest felszabadulásának dokumentumai* [Documents on the liberation of Budapest]. Budapest, 1955.

Tóth, Sándor. "Steinmetz Miklós." In *Forradalomban, háborúban.* ["Miklós Steinmetz" in In revolution and war.] Budapest, 1974.

——. *Budapest felszabadítása* [The liberation of Budapest]. Budapest, 1975a.

Tóth, Sándor. (ed.). *Hősök: A Szovjetunió Hősei a magyarországi felszabadító harcokban 1944–1945* [Heroes: The heroes of the Soviet Union in the Hungarian battles of liberation, 1944–1945]. Budapest, 1975b.

————. *A Budai Önkéntes Ezred* [The Buda Volunteer Regiment]. Budapest, 1980.

————. *Budai önkéntesek* [Buda Volunteers]. Budapest, 1985.

Újlaki, László. "A galántai zászlóalj és a 'vörös Csepel'" [The Galántai battalion and "red Csepel"]. In *Egyesületi Értesítő* 19, 1973.

Új Magyarság [New Hungarians (newspaper)].

Újpest története [The history of Újpest]. Budapest, 1977.

Új Szó [New word (newspaper)].

Új Tükör [New mirror (newspaper)].

Új Világ [New world (newspaper)].

Varga, László. *Kérem a vádlott felmentését* [I request the acquittal of the defendant]. New York, 1981.

Vas Zoltán polgármester jelentése a Székesfőváros közigazgatásának működéséről 1945. május 16.1946.–november 16. [Mayor Zoltán Vas's report on the activities of the capital's public administration, 16 May 1945–16 November 1945]. Budapest, 1946.

Veress, Csaba D. *A Dunántúl felszabadítása* [The liberation of Transdanubia]. Budapest, 1985.

Vigilia [Vigils (newspaper)].

Világosság [Light (newspaper)].

"Vízművek az ostrom alatt" [The waterworks during the siege]. In *A Szabad Nép naptára* [The free people's diary]. Budapest, 1947.

Walendy, Udo. *Einsatzgruppen im Verbande des Heeres* [Einsatzgruppen within the army]. Preussisch-Oldendorf, 1983.

Wiking Ruf [Viking call (newspaper)].

Woche, Klaus. "Die Soldaten der 'Feldherrnhalle'" [The soldiers of the Feldherrnhalle Division]. In *Zeitschrift für Heereskunde* 272, 1977.

Zaharov, Matvej Vasziljevics. *Délkelet-és Közép-Európa felszabadítása.* [Matvei Vasilevich Zakharov, The liberation of southeast and central Europe.] Budapest, 1973. [Matvei Vasilevich Zakharov, *Osvobozhdenie Yugo-Vostochnoy Tsentralnoy Yevropy voyskami vtorogo i tretyego Ukrainskikh frontov.* Moscow, 1970.]

Zákó, András. *Őszi harcok 1944* [Battles in autumn 1944]. Budapest, 1991.

Zamercev, Ivan Tyerentyevics. *Emlékek, arcok, Budapest: Egy szovjet városparancsnok visszaemlékezései.* [Ivan Terentevich Zamertsev, Memories, faces, Budapest: Memoirs of a Soviet city commander.] Budapest, 1969. [Ivan Terentevich Zamertsev, *Cherez gody i rasstoyaniya.* Moscow, 1965.]

Zayas, Alfred Maurice de. *Die Wehrmacht-Untersuchungsstelle: Deutsche Ermittlungen über alliierte Völkerrechsverletzungen im Zweiten Weltkrieg.* Munich, 1980. [*The Wehrmacht War Crimes Bureau, 1939–1945.* Lincoln, 1989.]

Zeitschrift für Heereskunde [Journal of army studies].

Zentai, Gyula. "Budapest felszabadítása" [The liberation of Budapest]. In *HK* 1, 1955.

Zolnai, László. "Egy SS-főhadnagy leleplezte a Margit híd felrobbantásának titkát: Nyilas gonosztevők okozták a sokszáz ember halálát előidéző borzalmas szerencsétlenséget" [An SS first lieutenant has revealed the secret of the blasting of Margit Bridge: The terrible disaster that cost the lives of several hundred people was caused by Arrow Cross criminals]. In *Világosság* 77, 1947.

———. "Decembertől februárig" [From December to February]. In *Népszabadság*, 9 February 1985.

———. *Hírünk és hamvunk (Tények és tanúk)* [Our traces (Facts and witnesses)]. Budapest, 1986.

Zsolt, Béla. *Kilenc koffer*. Budapest, 1980. [*Nine Suitcases*. Trans. Ladislaus Löb. London, 2004.

Zsombor, János. *Így történt* [This is how it happened]. Budapest, 1955.

Archival Material

Hadtudományi Levéltár Budapest [Archive of Military History, Budapest] (HL)

CONTEMPORARY DOCUMENTS

Documents of the operational section of the Hungarian army general staff (VKF) 304, 304/a, 305, 306, 306/a, 306/b.

Documents of the Hungarian 10th Infantry Division, box 90.

Daily reports of the Hungarian 12th Reserve Division, box 29.

Documents of the IX SS Mountain Army Corps and the 13th Panzer Division. No number.

Documents of the national Chief Inspector of the Royal Hungarian Police, box 21, I. 107.

War diary and attachments of the Army Group South on microfilm, 896–901.

Hindy's trial file on microfilm, 1068.

Winkelmann's notes on microfilm, 1053, 1071.

COLLECTIONS OF STUDIES (TGY)

Almay, Béla. Lecture and private diary. TGY 3091.

———. *A Budapestért vívott harc* [The struggle for Budapest]. TGY 3314.

Bakos, Tibor, and Erno Gödry. *Feljegyzés az egykori M.Kir. 153. kerékpáros utász századról* [Note on the former Royal Hungarian 153rd Bicycle-Pioneer Company]. No number.

Berthold, Hermann. *Visszaemlékezés a második Ukrán Frontnál eltöltött időre* [Recollections of time spent with the 2nd Ukrainian Front]. TGY 2814.

Bíró, József. *A Tatárhágótól Budapestig* [From the Tatárhágó Pass to Budapest]. TGY 3053.

Bíró, József. *Budapest védői* [The defenders of Budapest]. TGY 3251.

Botár, Elek. *A Morlin-csoport* [The Morlin Group]. TGY 3368.

Darnói, Pál. Collection of documents, including correspondence with former officers of the Royal Hungarian Police and Gendarmerie about the siege of Budapest. TGY 3070.

Egyedi, Balázs. *Sorstól űzve, hányavetetten* [Persecuted by fate]. TGY 3029.

Elischer, Gyula, *Visszaemlékezés a M. Kir. I. Honvéd Egyetemi Rohamzászlóalj megalakulásának napjaira 1944-ben* [Recollections of the days of the foundation of the Royal Hungarian Honvéd I University Assault Battalion in 1944]. TGY 3180.

Horváth, Dénes. *A 201/1 légvédelmi ágyúüteg részvétele a budapesti harcokban* [The 201/1 Antiaircraft Battery's participation in the fighting in Budapest]. TGY 3078.

Kokovay, Gyula. *Kitörés és átjutás* [Break-out and escape]. TGY 3369.

Konkoly-Thege, Aladár. *Tépett lobogó* [Torn flag]. TGY 3273.

Lám, Béla. *Emlékek gyertyafénynél* [Recollections by candlelight]. no number.

Lisszay, Aurél. *A Budapestért vívott harc* [The struggle for Budapest]. TGY 3072.

Marosújvári, Géza. *Ejtőernyős katonai szolgálatom emlékei* [Memories of my paratrooper service]. TGY 2904.

Mucsy, Iván. *Békéstől Békésig: Egy volt hadapródiskolai növendék emlékiratai* [From Békés to Békés: Memoirs of a former cadet]. no number.

Paulics, József. *Budapest végnapjai* [The last days of Budapest]. TGY 2829.

Péchy, György. *Csapattiszt voltam a Magyar Királyi Honvédségben* [I was a combat-troop officer in the Royal Hungarian Honvéd Army]. TGY 3184.

Pothradszky, Ádám. *A Hunyadi hadosztály* [The Hunyadi Division]. TGY 2830.

Rakovszky, István. *A M. Kir. Jurisics Miklós Honvéd Tüzér Osztály harcai Budapest védelmében* [The battles of the Royal Hungarian Honvéd Artillery Battalion: Jurisics Miklós in the defense of Budapest]. TGY 3269.

Rhédey, Tamás. *A Morlin-csoport története a budapesti ostrom idején* [The history of the Morlin Group at the time of the siege of Budapest]. TGY 3271.

Salamon, Aurél. *Budán történt* [It happened in Buda]. TGY 3116.

———. *Az elsüllyedt hadosztály* [The sunken division]. TGY 3179.

Salamon, Zsigmond. *Katonai szolgálatom a 202. fényszóró osztálynál* [My military service with the 202nd Searchlight Detachment]. TGY 3365.

Sárközi, Sándor, and Barnabás Csécsi. *A Budai Önkéntes Ezred kialakulása és harcai* [The development and battles of the Buda Volunteer Regiment]. TGY 2856.

Soltész, Emil. *Adatok a M. Kir. "Árpád fejedelem" 2. huszárezred történetéhez* [Data for the history of the Royal Hungarian "Árpád fejedelem" 2nd Honvéd Hussar Regiment]. TGY 3054.

Szalay, István. *Memoir*. No number.

Tassonyi, Edömér. "Zuhanóugrás" [Free fall]. In *Kritika,* 12 January 1982. No number.

Vajda, Alajos. *Az 1. páncéloshadosztály története* [The history of the 1st Armored Division]. TGY 2772.

———. *Budapest ostromának anyagi tanulságai* [The material lessons taught by the siege of Budapest]. TGY 2832.

Vass, Dénes. *A M. Kir. I. Egyetemi Rohamzászlóalj 2. századának története* [The history of the 2nd Company of the Royal Hungarian I University Assault Battalion]. TGY 3302.

Bundesarchiv—Militärarchiv Freiburg [Federal archive—Military archive Freiburg] (BA-MA)

WEHRMACHT DOCUMENTS

Heeresgruppenkommando RH 19 V/ 58-63 (Bestand Heeresgruppe Süd).

Generalkommando RH 24-72 (LXXVII. Armeekorps).

RH 24-202 (I. Kavalleriekorps).

OKH Generalstab RH 2/96k, 332, 720–723, 1387, 1398, 1418, 1420, 1421, 1426, 1428, 1468, 1950, 2338, 2358, 2468, 2960, 2883.

RH2 Ost Karten 4999-6257 (Panzerlage).

General der Panzertruppen RH 10/105, 139, 151, 206, 328, 350.

General der Pioniere und Festungen RH 11 III/25.

Inspektion der Infanterie RH 12-2/69.

13. Panzerdivision RH 27-13/160–165.

RH 80/B 11.

Wehrmachtführungsstab RW 4/44, 79, 84, 460, 482–485, 494, 584, 670, 714, 801, 802, 845, 900.

Amt Ausland/Abwehr RW49/145.

N 643/v13, documents of Helmut Wolff.

MANUSCRIPT COLLECTIONS

Balck, Hermann. Documents from the estate. N 647/12–23, 41–43.

Hübner, Werner. *Geschichte der in Ungarn eingesetzten Panzereinheiten* [History of the panzer units deployed in Hungary]. MSg 2/238.

Mückl, Ludwig. *Zwischen Don und Donau: Lebensweg eines Volksdeutschen aus Siebenbürgen* [Between the Don and the Danube: A Transylvanian ethnic German's journey through life]. MSg 2/5407.

Nachtmann. *Die letzten Tage im Ausbruch aus Budapest* [The last days of the break-out from Budapest]. RH 39/524.

Pfeffer-Wildenbruch, Karl. Documents from the estate. N 370/1–11.

Schweitzer, Ernst. *Der Kessel von Budapest* [The Budapest cauldron]. MSg 2/4631.

Manuscript Collection of the Országos Széchényi Könyvtár
[National Széchényi library] (OSZK)

Faragó Ödönné báró Urbán, Jusztina. *Buda ostroma és ami utána történt a Logodi utca 31. sz. házban: Naplóm, 1944. december 22-től 1945. március 16-ig* [The siege of Buda and what happened afterward at 31 Logodi Street: My diary, from 22 December 1944 to 16 March 1945]. Fol. Hung. 3646.

Csécsy, Imre. *Napló* [Diary]. OSZK Fond 36/1589.

Lichtenberg, Judit von [Judit Láng]. *Visszaemlékezések 1945-re* [Memories of 1945]. Analekta 11.579.

Ney, Klára Mária. *Budavár Ostroma* [The siege of the Buda Castle district], Analekta 12.172.

Rácz Pálné Újfalussy, Klára. *Naplóm* [My diary]. V. 139/57/95.

Szuly, Gyula. *A "Háttér a vár" háttere* [The background to "The background is the Castle district"]. Fol. Hung. 3568.

Szép, Anna. *Feljegyzések Szép Ernőről* [Notes about Ernő Szép]. Fond 81/820.

Tonelli, Sándor. *Budapest szörnyű napjai: Az ostrom története 1944 október–1945. május* [The terrible days of Budapest: The history of the siege, October 1944–May 1945]. OSZK, Fol. Hung.

———. *Az ostrom története: Emlékek* [The history of the siege: Memories]. Canada before 1950, Fol. Hung. 3629.

Újfalussy Lászlóné Murányi, Klára. *Napló: Budapest-Nyiregyháza. 1944. december 24–1945. május 7* [Diary: Budapest-Nyiregyháza, 24 December 1944–7 May 1945]. QH 3171.

Private Collections

I am indebted to the following researchers for allowing me to use material from their collections: Péter Gosztonyi, Pál Dobay, Dénes Vass, Péter Zwack Jr., Sándor Tóth, and László Hingyi. Further material, in written or oral form, was provided by the individuals listed in the section entitled Interviews and Letters.

Anon. An unknown student's memoir of the break-out and escape. Dénes Vass collection.

Billnitzer, Ernő. *Memoir*. Sándor Tóth collection.

Bolyos, Rezső Ákos P. *Pálosok magyarországon a XX. század első felében* [Pauline friars in Hungary in the first half of the twentieth century].

Csongrádi, András (Budapest resident). Letter.

Dalmy, Tibor (Budapest resident). Letter.

Dávid, András. Notes.

Dema, Andor (1st Armored Division). Manuscript.

Esterházy, Kázmérné. Diary.

Farkas, Erik. Diary.

Friedrich, Helmut. *Wanderer zwischen Krieg und Frieden* [A wanderer between war and peace]. Manuscript.

Galántay, Ervin. *Boy Soldier: Five Days in the Life of a Dispatch-Runner: Excerpts from the Defense of Budapest, 1944–45.* Self-published.

————. Letters to the author.

Garád, Róbert (assault artillery first lieutenant). Memories of the 7th Assault Artillery Detachment's Battles and Break-out.

Gödry, Ernő. Notes of the former commander of the 153rd Bicycle Pioneer Company.

Gömöri, György. *Budapest ostroma (napló)* [The siege of Budapest (Diary)].

Hanák, Sándor (captain, commander of 10th Infantry-Artillery Battalion). Report no. 6 about the fighting at Baracska on 8–9 December 1944.

Herbert, Jakob (8th SS Cavalry Division Florian Geyer). Memoir.

Hingyi, László. *Nyilas Hungarista pártszolgálatosok bevetései a budapesti harcokban* [The deployment of Arrow Cross Hungarist Party militiamen in the fighting in Budapest]. Manuscript.

Klein, Erich. Contribution to *Das Soldaten-Jahrbuch* [The soldiers' yearbook]. Manuscript.

Kovács, Ferenc X. *Villanások* [Flashes]. Manuscript.

Litteráti-Lóotz, Gyula. Letter to Péter Gosztonyi.

Lukács, Gyula. *A pokol stációi: Emlékirat a II. Világháborúból* [The stations of hell: Memoir from the Second World War]. Manuscript (by courtesy of Mrs Ernőné Lakatos).

Major, Norbert. *A 102. fogatolt vegyiharczászlóalj Buda várának védelmében* [The 102nd Horse-Drawn Chemical Warfare Battalion in the defense of Buda Castle]. Manuscript.

Monspart, Gábor (hussar colonel). Memoir.

M. v. K. önkéntes ápolónő visszaemlékezése a Sziklakórházban töltött időkre [Voluntary nurse M. v. K.'s memories of her times in the Rock Hospital]. Manuscript (Dénes Vass collection).

Ney, Klára Mária. *Budapest ostroma* [The siege of Budapest]. Manuscript.

Nyiredy, Szabolcs (private). Memoir.

Portugall, Kurt (Hauptsturmführer antiaircraft battalion commander, 8th SS Cavalry Division Florian Geyer). Memoir.

Schlosser, Franz (8th SS Cavalry Division Florian Geyer). Memoir.

Schöning, Wilhelm (reserve lieutenant-colonel, 13th Panzer Division). Documents, notes, and contemporary maps.

Schreiner, János. Diary.

Schweitzer, Ernst. Report of 26 February 1945 on the engagements of the 13th Panzer Division and the break-out. Manuscript.

Seidl, Marietta. *Ostrom* [Siege]. Manuscript.

Sipeki, Balás, Lajos. *1945. január 1-i Mikó-Bondor akció története* [The history of the Mikó-Bondor action of 1 January 1945]. Manuscript.

Szirtes, Tibor. *Három hónapom a székesfővárosi autóbuszüzemben: 1944–1945* [My three months with the bus company in the capital, 1944–1945]. Manuscript.

Teske, Hans Georg (8th SS Cavalry Division Florian Geyer). Memoir.

Tomka, Emil. *A szentesi M. Kir "Árpád feldjedem 2/I. honvéd huszárosztály harctéri naplója 1944–1945* [Battlefield diary of the Royal Hungarian "Prince Árpád" 2/I Honvéd Hussar Battalion, 1944–1945].

Válas, György. Letter.

Vályi, Lajos (1st Assault Artillery Detachment). Memoir.

Varga, József. *Átélt események 1944. december 23. és 28. között* [Events experienced between 23 and 28 December 1944]. Manuscript.

Városy, Péter (1st Assault Artillery Detachment). Memoir.

Vass, Dénes. *Egyetemisták az ostromgyűrűben: Az I. Honvéd Egyetemi Rohamzászlóalj története* [University students in the encirclement: The history of the I Honvéd University Assault Battalion]. Manuscript.

Wachter, Hans-Otto (8th SS Cavalry Division Florian Geyer). Memoir.

Interviews, Letters, Memoirs

My special thanks are due to those named below. This book could not have been written without their help and advice.

Men on active service during the Battle of Budapest are listed with the rank they held and the unit to which they belonged at the time. Local residents and researchers from whom I have received assistance are identified as such. The interviews were carried out in 1993–1997 and are recorded on cassettes or in manual notes.

Aczél, Ferenc (Budapest resident)

Alberz, Péter (271st Volksgrenadier Division)

André, Dr. László (deputy commissioner, Galántai Gendarmerie Battalion)

Antalóczy, Mrs. Tibor (Budapest resident)

Árvay, Rezső (University Assault Battalion)

Baki, József (researcher)

Baló, Zoltán (second lieutenant, 1st Armored Division)

Barabás, Béla (captain, head of operational section, 1st Armored Division)

Baranyi, László (University Assault Battalion)

Baross, Dénes (first lieutenant, 4th Hussar Regiment)

Baróthy, Miklós (captain, 1st Armored Division)

Bartha, Endre (KISKA)

Bartha, István (second lieutenant, 101st Military Police Company)

Baumgart, Leo-Franz (241st Flaksturmregiment)

Benefi, Géza (Budapest resident)

Benyovszky, Győző (captain, chief of staff, 10th Infantry Division)

Berend, Károly (captain, Berend Group)

Betzler, Wolfgang (lieutenant, diarist of IX SS Mountain Army Corps)

Bierwirth, Willibald (Feldherrnhalle Panzergrenadier Division)

Bődy, Oszkár (Morlin Group)

Boosfeld, Joachim (SS Hauptsturmführer, Florian Geyer 8th SS Cavalry Division)

Böttcher, Heinz (captain, 13th Panzer Division)

Csány, Balázs (lieutenant, 16th Assault Artillery Detachment)

Csipkés, Ernő, Jr. (Budapest resident)

Csongrády, András (Budapest resident)

Czagány, József (Prónay commandos)

Czeczidlowszky, Béla (lieutenant, 40th Artillery Detachment)

Dalmy, Tibor (Budapest resident)

Deseő, László (Budapest resident)

Dobay, Pál (forester and researcher)

Emmerich, Wolfgang (son of survivor)

Entzmann, Martin (Maria Theresia 22nd SS Cavalry Division)

Finger, Johannes (Florian Geyer 8th SS Cavalry Division)

Finta, József (Budapest resident)

Friedrich, Helmut (captain, 13th Panzer Division)

Galántay, Ervin (Vannay Battalion)

Geiss, Erhard (13th Panzer Division)

Gencsy, Tibor (lieutenant, 4th Hussar Regiment)

Gencsy Tiborné Hellenbach, Klotild (Budapest resident)

Grelle, Martin (13th Panzer Division)

Hanák, Sándor (captain, 10th Assault Artillery Detachment)

Haraszti, István (Budapest resident)

Héjj, Ervin (Budapest resident)

Hellenbronth, Gusztáv (commander, II Budapest Assault Battalion)

Hermándy, Iván (first lieutenant, 1st Armored Division)

Hernády, Béla (captain, 1st Armored Division)

Hingyi, László (researcher)

Horváth, Dr. Lóránd (Budapest resident)

Irmay, Ferenc (general staff captain, head of operational section, 12th Reserve Division)

Jerezian, Ara (Arrow Cross deputy district commander, rescuer of Jews)

John, Adolf (SS Unterscharführer, Florian Geyer 8th SS Cavalry Division)

Joó, Oszkár (12th Reserve Division)

Kákosy, Dr. László (Budapest resident)

Kamocsay, Gyula (Honvéd, train group)

Kaszás, István (first lieutenant, 1st Armored Division)

Katona, Dr. Tamás (historian)

Keller, Ernst (corporal, Feldherrnhalle Panzergrenadier Division)

Kerekes, Medárd (University Assault Battalion)

Kézdi-Beck, Géza (Budapest resident)

Klein, Andreas (22nd Cavalry Division)

Klein, Erich (captain, Feldherrnhalle Panzergrenadier Division)
Klein, Michael (SS Unterscharführer, Maria Theresia 22nd SS Cavalry Division)
Kohánszky, Béláné (Budapest resident)
Kokovay, Gyula (cadet, University Assault Battalion)
Kovács, Ferenc X. (general staff captain, head of operations, I Army Corps)
Kovács, Ferencné (Budapest resident, wife of Ferenc X. Kovács)
Kováts, László (201/2 Antiaircraft Artillery Battalion)
Kövendi, Dénes (Budapest resident)
Kükedi, József (Budapest resident)
Kurdi, József (10th Infantry Division)
Kutscher, Otto (13th Panzer Division)
Lakatos, Ernőné (Budapest resident)
Lám, Béla (first lieutenant, Galántai Gendarmerie Battalion)
Lénárt, Lajos (ensign, 16th Assault Artillery Detachment)
Létay, Gyula (captain, 10th Division, Buda Volunteer Regiment)
Linkowski, Alfred (8th SS Cavalry Division)
Lőrincz, András (University Assault Battalion)
Maczkovits, István (Budapest resident)
Major, Norbert (ensign, 101st Horse-Drawn Chemical Warfare Battalion)
Mányoky, István (first lieutenant, 1st Assault Artillery Battalion)
Marthy, Dr. János (local historian)
Martin, Kornél (ensign, Szent László Reserve Division)
Máté, József (local historian)
M. K., Mrs. (Budapest resident)
Mucsy, Iván (Morlin Group)
Nádasdi, Richard (Budapest resident)
Neuburg, Pál (former Budapest resident)
Ney, Klára (Budapest resident)
Nyárády, Gábor (1st Armored Division)
Nyárády, Richárd (Budapest resident)
Paál, Zoltán (Budapest resident)
Pataki, László (Budapest resident)
Pintér, Géza (lieutenant, Antiaircraft Group Buda South)
Prach, Hans (4th Assault Pioneer Company)
Prágay, Dezső (University Assault Battalion)
Rácz, Ernő (Budapest resident)
Rádi, Mrs. László (Budapest Resident)
Ringhoffer, Josef (Maria Theresia 22nd SS Cavalry Division)
Rüblein, Richárd (a.k.a. Szuly, Gyula; Vannay Battalion)
Ruszti, György (Budapest resident)
Safáry, Endre (general staff captain)
Salamon, Aurél (lieutenant, military hospital commander, 4th Hussar Regiment, later Buda Volunteer Regiment)

Salfay, István (Budapest resident)
Sasvári, Endre (researcher)
Schäffer, Georg (Maria Theresia 22nd SS Cavalry Division)
Schönfeld, Rolf (5th SS Panzer Division)
Schweitzer, Ernst (first lieutenant, diarist 13th Panzer Division)
Seidl, Gábor (Budapest resident)
Seidl, Marietta (Budapest resident)
Sélley-Rauscher, Aurél (captain, 25th Assault Artillery Detachment)
Solt, Pál (general staff captain, chief quartermaster, 12th Reserve Division)
Spanberger, Maria (Dorog resident)
Stanley, László (Budapest resident)
Sulyánszky, Jenő (cadet)
Sulzer, Michael (IX SS Mountain Army Corps)
Szablya, János (Budapest resident)
Szabó, Dr. László (cadet, 25th Assault Artillery Detachment)
Szántay, Lajos (University Assault Battalion)
Szentendrei, László (first lieutenant, 10 Infantry Division, Feldherrnhalle Panzer-
    grenadier Division)
Sztrilich, György (researcher)
Takács, János (private, University Assault Battalion)
Tasnádi, Frigyes (Maria Theresia 22nd SS Cavalry Division)
Tesszáry, Zoltán (lieutenant, 1st Armored Division)
Tomcsányi, Ágnes (Budapest resident)
Toperczer, Oszkár (captain, 1st Armored Division, researcher)
Török, László (first lieutenant, Guard Battalion)
Tóth, Sándor (Budapest resident)
Ungváry, Gerő (12th Reserve Division)
Ungváry, József (Morlin Group)
Vadász, Sándor (university professor)
Vajna, Edéné (Budapest resident)
Válas, György (Budapest resident)
Vályi, Dr. Lajos (ensign, 1st Assault Artillery Detachment)
Városy, Péter (cadet, sergeant, 1st Assault Artillery Battalion)
Vass, Dénes (private, University Assault Battalion)
Vasvári, Tibor (lieutenant, Viharos Group)
Wáczek, Frigyes (general staff captain, chief of staff, 1st Armored Division)
Wohltman, Willi (first lieutenant, 13th Panzer Division)
Wolff, Helmuth (lieutenant-colonel, Feldherrnhalle Panzergrenadier Division)
Závori, Lajos (lieutenant, I Army Corps)
Zeisler, Erwin (13th Panzer Division)
Zsohár, György (Maria Theresia 22nd SS Cavalry Division)
Zwack, Peter, Jr. (researcher)

Photo Credits

Index

Notes: **Boldface** page numbers indicate photographs.

The following Hungarian place-name equivalents may be helpful: avenue = fasor; baths = fürdő; boulevard = körút; bridge = híd; cemetery = temető; island = sziget; palace = palota; road = út; row = sor; square = tér; station = pályaudvar, (vasút) állomás; street = utca.

457